Johann Sturm
on
Education

Johann Sturm

1507–1589

Johann Sturm was called the "Perpetual Rector" of the Gymnasium, then of the Academy. This portrait by an anonymous painter is preserved in the Chapter House of St. Thomas. Courtesy of the Archives de la Ville de Strasbourg.

The Reformation and Humanist Learning

Johann Sturm
on
Education

LEWIS W. SPITZ
AND BARBARA SHER TINSLEY

CPH™
SAINT LOUIS

Copyright © 1995 Concordia Publishing House
3558 S. Jefferson Avenue, St. Louis, MO 63118-3968
Manufactured in the United States of America

Library of Congress Cataloging-in-Publication Data

Spitz, Lewis William, 1922–
    Johann Sturm on education : the reformation and humanist learning /
Lewis W. Spitz and Barbara Sher Tinsley.
        p.   cm.
    Includes bibliographical references and index.
    ISBN 0-570-04253-4
    1. Sturm, Johannes, 1507–1589. 2. Education—Philosophy.
3. Education, Humanistic—Philosophy. 4. Reformation. I. Tinsley, Barbara
Sher, 1938–   . II. Title.
LB275.S882S65   1995
370´.1—dc20   94-46603

1 2 3 4   5 6 7 8 9 10   04 03 02 01 00 99 98 97 96 95

*We dedicate this work
to our students
and
to professors of history
and the humanities.*

Contents

Engraving of the "old Gymnasium," the design and reconstruction by Salomon, an architect, after 1870, showing the former Dominican Convent, the "new church" of St. Thomas, with the cathedral in the background. It corresponds to the actual Gymnasium, according to the plan of 1726 conserved in the Historical Museum of Strasbourg. Courtesy of the Archives de la Ville de Strasbourg.

Acknowledgments

Gratitude is the heart's memory! We wish to express our heartfelt appreciation to a number of people and institutions without whose help the publication of this work could not have been realized. We would like to thank Dr. Anna Shaw Benjamin, for many years professor in the Classics Department of Rutgers University, who reviewed, corrected and improved upon our translation of Sturm's difficult Ciceronian Latin. We are grateful to the National Endowment for the Humanities and to the Fulbright Commission for fellowships that enabled us to make substantial progress on the work of translating and to gain a fresh perspective on Sturm's educational program by working in the European archives and libraries. At the Archives de la Ville de Strasbourg, with the St. Thomas archives, where most of Sturm's manuscripts are preserved, Dr. Jean Rott, Dr. François-Joseph Fuchs, and Dr. François Schwicker were extremely cordial and helpful during our research in Strasbourg. The staff members at the library of the University of Strasbourg were very good to us also, as were those at the library of the Sorbonne and at the Bibliothèque Nationale in Paris. At the Institute for European History in Mainz, Germany, Professor G.A. Benrath, Dr. Rainer Vinke, Dr. Rolf Decot, and Dr. Markus Wriedt were most generous in encouraging and facilitating the final research and preparation of the manuscript. We are grateful to the Huntington Library and to the Folger Shakespeare Library for making several Sturm texts available in photocopy and to the Stanford University librarians for their constant support and helpfulness, especially Dr. Mary Jane Parrine, Dr. Peter Frank, and Mr. Henry Lowood. Mr. Hinrich Dierks of the Bibliodata Center of the Staatsbibliothek Preussischer Kulturbesitz, Berlin, ran a bibliographical check for completeness in our listing of the significant Sturm bibliography. We wish especially to thank Dr. Ronald A. Davies for preparing the text for publication and Dr. Wilbert Rosin for seeing this volume through the press. Our sincere thanks to these and many others who are not named here, but who know all they have done for us and for the educational tradition to which Johann Sturm belonged.

Lewis W. Spitz
Barbara Sher Tinsley
Stanford, California

Introduction

At no time in history other than our own has so much attention been paid to educational theory as in the age of the Renaissance and the Reformation. The humanists had a lofty view of the rationality and educability of the upper strata of human society and were naively optimistic about the educability of man. The Italian humanists expressed their thoughts on education mellifluously, as Pietro Paolo Vergerio (1370–1444) did in his *De ingenuis moribus*, where he drew heavily on Plato, Plutarch, and the ever-present Cicero. In this work, Vergerio stressed the importance of the liberal arts for teaching the secret of true freedom and developing each individual to his full potential.[1] Putting these lofty ideas into practice was another thing and, as is well known, Vittorino da Feltre (1378–1146) and Guarino da Verona (1370–1460) founded schools based on the humanist educational philosophy at Mantua, Verona, and Ferrara.[2] The final word belonged to Leonardo Bruni, Chancellor of Florence in a time of crisis, in his treatise *On Studies and Letters*, written between 1423 and 1426: "That high standard of education to which I referred at the outset is only to be reached by one who has seen many things and read much. Poet, orator, historian, and the rest, all must be studied, each must contribute a share."[3]

Years of research into the theories of an indigenous origin of humanism during the northern Renaissance have led us to a Reception Theory based on the view that the Italian Renaissance and its classical revival set the pace and shaped the contours of the Northern Renaissance including ideas on education. This understanding, in contrast to a number of other theories, such as the one that postulates that the Prague Court of Charles IV was a model for emulation, or Heinrich Hermelink's notion that the stress on reason over will in the *via antiqua* provided a warm womb for humanism, obviates the necessity for sorting out the priority or the "pre-established harmony" notions that these other theories assume.

That the magisterial Reformers were great protagonists for education from early childhood to the university level is well known. One need merely be reminded of Luther's *Address to the Municipalities* or Melanchthon's role in the founding of gymnasia such as that at Nuremberg and his famous inaugural oration there. He earned the title *Praeceptor Germaniae*! But he remained a brilliant university professor and theologian. An educator who developed a liberal arts curriculum for schools from the lowest grade (begun at age five or six) through the university level was Johann Sturm of Strasbourg. His academy eventually became the University of Strasbourg and some of his teachers were to found and reform gymnasia which in due course matured into universities thriving today. John Calvin taught for Sturm and founded the academy which, transformed, is the University of Geneva. Claude Baduel moved on to Geneva from Strasbourg and then later reformed the University of Nîmes. Sturm directed and was consulted on the development of several municipal and princely gymnasia, his most extensive treatise being that on the foundation of the gymnasium at Lauingen in Bavaria.

Johann Sturm (1507–1589) lived his life across nearly the entire span of the sixteenth century in a highly exposed part of the Empire on the French border, a city for which both Valois and Habsburg rulers contended. Not only was his school an archetype widely emulated, like that of Vittorino da Feltre in Mantua but through his treatises on education and the editions of classical texts he provided, Sturm had a broad influence on educational thought throughout the Protestant world, and was not without influence even in Catholic education.[4] Although they never knew each other in person, Sturm and Roger Ascham had a sustained and intimate correspondence. Ascham, one recalls, was the tutor of Queen Elizabeth I, and he even named a son Johannes Sturm Ascham, but the unfortunate child died young.[5]

Of Sturm's thirty-six publications, nine can be considered his foremost writings on education, but they remained securely encased in formidable Ciceronian Latin, except for one published in the vernacular three centuries ago, and the classical letters translated into French by Jean Rott, the great Strasbourg Sturm scholar. In a day when a knowledge of Latin is so rare that even some professors of Renaissance history at prestigious universities cannot read it, it seemed to us that turning into English the major writings on pedagogy of the leading educator of the sixteenth century might be a useful service on behalf of the continuity and perpetuation of Western Civilization in a day when multiculturalism and political correctness for the time being hold sway. It is possible that current attitudes toward learning and the classical tradition may prove ephemeral, but in the meantime, we thought it prudent to make accessible what in their original tongue could only remain inaccessible, foreign and threatening. We undertook this enormous labor in the conviction that the translation of Sturm's key treatises and letters into English was not only educationally worthwhile, but culturally conservational.[6]

Included here are Sturm's original *Advice on What Organization to Give to the Gymnasium in Strasbourg*, written for the City Council and Scholarchs, an authoritarian board of education; followed by, in chronological order, his *De literarum ludis recte aperiendis, The Correct Opening of Elementary Schools of Letters* (1538); *De Amissa Dicendi Ratione, On the Lost Art of Speaking* (1538); *Ad Werteros Fratres, Nobilitas literata, Liberally Educated Nobility, for the Werter Brothers* (1549); *De educatione principis* (or *principum*), *On the Education of Princes* (1551); *Epistola de nobilitate anglicana, Concerning the English Nobility* (1551); *Scholae Lavinganae, The Lauingen School* (1565); *Epistolae Classicae, Classical Letters* (1565), some twenty letters that lay out Sturm's philosophy of education in exchange with other leading Renaissance and Reformation educators of the time; *Epistolae Academicae, Academic Letters* (1569), the practical "how to" letters on setting up curricula that reflect the philosophy of education revealed in the treatises and more theoretical letters.

No doubt the premiere work of translation during the sixteenth century was Luther's translation of the Bible. In his *Vom Dolmetschen* he described the art of translating in a timeless classical way: "To be a translator," Luther observed, "requires a stout heart." He translated the entire New Testament into German in just eleven weeks while in hiding in the Wartburg castle and hoped to show that "German nightingales can sing as beautifully as Roman goldfinches." As he worked away in 1522 he wrote: "I have undertaken to translate the Bible into German. This was good for me; otherwise I might have died in the mistaken notion that I was a learned fellow. All those who think they are learned ought to do some such work."[7] Putting the Hebrew Old Testament into German was even more difficult and required the advice of his entire Sanhedrin! And when it was done Luther reflected that doing a translation is like building one's house by the side of the road, for one passerby will say the word should have been rendered with another, and another that this difficult construction should have been done in some other way. But, he concluded with typical verve, that when all is said and done you built the house and they didn't. Having rendered several hundred pages of Ciceronian Latin into English, we can well appreciate Luther's sentiments and hope we have done Johann Sturm justice.

Sturm was born at Schleiden in the former Duchy of Luxembourg on October 1, 1507. His father sent him to the College of Saint Jerome in Liège. This school was founded in 1495 by the Brethren of the Common Life and they directed the school until the Jesuits took it over in the 16th century. From his correspondence over the years it is evident that Sturm was very happy with the course of studies there and introduced many features into his own plans for educational reform. Sturm studied there for four years, the sixth through the third form or grade and then enrolled at the University of Louvain at the end of 1524 in the faculty of the Arts of the famous *Collège des Trois Langues*, where he studied Greek, mastered Latin, and became a great admirer of Cicero and the power of oratory. There he learned to cherish the trilingual corona or the "triple linguistic tiara" of Latin, Greek, and Hebrew. Among his associates there were Latomus, Sleidan, Vesalius, and Claude Baduel. He had great enthusiasm also for the sciences, mathematics, physics, and astrology, and took his M.A. degree in Civil Law. He entered a classical printing house created by Rudiger (Rudgers) Rescius as an associate, with money advanced by his father.

He travelled for the firm and in Strasbourg in 1528, was moved by Martin Bucer's sermons and lectures on the Psalms toward an evangel- ical moral reform point of view. His contacts there helped prepare the way for his later call to school reform in Strasbourg. In 1529 he was in Paris where he did further publishing, and married a learned French woman. The couple opened a residential hotel, which soon became a hospice for German and French intellectuals such as Louis Carinus, a friend of Erasmus, of Melanchthon, and of Bucer. Sturm was drawn fur- ther into the nexus of evangelical reformers. The Affair of the *Placards* in Paris in October 1534, and in Germany the formation of the Schmal- kald League, changed the reasonably benign attitude of Francis I toward the Protestants and the Germans. One recalls the fate of Calvin, his brother, his cousin, Olivetan, of Nicholas Cop and of Protestants burned by the dozen. Sturm was more than happy to accept the invitation of the city council in Strasbourg to reorganize the educational system in that city. He left Paris on December 30, 1536, and arrived January 4, 1537, in Strasbourg.

In February 1538, he presented his proposal to city officials under the title "The Advice of Johann Sturm on what Organization to give to the Gymnasium of Strasbourg." Note that the references in many books to Sturm as the founder of the gymnasium are mistaken. On March 7, 1538, the Scholarchs, Jakob Sturm, Nicolas Kniebs, and Jakob Meyer, members chosen by the Council, not unlike a Board of Education, approved Sturm's Plan in its entirety. Sturm elaborated on this outline in what was to be his most important work on education, *The Correct Opening of Elementary Schools of Letters* (1538). On June 24 the Schol- archs offered the rectorate of the gymnasium to Sturm, and he devoted most of the remainder of his life to that calling.

The elementary Latin schools had no common curriculum and needed to be standardized with the beginning classes of the gymnasium by way of preparation for the university. Liberal arts, including the study of history, served as preparation for the study of law, theology, and medicine. Then Johann Sturm did something of which many will not approve. He segregated students along financial lines. In the medieval university when a poor student registered he was listed as a *pauper* in contrast to the *nobiles* who could pay their own way. But as a top administrator, Sturm in 1544 assigned the poor students, who had existed at the gymnasium from 1523 on, supported by the magistrates, to the Collège St. Guillaume, a place for scholarship students, *Collegium pauperum*, on the model of an ordinary Latin school. Sturm taught a bit, but basically became an administrator. What a horror he must have been, judging from his letters and instructions that every one of his instructors received as to how to prepare for classes, how to teach them, how to follow up on them. Whether in oratory, religion, mathematics, or science—Sturm was, or thought he was, "allwissend." Yet he got the job done for several decades, before he ran afoul of dangerous political circumstances and encountered deeper religious currents.

The purpose of this introduction, however, is not to describe the internal stresses in a churning municipality, a story often told in the German volumes on Strasbourg, without Marxist or sociological spoliation, nor to describe the French assaults on the German border, nor the Habsburg and Catholic attacks on what had been in Sturm's earlier years a fairly free city in the Empire, but to discuss briefly the educational methodology of this leading educator, Johann Sturm.

A methodologist he certainly was and his papers in the St. Thomas Archive in the *Archives Municipales* in Strasbourg as well as in his printed correspondence are replete with careful instructions to his staff in each of the disciplines. Conrad Dasypodius, who was in charge of mathematics, astronomy, and geography must have felt unusually insecure in view of the many instructions on procedure he received from Sturm. Dasypodius, after all, was the brilliant mathematician who, with the brothers Habrecht created the astronomical clock (1571–1574) which is to this day admired by tourists in the right wing of the cathedral. The rector believed that patient instruction and constant drill would develop young minds. Moreover, he worked out a progressive schema for eight years of schooling (later, increased to ten), and followed up this elementary and secondary education with a plan for public lectures for the graduates, before they went off to the university, a kind of junior college where one completed one's liberal education before embarking on professional training. He also provided for a quicker passage through the forms or grades for the exceptionally gifted students. Even in Lutheran academies in America, much of his terminol-

ogy persisted into the twentieth century and much of the curriculum
including the classical languages and the Latin terms for the classes from
sexta to *prima*. Pierre Mesnard has described Sturm's universal method
as resting on three principles—impregnation, continuity, and progression.[8]

Sturm had his shortcomings as a pedagogue and as an administrator, and no doubt as a politician and a man.[9] He was not always right,
nor was his judgment always sound. We have already mentioned his
desire to control the instructional liberty of classroom teachers, a practice which, even in the United States until quite recently, was not considered so unfortunate as it now seems to be. There was not much
development in his educational philosophy and insight, perhaps none
at all. But then, there was little difference if any between a Sturm, a
Melanchthon, or an Erasmus on the philosophy of education, although
considerable difference on the appropriate methodology. Renaissance
and Reformation educators held tenaciously to the notion that the best
education combined Christian piety with classical style and wisdom.
Their tenacious grasp of these principles gave little scope to alternative
education. On the other hand, Sturm's inflexible standards fueled his
determined optimism that the elite, and thus only a very small fraction
of the youth, who were trained in the classics, could achieve the highest
cultural goals their society had to offer them. Many of them did brilliantly, and went on to become very able civil servants and teachers,
lawyers and judges, pastors and theologians, professors, scholars, and
physicians. A few went home to rule their states, municipalities, and
principalities, and were probably not the worse rulers for their knowledge of religion and the classics.

That he expressed little interest in education for any but noble or
bourgeois boys and men and a small number of poor students leaving
the educational requirements of girls and women to others leads one to
conclude that in this respect, Sturm was not so progressive as were a
number of other Renaissance and Reformation educators, including men
like Thomas More, Vives, Luther and Melanchthon. Luther's concern
expressed in his *Address to the Municipalities* and in many other places
for a basic, though not a classical, education for all girls is well known.
Luther's close colleague and dear friend, Philipp Melanchthon, seems to
have been more progressive than Sturm in this regard, and to have envi-
sioned a course of study more in accord with that of the male sex.
Melanchthon's student Melchior Acontius composed a poem urging
humanist learning for women:

"On the Education of Women"

In our time they are teaching tender girls to love books
    And the female sex to make use of its gifts.
They make intellect flow into the arts, beauty
    Into its culture.
Nor let such learned ones now be men alone.
Let sweet girls vie with the males,
As I see it, your glory will not be light
For both sexes share the muses by common consent,
    I judge them to be less difficult for you![10]

Sturm was no less devoid of political instincts, including the instinct of self-preservation, than any other civic administrator and courtier of the Renaissance. He did not, however, limit his interest to self-preservation, and kept foremost in his mind the preservation of Protestants throughout Europe, even those with whom he disagreed doctrinally. He was engaged as a Protestant diplomat as much as he was an educator—he knew how to navigate in deep political waters and was not above taking presents and pensions from a variety of rulers. This did not make Sturm a spy, nor would any of his contemporaries have considered him unethical for accepting pensions and presents, for such was the custom. The test of his political ethics was his loyalty to the cause of Protestant liberties. He spent his own money, and encouraged friends and businessmen to spend theirs, on the support of wealthy or royal Huguenot refugees, most of whom never repaid their indebtedness to him. He struggled to pay back those whom he had tapped for such emergency funds. His failures were not of principle, nor of piety, but sometimes of judgment. It is debatable if his flattery of the Catholic Conrad Heresbach, a fellow schoolmaster, and his Catholic prince, to whom Sturm dedicated his *De educatione principis*, exemplified a desertion of Protestant loyalty more than it did an example of Sturm's dogged ecumenism, for which he was frequently criticized. For example, in 1565 he twice praised the Jesuits for introducing the classical and Christian humanist curriculum into their Catholic schools. This tendency ultimately destroyed him as a leader of Strasbourg's intellectual and civic life. While Sturm's critics might still fault him for not having grasped the depths or heights of evangelical theology, he remained one of the most tolerant and ecumenical humanists of the Reformation, cast in the mold of Erasmus, Melanchthon, or Bucer. He was not always comfortable in his own century, nor in touch with the sentiments of those who sought to define dogmatically the meaning of the evangelical and reformed faith.[11]

When political conditions in the Empire forced things in Strasbourg into a more conservative mode, Martin Bucer and others moved from Strasbourg to England. Sturm did not see the need to trim his sails, and in any event was too dedicated to his post as rector to relinquish an educational experiment that was sometimes more frustrating than rewarding or satisfying. His lack of consideration for his own safety and ease, plus the support of many of his faculty and of the Strasbourg Scholarchs combined to preserve him in authority as rector until his infirmities, his enemies, and his intemperate and ill-tempered polemics called the *Anti-Pappi* combined to relieve him of his post in 1581. In self-imposed exile at Northeim, near Strasbourg, he ended his life in 1589, blind and impoverished, living under the care and protection of Duke John Casimir at Neustadt.

If it is true, as H.G. Wells once said, that "Civilization is a race between education and catastrophe," then of Sturm it can be said that in this race he was a most competitive long distance runner, who could not stave off the catastrophic consequences of having "outrun" those intellectual athletes with whom he was most in sympathy—the Christian humanists.

1
Johann Sturm
(1507–1589)

Johann Sturm was born in the hamlet of Schleiden, near Aachen, in that part of the Rhineland called Eifel on October 1, 1507. His father Wilhelm was the financial officer (receiver) of the Count of Manderscheid, whose castle dominated the town's overhanging bluff. His mother, Gertrude Huls Sturm, was a member of a bourgeois family from Cologne. The Eifel region, though German-speaking and part of the Holy Roman Empire, looked west toward France and northwest toward Flanders for cultural guidance as much as to Germany. Johann Sturm grew up familiar with both French and German culture.

In Schleiden he spent his first fourteen years. Since his parents had fourteen children to raise, his acceptance into the Manderscheid family as a companion to their son was fortunate. At their castle he received much of his elementary education.[1] The kind and cultivated atmosphere of that setting may account for the fact that Sturm, though not a nobleman, showed a marked affinity with the titled class, as was later apparent in his relationships with European aristocrats. In Schleiden he formed one of his most enduring friendships with a boy named Johann Philipson, later the great historian Johann Sleidan and later Sturm's own colleague at Strasbourg.[2]

To the brief years Sturm spent in his native town must be attributed that respect for nurturing and nurturers that made him not only an advocate of the parental role in the earliest years of child training, but also a respector of the role of teachers generally as nurturers of the mind. In his letter to Abraham Feis, Sturm would recall (1565) with emotion the happy hours of his childhood spent with parents, grandparents and even a great-grandmother, and of his first teachers.[3]

That Schleiden phase of his education ended in 1521 when Sturm was sent to Liège to study at the College of St. Jerome, run by the Brethren of the Common Life. Later, when recalling his experience there he wrote mentioning four more of his childhood teachers.[4] The Brethren had been engaged in educating boys since the late fourteenth century and had gradually produced a program of educational reform, blending personal piety with some of the safer classical texts. These efforts, intermingled with other currents of the Renaissance, and especially with Italian humanism, so that, by the time young Sturm was preparing to be grounded in classical languages and literature, he was following a succession of boys who had received similar training, among them Desiderius Erasmus[5] and very likely, Martin Luther.[6] The College of St. Jerome was one of the better ones run by the Brethren, a fact attested by Sturm himself in several of his writings. Founded in 1500 it reached its most brilliant development after 1515 largely due to the influence of Nicholas Nickman, a brilliant teacher, whose influence brought the college to a point where it served as a model for Liège, outstripping the parish and chapter schools there.[7] More importantly, the College of St. Jerome served as Sturm's own model when he presented the school authorities of Strasbourg with a famous memoir in which he alluded to their program as his inspiration for the new Strasbourg Gymnasium.[8] At its height St. Jerome's enrolled some 1,600 students, but after 1581, it became a Jesuit school, although some of the original goals of the school were still preserved.[9] This is not surprising considering that Jesuit schools frequently patterned themselves after those Sturm designed or counseled. In Sturm's day the school provided eight classes for as many years of attendance. The first three were devoted to Latin, grammar and literature. Greek was introduced in the fourth year; literature in the fifth. Rhetoric and logic, or dialectic, were introduced then too, and completed in the sixth year, when the imitation of classical authors was begun. The last two years of schooling were devoted to oratory or declaiming, and to composition. Such aspects of the program as promotions at the end of one grade before passing to the next; prizes for excellence; and the enactment of plays[10] made a deep impression on young Sturm, and along with other features of the program, were later incorporated by him into the Strasbourg Gymnasium.

At seventeen (1524) Sturm left St. Jerome's for Louvain, enrolling at the famous College of Three Languages at the university.[11] Although Sturm did not learn Hebrew until he was in his fifties, he was delighted with his Latin and Greek studies. His Latin professor was Conrad Wackers (Goclenius), the first professor of Latin the University had ever had, of whom Erasmus once observed that one had to excuse him for publishing so little since he taught so well.[12] Sturm admired his knowledge of Cicero, who became the touchstone for his own approach to the art of teaching rhetoric and oratory. For Greek Sturm studied under Rutgers Ressen (Rescius), a brilliant Hellenist who had been named to the chair of Greek in 1518, but had become interested in the printing trade as a result of some work done as a proofreader and corrector of Greek texts for a printer named Martens. Meanwhile, Sturm had taken a

Master of Arts degree and for two years (1527–29) lived on his meager wages as a tutor.

In 1529 Sturm and Rescius, who had taken over the printing business from Martens, formed a partnership, capital for which was provided by Wilhelm Sturm. The previous year Johann took a short trip to Strasbourg where he attended some lectures on the Psalms given by the city's celebrated reformer, Martin Bucer.[13] He liked the city and although he would spend several years in Paris before taking up residence, when he did return he would make an indelible mark on the city the Romans had called Argentoratum.

In Paris he sold his firm's classical texts, for that city was then attracting some of the best scholars of the late Renaissance. Sturm took up the study of medicine, and edited a Latin translation of Galen,[14] which he finally published (1531) at Basel. By then he had given up his partnership with Rescius. He never completed his medical degree, as did his friend Andreas Vesalius.[15] A long illness had obliged him to halt his medical studies, but did not prevent him from making important social and intellectual contacts, for shortly after 1531, he was able to claim as protectors and benefactors Guillaume Budé (Budaeus), the great French humanist,[16] Queen Marguerite of Navarre, sister of Francis I and patroness of many humanists and reformers,[17] and the brothers Guillaume and Jean, Cardinal du Bellay.[18] These well-placed people gave scope to Sturm's ability for both intellectual and diplomatic activity, and enabled him to participate as one of a group of young, learned Germans who were promoting the cause of letters, science, and after 1534, of peace to balance the power of the Habsburg monarch, Charles V, against that of Francis I and the dissident reformed princes of Germany. Whatever future acts Sturm was to engage in as a diplomat, no matter in how much secrecy these were necessarily submerged, he never lost his interest in trying to obtain a general European peace so that some form of the reformed religion would benefit and an extensive, if not perfect, liberty of conscience endure. Among these young men were Johann Gunther (Andernacus), only two years Sturm's senior but nonetheless his teacher in medicine, as well as Vesalius, and even the Spaniard Michael Serveto (Servetus) whose later condemnation as a heretic Sturm would one day approve.[19] Yet another student of medicine at this time numbered among Sturm's friends was Ulrich Geiger (Chelius), and his role was also that of a political agent. Sturm's oldest friend, Philipson, became attached to the Du Bellays through Sturm's recommendation in the enduring capacity of secretary to the Cardinal.

Between 1531 and 1534 the major preoccupation of Sturm was not diplomacy, but letters. It may have been Guillaume Budé who was ultimately responsible for Sturm's first academic appointment, that of lecturer in the new Royal College (Collège de France) where he made his reputation giving public lectures on Cicero. When perplexed, he consulted Budé on certain knotty problems.[20] He also lectured on the new logic (dialectic) pioneered by the anti-Aristotelian Roelof Huysman (Rudolph Agricola).[21] Sturm had in his capacity as professor of logic, a keen-minded disciple whose ultimate fame as a logician would one day surpass his own, namely Peter de la Ramée (Ramus).[22] During his short period of service at the Collège de France, Sturm and his fellow countryman, Bartholomew Steinmetz (Latomus) were the two most popular professors there. Latomus was professor of Latin eloquence whose specialties were Cicero and Agricola's logic. Not even future differences of opinion concerning religious reform would prevent Sturm from admiring a man whose literary formation was so much like his own.[23]

Sturm's own fame as a teacher resulted in the offer of a position in the new university that Queen Marguerite was planning to establish in Béarn. Sturm declined the offer, perhaps because his life in Paris had become still more interesting to him after his marriage to a woman named Jeanne Pison (Johanna Ponderia).[24] Together they transformed their home in Paris into a pension or boarding house that attracted learned foreigners, including one Dr. Ludwig Carinus of Lucerne, a friend of Erasmus, Melanchthon, and Bucer, who may have helped encourage Sturm to take a reformed view of religion.[25]

Meanwhile, Guillaume du Bellay had been trying to coax Francis I to a reconciliation of the churches whose schism was still in the 1530s regarded by Christians a reproach to conscience. Chelius had been sent to Germany to sound out Philipp Melanchthon, Bucer and Hedio. These hopes were frustrated by an outbreak of radical reform sentiment in Paris that reached fever pitch on a certain day (1534) known as the Day of the Placards, when *placards* or posters that defamed the Catholic Mass were tacked up in public places around Paris and other cities, and even attached to the King's bedroom door at Amboise. Sturm disapproved of these reform tactics, and wrote to encourage Melanchthon to continue to think in terms of reaching an agreement with Francis, who would, he trusted, find Melanchthon's skill and moderation reassuring despite the unfortunate *placard* affair.[26] After this event, Francis initiated a policy of repressive legislation to curb the reform. Because this included the burning of a number of heretics Sturm and his young reform-minded friends found it harder to persuade Melanchthon of

Francis's willingness to cooperate with the Protestant princes of Germany, and only Bucer appeared still willing to be persuaded. In the end neither Bucer nor Melanchthon came to France to confer with Francis I. For a while Sturm continued to believe that Francis I was willing to be ruled by reason where his own honor and safety were not under attack, as they had been during the *placard* crisis. No doubt he was lulled by his own optimistic nature, for his failure to assess Francis correctly was naive. He wrote in the summer of 1535 that the king's nature was frank and open, apt to be guided by prudence, but also and as much by reason.[27] What Sturm hoped for was that the reform of religion might be accomplished in France, as it had not been in Germany, under a cooperative monarch and without the horrors of civil war and bloodshed.[28]

Only when Sturm saw his efforts were ineffectual, did he consent to leave France for Germany. Considerations for his personal safety contributed to that decision. He began his trip on December 30, 1536, arriving in Strasbourg on January 14, 1537. There he accepted a position teaching rhetoric and dialectic and must have been gratified to receive two salary increases within the space of several months, more than tripling the forty florins he had originally accepted. The reason for such marks of favor was his own merit: his courses were so popular that within a few months he was attracting other teachers of his school who preferred to audit his course than to conduct their own. The increased salary was meant to discourage him from accepting job offers from Basel or Wittenberg.[29]

One cannot assess or appreciate Sturm's subsequent educational triumphs—or disappointments—without some knowledge of Strasbourg's cultural history, spiritual as well as intellectual, before his arrival there in 1537. Throughout most of the Renaissance period the city was not particularly known for its prominent role in arts and sciences.[30] There was no university there, nor even a Latin school of note, although the nearby city of Schlettstadt was famous for schools set up by the Brethren of the Common Life and all around Strasbourg were universities of some standing—those of Basel, Tübingen, Freiburg, and Heidelberg. The only Latin education available in the city was that offered by monks for prospective clerics, but lay education was not a great concern of the city fathers until the very end of the fifteenth century, when a general unrest among the laity, caused in large part by disapproval of clerical laxness, began to feed their dissatisfaction with the educational status quo. Of course, Strasbourg did have its share of outspoken and learned critics of social behavior, the chief of whom being Sebastian Brant, author of the satiric and popular *Ship of Fools*,[31] and pre-Reformation preachers such as Johann Geiler von Kaisersberg[32] and Jacob Wimpheling,[33] his former pupil and disciple. These three men were friends. Geiler was a Savanarola-like character who delivered fiery sermons on the evils of monopolistic business practices while trying at the same time to win his Bishop's approval for a new secondary school or "Hochschule" that would produce a more competent priesthood. In this he was unsuccessful. His sensitivity to the need for education was reflected by his disciple, Wimpheling, who provided a secular twist in his book *Germania* (1510), which was dedicated to the Strasbourg city council. In it he proposed that a secular and community-sponsored school be set up along humanist lines, that is as a general preparatory school that would equip its graduates to enter the professions as civic and military leaders, notaries, teachers, merchants, etc. Although he received twelve florins for his plans, Wimpheling's school never materialized, though the proposal was renewed in 1504 and in 1507.

For the next twenty years some progress toward expanding the educational base in Strasbourg was made. During the 1520s a number of primary schools taught by former clerics were established, and there were at least two Latin schools as well as series of public lectures for adults that formed the basis of scientific education available in the city. But the general sentiment was that the schools were poorly organized and that faulty grammar impeded instruction. As yet no one had appeared who could provide a solution to these criticisms.[34]

Certainly the deficiencies in the offerings were not due to an absence of progress in humanistic studies. By the 1520s German concerns for improved spiritual and moral leadership had fused with the intellectual concerns of the German humanists. The activities of men such as Erasmus and his friend and former pupil, Beatus Rhenanus,[35] in disseminating the Italian scholarship of the previous century had become prime. Sturm, in his life of Beatus (1551),[36] cited a modest list of Italian humanists who had been flourishing and productive when Germany was scarcely out of its literary infancy. He noted that before such northerners as Rudolf Agricola, Alexander Hegius,[37] and Erasmus there had not been sufficient interest among young men in the beauties of pure language.

By 1537, however, the problem was clearly not one of insufficient motivation, for who was not convinced by then that a thorough grounding in classical literature was a necessary accomplishment? On the acquisition of such knowledge depended preferment in the church or at court. A classical education opened new doors to positions formerly reserved only for the well-born and noble. Indeed, with the coming and the flourishing of Protestantism, the lines between scholar, clerk, and layman became increasingly less distinct. A classical education was no longer just the concern of professionals, but of earnest Christians generally, for the humanists had demonstrated that mere literacy and Bible reading were not the only keys to understanding the meaning of one's faith. The possession of classical language and logic was also very helpful. Indeed, one is tempted to think that education in the sixteenth century had become, for those who could afford it, a significant status symbol.

If fifteenth-century Strasbourg had been in its literary infancy, as Sturm had observed, sixteenth-century Strasbourg nearing the century's halfway mark had come of age. It had the printing establishments necessary to supply a learned community. It had support and encouragement from the reformed and their clergy. It had humanistic sodalities or clubs devoted to the cultivation of letters. It was surrounded by a plethora of secondary schools and universities in neighboring regions. It could draw on a community of German humanists for support, and its reformed inhabitants had not yet entered upon sectarian divisions that would in another generation be straining the fabric of community spirit. The community was governed by a class who had managed to overcome their rivalries and work together in relative harmony for the common interest. This group of influential governors had during the dozen years or so before Sturm's arrival in 1537 shown a mutual interest in remodeling the old educational system in the interest of the new and progressive humanist sort.

Humanism was not, however, the only concern of the reformers, for as early as 1524 they had been laboring on behalf of education in Strasbourg. Reformed piety provided theologians such as Martin Bucer, and with him Wolfgang Capito[38] and Caspar Hedio[39] the moral justification that the city magistrates needed to re-structure the educational system inherited from the Catholic past. The twin necessities of the new educational program would be a reformed theological education for prospective clergymen and a classical or humanist curriculum for young men interested in any of the other professions, but especially in public service.

It was greatly to Sturm's advantage that precedents for a public school system had been set as early as 1528, with a ministry of education in the form of three appointees called Scholarchs to direct the new program; that the traditional public lecture system of the city had been enlarged to include rhetoric, mathematics, poetry, Greek and Hebrew, in addition to theology and jurisprudence; and that the public had been thoroughly prepared for an expanded intellectual offering. In fact, the need for a real university had already been broached by Bucer and introduced before the city council and other municipal bodies,[40] though a university was then considered to be too costly and the scheme was rejected. Yet Bucer's prior work in preparing a plan for secondary education should be regarded as a contribution to the ultimate formulation of the Strasbourg Gymnasium and (after 1565) to the Strasbourg Academy, even if the final formulation for the founding of those institutions was submitted by Sturm, rather than Bucer.

By the time Johann Sturm entered upon the Strasbourg educational scene there was scarcely more to be done than to fulfill the high expectations which reformers like Bucer and Melanchthon had formed of him. His immediate tasks were to state the educational needs of a city that had already gone far to meet them, to provide a model or schema that would command the attention of the city's governing bodies and the support of an already supportive community. The memoir that did that was submitted by Sturm to the Scholarchs at their request.[41] It provided for the consolidation of the three Latin schools then in existence; recommended a logical progression of subject matter from one grade to the next, as well as one methodology; alluded to the College of St. Jerome as a curricular model; recommended lodging the new school in the former Dominican monastery; and prescribed a course of liberal studies—philosophy, ancient languages, history, mathematics and theology—for those who completed the nine classes of the new gymnasium. This memoir also provided for some de-centralized elementary schools on the outskirts of the city, a concession to parents of very young pupils who were worried about a long walk for their youngsters if the school were in the center of town. As for the position of rector, Sturm urged for reasons of prestige that he be chosen from among the teachers of the public courses, not from the group of regular gymnasium masters. He was himself appointed in June of 1538 to fill the position, a year's trial appointment that lasted for forty-three!

From its inception the gymnasium was well regarded. Sturm attracted some of the students he had taught in Paris, and many came from other countries as well. The staff was more than usually able and included some reformers of note during the first decade: John Calvin,[42] Wolfgang Capito, and the Florentine refugee, Peter Martyr Vermigli,[43] who became Sturm's close friend.

Two years of plague (1540–1541) caused some inconvenience and considerable grief to Sturm and his school,[44] and made it necessary to leave Strasbourg temporarily. Nearly as discouraging to Sturm was a disagreement (soon resolved) between him and Martin Bucer, who would have preferred to see the income from the Chapter of St. Thomas used solely to support prospective preachers. When Sturm objected that the Chapter must decide for itself without interference from the magistrates Bucer deferred to Sturm's view of the matter, which revolved on the issue of independence from magisterial interference. It was fortunate for their friendship that Bucer backed away from confrontation.[45] Though tempted occasionally to find a more challenging profession, Sturm stayed with teaching and administration, largely because his friend Melanchthon persuaded him that he was needed in that capacity.[46] He continued to enjoy a close rapport with his staff and took pleasure in the Strasbourg residence of his boyhood friend, Philipson, or Sleidan, as he was now called, who had moved to the city to do historical research. Also reassuring was the fact that the school continued to grow in enrollment.[47]

The major threats to the prosperity of the school in its first critical decade of existence were political and religious. The collapse of the Schmalkald League (1546) of Protestant princes had been followed by the publication (May 15, 1548) of a policy known as the Augsburg Interim.[48] This might have affected the gymnasium adversely but for Sturm's ability to dissuade the city's respected Catholic Bishop, Erasmus of Limbourg,[49] from restoring the income of the Chapter of St. Thomas to Catholic use. The Chapter had been converted at the gymnasium's founding to meet its financial obligations in a way that insured its independence. Sturm's efforts to preserve that independence were firmly supported by the Chapter's canons. Together they managed to persuade Bishop Erasmus of Limbourg that such independence was consistent with the requirements of the Interim to preserve public tranquillity.[50] The Bishop, a personal friend of the Rector's and a Catholic moderate, was persuaded at length to change his plans, while Sturm's ability to win concessions from other Catholic churchmen won for the school a coveted exemption from the Interim, and freedom from Catholic control. This triumph was not fortuitous, but the fruit of that goodwill and respect Sturm had derived from both Catholics and a variety of Protestants in more than a decade of activity on the international as well as domestic scene. He never ceased to involve himself in the cause of church unity and reconciliation.

The lack of unity among the reformed occupied Sturm as much as the opening of the new school, for between 1537 and 1538 he, Capito and Bucer were engaged in settling differences that had arisen in Basel between two reformers, and in Berne where they agreed to a formula of faith drawn up for the French churches. In 1539 he and Bucer attended a conference in Frankfurt called to determine a plan for reaching agreement among reformed churches on a number of diverse forms and practices. There Sturm met Philipp Melanchthon for the first time, although he had long been a correspondent.[51] The following year he was sent with Calvin and Jacob Sturm, the Mayor of Strasbourg,[52] to the Diet at Hagenau where the order of the day was again reconciliation between the Catholic and reformed churches. During this period Sturm worked quietly at the behest of Francis I to align the reformed princes with France. In the event, the Protestants dithered, and despite the best efforts of Sturm, Sleidan and the Du Bellays, the Catholic intransigents surrounding the French king managed to sabotage any alliance.

Similarly unsuccessful in effecting church reconciliation were colloquies held in Worms (1540) and Ratisbon (1541), both of which Sturm attended as deputy, along with Bucer, Calvin, Jacob Sturm and Capito. He developed a deep friendship with Joachim Camerarius[53] during these years, for the two men shared similar interests in classical literature, and his ideal of *pietas docta* was exactly congruent with Sturm's own "sapiens et eloquens pietas" (also referred to as *pietas litterata*), an obvious re-statement of Cicero's "vir bonus dicendi peritus."[54] Nor were Protestants alone proponents of such ideals. Sturm admired the legate Cardinal Gasparo Contarini[55] and exchanged sentiments with him at the Diet of Ratisbon on issues that divided their churches, but could not obliterate their common heritage—Christian humanism. In 1542 and 1543 Sturm accompanied Bucer to Cologne where both men worked to reform that diocese.[56]

It may be that in his efforts to effect the alliance between France and the Protestant princes during the 1540s, Sturm was unable to comprehend the lack of complete good faith of both parties. Francis I was not the most consistent of princes, and the German princes were ultimately to prove more fearful of the loss of their privileges and power than the loss of their religious liberty. Sturm's naiveté may have made him a less capable diplomat, but it increased his determination to continue his diplomatic service. A more realistic negotiator might well have become discouraged earlier and given up his efforts. There were, nevertheless, moments of disenchantment as when in 1544 the Protestant states decided to join the empire in a war against France. Again, Strasbourg profited from Sturm's reputation as a sincere peacemaker, and he was able to persuade Francis I to respect the frontiers of Alsace should there be a large-scale mobilization. Although the French and the Germans seemed intent on earning the suspicions of the other party, their needs for security were such that neither side could give up altogether the idea of an alliance. It was this interdependence which Sturm recognized, and he hoped that the price the French court would be willing to pay for German Protestant aid against an imperial consolidation was increased toleration of French reform within French borders. Yet not even the Vaudois or Waldensian massacre,[57] ordered by Francis against the reformed of Piedmont, discouraged Sturm from participating in the next round of negotiations that the German princes hoped would shelter them from the wrath of Charles V. Sturm was chosen in the summer of 1545 as an ambassador to the French court in an attempt to negotiate a peace between that country and England. Unfortunately for his high hopes, when the peace was made between those two powers it contained no provisions for the religious liberty of Protestants in either Germany or France.

Between 1545 and 1547 Sturm labored on behalf of the Schmalkald princes to cement the elusive alliance. His burden was not eased by Francis I's stubborn insistence upon the entry of England into the alliance, and his equally stubborn determination to get the German princes to elect his son, the future Henry II, as the new emperor. Sturm was dismayed by the intransigence of Francis I, but also by the obvious selfishness of the German princes, who reconciled with the Emperor and prejudiced their own liberties. The submission of Frankfurt, Ulm, Augsburg, and Württemberg to the emperor (prompted at least in part by the death of Francis I and the uncertainty of winning French support of any king against the emperor) were a clear blow to Sturm, who felt their capitulation was a reflection against their loyalty to German liberties as well as to their religion. The failure of the German Protestant states to effect an alliance with France was for the rest of his life a matter of disappointment to Sturm, although it appears that he distributed the blame equally on the indecisiveness of the dying Francis and the selfishness of the German Protestant princes.[58]

For Sturm, the years of the Interim (1548–1555) were discouraging by and large, though he continued to be honored by royalty,[59] entrusted with diplomatic errands,[60] presented with a variety of gratuities,[61] which he usually devoted to his favorite charity—helping Protestant refugees, usually of noble birth, relocate in Strasbourg. Since 1548 he had been without the company of Martin Bucer, of Paul Fagius,[62] and of Peter Martyr, all of whom had accepted the generous hospitality of Archbishop Cranmer and sought refuge in England. But friendships persisted even when proximity did not, as in the case of Sturm's friend John Calvin, who wrote him (December 1548) from Geneva to assure him that however bleak the international scene might then appear, however imminent the prospects of war or death, "...we shall have cherished a friendship in good faith, the bond of which is inviolable...."[63]

In late spring of 1553 the plague returned and obliged a short migration of the school, and in October of that year Jacob Sturm died, removing from the councils of government a moderate and friendly protectorship over the school. There were, however, compensations for the loss. In 1550 Sturm's long pen-friendship with Roger Ascham,[64] the English humanist and tutor to Princess Elizabeth, began. Ascham had made the acquaintance of Bucer shortly after the latter's arrival in England, and at Cambridge the two spoke of Bucer's Strasbourg days of his friendship with the rector of the gymnasium there. Ascham was drawn to Sturm in this way and through Sturm's writings, of which he was an ardent admirer. His first letter to Sturm, dated April 4, 1550, was a comment on the interconnection of logic and rhetoric, and in it he asked Sturm to publish his commentary on Aristotle's Rhetoric.[65] The eighteen-year-long correspondence between these two schoolmasters still offers a touching testimonial to the possibility of close friendship between people who meet only in a spiritual and intellectual sense, but meet fully. When Sturm wrote Ascham that he could not permit Ascham to love him more than he, Sturm, esteemed his English friend, the sincerity of such affection is unmistakable.[66] And because their bond was deep, they were able to learn from each other, to admire each other's work in progress,[67] and to ask each other for criticism and help.[68] Ascham's last letter to Sturm was a long one concerning the topic of imitation, or emulation of the classics, about which Ascham was almost consumed with curiosity, for he had been expecting Sturm to publish some examples that would make Ascham's own task of completing *The Schoolmaster* easier.[69]

Naturally the two men were eager to share their educational triumphs. In his first letter Ascham praised the English nobility for their zeal in learning, among them the princess Elizabeth. Perhaps he had read the work Sturm had published the year before for the benefit of the Werter brothers.[70] In any event, Ascham suggested that Sturm write something for Elizabeth that she would read with appreciation and perception. Sturm had his efforts printed up under the title *Epistolae Duae de Nobilitate* and this exchange of letters appeared with another of Sturm's works, *De Educatione Principum* in Conrad Heresbach's work on Greek eloquence.[71] The exchange with Ascham on the English nobility was intended to motivate their German counterparts to make similar strides in classical learning. Sturm sent Elizabeth a copy of his recently published *Liber Unus de Periodis*, dedicating the Preface to her.

It is probable that an undated letter from the princess to Sturm was written by way of a thank-you for his flattering attention to her. The princess began her note by calling Sturm her "Amice perdilecte" and acknowledging that from his writings she knew him to be a man of pure doctrine, great learning, and much kindness to herself.[72]

Aside from personal friendship, the compensation of the 1550s included the leisure that diminished diplomatic activity gave him. He could find more time for writing, and he took his writing seriously.[73] Nor, in Sturm, were humanism—the study of letters—and the requirements of humane behavior separate entities. During the 1540s and into the '50s and '60s he labored on behalf of the oppressed reformed of France and Germany. In the 1540s Sturm sought relief for the Protestants of Metz from the Empire, and when that city was captured by Henry II of France (1553) he continued to work for their betterment, trying in 1558 to intercede in negotiations between the empire and France. Neither side showed any interest. On the other hand, when William Farel[74] and Theodore Bèze[75] asked for Sturm's intercession with the French king on behalf of the oppressed Vaudois Protestants, Sturm drew up an impressive list of reasons why Henry II should treat them with consideration. His letter was perhaps instrumental in obtaining better treatment for the Vaudois.

The Vaudois, however, were on the periphery of France. When it was a question of Huguenots inside the kingdom there was more hostility on the part of the court. This was notably the case during the reign of young Francis II (1559–60), because Francis was still an adolescent and was dominated by his Guise in-laws, who were rabidly ultramontane and not interested in a nationalistic diplomacy. Sturm, together with John Calvin and Francis Hotman,[76] tried to enlist the help of German princes against the Guises outside France, and of Bourbon princes, especially Antoine of Navarre, within. Their efforts were hampered by the vacillations of Navarre and the prejudices of some of the Lutheran princes of Germany against the new Calvinist doctrine. The Lorrainers, for example, persuaded Christoph of Württemberg from a unified pro-reformed policy because Huguenots were naturally rebellious against all authority.

The Civil war that broke out in France after the massacre of Vassy (March 1562) caused Sturm the greatest distress. His old friend Hotman accused him of betraying the plotters involved in the conspiracy of Amboise, while Sturm protested his innocence.[77] The bulk of his efforts during these trying years (1562–66) was directed to finding funds for the Protestant troops sent into France, and in giving shelter to the Protestant mother-in-law of the Huguenot commander, Condé. This woman, Mme. de Roye, was the recipient of ten thousand florins of Sturm's own money, and several thousand more of which he was guarantor. Not only did he give all he had—literally—to this woman in distress, but he entreated other nobles and his own friend and publisher, Wendelin Rihel, to lend her money. In addition to that, Sturm found money for Condé's troops. He refused, however, a request by Calvin that he obtain the consent of the Strasbourg governors to raise the funds needed to pay off certain German troops who were occupying parts of France. Meanwhile, peace came (March 1563) but repayment of the money Sturm had provided these needy refugees did not. He was reduced to such an extent that he thought seriously of resigning his provostship of the Chapter of St. Thomas. At the same time he was busy receiving letters from parties testifying to the legitimacy of his demands for repayment. At one point Theodore Bèze's help was requested. Sturm had written asking him to intervene with Madame de Roye and her nephews, Admiral Coligny[78] and d'Andelot,[79] his brother. Bèze wrote back that he had done as asked, and hoped Sturm's mind might be eased, wishing he could think of something more to do for him.[80] In 1565 Sturm wrote Anthony Cook[81] to lament the fact that he was reduced to such extremes of poverty that he was obliged to enlist the help of various princes. He was sending a copy of a letter he had drafted and addressed to Elizabeth. Would she also be willing to write letters presenting the merits of his case for repayment? He thought hers might be especially productive.[82]

Although the magistrates of Strasbourg, aided by several of the princes, formed a commission that recognized the rightfulness of Sturm's request for repayment, he had only been partially repaid at his death for his generosity.[83] The lack of gratitude on the part of those he aided hurt him more than the dunning letters of his creditors. Yet he never regretted giving his all to protect endangered Huguenots.

Sturm lost more than time, energy and money in caring for the Calvinist reformed—he lost credibility and support from the orthodox Lutheran clergy and their supporters. His irenic point of view had become an object of suspicion to men like Johann Marbach[84] who insisted on adherence of all teachers and professors in the public courses to the Wittenberg formula of faith,[85] hoping that the provisions concerning the elements of the Eucharist would disqualify any but orthodox Lutherans from getting or holding a teaching position in Strasbourg.

The first rift indeed brought about the resignation of Peter Martyr from his philosophy post (1556), and at about the same time Sturm and

Hotman set about to prevent Jerome Zanchi, who held a chair in theology, from being dismissed over doctrine.[86] Sturm's intervention as provost saved Zanchi temporarily, but Sturm then became the object of Marbach's ire when Zanchi and Sturm attempted to prevent publication of an attack on Philipp Melanchthon.[87]

A letter written by Sturm to Bèze on February 20, 1558, quite dramatically reveals the author's frame of mind during these trying struggles against ultra conservative critics in the church. Sturm began by inquiring after Bèze's health, and moved on to discuss how the ultra conservative pastor, Melchior Specker,[88] one of that troublesome younger crowd which Sturm referred to as the "pueri" (boys), had determined to publish a book refuting Bèze's position on predestination. Sturm noted that there was absolutely nothing anyone could do to dissuade him from publishing.[89] Then, giving vent to an oratorical soliloquy of despair and irony, he added:

> Oh what a miserable century is ours, miserable you ask, for what reason? For our sins, yes, ours, I say, greed, ambition, how I wish these fine things were useful to the church![90]

The thrust of Sturm's campaign to defend the school and the reformed position against the ultra Lutherans was that to do otherwise would jeopardize Protestantism generally, making a union of European Protestant states difficult or impossible. The 1550s and first years of the 1560s were made difficult by doctrinal differences of opinion combined with institutional and political issues affected by religion. Sturm's method of fighting the Superintendent was to pen letters to influential people and to write prefaces to treatises of Bucer on the Eucharist in which he explained the dangers of such illiberal religious policies to European reform generally. The publication of these treatises with Sturm's impassioned preface to Anthony Cook,[91] Edward VI's tutor, made it necessary for Sturm to define and defend his beliefs concerning the Lord's Supper, which he did in October of 1561. For him there could be no ubiquitist or Catholic interpretations; rather, the supper was a spiritual communion with the body and blood of Christ entirely validated by faith, or invalidated by lack of it.[92]

Rumors soon spread that Sturm was opposed to the basic tenets of Lutheranism, and these probably discouraged him from publishing anything more of a theological nature at that time.[93] He did, however, circulate his religious views among friends. In defining those views regarding the chief mystery of the Christian religion—the Eucharist—

Sturm aligned himself with the more anti-metaphysical believers of his time, as had Bucer. His religious views were not original, but those of the Christian humanists and reformers of Strasbourg's recent past, characterized by moderation and human reason insofar as he felt it to be consistent with the written word of God.[94]

As a result of the publicity given Sturm's religious views, he was obliquely reproved from the pulpit by Melchior Specker, preaching in St. Thomas in October 1561 on the theme that seditious persons and heretics undermine the well-being of the world by treating, without any mission to do so, matters pertaining to faith. Sturm concluded that he was the object of Specker's sermon, which was in fact an attack on Sturm's probity,[95] and he threw himself into a whirlwind of activity to justify his positions and Zanchi's that he had defended. The theologians he consulted assured him that Zanchi's work was not heretical, but urged him to avoid further publicity.

Sturm and Zanchi certainly knew the extent to which genuine Lutherans were dismayed by the confluence in Lutheran circles of men who held to mere symbolic interpretations of the sacraments. On the other hand, in 1561 there was so much political uncertainty and tension that in France and Germany the possibility again arose of maintaining peace by making religious and civil concessions to opposing churches. Suddenly many men of good will grasped at any chance to improve international as well as to quell domestic strife. The motive of peace and Christian unity had given substance to German irenicism since its inception in the early decades of the Reformation. It had been reflected in Bucerian theology, the promotion of compromise re-statements of the Augsburg Confession (1530) such as *Apology to the Augsburg Confession* by Melanchthon or *The Confessio Tetrapolitana*; countless efforts at discussion (colloquies) at places like Marburg, Worms, Regensburg, and the interest in religious unity displayed by princes like Frederick II of the Palatinate,[96] and Christoph, Duke of Württemberg,[97] who seemed to put the material prosperity and the civic tranquillity of their subjects at a level as great as that of doctrinal purity. Strasbourg, having been home to Bucer and situated between France and the rest of empire, had been notoriously broad minded as to the pursuit of Protestant unity irrespective of doctrinal diversity. In France, the government of Catherine d'Medici[98] and her chancellor, Michel de l'Hôpital, proposed that the Colloquy of Poissy (January 1562) consider possibilities of rapprochement between Catholic and Huguenot practice, their position a reflection of some sincere interest on the part of a small number of Catholics who had labored for years to make accommodation with Calvinists.[99] In the final analysis, Poissy was successfully used by the intransigent Catholic party in France to divide the Lutherans from the Calvinists. Calvin warned his representative, Theodore Bèze, that the French were pressing for a Lutheran interpretation of the reformed faith.

Since Sturm was a friend and correspondent of Calvin, with plenty of contacts in the highest diplomatic and religious circles, it is unlikely that he was not aware of the larger implications of Poissy. But a scant month later found him attending the conference of Saverne (February 1562) requested by Charles of Guise, the Cardinal of Lorraine, and Francis, Duke of Guise, and held at the residence of the Bishop of Strasbourg. There too came Zanchi and the Lutheran theologian, Johannes Brenz,[100] Jakob Andreae, Chancellor of the University of Tübingen,[101] and Christoph, Duke of Württemberg. Brenz, along with others, told Sturm at Saverne that he ought not to be showing himself partial to Zanchi's cause, and added that he had observed that Sturm, in his old age (he was then fifty-five) was trying to become a theologian. To this Sturm replied facetiously that he was indeed partial to Zanchi in this sense: that he had lent one part (an ear) and another part (the other ear) to Marbach; that he was defending Zanchi so as not to damn him unheard; and that he, Sturm, was being held in line by both colleagues.[102]

The wedge that the Guise party in France had begun to drive at Poissy was pounded deeper at Saverne, where the French party made astounding and insincere declarations of their willingness to accept major aspects of the Augsburg Confession, and where the Cardinal of Lorraine exuded a charm that apparently threw Zanchi and Sturm off their guard. They were in short, completely taken in. The massacre of Vassy,[103] which followed immediately thereafter, disabused them of their naiveté.

Sturm felt that only a synod of theologians would serve to justify the positions he and Zanchi had taken as non-heretical. He petitioned the magistrates to sponsor a conference and one was called in March 1563. It was attended by theologians from Switzerland and Germany,[104] and it produced the Strasbourg Consensus or Concord.[105] This reaffirmed two earlier formulae, the Confession of Augsburg (1530) and the Wittenberg Concord (1536). The Strasbourg Formula presented a scriptural and basically Lutheran point of view in the doctrine of election. One is not to speculate on the act of eternal election as such *a priori* but should consider it *a posteriori* as manifested to one in the gospel of Christ. Although Zanchi signed it at Sturm's urging, it was scarcely a matter of rejoicing for either man. Zanchi left Strasbourg shortly afterward to become a pastor at Chiavenna in the Valtelline. Sturm, after contemplating a removal to Zurich, decided against it and settled down to devote himself once again to the problems of education, sadly neglected after so many years of tension.

Yet, despite their doctrinal differences, Sturm and Marbach were able to work in tandem to improve the quality of Protestant education. Both men were interested in the school reforms in the territory of Zweibrücken. Marbach had been hired in 1558 by Duke Wolfgang of Zweibrücken, a former pupil of Sturm's, to serve as Church Visitor there. In that position he had occasion to study the school program of Hornbach and had published a detailed memorandum on his observations that amounted to a plan for the restructuring of the school.[106] The staff of the Hornbach school was composed of graduates of the Strasbourg gymnasium, and they had been trained in accordance with Sturm's educational precepts. Those precepts concerning curriculum and methodology became an integral feature of the Hornbach program and served as a model for still more schools in the Duke's territory. What is noteworthy about this is that Marbach can be seen to have supported the Sturmian program even though religiously he was not in agreement, and was even in bitter disagreement, with Sturm. When, in 1573, the new Duke of Zweibrücken, Johann I, invited Sturm to serve as school visitor at Hornbach, it was agreed between them that the Lauingen school plan (which provided for six years of education, not four) should supersede that of Marbach.

The decade of the 1560s was an important time for the educational history of Strasbourg. Perhaps for Sturm a return to education represented a relief precisely because he was assured of the support of the Superintendent, and of the continued respect for his pedagogy that the magistrates preserved from earlier times. Yet their support of his expertise and their respect for his dedication to the city did not guarantee that funds would be forthcoming for the university he wished to see created there. In fact, Marbach and Sturm were fortunate that the city magistrates, having received (May 6, 1566) their written memoir urging the creation of a full-scale university, did not refuse further consideration on the subject of higher education. Only one man on the city council supported their ambitious project. The rest of the magistrates supported a more modest establishment of an academy rather than a university, and even then, it was necessary to bribe the imperial vice-chancellor with a gift of furniture, and the imperial counsel with a gift of new books! Nor did Sturm and Marbach escape reproach when it became known in Strasbourg that an extra five hundred florins were needed to bribe the imperial chancellery!

The creation of the Academy was not the fulfillment of Sturm's educational goals,[107] but he was pleased when he was at least named the Academy's first rector, and that for life. Although the offerings in all subjects but theology, literature and philosophy were scarcely satisfactory (since the Academy granted only bachelors' and masters' degrees in philosophy), Sturm concentrated his attention on improving aspects of education that were within the realm of the possible. Among these were encouraging his colleagues to take their jobs seriously, and recognize their duties to the community despite inadequate salaries. The latter were also of special concern to Sturm, and he wrote frequent messages to the Scholarchs on behalf of his underpaid faculty. He obtained a new home for the library which Jakob Sturm had founded, and assured the appointment of its first librarian. He wanted to see the creation of a botanical garden by a physician named Didyme Obrecht, but could not persuade the Scholarchs to fund it.

Sturm's relatively peaceful periods were always dependent upon the religious peace of Europe. When war broke out in 1567 between the Huguenots and the French court of Charles IX, his attention and energies were absorbed in the relief of the beleaguered reformed. Indeed, the next nine years were largely devoted to the problems of Huguenots in France and their survival as refugees. In the period 1567–1572 Sturm worked as an agent on behalf of the house of Navarre, the Protestant refugee Cardinal Châtillon,[108] Duke Wolfgang of Zweibrücken, the Elector of Saxony[109] and even of Queen Elizabeth I[110] to furnish money and troops to the reformed forces in France. Sturm underwrote a loan to Navarre of 10,000 écus and hoped that he would be reimbursed within the month. As it turned out, Navarre stalled, and the Landgrave of Cassel refused to honor Wolfgang's debts even though he was made tutor to the Duke's heirs. Such complications meant that Sturm waited unpaid for the loan made to Navarre. In April 1572, the Queen of Navarre, Jeanne d'Albret,[111] wrote Sturm to pledge her aid in his repayment. In fact, arrangements were under way to repay some 30,000 francs that were owed him. Unfortunately, the massacre of St. Bartholomew's Day (August 24, 1572) dispelled any hope he may have had for re-payment.

All things considered, Sturm would be the last person one might accuse of self-interest. He had heroically gone out on a limb for a number of princes and aristocrats because he wished to be of use in the honorable task of saving the reformed faith in France. Besides his own money and that of his friends he had risked his honor on their behalf, for he had always to answer in person to creditors whose generosity was in large measure a reflection of their confidence in him. His financial distress influenced his behavior negatively. He was made credulous by his debts, vulnerable to the manipulations of men less principled than he when his financial distress made him less than a wise judge of character. His plight was all the more humiliating because it was well known. Both he and his friends made numerous appeals to their debtors for repayment. Perhaps not all the tempting offers which his predicament probably encouraged have come to light, but on one occasion he was approached by agents of Catherine d'Medici and her son, Duke Henry of Anjou, who proposed repayment of his debts in return for his support for the candidacy of Anjou to the Polish throne.[112] Sturm agreed to write letters influencing opinion in Poland in favor of Anjou, being as yet unaware of the true horrors of the St. Bartholomew's Day tragedy. In 1576 Sturm found it necessary to remind the former Duke, now King Henry III of France, of his promises of repayment, as yet unfulfilled.[113]

Charles IX, who had engaged as well to reimburse Sturm in return for his help in securing a mediated peace between Charles's Huguenot enemies and the German Princes may have been prevented by the resumption of the war in France in April 1574 from paying Sturm the money owed him, and Charles's death in May of that year put an end to any hopes Sturm may have had for either peace or repayment.

To consider the last two decades or so of Sturm's life is painful. The ideals he had spent a lifetime implementing and defending—humanist education and Protestant unity—were coming increasingly under attack in the last third of the century. A theological literalism with less enthusiasm for classical studies was eroding the earlier cultural consensus on which Sturm's generation of Christian humanists had counted for support. In January 1570, Sturm petitioned the magistrates to let him resign, alluding to doctrinal divergences between the academic staff and the theological one, made harder to bear by failing eyesight. He had already served the school for thirty-three years. The magistrates refused to accept his request, and instead, made it plain that they wished the opposing factions to cooperate in a general reform of the major abuses.

Marbach and Sturm were asked to submit memoirs describing the problems. Sturm's revolved upon the encroachments Marbach had made in the old discipline of the school, and to the intolerant sectarianism he had promoted within the student body and among the theological faculty. Marbach revealed primarily sectarian grievances. He accused Sturm of heresy, of Calvinism, Zwinglianism, and even of recommending a Protestant-Catholic front against the Turkish threat.[114] We have already seen that Marbach and Sturm were not so far apart in their conceptions of what constituted the proper subject matter and methods for schools. So it seems difficult to accept the suggestion, put forth long ago by Walter Sohm, that the two men were definitively prevented from cooperating because each held a different conception of what it meant to be well educated.[115] Rather, it seems to be truer to see the two men as separated by different patterns of social intercourse, Sturm being the archetypal ecumenical Christian of good will, able to accommodate a broad range of Christian theological formulations,[116] and Marbach who was not, like Sturm, a diplomat, but a pastor, School Visitor, and church official, serving as the model of the earnest, but culturally limited provincial confined to intercourse within his own church and within the most conservative wing of it at that.[117] Marbach accused Sturm, furthermore, of an unrealistic platonism, which he said was made evident by Sturm's most recent publication, the *Academic Letters* (1569)[118] addressed to the members of the newly established (1566) Academy. That the Academy fell short of Sturm's expectations is well known. The objective of training students for higher degrees in professions other than the religious may in fact be what Marbach was referring to when he criticized Sturm's platonism. It is possible that Marbach feared the reduction of power and prestige that might befall the theological faculty if their students were not the only ones eligible for advanced degrees.[119]

In creating the Academy the pastoral union over which Marbach presided as president apparently managed to convince the city magistrates of Strasbourg that their own preferred plan was preferable to a full-scale university, and by such manipulation to defeat the university scheme even though the emperor and his counselors had given no evidence that they would oppose such a creation.[120] Marbach's sensitivity to "platonism" was a kind of shorthand for what in pre-humanist centuries many churchmen felt for the classical authors—disdain for having preceded the era of Christian truth, which they felt superior to the other. In any event, Marbach had only to glance at the first of the *Academic Letters* (from Sturm to the City) to note that there the familiar theme which Sturm sought to establish in the minds of the Council—that without a knowledge of ancient literature no modern society could expect to preserve or improve the laws or maintain the reformed faith.[121]

Yet, for all Sturm's pleading that it would be better to support a university than an Academy,[122] and for all the magistrates' unwillingness to be persuaded, it would be wrong to think they were lacking in sympathy for Sturm. They ordered (1573) the immediate reform of abuses according to the views put forth in the *Epistolae Classicae* and in the *Epistolae Academicae*. They encouraged Marbach to apologize to Sturm and both men submitted a formal agreement to the magistrates in which they promised to respect each other's sphere of authority. There were still problems which were to exacerbate the truce. One of these was Sturm's successful efforts to prevent the hiring by Marbach of the ultra Lutheran historian and publicist, Flacius Illyricus,[123] in 1570. The supporters of Marbach resented, too, that Sturm managed to protect the Calvinist refugee church in Strasbourg, which had been officially outlawed in 1563, and that he kept in touch with a variety of Protestant pastors and potentates—which included many influential members of Elizabeth I's government, and a good number of Catholic churchmen of good will.[124]

In 1577 the Formula of Concord was drawn up which became the definitive confession of most Lutherans throughout Germany, but which Sturm felt to be the epitome of a materialistic, anti-Bucerian interpretation of dogma. The Strasbourg theologians were decidedly in favor of subscription to it, and one of them, a young man not yet thirty, Dr. Johann Pappus,[125] for whom Sturm had once served as patron and benefactor, decided to generate support for the Concord by defending sixty-eight theses on the irenic subject of charity. The debates and written exchanges (1577–1581) between Pappus and Sturm were acerbic, even violent, and attracted other pens to attack the old rector, such as that of Lucas Osiander.[126]

The Pappus debates were Sturm's last act of devotion to the cause of a liberal Strasbourg confession of faith, and they attracted outside attention in Switzerland and all over Protestant Germany. Pappus was especially eager to attack the Calvinist concept of the Eucharist, and at the March 22, 1578, session tempers reached the boiling point. A Polish Calvinist who opposed Pappus was imprisoned.[127] Sturm felt it necessary to adjourn the session because some of the propositions Pappus had introduced had not been previously submitted to him for scrutiny, which was against the regulations. Although the Scholarchs forbade Pappus from continuing, the defense proceeded on the 5th of April, and Sturm took the podium himself, determined that the debates should not cut off Calvinists from Lutherans, but that a conciliatory spirit should prevail.

Pappus's reply was not conciliatory though Sturm pleaded continually for reconciliation. On April 14, he asserted that there could be no reconciliation between a wrong position and a right one. In all, Sturm delivered three replies to Pappus, and they were so pungent that the Stettmeister refused permission to publish. Sturm had again been sharply criticized from at least one Strasbourg pulpit and the magistrates imposed silence on both men.

Publication of the interchange had been enjoined, but when Sturm discovered that Pappus had sent copies of his first defense to various courts in Germany (Hanau, Stuttgart, Tübingen), he had all three of his own (the *Antipappi*)[128] printed in Geneva with the theses and two discourses of Pappus for an introduction. The gist of the attack by Pappus, joined by Osiander, was that Sturm was a Melanchthonian compromiser of the orthodox Lutheran faith, or else—they seemed unsure—a Calvinist in all but name—or that he had maintained his allegiance to the *Confessio tetrapolitana* that they felt had rightfully been discarded in favor of the Formula of Concord.[129] They were outraged that he had stopped attending church and had encouraged his family to do the same. They even faulted him for failure to pay his debts. When Sturm wrote on November 19, 1580, to the Scholarchs to complain of their harassment, he asked them to let him know if they still valued his services, and if they did not, to release him from his duties. If they did value them, he wished protection from his enemies.

In March of 1580 Pappus and the theologians made a complaint too, attributing all the divisions in the academic community to Sturm's heterodoxy and to the interference on his behalf of the foreign (English, Polish and Silesian) students, many of whom had grown up in households that professed Calvinist or anti-trinitarian ideas. These complaints led the magistrates to enact the decree of April 29, 1581, which prohibited further controversy by either side. The pastors, however, continued their polemics from their pulpits, and Sturm, somewhat rejuvenated by the need for self-defense, published no fewer than six pamphlets in the course of that year against Pappus, Osiander and Andreae.

There seemed to be no end to these disputes between the liberal old professor and his conservative critics and enemies. When the magistrates, in response to a complaint by the pastors, again enjoined silence on the old rector, the Senate passed a harsh rebuke upon him, which resulted in the intercession of the Landgrave William of Hesse and concerned Swiss Calvinists, and his old friend and antagonist, Hotman. The majority opinion was unsympathetic to Sturm and in September 1581, he decided to leave Strasbourg for the Palatine city of Neustadt, where the Palatine Elector, Duke Casimir, offered him refuge.

Despite Sturm's entreaties, the magistrates took decisive steps. On November 18 the city magistrates invited Sturm to resign his duties as rector, after declaring that henceforth, the rectorate would not be granted for life. To ease his humiliation the magistrates cited his advanced age—he was then seventy-four—as their motivation for their action.[130] Sturm refused to resign, but the magistrates nevertheless informed the academic senate on December 7 that their rector had been relieved of his post due to his advanced age and other, unspecified reasons. On the whole, the majority of the faculty acquiesced in the magistrates' decision.

Sturm's supporters were able to elect as his successor Melchior Junius—one of the teachers in the school, and a former protégé of Sturm's—who apparently took the job to prevent any of Sturm's enemies from taking control of the academy. Although Sturm appealed to the Aulic Council at Speyer against his removal, he was unable to undo what amounted to a constitutional re-organization of the school vis à vis the city council, which managed to win a clearcut victory over both academic and pastoral corporate interests in the control of school policy and discipline, but which was itself to become increasingly orthodox with regard to religious matters.[131] Sturm's suit against the city, and against two of Strasbourg's senators whom he believed to be prejudiced against him, dragged on the rest of his life. His opponents compiled a list of 272 offenses with which they charged the old rector. Although Sturm's supporters, who included the Scholarchs, tried to win the rectorate back for him, and even appealed to the emperor for swift justice, the emperor proved unable to alter the judicial process and only Sturm's death ended the proceedings.

Apart from these frustrating embroilments, and despite Sturm's manifest distress and financial suffering, his creditors continued to harass him for the debts contracted during the Huguenot wars.[132] Yet on one occasion in 1583 he was threatened with imprisonment by two merchants from Strasbourg over a loan of one thousand florins which Sturm had guaranteed in 1567 for the house of Navarre. Sturm had actually repaid the loan but had forgotten the details of the repayment, a bit of absent-mindedness that may indeed have betrayed his advancing years.[133]

To relieve the tedium of self defense he spent his last years occupying himself with his garden and hives. He sold their surplus in town for needed cash. After his second wife died, he married again. His third wife continued to live in Strasbourg, in a separate accommodation, and he interspersed the chores of gardening with writing, though near blindness prevented him from research.[134] His last writing mostly concerned the Turkish problem. He conceived of a permanent imperial army to be made up of Catholics and Protestants united against the foe. The army was to be well-disciplined, paid out of special taxes fairly apportioned on all subjects and led by an elite officer corps trained in a military academy by teachers well versed in history, law, literature, rhetoric, dialectic, and medicine, and in military science and gymnastics. During Sturm's enforced retirement at Northeim, he received visits from friends, many faculty members, and from visiting rectors, scholars, magistrates and foreign diplomats, of whom one was the Elizabethan courtier, Sir Philipp Sidney.[135] Theodore Bèze and the Landgrave William of Hesse continued to concern themselves for his welfare, and the new Elector Palatine, Duke Casimir, offered him a chair at the University of Heidelberg in 1583, which Sturm refused due to his infirmities. In 1581 one of his former pupils, a Polish count named John of Ostrorog gave a public lecture at the Strasbourg Academy extolling Sturm's virtues in the flowery rhetoric of the age. He alluded to the old rector's international reputation as an educator, and insisted that his name was on the lips of Europe's most studious youth.[136] Another former student published a poem in his old teacher's honor,[137] and still another wanted to publish his correspondence with Sturm, though the latter refused his permission.[138] There were other honors, too. Senator Heinrich Stroband of Thorn (Prussia) had all Sturm's principal treatises on education reprinted in 1586.[139]

Death came to Sturm on March 3, 1589. On the last day of that month during the Easter promotions ceremonies at the Academy, his successor, Junius, delivered a funeral eulogy to an assemblage of leading citizens, including pastors and magistrates. Among the poems read commemorating Sturm was one by Bèze and many by former students. These were collected and dedicated to Elizabeth I who had been Sturm's lifelong admirer and patron.[140] Sturm's name was praised again at the first centenary celebration in honor of the Strasbourg Academy's foundation,[141] and in subsequent centuries as well it became fashionable to invoke his memory.

Sturm's life was long and active, and his services to the European community though diverse, were singularly unified by the nature of his ideals. These were humanistic in the grand sense of the term. The goals he set for himself and recommended to others were service to the human community and reverence for the life of the mind and spirit. There is no doubt whatever that his whole life was a continual reaffirmation of this *modus vivendi* defined in 1538 when his first youth was already over, and he was just launching his new, scholarly career in Strasbourg. In that year he wrote in the Introduction to his work on logic[142] that the best lived life was that of the man dedicated to civic matters, and added that he had never regretted teaching and scholarship once he had decided that both his own nature and God's will had pointed him in that direction. It seems not inaccurate to observe that even if Sturm never felt called upon to profess the Calvinist creed[143] he certainly had a Calvinist's sense of calling. He would stake his claim to recognition for public service on the profession of teacher. Aside from this religious affirmation of the necessity to do God's will in a professional capacity, Sturm let nature and reason serve as his guides throughout the long decades of his public career. They were the two components of a Christian humanism that had so long been invoked to preserve Europe from the threat of a new barbarism, i.e., from religious intolerance and unenlightened self interest.

2
Johann Sturm's Method for Humanistic Pedagogy

Johann Sturm's classical curriculum and teaching method obliged students in the later Reformation period to strive for Latin eloquence and a thorough knowledge of classical literature. Their attempt to emulate the ancients' literary, artistic, and civic ideals made humanism the model for education at Strasbourg and at schools throughout Europe styled after Strasbourg's Gymnasium. Although Protestant piety was, with classical learning, a goal of education, humanism was not sacrificed to religious indoctrination; for Sturm, like other Reformation humanists, regarded pagan wisdom a harbinger of rather than a challenge to Christian morality. Luther himself compared the Renaissance revival of learning with its knowledge of the languages as a John the Baptist heralding the coming of Christ and the gospel.

That Classical Humanism in the sixteenth century is still viewed as having lost its impetus long before 1600 is a mistaken notion sown by Jacob Burckhardt's *The Civilization of the Renaissance in Italy* (1860). Whereas Burckhardt argued that the fall of humanism in this century was chargeable, in part at least, to the excessive ribaldry, pettiness, and skepticism of Italian humanists,[1] modern scholars contribute to the myth of decline not by blaming the Italians, but by inculpating Christian reformers to the north of Italy. Often their contributions to the myth are subtle, even unwitting. They concentrate on a sub-category of humanists, the Christian humanists, stressing the things that divide these from all other humanist scholars and authors rather than recounting the larger numbers of qualities that served to identify humanists generally. Occasionally, there appears a modern critic who is not subtle but who is concerned to establish that the sectarian interests of the Reformation were largely responsible for the decline of classicism.[2] Such an extreme analysis is unwarranted, particularly if we recall the excellent definitions of humanism offered by Paul Oskar Kristeller, i.e., that humanism was the "*studia humanitatis*"; "a phase... in the rhetorical tradition in western culture;" and "a clearly defined cycle of scholarly disciplines," among which grammar and rhetoric were the most significant.[3]

These scholarly definitions are well suited to the pedagogical program of Johann Sturm (1507–89) in sixteenth-century Strasbourg.[4] His persistence in promoting classical humanist ideals in that city will be illustrated in the course of this chapter by examining nine of his once widely read pedagogical treatises, the evidentiary base for this presentation of classical humanism in a school setting. After a brief biographical introduction, the rest of the text will be devoted mainly to the classical nature of the curriculum, which survived the sixteenth century and was continued into the seventeenth; and to the nature of Sturm's famous teaching method with which the curriculum was inextricably fused.

Sturm referred to the school of St. Jerome at Liège in his *Advice on What Organization to give to the Gymnasium of Strasbourg* (see Chapter 3) that he submitted, at the request of Strasbourg's school authorities, February 24, 1538.[5] Here he noted that the program of Saint Jerome's except for a few small defects, which he had corrected, was in essence that which he recommended for Strasbourg's new *Gymnasium*: "But while paying heed to former flaws, that earlier program is restored. Whenever any thing is good, it should be affixed to this program."[6]

After Liège, Sturm obtained his Master's degree at Louvain, and then went to Paris in 1529 where he studied medicine for a while. He began to publish, too, an edition of Galen, and commentaries on Cicero. Having changed his major from medicine to letters, his patrons soon included Guillaume Budé,[7] Queen Marguerite of Navarre,[8] and Jean (Cardinal) du Bellay.[9] By 1534 he was lecturing at the new *Collège de France*, a post he may have held through Budé's patronage. His commentaries on Cicero and on logic earned for him fame as a humanist scholar and an outstanding teacher. Won over to the reformed religion,[10] he was asked by du Bellay to invite Bucer and Melanchthon to discuss diplomacy at the French court. Such overtures were fruitless in the wake of the *Placard* repression,[11] and in December 1536, Sturm fled France for Strasbourg. He was hired to teach rhetoric and logic in the proposed new school, and found himself formulating curriculum and proposing methodology, tasks he assumed in cooperation with Martin Bucer, whose acquaintance he had made in his student days several years earlier.[12]

The support of Bucer and of Jacob Sturm (no relation), mayor of Strasbourg and a school trustee (*Scholarch*), gave Sturm, after 1538 Rector of the *Gymnasium*, an audience to which his Paris reputation alone could not have entitled him. This patronage represented the official approval by the authorities of a half century of intellectual humanist activity at Strasbourg.[13] Helpful to Sturm's career as a pedagogue (and diplomat) was that city's receptivity to humanist instruction. There were already several private Latin schools operating before Sturm arrived in Strasbourg. He recommended that these be replaced by one consolidated school in the interest of economy, and to encourage a better performance among pupils by ensuring that there would be a larger number against whom each pupil would be obliged to compete. Far from it having been the case that the city, two decades after the start of Luther's reform movement had suffered any loss of its cultural values,[14] Strasbourg had used the years 1518–38 to build a consensus for classical studies. Sturm would in turn build upon this foundation a program capable of enduring for several generations.

The proof of this endurance is not hard to establish. One need only consider a document that provided for a reform of the city's school system in 1604, twenty-five years after Sturm's removal from the rectorship (1581)[15] and sixty-nine years after the school system was founded:

> Finally, with regard to the authors and exercises, which are to be read and treated in the grades, it is our feeling and opinion, because these same things were well and usefully regulated and provided for by Master Johann Sturm, who also, concerning these matters left his *Classical Letters*, that these in every way remain as he had it therein previously in such manner and measure as the organization of each grade set out prior to this testifies.[16]

The reforms of 1604 did not dismantle the humanist program but, instead, reaffirmed its value, just as the *Classical Letters* (1565) reaffirmed the first formulation of the program in 1538. Left undisturbed were the *Gymnasium* classes, their textbooks, including those written by Sturm, and the learning method. In their turn, the *Classical Letters* looked backward to the single most important document relative to pedagogical humanism at Strasbourg, a treatise Sturm had prepared as an elaboration of his first *Memoir*, entitled *The Correct Opening of Elementary Schools of Letters* (1538).[17] This treatise, with its famous instructional goal, "wise and eloquent piety,"[18] offered a detailed description of the methods, textbooks, and tasks deemed suitable for each of the nine (later ten) grades of the *Gymnasium*. In addition, it described the five-year cycle of public lectures that provided boys from sixteen to twenty-one with a liberal education: some of the basic principles of law, medicine and theology, and the opportunity to continue their studies of philosophy, literature, and oratory. Sturm thought that any boy thus trained ought to be able "to move freely about in all writers without an interpreter."[19]

If this treatise were merely a discussion of books, classroom procedures and teaching techniques, it would still be fascinating; for its description of Sturm's expectations for boys astonishes modern readers who find it hard to believe that seven-year-olds, often brought to their first year teacher without knowledge of the alphabet, were by the end of that year expected to be reading Cicero's shorter letters! In their third year they were reading Vergil's *Aeneid*, and in their fifth, the one in which they began Greek, Aesop. Then, during "their last year of boyhood" (at twelve) they were studying Aristotle's logic. At fourteen, the year they would have acquired "ornate speech,"[20] they began to study Hebrew. In their final year of the *Gymnasium*, they were to perfect "apt speech," which Sturm expressed as "instructed, liberal, and accommodated to things" and to have begun (!) "the science of numbers," and astrology.[21]

This treatise was more than a handbook for administrators. It was also a humanist's application of his professional values to a school setting. Like all humanists, Sturm favored the reading of original works by the best authors, leaving the rest to home study. He felt commentaries, the bane of scholasticism, should be read in private, not at school. Hippocrates ought, for example, never to be explained by Galen, and only Moses and the other prophets, the evangelists, and the apostles had written commentaries worthy of school study. The Fathers were not to be taught even in schools for theologians, but privately at home.[22]

While Aristotle, Plato, and Cicero were "authors in whom one cannot err,"[23] Cicero was the hands-on favorite and the staple of instruction in the lower grades, with Vergil, Horace, Terence, Plautus, Caesar, and Sallust trailing after. Among Greek writers, Homer and Demosthenes were prime for the boys nearing the end of *Gymnasium* studies, as was Aristotle (logic, poetics). All these authors and more were cited for the public lecture program, where the emphasis would be more on knowing things than on the elements of writing and speaking. Public lectures would include the Greek comedies. For historians, the young men would read Herodotus, Thucydides, Xenophon, and Livy. Aristotle would be read on nature, and they would also read Plato's *Phaedo* and *Timaeus*. Aratus and Dionysius would serve the mathematicians.[24]

The public lectures were not a degree granting program, but were designed to give young men an introduction to professional studies in letters, medicine, law, and theology before they went off to distant universities. To make the lectures attractive, Sturm did not require attendance, but he hoped young men could be persuaded that four hours of lectures each day were not unreasonable. Partly because there were only six or seven lecturers, and not many courses, he insisted that "All things in nature whether... waxing or waning are inter-related."[25] Therefore, he urged students to attend lectures outside their specialty.[26] He was anxious for professional men to avoid a too narrow specialization, for men liberally educated would stand up for "concord in life, letters, and opinion."[27] To Sturm, learning rendered men peaceful.

Peace was not easy to find in sixteenth-century Strasbourg. He wrote:

> Indeed, before tempests arise and serenity is disturbed, humane studies must be cultivated lest they be cast away by the floods, and render us unable to predict evil and destitute of counsel if evil is of long duration.[28]

It was absolutely necessary that "the ancient disciplines" be restored for the state's survival. That humanist education helped obviate, if not avoid, problems that befell states was already a commonplace in fifteenth-century Italian humanism. Sturm's fascination with Cicero would in any case have made civic humanism appealing, for much of Cicero's thought concerned civic behavior. Sturm wrote that the only justification for government was the promotion of education, for only then would society flourish.[28] Educated men, whatever their profession, could not ignore oratory or disciplines required for effective speaking. Eloquence without knowledge was as dangerous as knowledge without eloquence; either one made men incapable of effective action.[30] Sturm did not distinguish between good learning and good morals in public life, since "nothing in the nature of things cultivates morality as does the study of letters."[31] He echoed Cicero's lament for the excesses of his own day (*O tempora! O mores!*) when he observed:

> But if there have ever been times when civil affairs were imperiled by the rarity of good and wise men and the multiplicity of evil and inexperienced ones, ours are such.[32]

It was nearly impossible to speak of morality without speaking of piety—that "wise and eloquent piety" that was the hallmark of the good man who spoke eloquently.[33] There were good and pious men in Strasbourg who believed that a classical curriculum might leave too little room for religion. This apparently was the sentiment of men like Wolfgang Capito.[34] But there were others, like Otto Brunfels,[35] who taught in his private Latin school during the years prior to Sturm's arrival, and shared with Sturm a confidence that liberal education was wholly consistent with evangelical piety. This was also the attitude of Martin Bucer.[36] In that first treatise on schools Sturm had little to say about teaching piety, observing that on festival days students would study the history of Christ and "certain things" from Moses. Younger boys would be catechized then, while older ones studied Moses in Hebrew. One should not forget about God in between, but "it was permitted to reflect upon the studies of eloquence and philosophy as long as they are undertaken for the illustration of religious teaching."[37]

> The highest goal of studies is God's religion and the knowledge of godly things. Religion will be studied by teaching and by good speech.[38]

Accordingly, the approach to "godly things" and to religion was to be gained primarily by studying literature and language; to a lesser degree by studying Scripture and the apostles. Dogma as such (except for catechism) was largely ignored. How this learned piety affected pedagogy is difficult to determine, since the pedagogical writings offer little explanation. They do suggest that the emphasis was on classical authors, not Christian ones. Sturm held the traditional humanist attitude towards classical writers, which was that they were divinely inspired, hence, not opposed to Christian teaching. Indeed, they were necessary to understand God and his religion properly.[39]

One can hardly leave the consideration of Sturm's curriculum for that of his method, since the method, rhetorical and oratorical, was so narrowly suited to the literary curriculum that they were as the two sides of one coin. This was one reason why the method was consistently supported by the school authorities. As Sturm notes, "the primary task is to inform and educate the tongue."[40] Hence, the methods used were those which encouraged good pronunciation; grammatical facility; rhetorical style; and the ability to store a large number of words and to use them effectively. The teaching techniques were not original with Sturm, but were in use during the fifteenth century at schools run by the Brethren of the Common Life. Indeed, more than their *devotio moderna* Sturm copied the Brethren's techniques of teaching—imitation of models, disputations, declamations, directed conversations, word-diaries, performance of plays, written and extemporaneous exercises, and above all, memorization.[41]

It should not be imagined that these methods had displaced the systematic resort to logical analysis that had, in its scholastic form, so offended the reformers. Instead, Sturm drew upon the work of Rudolf Agricola in dialectic, a rhetorical rather than deductive approach to logic, and adapted it as a teaching tool for students of literature.[42] The method was supported by a number of devices that reflected Sturm's astute observations of child psychology and learning psychology. Among these were his use of prizes and praise to motivate and encourage boys to perform; his recognition of the fact that not all children develop at the same rate, that some are destined to be late-bloomers; his appreciation of the competitive spirit and its usefulness in stimulating effort. When such things failed, as they did at times, he was not averse to whipping boys, for pain administered to the body improves the spirit.[43] But men who enjoyed whipping boys had no business teaching, and the spirit was also improved by recreational activities such as games and nature walks.

The heart of Sturm's method was the rhetorical *loci communes* of which Philipp Melanchthon's own work on dialectics, published at Strasbourg with an introduction by Sturm (1538), provides a more familiar example to students of Reformation education.[44] Erasmus had written that knowledge requires both word and thing. Sturm used memorization to tie these two together.[45] He was the first to treat of method in a logic manual; the first to consider it a separate subject. Walter Ong, the Ramist scholar, claims that this triggered the onset of the modern mentality, though he doubted the pedagogical fruitfulness of Sturm's method.[46] Sturm defended it, however, with a rigidity belied only by the suppleness of the method itself.[47] In fact, his method involved so many different techniques that it would have been odd if many boys in the gymnasium could have remained impervious to all of them. Sturm wanted the individual differences of students to be accommodated by means of this variety.

One factor that helped in the acceptance by parents of this predominantly rhetorical learning method was that of selection. Boys whose families did not wish them to enter the professions—law, theology, or teaching—were not likely to be enrolled at the school in Strasbourg nor in any of the numerous schools throughout Europe that were patterned after it.[48] Among the latter were the Jesuit academies, for their *Ratio Studiorum* contained a similar classical curriculum.[49] Sturm noted this similarity in a letter to the Strasbourg Scholarchs:

> They teach languages and grammar. I rejoice for two reasons. They are helping us cultivate the sciences. I have seen the authors they read, the exercises they do, the meth-

ods they use. It is so close to our rules and our schools, that
it would seem to be derived from us.[50]

While merchants in the later Renaissance would look to more practical
training for their sons and find it outside the orbit of classical institutions, humanism continued to find its own clientele in the upper strata
of European society.

In the same year (1538), Sturm published a treatise on the "lost" art
of speaking or eloquence.[51] He addressed it to Franciscus Fross, a lawyer and city councilor at Strasbourg who was also a patron of the school
just established. To Fross, Sturm stressed the difficulty in every age of
achieving eloquence. He thought it had only once been done, in
Cicero's lifetime. He thought that everything needed for it was already
at hand, since Germans had made great strides in rhetoric and in letters.
What was needed now was concerted effort, and above all, "method
and order." Books were all well and good, but the body politic would
not flourish simply because there were learned volumes lying about.
Sturm pointed to a problem—a disturbed civic order—the solution for
which—eloquence—may strike modern readers as inappropriate, even
ridiculous. Some critics of Sturm's pedagogy have been skeptical of the
value that he placed on speech.[52] But eloquence was appropriate
enough for an age in which, though books were relatively plentiful, the
exigencies of policy making—often during periods of extended warfare—were such that the policy makers had little time for reading. Furthermore, the most difficult problems were not those which depended
on knowledge so much as on opinion; for policy hinged on ethical and
religious points of view more often than on technical circumstance. In
late twentieth-century policy making, mass media serves the function of
rhetorical eloquence with this difference: the media are less concerned
with apt or elegant rhetoric. Instead, they emphasize speedy delivery,
quantification, and visual impact. In the Renaissance, such opinion-
molding factors were not readily available. Men were more sensitive to
the spoken word uttered in courts and in audience chambers. The policy makers, to a large extent noblemen, could not afford to be undered-
ucated.

We can see how seriously Sturm regarded the need for an educated
nobility trained in oratory by glancing at his 1549 treatise written for the
benefit of two brothers of noble birth, Anthony and Philip Werter.[53]
They had written to him for advice on how best to complete their education at home. Sturm noted that they had already attained to considerable Latin and Greek and were familiar with logic as well as rhetoric, so
it is probable that they had graduated from the gymnasium. Sturm pre-

scribed an accelerated three-year independent study plan that would give them the equivalent of the education dispensed in the five-year public lecture program. This would necessarily require their diligence, temperance, and constancy. There would be no time for "gadding" (carousing), he warned; but if they adhered to the reading list and performed the written and oral exercises, they would achieve elegant Latin style and a knowledge of political science. It is not necessary to rehearse again the authors Sturm preferred, other than to note that their first year would be devoted largely to imitating Cicero. The object of this was not so much to improve upon the model, but to improve upon self, and possibly to excel the original.

> Imitation ought to be free, not servile. It is our wish that an imitator should not always follow in the footsteps of another, but should, whenever possible and he is decently able, outrun the one ahead.[54]

To that near art form of Renaissance letters, advice concerning the education of princes, Sturm also contributed.[55] His treatise, addressed to Prince William, Duke of Jülich and Cleves, stressed the usual things, i.e., the need to prepare the prince in both history and true religion, so that he will make wise and spiritual decisions. His explanation of how teachers may do these things wisely so that their royal pupils became wholly engaged learners is interesting. The teacher is the key to successful learning, although it is helpful if his pupil is bright and willing! Only the teacher who is truly learned, who enjoys his work, and puts thoughts for his own advantage out of his mind can succeed. Such a man was Prince William's own former master, Conrad Heresbach.[56] Such teachers make the very difficult work of learning letters truly pleasurable, for their method makes clear the inter-relationship of all knowledge. Every activity has what modern educators would term "transfer value."[57] The good teacher eliminates violence in education, and promotes "a playful didactic discipline" that provides the body with sports, and the mind with grave but pleasant learning.[58] As for the prince's companions, these must represent "the whole people" and also foreign folk and not just the nobility.[59] Only those boys who accept such discipline may remain in the prince's classroom. Many pages of this advice to princes deal with the penalties incurred—superstition and intellectual arrogance—when a proper education is not available. Sturm was highly critical of the mischief derived from pagan mythology, from failure to read the Old Testament properly (i.e., Jewish "stubbornness") and from the tyrannical inventions of the Turks.[60] Therefore, he cautioned that a royal tutor needs more than just learning; he must have a correct religious outlook. "In the ignorance of the divinity, there can be no true religion...." The teacher must be a fountain from which the prince may draw the "heavenly waters of life."[61]

Published simultaneously with the former treatise was Sturm's letter to Roger Ascham, tutor of Princess Elizabeth Tudor, and Sturm's devoted admirer and correspondent.[62] Sturm wrote primarily of the preservation of true religion by eloquence and letters, and the mastery by noblemen of both these arts. Eloquence without knowledge was, he wrote, mere "inflated verbiage." True learning must eschew scholastic commentaries, whose speech was "of shabby purity" and "hideous." Such were written by men whose teachers were "manumitted barbarians." The products of such learning were "unintelligible" and "polluted."[63]

As for Ascham's English nobility, they had succeeded to a period of domination by Italians and Frenchmen, for Ascham had informed Sturm that Englishmen had gained mastery of speech. Sturm told him that he was of the opinion that the German nobility had amongst it only a few who understood the value of learning for the governing class.[64] He congratulated Ascham and the Princess Elizabeth for their labors in the classroom. He recommended "discipline and the art of speaking" for the female sex (married and unmarried noblewomen) and hoped Elizabeth's example would enable them to be regarded for more than their "propagative powers" as had formerly been the case, for they were indeed capable, he knew, of knowledge and eloquence.[65]

In 1565 Sturm published two treatises of pedagogical importance. The first was a plan for the remodeling of the Lauingen school, requested by Duke Wolfgang of Zweibrücken.[66] The new plan was an accelerated learning program of five classes to which a public lecture series was added. This scheme preserved the essentials of Strasbourg's school philosophy. It was in turn used as a model for Polish Calvinist schools, and as the basis for remodeling the Hornbach school in Germany.[67] The plan was written at a time when Sturm's educational ideals were struggling against the waning enthusiasm of his staff and increasing restiveness among the theologians of conservative Lutheran stamp over Sturm's domination of the school system.

The second work was the *Classical Letters*.[68] These were addressed to each of the gymnasium teachers, and to the Duke of Prussia, the scholarchs, and the rector of the Lauingen school. Of the last three letters, that to the scholarchs is the most revealing, for it touched on the Jesuits' schools; the rectitude of educational disbursements, of which Sturm, as Provost of the Chapter of Saint Thomas was responsible;[69] and the need for leaving unchanged his methods and textbook choices.[70] Through these letters Sturm made it clear that oratorical excellence was a non-negotiable goal of learning. He realized that some teachers neither understood nor practiced his method, which he insisted be applied. In a poignant passage he described the exposure which Greek and Roman (but not German) boys had once had from their mothers' breast to classical languages, an exposure reinforced by their nursemaids, playmates, servants, parents, and public magistrates. "This method of learning," he admitted ruefully, "no longer exists." That boys were no longer able to hear Latin at home was a "public and widespread calamity" that could be corrected only by schoolteachers using his method,[71] a method that consisted, we may add, in total immersion of a boy from the age of seven through twenty-one in a contrived Latin-speaking culture. For Sturm made the school into a giant language laboratory whose only equipment was children, books, and teachers. In such an environment a boy could absorb, or so he hoped, the culture of a bygone era. That the environment was artificial did not daunt him because he was convinced that it had already turned out large numbers of youth with sufficient classical competency to make the enterprise worthwhile.

In the letter to Dr. Marbach, President of the pastoral corps (*Kirchenkonvent*), Sturm wrote of the need for adherence to the program. He was convinced that they were on the brink of oratorical excellence. If Dr. Marbach would follow through by keeping the theological students mindful of his requirements—that is, to avoid the use of commentaries and use only the best humanist texts—he would soon see a difference in result. Marbach would be able to determine what benefits oratory would confer on sermons, his special province.[72]

Although the *Classical Letters* were written during that dismal latter portion of his career when he was on the defensive because of his liberal and irenic stance in religion, he did not let this detract from a concern for the needs of teachers and students. The latter he viewed not in terms of intellectual progress only, but in terms of the emotional welfare of his charges. In his letter to the first year teacher, Abraham Feis, he recommended pleasant "visual and sensory" exercises.[73]

> Just as milk and light food are most suited to the delicate stomach of a child, so is instruction which is pleasant and easy for him to assimilate.[74]

The heart of learning for Sturm was memory. This faculty required constant practice and review, and minimal theory. He told Theobald Lingelsheim, the fourth year teacher, that he did not want boys "weighed down with rules," but wanted them instead to learn as much vocabulary as possible because it increased their capacity. Practical exercise rather than abstract theory was greatly valued by him. He faulted the substitution of another catechism for that of Bucer, in use in the lower grades. The new one (David Chytraeus's) was but superfluous work for the boys and would sidetrack their memory to no profit.[75] It was diagnostic of Sturm's irenicism that he did not view catechetical knowledge as liberating in the same way that letters liberated men, and he spoke of the "natural energy" or "divine force and power" inside man as the more powerful emancipator.[76] He told Elie Kyber, the Hebrew teacher, to "follow his young soldiers' nature" as good teachers must.[77]

Whatever acceptance problems beset his method among the faculty, he stood staunchly by it. Nor did his classical curriculum change, except to become more intense. So when Dr. Marbach and Sturm jointly addressed the city fathers on the need to transform the gymnasium into an Academy that could grant the Bachelor's and Master's degrees, they proposed no changes in curriculum or method.[78] They told the magistrates that something more was needed than had been put into effect in 1538 if they were to retain upper class students. Boys who completed the last two classes in the gymnasium were, after this transformation which resulted in the Academy (1566), to receive the Bachelor's degree; those who completed the public lecture series, the Master's degree.

The city's response was to petition Emperor Maximilian II, and to praise the school for its recent improvements, including "more famous authors," and for its famous, well-organized liberal arts program.[79] The letter from Maximilian did indeed establish the Academy along the lines just described, and in the same document praised the school for its fine liberal arts program, its declamations and disputations, and its methods. This letter noted as well that the school had already made an outstanding contribution to the arts and to government by virtue of its accomplished graduates.[80]

Such praise and recognition from the municipal and imperial authorities permit the historian of Strasbourg's educational past to state that the reputation of its schools under Sturm's rectorate was one with his personal contributions to its forms and format, its method and curriculum. The threat which Sturm's persistent and even, on occasion, tactless defense of Zwinglian and Calvinist theology, posed for Strasbourg's increasingly conservative Lutheran pastorate, resulted in his removal from office (1581). But that enforced retirement should not be regarded as a reflection upon, nor diminishment of the status of his pedagogy or the prestige of Strasbourg's educational institutions.

Sturm's last pedagogical statement, the *Academic Letters* (1569), contained nothing new.[81] These letters simply reminded the staff of the new Academy that the old principles would still apply. The Academy provided more instruction in natural subjects (mathematics, physics, astronomy, medicine). Sturm did not object to such studies, but remarked that "even Pallas preserved jars of pickles."[82] Yet he thought it well to point out that literary studies remained more important than any other kind. Bodies, after all, could be healed by medicine. The soul, nourished on the wisdom of the ages, could not. Thus, cultivation of the soul through literature was still the prime educational task.[83]

Accordingly, he did not wish the faculty to neglect literature for the practical arts. He asked the law professor to use Justinian as a text, even if some of his students protested its use.[84] The teacher of astronomy, geometry, and physics (one man!) should use Aristotle and Euclid.[85] The mathematician was not to let mathematics cause any neglect of language, since "barbarous expressions" contaminate any pursuit.[86] In a second letter to the same teacher, he said that "men are made tense by mediocrity, not by perfect understanding." He added that those who did not teach philosophy and literature ought at least to acknowledge their value.[87]

Obviously, some teachers and students did not share the same enthusiasm for the classics, nor for Latin eloquence, as did Sturm and his supporters. Some teachers introduced "inferior authors" into the program. Some students had begun to "slip away to places where they teach new things (and) where there are lawyers...." If lawyers (and scientists) were willing to work for the same salary as literature professors, Sturm wrote, he did not object to hiring them. The *Academic Letters* reveal that at age sixty-two, Sturm viewed his role as that of a defender of values rapidly being challenged. He wrote as "a veteran of wars" to the rhetoric professor, promising to remain "brave until the reigning in of his steed and that final fall onto the dusty battleground."[88]

As a young professor Sturm enjoyed a culture with fewer contradictions between academe and the public forum. In such circumstances his verbal methodology and literary curriculum were judged eminently practical. As an old man, Sturm was living in a period of transition and his program was beginning to attract criticism from a variety of provincial, sectarian, and professional sources. It would, however, be exaggerating to think that such critics had undermined the classical position to such a point that it was incapable of self defense. The erosion of classicism in German universities was a phenomenon of the close of the seventeenth century, and not of the sixteenth.[89]

Classical letters or humanism, piety at once liberal and unobtrusive, and a teaching method that sought perfection of learners in Latin expression—these were the pillars on which Sturm's pedagogy rested. These were the ideals his admirers perpetuated in the schools they set up along the lines of Strasbourg's. While Sturm did not claim to have founded the Strasbourg system, his ideas served to give it form and substance.[90] The specific requirements of education were just beginning to change during his long lifetime, and the classical model eventually gave way to make room for science, technology, and vernacular languages. Yet Sturm's pedagogy lingered a long while, even when his educational ideals were no longer served by it.

Those ideals were not merely Latin or Greek, but classical in a profound sense,[91] for they illuminated a problem that is still a legitimate educational issue: how to provide learners with information that will let them serve the needs of self and community without destroying the spiritual satisfaction without which they can do neither well. We are still trying to make education what Sturm hoped would prove "the business of every man."

3
The Advice of Johann Sturm on What Organization to give to the Gymnasium of Strasbourg
(February, 1538)

Introduction

Scholars have long recognized the importance of humanism for the success of the Reformation, using phrases such as "no humanists, no Reformation." Since the nineteenth century learned histories of the Reformation in the imperial cities and in others have done full justice to the importance for both religious and educational reformation. The history of few cities is so well documented in this regard than that of Strasbourg. It provides a premiere example of the process particularly for Southwest Germany. Switzerland is an analogous but quite another case. As noted in the Introduction and Chapter 1, in Strasbourg the City Council with its upper bourgeois concern for learned leadership in church and state took the initiative in working for educational reform and initiated the move to found the Gymnasium or Academy.

Around the year 1535 the schools of Strasbourg had a disorganized and fragmentary character. There were three small Latin schools, the public lectures, and two religious convent schools. The best of these schools were those led by Johann Sapidus, who had served as the rector of the school in Schlettstadt, a smaller city in Alsace, and the schools of Peter Dasypodius and Johann Schwebel. But they had very limited plans of study. The scholars worked together with the reformer Martin Bucer and two visitors, Caspar Hedio and Jakob Bedrottus, and in January, 1538, published a report on the situation in which they suggested that a central school for the entire city be established in the former Dominican monastery, dominated by the Church of St. Thomas. A month later the council through its scholars invited Johann Sturm, noted for his knowledge of dialectic and rhetoric, who had come from Paris the previous year, to provide a detailed program for the new school.

Sturm's response was his *Advice* to the City Council in which he laid out a program of studies and a plan for organizing the school in forms and classes, for he was concerned both for the learning content and for the administration of the school. In his next most important work on *The Correct Opening of Schools of Letters* which follows, he elaborated on this brief outline. As we have noted, Sturm was amazingly consistent through the decades in his firm convictions regarding the substance and method of education.

The most readily available edition of Sturm's *Advice* is to be found in Marcel Fournier, *Les Statuts et Privilèges des Universités Françaises depuis leur Fondation jusqu'en 1789*, vol. 4, *Deuxième partie: Seizième siècle* (Paris: Réimpression de L'Édition, 1894; Scientia Verlag Aalen, 1970), pp. 18–22. The authoritative account is in Anton Schindling, *Humanistische Hochschule und Freie Reichsstadt: Gymnasium und Akademie in Strassburg 1538–1621* (Wiesbaden: Franz Steiner Verlag GMBH, 1977), pp. 30–33. Anton Schindling and Walter Ziegler are the editors of a multi-volumed series most useful for those unfamiliar with the territorial divisions of the Holy Roman Empire in the sixteenth and seventeenth centuries, *Die Territorien des Reichs im Zeitalter der Reformation und Konfessionalisierung: Land und Konfession 1500–1650*, vol. 5, *Der Südwesten* (Münster: Aschendorff Verlag, 1993).

The Advice of Johann Sturm on What Organization to give to the Gymnasium of Strasbourg

(February, 1538)

It is more useful for schools of letters to be gathered in one place than to be scattered about in various locations. For it would be ridiculous to assign individual teachers and one pasture to ten sheep if one place and one pasture would be enough (for all). It is accordingly not laudable that one or more (schools) in the same location scatter, but rather that they be brought together from their diverse locations.

Even though bringing sheep together is useful, it is almost necessary for men to compare themselves to the multitude and variety from which first, imitation is stimulated and next, pleasure derived. For by that which many or all praise, and by which men customarily catch fire is the tedium of diverse studies removed.

I also think this to be the reason why in his *Republica* Xenophon writes in one passage that the free assembly was built in a place far from the madding crowd and the loud noise. For this reason one ought to have good order, a common enthusiasm and a splendid agreement, so that all things are done in order and in moderation, so that common studies and related strengths may appear as if under one field of vision. Hence, it is to be organized like those Persian places about which Xenophon writes; however youths, adolescents, men and those too old for military service dwelt there in the same buildings. But in joining together more examples and occasions for speaking are displayed. For that reason Socrates, according to Plato in the *Phaedrus*, disapproves of solitude when he says: "By no means does he wish to teach me in the country places and (among) the trees, but among men in the city." Therefore unless there is such a large number that one location is inadequate, it is more useful for studies to be brought together rather than scattered. They have schools at Liège, Deventer, Zwolle, Wesel, called academies, with one designated location, organized by grade and from these schools go forth more fortunate and greater talents than from neighboring schools. It is often so that those who have been instructed learnedly and piously are corrupted in those gymnasia of greater masters. For in truth more hay can be gathered where many can be grouped together. Since a large number and diverse populations of students come together in Paris, many colleges have been established. Moreover, among these it is very rare for them to provide unfortunate students with bad literary exercises or inferior progress. Moreover, it is most frequently the case that teachers there have more diligent pupils. For highly enthusiastic teachers and pupils languish in solitude. But that multitude of colleges can also hinder because those (pupils) who live with townspeople do not gather in one place but meet at all hours submitting to their own individual bent, not following what is the very best.

When I was at Liège the teachers were variously located and they had determined that each could teach separately; but if these counsels had succeeded, the College of St. Jerome would have been destroyed. But when anyone is interested in attracting youth they choose not what is best but what pleases most and they cater more to the taste than to the reason of the auditors. Moreover, all who disparaged this shallow interpretation of weighty matters were thought to be constrained by the times to hold youth back. This dissension weakened studies, turned the order of studies upside down, and impeded all advances. But when the disadvantages were once noted, the original plan was restored. Since that is the very best, it is proper that the institution should be established according to this model.

1. The whole student body has been divided into eight classes. The first class consists of those who must learn to read, to write, to inflect nouns and verbs. This is called the eighth class.

2. The seventh class constitutes those who have been taught about the connection of words with which reason more diligently dictates the inflection of words so that some things of the poets and orators are more easily understood. Their meaning can be better comprehended and the nature of individual things openly and familiarly explained. These matters are again conjoined with other sentences, so that the way is opened up to composition.

3. In the sixth class certain hours have been set for grammatical precepts. Certain things that are not new should be offered, but those things should be retained which they learned earlier and certain things should be added, which, moreover, are very necessary to learn, but which in the seventh grade were still untimely. The explication of the writers should here be begun

and should be practiced by writing, but should be made with familiar and unencumbered arguments and what they call eloquence. However, they should sometimes turn to certain prescriptions for singing and begin to learn them.

4.   In the fifth class grammatical rules which they learned before should be repeated and with the same plan held by their authors whom they previously learned. They should add new authors and the historians should be set forth and their mode of writing should be more polished. Their speaking manner should be improved by writing poems and certain Greek precepts should be introduced.

5.   In the fourth grade Greek grammar should be introduced more diligently, dialectical and rhetorical precepts should be instituted which in the fifth class were merely referred to. Nor should the boys merely exercise style, but after thought and deep reflection they should recite something that has been kept in reserve for public speaking. The reason for this truly is that they ought to have to write something original down separately.

6.   In the third class dialectical and rhetorical precepts should be investigated once again. Then the Greeks and the Greek orators should be explained. They should never work only in the Latin style, but also in the Greek style with a very diligent perception and very accurate imitation. Moreover, this plan of imitation (mimesis) must be laid out and a certain habit of working diligently must be prescribed.

7.   In the second class Aristotle's *Organum* should be explained. The rhetorical principles should be perfected. Plato, Euclid, the laws should be read and they should do the orations.

8.   The first class should be devoted to the diligent interpretation of theology. Having proposed the questions, it should begin with disputations. But these should be tied in with those which were first discussed in the second class.

The first six grades ought to have individual teachers, but in the second and first classes it is more useful to have more, because of the variety and difficulty of the subjects, for all of which the industry of one person does not suffice. And in the times before Plato's Academy came into being, they learned by listening to mathematicians. Therefore it is fitting to teach mathematics separately. It is also proper that they should learn from the first book of the Orators what Carneades, Clitomachus,

Aeschinus as well as the Academy maintained. Crassus in his third book points to individuals to know in different arts. For it is one thing to transmit and to teach, but it is another thing to learn. All things can be learned in order, but no individual can teach everything at the same time.

One thing must most carefully be cautioned against so that the grammatical, dialectical and rhetorical precepts be retained. Nothing is more pernicious than mixing them together. By these means, moreover, these dialectical and rhetorical principles ought to be handed on in the fourth and third classes, so that it may be added to the second class and to Aristotle, so there it will not be necessary to teach and to communicate things already known.

Moreover, on festival days they should read individually in their own classes, twice, once before breakfast and also once after breakfast. May it be the case that youths with their teachers may move on to the public lectures. For these have been continuing things to attend to.

The day of Jupiter (Sunday) was not altogether devoid of lectures, but it depended upon the decision of the rector, about whom it is now necessary to speak.

There was one who was outstanding in all classes, who prescribed which books should be read, who divided the various classes into decurions of ten students, who judged the boys' learning, who observed everything. For his duty was directed toward his four classes.

For no one followed such practice eagerly who consulted his own will more than he did better judgment. Such a teacher might often act in a way that later classes might disapprove of those preceding, bringing together new grammatical, dialectical and rhetorical precepts, and be ruined by new and superficially brilliant labor. Others, sooner than the boys, began to loathe the daily routine in the same book and before it had been completely studied, rejected it. Others asked the boys for their advice about their own studies, whether because they were satisfied with the outspoken desires of youth, or were crying up a fuller teaching of those writers not suitable for the boys' age level. Others, however, were reading the sort of things that go against morals or pervert good judgment. Therefore, whoever presides over such things, by whose decision and authority the readings, exercises, and finally all studies should be formed, must oppose such evils.

At Liège, however, the director of the Convent of St. Jerome thought of himself as a monk and that whoever referred to him as rector was in error. Men can, however, grow accustomed to do many things eagerly. Therefore it is valuable to be a "scholarch" of such a kind that all things never depend on just one person, but that an individual's authority be shared.

Therefore the first principle of the office should be concerned with the authors to be assigned, secondly to the division of classes into decurions or groups of ten. For the individual classes of learned and more fully developed youths can be grouped into tens or eights. Among them one person could be appointed who would observe and take note of the mores, how often anyone erred, which he would report to the rector, who would moderate the punishment according to the magnitude of the delinquencies. The head of a body of ten or eight pupils appointed anew every seven days should (not) be negligent, but should make notes and give wrongdoers over for punishment. Moreover, for particular months individuals should contribute coins with which a book or something of that sort should be bought in which should be recorded who failed in his duty, who repeated the lessons better, who composed more elegantly, concerning which things the teacher of this class should judge.

The third was that he (the rector) should judge concerning the learning of the boys. For once an individual has made progress, he should go on to the next class. Here they should be constituted in a single class so that they may excel in instruction. This class must be selected by the teacher. But since he may go wrong either by error or by benevolence, it was permitted that inferiors contend against the superior, with a theme proposed unexpected as to style and diction, or some similar debate. If the lower (boy) triumph, let him be given the honor and the other be reassigned by the rector. It should be held to be the highest honor to conquer an adversary, just as it is a shame to be conquered and to leave that position. The first so elevated and the second would receive rewards proposed by the College of St. Jerome. But the rewards were better for the first than for the second. Thus, if to the first a complete Vergil was given, to the second only Vergil's *Georgics*. But if the second contended equally well with the first, they received equal prizes. Moreover, the time for moving up to higher places was the Calends (first day) of October, my sentiment completely. For minds usually are languorous and studies yield to heat. But that censor's dignity which established it for the Calends of October aroused them so that each one prepared for future disputations, so that he would be capable of attacking and defending. Afterwards, when winter is near so that the tedium of the winter burden be removed they preferred to make new beginnings then, which usually stirred up greater interest, rather than the middle and end. That time is also suitable on account of those who come from other states and places in order to learn letters. For since all migration and change from a sound place should be resisted if the atmosphere worsens, nevertheless there is less peril in winter.

What books, then, should be read in individual classes, how they should be explained, and what plan of studies should be instituted in individual classes can not be set forth at this point, for that would require a lengthier explanation.

It seems to me that this institution can best be established in this city, for since locations have been assigned and constructed, I do not see anything more that remains to be taken up. For it will be housed in the Dominican friary, nothing must be changed in Sapidus's school. But the school must be divided into three classes, into eight, seven, and five. For the youths of Suebellius who are more informed should be placed for their teaching in the eighth, seventh, or sixth class. The boys of Dasypodius, because they are more advanced, should make up the fourth and third class, and in part they should strengthen the lower classes. Therefore the first six classes have been constituted in this way. The seventh is made up of public readings, that is the second *class*. The first is indeed theology.

Whoever is appointed director of the classes, where both erudition and diligence are in evidence, must be considered especially carefully. But I hear that there is some difficulty with this eighth (i.e., beginning) class. For since that age is weak up until then, some citizens will perhaps not be willing for their own children that the gymnasium be located far away. Nevertheless, in other respects both the labor and the utility of studies must be set forth and that softness would be pernicious; moreover, it must be remedied in this way. For since Dasypodius should have two teaching assistants, the one should remain where he is and should teach the small children. Sapidus should remain in the same place, for he is suitable for them. One at least could be transferred to Suebellius for he will then be of greater use to Simon, who should be appointed as superintendent of one of the more advanced classes.

Moreover, once a director is appointed the plan is not difficult, if only one holds fast to the idea that no privately chosen readings be selected for the six classes, nor anyone question sending a pupil back (i.e., not promoting him) as often as necessary, or if false accusations arise in private conversation; but so that he should have that duty and authority more to *himself,* I will be silent about remaining subjects. Moreover, he should be subject to the judgment of the scholarchs, to whom complaints should be brought in the presence of two or three (others), who in general should visit (the classes) as often as four times (annually).

There is no more work here nor is it to be counted as more work than formerly. For nothing more is committed to the rector but if anything more is, then he will have the third part of whoever hitherto was used to being paid for it, the same amount formerly paid a teaching assistant.

If the Senate should decide something about thirty poor students, it must be seen to that a careful disbursement be employed which can be useful and safe for studies.

This institution will be useful to our citizens, generous towards neighboring city-states and people, necessary for posterity. For all the hope of the republic rests on the instruction of the youth. Nor do I see how that paucity of studies which exists throughout Germany can be avoided and alleviated without this kind of education for the first time of life.

4
The Correct Opening of Elementary Schools of Letters
(1538)

Introduction

The most important overview of Sturm's educational ideas is presented in this treatise. Having presented to the scholarchs and the council his brief *Advice*, Sturm in this treatise elaborates on the principles, contents, and organization of the educational system he proposed for the gymnasium in Strasbourg. The school was destined to have a great future, a tribute to Sturm's solid foundation and careful planning. In 1566 Emperor Maximilian II bestowed on the school the privilege of an academy, a prerequisite for becoming a university. In 1621 Emperor Ferdinand II extended to the Academy the privilege of a university, the University of Strasbourg. The educational program of this gymnasium, academy and university was emulated by many other institutions of higher learning in the Empire, Switzerland, and France.

The key sentence in this treatise is clearly *Propositum a nobis est, sapientem atque eloquentem pietatem finem esse studiorum*, we have proposed that the goal of studies is a wise and eloquent piety. There springs immediately to mind the Ciceronian ideal of education in the republican virtues of gravity, dignity, piety, eloquence, and the like. "What greater or better gift can we offer our youth," asked Cicero, "than to teach and instruct our youth?" In one of his *Table Talks*, Luther is said to have asked, "What prevents us from praying for the salvation of that good man Cicero?" Humanists and the reformers converged on Ciceronian ideals of education for the servants of the republic and the church.

The importance of this work is such that it was published a good many times into the seventeenth century, here for the first time in a modern language. The editions are therefore available in the better libraries, but the most readily available is the reprint edition in Reinhold Vormbaum, ed., *Die evangelischen Schulordnungen des sechzehnten Jahrhunderts*, I (Gütersloh: C. Bertelsmann, 1960), pp. 653–77. The most comprehensive discussion of the educational ideas expressed in this work is that of Anton Schindling, "Das Lehrangebot der Hochschule," *Humanistische Hochschule und freie Reichsstadt: Gymnasium und Akademie in Strassburg 1538–1621*, pp. 162–210.

The Correct Opening of Elementary Schools of Letters
(1538)

Dedicated to the most prudent of men and most distinguished of people, the noblest citizens: Jakob Sturm, Nicolaus Cripsius, and Jakob Meier.

The Usefulness of Letters

On the Nones of March, when it became known that a resolution of the Senate had been passed by which the improvement of elementary education and the establishment of a new school were entrusted to you, good men were overjoyed. Since you are the authors of this undertaking, most of the praise and congratulations are yours. You brought the questions before the Senate. The senate gave you the power to effect whatever you would regard right in this same matter. You made this project a reality; you conceived it; you instituted it and established it on a firm basis. You laid the foundations of a beneficial resolution and of a most sacred education.

People by nature possess many common vices. We are born with a large measure of barbarity. Historic periods, peoples, undertakings have, as well, their own characteristic false morality and each individual man is fashioned by his own peculiar nature. Finally, we imprudent men have lapsed into the worst habits through this very morality. And unless a remedy is found for these evils, what, in the future, can be uncorrupted or enduring in the state? Therefore I regard it absolutely necessary to restore to the states the ancient education which will then destroy, group by group, whatever is evil in morals, nature, habit, age, opinion, or ability. For just as lawfully constituted states must have different kinds of artisans and artists, so they must have separate kinds of education. There remain to this day in most states examples of the ancient custom which though corrupted, nevertheless proclaim what those famous men accomplished who prior to us administered the state justly.

While honorable acts are in the purview of all men and there is no one who should not live according to nature and virtue, there is no class of men who should establish and preserve a holier and stricter discipline than the class of men of letters. For there is nothing in the nature of the universe that cultivates morality as does the study of letters. Nothing has advantages so widely spread as humanity and learning. For as it was almost always useful for individual private citizens to have their children conversant with the discipline of the liberal arts, so in the public realm it was essential for all for the preservation of the state that some persons stand forth who, in periods of crisis and danger, would look after the needs of state not only advantageously, but also wisely. But if there have ever been times when the state has seen a change of fortune and many great perils stirred up because of the scarcity of good and wise men and the plethora of evil and inexperienced men, ours surely are such times. In our times, there are more traces of foolishness and greed than of prudence and probity. Not only in peaceful times but also in wretched circumstances, the most ancient and mightiest peoples desired that room be left for wisdom—a thing which we rarely do. Indeed as tempests arise and leisure is disturbed, the pursuit of letters and of wisdom must be cultivated. Amidst the storm waves they should not be suppressed and cast away so that even in dangers, we can foresee evil and in the midst of difficulties, if they are of long duration, we may not be deprived of rational judgment. Yet it often happens that we do not even avoid the very things that are foreseen, because they are joined with infamy and danger. Medea was a person of this sort:

"I see the better and approve
Yet I follow the worse course."

Therefore knowledge and wisdom do not contribute much to states unless we also add the cultivation and teaching of virtue by which we become accustomed to do what we have learned. For there is true wisdom only where there appears no inconstancy in speech, no error in opinion, and in actions no infamy or any fault. Even though virtue needs not only to be taught but also to be practiced, nevertheless there have always been teachers of good who are useful to the society of men and we must learn much before we can see what ought to be done and what is suitable. A man will not live virtuously who will be ignorant of what is common to all or many, or what is private, and what is praiseworthy in nature or honorable in habit. Faults of which we are unaware and which we commit because we are imprudent, we cannot avoid. But faults which are pointed out and censured, even if there are many of them, nonetheless are removed by education.

There are three things—and these are important—that produce prudence together with wisdom: namely nature, experience, and learning. The former two are common to nearly all people; nevertheless their nature is such that unless the third factor, i.e., learning and discipline, is joined with them, the one (nature) cannot be developed and the other (experience) cannot be employed in practical matters. For God has given us the power of mind together with life; some experience must exist in the man who has been given a rather long life and endowed with some diligence. But either one becomes worth more if a teacher of letters is brought in. When God has given to the teacher a good nature, he stands out always as useful and often as wholesome for the citizenry. But when literary elegance has been improperly applied to corrupted minds, frequently evil and very often wicked examples are apt to result.

For there is nothing more potent than learning. It has the greatest potential both for harming and for helping man. Many wise men have been nonchalant and contemptuous with impunity before the threats of kings and tyrants who could not bear the enmity of poets or the shouting of orators. Therefore the arts and disciplines should be taught not only in conformance with the rules of the arts, but also in a way that promotes wholesomeness—both of which in our times have been vitiated. For many do not follow in their teaching either the method or the program which the subject requires. In not a few cases a system of morality is maintained of the sort that because of long-standing habit either does not foresee or else excuses faults. Rightly therefore our Senate which wished you to be in charge of education, has arranged for you who have the desire, the zeal, and the ability, to give counsel as to what is best for a free people. Inasmuch as you have requested some advice from me, I have decided to explain my counsel and my thoughts in writing, and likewise to reveal what kind of schools seem best and which system of teaching I regard most expeditious.

The Goal of Studies
The Office of Teachers of Letters

The best kind of school, therefore, is one in which a system of teaching and of morality is scrupulously observed. For although the goal of our studies is a knowledge of the physical world, still, as we said before, if life is separated from teaching and letters, what usefulness does elegant and liberal education have? Accordingly, let piety and religion be set forth in schools and let the youthful spirit be trained for this through the cultivation of letters.

But the knowledge of the physical world without elegant speech is usually base and barbarous and along with the decay of speech we see that a certain captious conviction of what wisdom is insinuates itself in men. Therefore we must see to it that the early period of children's lives be given over to the formation of their speech. For men are naturally more ready to speak than to think or to make judgments and in education we ought to begin with what is appropriate for each individual. As with speaking, so too young boys are most easily habituated to behaving properly. For up to this point, poor behavior has not yet taken root firmly and those very faults in the beginning when they are not yet implanted can be rooted out more easily than they can be put aside once they have been implanted a long while. Thus, in the first years, let the control of speech and of life be joined together so that they may more easily achieve excellent education and religion—things which must be acquired afterwards. Of these, the one is necessary to mankind, while the other adds just and due ornamentation to what is necessary.

But whatever we want planted in our children's minds ought also to be clear in their teachers', so that teachers surpass the rest of mankind in education and piety. For nobody willingly follows an inexperienced man, and more people have greater confidence in a good man than in an evil man. Although the first hope rests in the innate capacity for virtue and talent with which the boys of necessity are endowed, and the second hope is in teachers, without the magistracy and parental effort too, the conscientiousness of instructors is frequently abated, and the pleasure of industriousness extinguished in adolescents' spirits. The well-being of the state obliges the magistracy to practice liberality toward those in charge of the education of youth, while privately in domestic affairs, it is useful for the father to want his boys to excel and for this purpose to study with teachers of letters.

But in those teachers who are to be selected, three kinds of zeal should be observed: for the humanities, for virtue, and for teaching. For many may bear certain marks of distinction in teaching, but nonetheless possess faulty habits that make them unfit role models. There are not a few from the noble class who prefer private, domestic leisure to public employment. All the more reason then why one should see to it that the conscientiousness of teachers is not roused by money more than it is valued as a result of consideration of their talents and an examination of the lives they have led. For steadfastness and a mature disposition are rarely found in men excited by zeal for money. Those whose motivation is above that and who flee from moral dishonor deserve greater trust. Thus the teachers of letters should be not only learned but also endowed with virtue and be most avid for the fatherland and for public service. Although there are three things that customarily stimulate men's minds toward distinguished acts—love of the honorable, desire for peace, and zeal for money—nevertheless wise men discriminate not only among dissimilar objects, but also among objects of nearly the same nature. Furthermore, as to this point, care must be taken that, once the talent of those who are the best qualified is established, we always prefer those who combine ability to achieve with determination and zeal. For though the desire for praise has often been lauded, in most instances it is combined with the corruption that ambitious men have. Avarice and inexhaustible ardor in acquiring riches cannot but be condemned by good men. The enthusiasm of the mind by which men of their own will are inflamed to acquire virtue always retains the approval of the greatest men.

But no one is good who does not rejoice at the signs of virtue in other people, and with many men the ingratitude of the wicked often lessens their enthusiasm. Pre-eminent talents desire both to practice and to experience liberality. No one at all can always help the unwilling and the ungrateful. Virtue is moved with profound sorrow when it sees itself overcome by vice. But although virtue desires to expand even after it has been reduced, it has something with which to be comforted. Whoever wishes, whoever desires virtues, for him it is always present. Whoever rejects or disdains virtue is not abandoned by that by which he should be saved—rather he avoids or does not embrace that by which he could remain unharmed.

The studious not only merit our good will but also should be favored with rewards and stipends and honored by benevolent decrees that are customarily regarded as a sign of outstanding good will. Therefore we require discrimination and liberality in the magistracy. Liberality must be extended so that the teachers do not lack what they need and so that as many teachers as possible, as well as parents and adolescents, may be stirred to action. For things that are honored are usually attended by crowds, but those which lie despised or neglected, even when they are very good, have only a few followers. But as has been said, those teachers must be selected who have as much learning as possible and to whom heaven has given such a nature that they desire to benefit the community.

The Kind and Amount of Stipends and from Whom They are to be Sought

A fixed amount and specific system in reckoning and granting stipends must also be maintained. First, the basic needs must be determined.

Then one must proceed to those rewards which are conferred for intellectual breadth and dignity. I shall call these stipends designated for grammarians "basic needs." There should not be any place, especially among Christian communities, where there is no one who can teach the elements of Latin and Greek. The states that can do more should also provide those who teach the arts of divisions[1] and of speaking. The dignity of the greater states demands that they provide professors of the major arts and supply theologians, physicians, and lawyers for states less able to provide them. The method of payment should, however, be so determined that the guiding principle of liberality is not violated, namely that what one man lacks, another man should not have in excess and allow to flow away. For that is an important sign of an unjustly constituted state. Therefore those who are deprived of the basic needs without which a suitable leisure for letters is not possible, are often constrained by poverty to ignore duty and undertake work casually, even greedily, in ways unbecoming and unsuitable. The amount of the stipend should be established first of all with reference to the state's resources and the usefulness of the studies. After this, the calculation should be made with regard to honor and dignity. I shall maintain, therefore, that a state flourishes by the teaching of letters where there is no lack of men who are closely connected and who can bring honor to the citizenry and where no one goes away or causes an interruption without leaving behind a successor or an assistant in place of himself. For states that are able should, from the very beginning, provide two teachers in each category. As long as they can, states should work so that they appear developed by their own resources and content with their powers; and they should not seek elsewhere what they can find at home.

There should be sufficient resources for what we have proposed if the wealth of the church is rightly disbursed. If only other states would follow the example of our republic! And if they cannot carry out all that should be done, yet will still want to do as much as they can, however little that may be! Three elements are necessary in every great and arduous matter: first that states have the desire; second that they are able to do what they desire; and third that after the work has been undertaken, they carry out what they can. The middle element is characteristic of only a few great states. Where the other two elements do not exist, censure and reproof are really in order. You must strive and sensibly try to bring about for the citizenry whatever you decide upon as most useful. Our forefathers provided the wealth of the church so that, with the highest reverence and devotion of life, worship and service might be rendered to God and Christ. However, that service is discharged in the midst of a dearth of things of which the body and soul cannot be deprived—namely teaching and beneficence. Times are terrible indeed when Christ's gifts are bestowed on men who do not wish to practice charity and who are not able to teach and who are incompetent to undertake their duties in Christian assemblies and, so as not to say something worse, who have a talent more suited to dishonoring than to adorning religion. I say these things about evil men whose number in our times is altogether too large. If only good people might be stirred by a mutual desire to drive out the men who brand with a shameful stigma a most honorable class of people! Let this suffice, if it is now agreed that the resources of the church have been provided first for teaching and poverty, then for letters with which teaching is helped most and, in our time, are necessary. If we maintain this policy, the ancient custom and discipline of our forefathers will sometime be restored. But these are my reflections up to this point regarding the duty of the magistracy and the payment of teachers.

The Duties of Parents

At home, the care of parents must complement the counsel of teachers. For it disturbs the educational process of children greatly when they harbor antipathies. Thus a father must see to it that his boys are praised, motivated, and loved as well as admonished, reprimanded and punished. For in schools of letters, as in a great nation, laws are passed; so with a crowd of youths let rewards be proposed for praise, and let punishment be proposed for censure in the same way as is usually done by legislators in citizen assemblies.

But love is often a poor critic and judge and does not allow anything to be corrected except by itself; and frequently, although it says otherwise, hates rather severe punishment. It is mean to be punished and corrected with the rod! Since most youths have defective natures, when it is necessary and cannot be ignored on account of his fellow students and when it is useful for the boy, the parent should think that duty takes precedence if in order to correct the soul, pain, which is more serious for the soul than for the sense of touch, is administered to the body. Cruelty and cupidity in men who instruct and teach ought to be censured and whoever derives pleasure from beating pupils ought to be removed from elementary school teaching. On the other hand, indulgence often brings with it many great disadvantages. Those who cannot maintain moderation in punishing or pardoning faults should be expelled from educating gifted minds. The children of parents who refuse to abide by such regulations will not be permitted to be included in the student body. The goals of the fathers and teachers ought to be united, for there is no proper compliance when the boy observes their disagreements. Domestic duties and the hindrances of worries should not impede or disturb the study of letters and other school subjects. When the mind is properly motivated, letters require a free mind. Chores are a hindrance and though wholesome for the body, they so affect the mind that it becomes unfit to study.

There are, in all, four things that the father should strive for on behalf of the teacher when the adolescent is at home. First, he should motivate his love of letters and increase his application to his studies. Second, his son should recognize that the utmost attention must be paid to his teacher from whom he will receive beneficial precepts for the education and formation of his mind. Third, the boy's application to his studies should not be distracted by domestic chores. Last of all, let nothing be done in conversation and training of the body and nutrition which might compromise his studies or upset the keenness of his talent or in any way interfere with his morals. In fine, both parents must act in such a way that they seem to want and desire the same subjects that are taught in school even if they themselves cannot pass them on because they are prevented by ignorance or desire or work. For in this way the unlearned parent will train the boy to discipline.

The Selection and Duties of Boys

In the beginning, the boy's nature must be carefully evaluated by his parents at home and by the teacher in the public school to whom he has been committed for instruction. For not only ought those born with slow minds be excluded from this education, but also those who, while not endowed with a base nature, are yet nevertheless unfit for letters. Then too, some boys of an exceptionally fine nature are yet better suited for military service or for public service rather than for education in the arts. As it is the business of a very good physician to judge who can enter upon marriage with good prospects of producing children, so it is in the province of a diligent teacher and master to decide which student is suited by nature for a particular art. It is the task of a diligent teacher to examine; of an experienced teacher to know; of a good and true teacher to advise the parents. For he ought to have the best possible students, not as many students as possible. Therefore, so that a fine, outstanding training and education of talents may be undertaken—just as the selection of soldiers must be held—so no one must be enlisted through whom you anticipate that you will accomplish nothing. Fitness of the body must indeed be looked at, but not to the extent that it takes precedence over the superiority of the mind. For though the body's appearance and health is a great thing and much to be desired, nothing is more glorious than the mind. Therefore the judgment always ought to be made with the mind in view which has a journey better fortified for work and authority if the body is elegant and of commendable form.

The virtues of the mind are ardor in undertaking, zeal in searching, acumen in comprehending, industrious in accomplishing, and memory in preserving. For where these exist, there is also that integrity of mind of which Plato speaks—love of truth and hatred of what is false. It would be desirable if all such virtues were everywhere found alike in everyone, but this has not been ordained for man's nature which varies widely and is of many types. Those whose talents are found to be but mediocre, should not be rejected from school and elementary education. A judgment cannot be reached hastily and quickly. For some youths of keen mind and nature are at first slow to perceive, but in time and with practice later acquire speed in comprehension. Many youths display natures which lie asleep, oppressed by the dullness of the body. When informed and instructed they nevertheless emerge excellent and distinguished. In some there are excellent gifts of mental perception, but memory is at times slow and at times unreliable. Yet memory can be aroused by teaching and use. The primary concern is for the will which, when present, may be the hope for mental processes. If absent it must first be stimulated with praise and promises, for many things that do not appear are merely latent. If success is not forthcoming in this manner, reproof is in order and one ought not to abstain from the use of rods before giving up. There is also another kind of mind of which Plato speaks in the books of the *Republic*,[2] which has a "defective attentiveness"—as he calls it—given more to hunting and wrestling than to letters and teaching. Such a mind Socrates barred from the dialectical discipline. We also do not regard it as suitable for letters even though we would want all youths to be perfect. Yet the mediocre minds must also be endured and the poorer impulses of the mind can be improved with teaching and practice.

The Culture and the Speech of Youths

Finally, instruction is properly accomplished when the nature of each youth has been examined and when all activities and studies are directed toward a kind of life. Why? So that the lifestyle, culture, and speech of students may be distinct from those of the unlearned. And in these matters, attention especially should be given to what is appropriate. What is not alien to one's profession in life is most appropriate. Indeed, inasmuch as the scholarly profession should consist in using reason and speech more prudently than others, every action and speech ought to be free of rashness and carelessness. Order, consistency, and moderation must be employed in every word and deed. Pleasure and self-gratification on the other hand should be hidden if they cannot fully be curbed. Therefore, if love is to be avoided or concealed in the adolescent, it will be suitable to remove from him his pursuit of a beautiful person. If minds drawn to the pursuit of warfare or hunting are to be corrected, it is essential that those who by their appearance and dress suggest the soldier and hunter more than the boy devoted to his studies, should be admonished and reformed. Loose garments can be taken in at the shoulders, and torn ones sewn together. Hence there is no excuse for sloppiness in clothes, but only censure. Whatever is mean, petulant, shameful, and offensive in a boy's speech must be noticed and eliminated. Certain natures have faults which may be removed or corrected with words rather than rods. So it is in speech: barbarous slowness or precipitous speed can be eliminated. Words and sentences in which the hearer appears to be held in contempt must be corrected. Yet, if they are the product of convention or ignorance they are not to be corrected harshly or painfully. The best speech is one that is prudent, well thought out and restrained. What is foolish should be censured. What is unlearned and confused, corrected. But whatever is immoderate, particularly if shameful, as for example, ostentation, must be punished with words; if it is lewd and shameless, such as obscenity or lying, then more harshly. Finally, culture should be judged by reference to the health and harmony of a profession, while speech by reference to prudence and moderation. Men who do not abide by these are evil and have rejected obedience which should take precedence in discipline.

Respect is always to be shown to all people. It is bad not to stand, bare one's head, or respond properly to a magistrate, a theologian, a teacher, a parent, or an elderly person. Those who play when no recess from studies has been granted, disregard obedience. They also act disrespectfully who play at a time when they are seen by other citizens in whom the habit of discipline has been observed. Those who do not practice moderation in sleep or, when at leisure, in play, even when it is permitted, nevertheless, because they are intemperate, damage discipline—although this is no serious crime. That group of pupils is truly, praised in which there is superior character, passionate love, constant attentiveness, and respect worthy of a free man.

The Poor

It truly behooves large states especially, to take account of the poor. For it has always been a matter of honor to cultivate liberality and benefi-cence, and Christ left the poor to be cared for in his absence by his flock. But there is no one kind of poverty. There are those for whom work is hateful and idleness more pleasant. The class of beggars who are not deprived of bodily strength, should be thrown out of the state that has been founded justly. For they are either useless and stand in the way of others, or else are wicked and given to brigandry and robbery. But those who, though physically strong and enabled by their natural abilities to do something, are hindered by the numbers of their children or by their parents' creditors, or by their friends' misfortunes, or their personal misfortunes—these if they love virtue and want to escape deg-radation should be saved from affliction by all the noblemen. For although they are miserable, yet because they are not also criminal, they ought to be aided. If the goal of public affairs is happiness, the state in which good citizens are hard-pressed by want can be considered mis-erable. To this kind of poverty a third ought to be added: those afflicted with protracted sickness, physical debility, or advanced age. These three kinds of poverty are not of concern to our institution.

But there is in addition another class of men who possess whole-some physical energy and highly capable minds but are afflicted by nothing more unfortunate than having been born to indigent parents. This class has excellent abilities for letters and is instinctively attracted to their study. Its indigence should not only be excused but even praised and should motivate others to goodness. In our times it is indeed very necessary that this be the case. For the study of letters are antithetical to riches and poverty, virtue and vice, liberality and greed. Where ample rewards are offered for the study of letters, a larger num-ber of students present themselves than in the case of those societies for which barbarity is more agreeable than the elegance of learning. Of the rich and noble, except for some endowed with unusual goodness of nature, by far the greatest part which is given over to effeminate self-indulgence and to certain other vices which are inherent, has poor judg-ment and is driven to seeking popularity and pursuing money in the face of which it has always been difficult to maintain moderation. According to such men, bidding up goods for speculative gain irrespec-tive of moderation and religion is thought to be virtue. Whereas those who observe religion and cherish the dignity of virtue make greater advances and progress farther than those who chase profits and power through favor and riches, and, with no education or holiness in their lives, make a sudden ascent to the fullest honors. Poverty indeed arrives slowly and late where it wills, but nevertheless gives us many men who perform and complete great and arduous deeds. Selection, moreover, is easier from large numbers and diversity than from small numbers and uniformity. From men who are afloat in wealth and inherit nobility from their forefathers, few feel that letters are their concern. Although in every instance, something very good is exceedingly rare, poverty yet arouses more men to study and to the love of letters. Poverty itself has great power for enterprise. Yet extreme need is a hindrance to accomplishment if no support is available. Therefore, it is not proper to banish from among citizens the beggary which burns with love for wisdom; and contributions, i.e. that they be supported free for virtue's sake, should be made not only to the children of citizens, but also should go to foreigners and aliens in whom the light of genius and hard work appears to have been kindled. The highest and greatest praise has always been for hospitality and goodness and among us who are Christians in name are very necessary. For religion is in disagreement with elegance and greed for gain in this respect: They both offer hospitality to the illustrious and prosperous, but religion keeps its house open to those from whom it expects neither thanks nor wealth nor profit. But order and moderation must be maintained among the poor so that the children of the citizens (especially if they are good) are not in want and so as to take an account of the better sort and always give preference to what is best. It is shameful that the children of citizens should be in want and honorable that foreigners not be in need. A certain number of children who, it is agreed, have high native ability should be designated for state support. Others should seek their needs from citizens privately. All, moreover, both those who are the objects of private charity and those who receive support from public resources, ought to bring to the school and education grace and usefulness, not trouble. If they do otherwise than is fitting, they ought to expelled. For we do not want to shackle the benevolent generosity of the citizenry. He serves as a shining example who cultivates virtue and religion. He is useless who cannot so serve but sets a bad example.

Privileges

Privileges are not offered for the purpose of exemption from punishment or the defense of wrong-doers. They are imposed, rather, so as to punish the guilty and have been instituted to protect the innocent and preserve the state. The laws employed by Paris, Louvain and other states where arts and learning are taught, seem to have been established on account of the scarcity of scholars. For there were times when letters and all teaching were in a desperate state. To obviate this calamity, magisterial enterprise was aroused. Rewards were offered. An entrance and an ascent to honors were opened up and privileges were proposed as protection against insolent citizens who manifested a disagreeable and despicable attitude toward teachers and students. In order to encourage talent, rewards and honors were offered and laws were passed to preserve leisure and maintain status. But even so the same thing happened that happens with everything else that is good: namely, that little by little men abuse them. For in bestowing honors, circumstances and money are of more account than virtue and teaching. Excellence is not considered and ranking is subverted. We apply our law in such a way that an empty and false conviction about wisdom seems to have instituted the law to be used as an exemption from punishment for crime and a shield for evil. But as the magistracy can, by giving rewards, exert influence with them, so it can also punish by withholding them.

Among the Greeks, the citizenry granted daily sustenance in the Prytaneum to those who were eminently deserving of the state. But if anyone later attempted to betray the fatherland and began to abuse this benevolence by some criminal act, they not only stripped him of his honor but even passed a law to force him to plead his case under the threat of capital punishment. That way they maintained honor in the republic and punished evil. Men ought to enjoy laws who have those very qualities for the sake of which the laws were passed: namely, knowledge of the world and love of letters. Every rank and magistracy ought to be rebuked if the men who break the law and dishonor traditional rights should not be punished. Therefore, we desire that privileges be long lasting and made public, but in such a way that the strictness of discipline and ancient tradition are maintained. These are the privileges which briefly and in general terms, it appeared, must be recorded and recalled in regard to the universal principles which seem to pertain to schools of letters.

For it clearly suffices if all studies are directed toward piety and wisdom; if the number of those being educated is large enough to make possible a selection of distinguished talents; if magistrates set up awards and increase the honor for education; if the zeal and will of parents and teachers are joined together; if teachers are of such quality and possess as much learning as they can, and are gifted with that virtue that makes them want and desire to elucidate and increase the influence of letters; if the poor are taken into account, and if we use laws and privileges for their intended purposes. In fine, then at last all will flourish when each individual does only what reason and a dignified life style prescribe.

God has not laid upon us more than we can bear, nor does any prudent man undertake what he cannot carry out. In free states only as much is demanded of each individual as his powers and talent can sustain.

One General and Public School[3] Ought to be Established in the State

Next, an announcement in writing must be made about the schools to be established. Grades must be designated and also a method of instruction and a plan of education must be handed down. For whatever is done rashly, in confusion, and heedlessly, is rarely wont to make progress. And so, in the works of Plato, Protagoras (though an unwise orator is being cited), correctly states, "For the whole life of man requires harmony and rhythm." (Πᾶς γὰρ ὁ βίος τοῦ ἀνθρώπου εὐρυθμίας τε καὶ εὐαρμοστίας δεῖται.).[4]

As there is one goal for true studies, so it is more useful for elementary schools to be located in one place instead of being divided throughout various places in the city. For just as it would be inept to assign to every ten sheep one shepherd and one pasture, so it is not commendable to divide up and entrust to more teachers what can be done by one or a few teachers at the same location equally well as by many. Then too, man is happy in society and in a group. There are few for whom solitude is pleasant. Rarely too does a large group lack variety and excellence, offering thus a selection and examples. Xenophon writes[5] that the Persians constructed a "free forum" (ἐλευθέρη ἀγορά) in one place, removed from the crowd and noise. For all liberal education must have good conduct (εὐκοσμία), discussion (συζήτησις) and the prowess that arises from unity (συμφερτή ἀρετή),[6] so that everything may progress in order and in due measure and shared studies and a united effort may appear as if in one guise. This is why the Persians—if we may credit Xenophon—who generally lived in scattered localities that are called country villages (χῶραι) nevertheless made their boys, adolescents, and young noblemen who had already completed their military service, all frequent the same place. For a large group offers more and better examples to follow and more opportunities for learning than a small group. Thus cities are better sites for learning than deserted climes, as Socrates says in Plato's *Phaedrus*.[7] Furthermore, if the numbers involved and the size of the city is so large that a single location does not suffice, as is in the case of Paris, it is more beneficial for the various schools[8] to be brought together than to be scattered about. For both those who teach and those who listen are spurred on by variety and numbers but languish in isolation and sparse numbers. Therefore, there should be one school[9] of liberal studies constructed in a convenient, central location inside the city if distances and numbers permit. But this school shall be divided into individual classes which in turn will have been divided according to the kind and different types of instruction and by periods of time for work and training. Regarding this we must now give advice.

The Division into Grades

We have stated that wise and eloquent piety is the goal of studies. For it behooves all men to cultivate piety. But the educated man is different from the unlearned in the following way: the former excels in reasoning and in speech. Therefore the knowledge of the world, combined with a pure and graceful speaking manner must be made available to the man who wishes to be considered worthy of the title "educated." To this end, they should assign general studies to those who wish to engage in and hear such discipline. And though the studies of philosophy and languages[10] are related, it is nevertheless more suitable for human nature if instruction begins with the elements of speech. But even so, the teaching of morals, as already stated, must always and continuously be maintained. Inasmuch then as the primary task must be to inform and educate the tongue, this will occur if we adapt the class levels to the divisions of speech. For the best authors desire that perfect speech should first be pure and clear; then richly adorned; and later, consistent with and appropriate to the topic at hand. The first two (elements of language and pure, clear speech) entail nearly the same, surely closely connected, kind of instruction and in our time-schedule are learned from the moment when the boy is placed under teachers and tutors. The third (richly ornamented speech), since it is of more significance, also requires a more liberal training; nevertheless not free of all rules, but enough that a mere adolescent may be in awe of it. The fourth requires a mind firmly grounded in the study of letters, and therefore demands rules so that the students will give their attention, so that the teachers may maintain their authority, and so that strictness may be ample enough for securing obedience of will and for giving instruction. On this basis we divide all grades into two categories. The first is that of boyhood which entails essentials and constant learning. The second is adulthood which requires public and liberal lectures. To boyhood education we allot nine years. Advanced public lectures absolutely require five. So, if the boy happens to be brought to the teachers in his seventh year, by the time he is twenty-one he will have progressed through all the grades.

When a Boy Should be Brought to the Teachers

But the light of talent is not the same in everyone. There are certain excellent natures that can grasp the function of letters and the principles of reading by their fifth year. Some are scarcely ready by their seventh, although those who exceed that time rarely succeed if their mental fog does not lift. But just as those who begin early and make rapid progress are sometimes inclined to be over-hasty and to be misled by their age, so those who are scarcely ready to begin at seven often achieve sounder judgment and a more steadfast will. Therefore we designate the sixth year, the middle time, as suitable for everyone for learning, so that as soon as the boy has passed his fifth year and has about reached his sixth birthday, he should be handed over for education. But those who can before that age attain to greater things, display signs of such a nature as Socrates wished for dialecticians calling them "thoroughly competent" (ἐντρεχεζάτους)[11] who have, as it were, quick impulses toward understanding.

The Number of Required Lectures

As soon as the years of infancy begin to pass and boyhood begins to arrive, the boy should be handed over to the teacher of letters and led gradually through all grades of this instruction. We limit the number of these grades to those years which we devote to boyhood education. Thus there should be nine grades, divisions, classes, or even tribes or whatever term it is agreeable to use, even as there are nine years. Of these we have set aside seven for teaching clear Latin speech. The remaining two are sufficient for developing the ornate style. The basic instruction in this style is passed on in these two grades. More correct practice and greater skill will accrue in those next five years which we think are necessary for free schools and for a method of speaking suitably. Just as pure and clear speech involves a number of skills which are co-related (ἀντίστροφα), so the ornate style of speech can hardly exist if it is foolish and nothing suitable is said because it is crude. I was once of the opinion that six grades were sufficient, but experience taught me this more useful division. Therefore we give seven years to the boy's mother for her to bring him up and play with him. Fourteen years belong to the teachers. The boy should not regret not graduating before his twenty-first year. For before that time, matrimony and public life are premature. But this course[12] is the most suitable for a palaestra and school of letters.

The Benefits of the Grades. The Distinctions between the Individual Grades. How Boys are to be Motivated.

There is in this division sometimes a certain necessary benefit and sometimes a pleasure of the sort which accords well with boys' studies. For one cannot possibly teach everything, and unless a fixed and declared approach is found, it often happens that we stray from the true path, not only from ignorance but also from greed. Is there indeed in our own times anyone who has achieved excellence in teaching by his twenty-first year? We scarcely reach in the fiftieth year what youths are expected to excel in at once. Marcus Cicero was only twenty-six when he delivered the oration for Publius Quintus and Sextus Roscius. Who is there in these last centuries who has departed this life, even as an old man, who has left behind such an example? We do not lack books; our people are not in want of talent; perhaps they do not even shy away from hard work. They are lacking in only two things: the Roman language and right reason, which is the old discipline, both of which must be acquired before we can expect anything perfect. But there are many other useful things that we need not mention here. There is indeed delight in the fact that the division represents as it were the image of a city-state and a whole republic: For those three men whom the state made prefects of all, represent the face of aristocracy. The other three who are the intermediaries between those I mentioned and the directors of discipline are like assistants if something outside the grade is to be deliberated. Then too, the entire group is separated, as are all citizens, into grades, as it were, into tribes and classes, over which individual teachers are placed like curators over the people or masters over tyros. The grades are divided according to bodies of ten from which captains of the ten are elected: the observers of morals and supervisors of duties. The moderator himself is in charge just like an unharmful dictator who, subject in his turn to a higher magistracy, then obtains praise if he rules properly, and produces fine, useful fruits. Rewards are also given to individual classes, or to brave citizens, when the annual promotions are made to the next grade. This we must now also explain.

Promotion to Grades

It motivates youths greatly when they note how much progress they have made. They generally think the later grades are easier than those they have mastered. Such was the encouragement of Aeneas:

"O you who have suffered graver things, God will
make an end also of these"

So a solemn annual promotion to the higher grades should be held to which the teachers will come, and also the prefects together with the theologians, and the boys' parents and friends. To the two boys in each grade who have made greater achievements than the others, awards ought to be presented for conscientiousness and virtue. And inasmuch as favoritism is often suspected of influencing such matters, those who are inferior should have the right to confront those who placed first and to challenge them in writing, speaking and debate, so that if one of them should prove equal to his rival, he will be given the same reward; if poorer, he may still return to his place without disgrace. The Calends of October are good for the promotion, because then sickness is at its lowest or is minimal, or, if it exists, can be avoided. It is also midway between the times when the bad weather of winter is not a hindrance with its new hardships and when the end of summer does not cause disgust in youths who have prepared for the Calends of October.

The Last Grade—Grade Nine

The beginning, moreover, must be derived from the end. And so, at about his fifth or sixth year a boy should be brought to a teacher who will teach letter forms, compound forms, and sounds. To the instruction in these we devote the ninth grade as well as the first grade for one year. But since two topics are offered to which these three subjects (letter forms, etc.) are basic, namely reading and writing, this first grade ought to contain what is to be taught to everyone so that the best part may follow. Therefore, the teacher should teach how to draw and to represent the forms of letters in the most elegant way possible and to pronounce fully the sound of these as they ought to be. He should teach control of the tongue, of the breathing, and of the voice in a way which sees to it that nothing is expressed which is shoddy, obscure, lifeless or terribly bombastic. The voice ought to be subdued and steady, not loud or cracked or provincial. Apropos of this one may rightly disapprove the habit of speech of the crowd. What the most educated do should always be maintained. Those who pronounce best have many things in common with Greeks and Italians, but certain pronunciations are unique to them. Many must be corrected among the Germans, but more among the English and the French. The Italians err less. But no one is without fault in pronouncing some letters, either in single letters or in combinations.

It is also proper in teaching to look after morals. Therefore one should be instructed in the catechism. This should be brief, so that an immediate transition can be made to the inflections of nouns and verbs. Of these, certain general examples should be selected. If the instruction will be carried out properly, then anyone who is not of a base nature will learn in one year both to read and to commit to memory the general forms of inflections. To those who have some time left over, the easier and shorter letters of Cicero ought to be introduced, for instance, those he wrote to his wife Terentia and some of those to his freedman Tiro. From all the volumes of letters, we have selected three books in which we saw nothing extremely learned, but have gathered what is most suitable for boys of this age. I do not know anything which can be more usefully introduced at the beginning.

The Eighth Grade

At the eighth grade, after the foundations of which we have spoken have been laid, students will receive their first promotion in their studies and the first training in conscientiousness. For those who have received awards will try, for the rest of the year, not to lose the honor they won and will build their way to new praise. Those who were the last, will not try to be defeated again and will strive to equal, or even excel, their teachers. Then in the first six months, grammatical distinctions[13] should be taught with the greatest care but not the points that are obscure or drawn from all sorts of exceptions. For the explanation of this, two hours a day are needed. Whatever time is left over should be devoted to the *Eclogues* of Vergil and the letters of Cicero. That is two hours; since instruction should last about four hours, I give this advice. The letters ought to be analyzed. Individual words must be inflected, interchanged, and again combined and the reason for each word's sequence given. I postpone the process of construing speech to the last six months. For teaching, this two hours daily should be set aside. The other two should, as in the previous six months, be assigned alternately to the letters of Cicero and the *Eclogues*. At this point the boy begins to be accustomed to Latin speech and to translate sentences from everyday speech into Latin form. This exercise properly precedes composition.

The teacher should then also read the poems in meter and the boy should imitate more by habit and practice than by reason. But whatever is being taught, unless it is very clearly explained, is flawed.

The Seventh Grade

By the time the boy reaches the seventh grade, his time of life will begin to integrate the powers of his talent and to reveal something of his promise. For at this point he has learned, for the most part, classes and inflections of nouns and verbs; the rules of coherent speech are also not unknown. These must be repeated from then on and his memory refreshed. Yet the time spent on review ought to be carefully allotted so that the review does not impede the knowledge of subsequent subjects. The length and quantities of words and syllables must be thoroughly learned without ignoring the types of speech and the kinds of verse. But one hour each day is enough to devote to such learning. Many teachers ought not to teach this even if something is to be skipped because one ought to be careful not to include too much. Nevertheless, if anything will be skipped, it will be picked up in the sixth grade.

Here, those two great books by Cicero should be introduced, both elegant and pious and easy to understand: one *On Friendship* and the other *On Old Age*. For these, we need a second hour free from other work. The third, the poets claim for themselves. Vergil's *Aeneid* has all the virtues of heroic verse. Other kinds of verse are to be chosen from Catullus, Tibullus, and Horace. More kinds of poetry would be from Catullus and Tibullus if they were chaste. But if this may not be so and if some kinds are not available (for you would find better only with difficulty in other poets), nevertheless, the kinds of poetry not available from Catullus and Tibullus should be selected from Horace. Nothing should enter the boys' ears and minds that is not chaste, pious, elegant, and worthy of a free man.[14]

A fourth of that time devoted to rhetoric should be given over to composition because the usefulness of developing arguments and correcting writing is considered great and more time is used. But if any time is left over, it may be quietly taken to explain a subject that needs it more. Arguments should be collected from material the boys have already heard so that they recognize the passages from which they should take their vocabulary and sentence structure. Poetic words and figures of speech should also be carefully distinguished from the pure style of the orators. Boys must keep in mind that nothing not used by Cicero or not permitted by the teacher is true oratory. The boy's task is to be lightened by composing poems. For by itself the habit of writing is burdensome, particularly in the beginning. Truly the more tightly constructed and more succinct their sentences are, the more difficult the speech of poets is. Therefore the words of good poems should be transposed during the first months so that the boys work only with structure. Later they should be exposed to free sentences, but nevertheless the sentences should all be such that they have no need of inquiry into them and their task consists wholly in finding the right words and determining their grammatical connections.

Training the Memory

These three grades, the ninth, eighth, and seventh, require training the memory. For the teachings are the kind which are handed on so that they all ought to be retained in the memory permanently. So, no more should be read than the power of memory can support. Nonetheless, some topics of learning (such as exceptions to the rules) are marked down more usefully than the subject itself which is being immediately engraved on the mind. But there are some things that must be memorized right away, such as the apprehension (κατάληψις) of a subject, forms of inflection and examples. I do not know whether it is more useful to be able to relate from memory all that is read in Cicero and Vergil, or only those passages that are the most worthy of imitation. For at this age, boys are still injudicious and must be given many assignments which they will not do of their own volition. Knowledge which escapes being used when needed is not learned thoroughly enough. Therefore students must daily be given something which trains both understanding and memory. Indeed, as I said before, as much must be offered as the powers of their memory and the nature of the subject matter can accommodate. Even material which they have already learned once must be repeated at brief intervals, often and regularly. The perceptions of the mind become clearer, the faculty of recall becomes brighter, and the discovery and use of each are easier, if they may be divided up according to certain common criteria, limb by limb as it were, and by short phrases, and collected under general headings so that what the orderly mind itself can recite from memory, it may also know where to find the same information divided neatly into its basic components. For just as cosmographers' maps which depict the very places we once frequented strongly excite us and enlighten our perceptions, so even desolate expanses are put into order when we grasp them with the mind. Although the pen does not include everything in one illustration, yet when all the facts are piled up in one place by making observations, they reveal themselves and explain the observations more clearly.

The Method of Teaching and Time Schedules

A method of resolving information into basic components[15] must be taught at another time. Now before we come to the sixth grade, let us briefly interpose some comments on method of instruction and the time schedule by which we should teach. For boys should not be burdened with long lessons. It is not enough for the teacher to assign excellent material and to understand it. He ought rather to discern and choose the most expeditious and useful method of explanation. And apropos of this, one must condemn the practice of men who fill the ears of their audience for hours on end without a break, and think that it is not enough to explain only what is in the author. They often think that introducing the study of a topic cannot be sufficient. They try, rather, to teach everything at one sitting and they bring in much inappropriate material so that they may appear very thorough and very learned. I do acknowledge that something must be heard, read, written, or thought about and questioned. But continuously, highly detailed treatment produces boredom, while variety removes the discomfort of being over-fed and maintains pleasure. A relaxed effort at exposition encourages private study and individual ideas. Four or at most five hours (not less than four nor more than five) should be demanded daily by teachers. These should be divided up according to a plan made with a view to subject matter, time schedules, and normal practices. Explanation should be kept easy so that the boys will understand whatever they hear. In the last (i.e., first) grade only words and phrases shall be taught and sentence structure should be so explained that they follow the meanings of these and learn where they may use similar expressions. But the most important of customs, histories, counsels, ornaments, and famous topics contained in any work of art require explication. But all topics are to be given their own allotments of time, nor is it the sign of an accomplished teacher to explain or mention something out of the allotted time. Therefore one ought always to consider the subject matter and the powers of the mind. It is foolish to wish to make mercury from any wood you please.

Even to remain fixed in one spot for a long time hinders and impedes quickness and promptness of mind. But precipitous haste tires the senses and disturbs the memory. A mature teacher maintains a measured pace, does not propose more than the intellect can bear, and does not dwell on a subject that is being presented to be learned any longer than it may seem to require. Too much diversity all in one day is also to be avoided and is injudicious when it occurs every single hour or in the same hour. Subject matter that is reintroduced after an interval of days is usually more useful, but one must never approach the new before the old subject has been completed. For to interrupt a subject once it is begun, or a narration, or the main part of an art, and to interpose something else distracts the understanding, confuses the memory and burdens the mind which always strives to arrive at perfect understanding. To practice more than three subjects on the same day should be disparaged. It is more beneficial to stop with two, but at times it is necessary to proceed to a third. Teachers can easily find out how much the boys know and have attained when, in response to questions which are brief and clear, the boys repeat, as it were, what they have heard. Long rapid speeches in periodic style should be wholly avoided in schools, for even if agility of mind may be attained, they are always inimical to accurate memory and are also unfavorable to the stimulation of the intellect which often requires time for meditation.

The Sixth Grade

I have no doubt that a boy can achieve in these three years what we promise; namely, that he will master the rules of Latin and clear speech and will acquire some ability to do similar things himself, provided that he has both talent and motivation and has been properly instructed according to this plan. After the ninth or tenth year, therefore, a boy ought to reach the stage where his education should be continued by reviewing principles already in the memory rather than by introducing new material. Unless it is absolutely necessary that something should now be taught which could not be previously, this year should be a respite from new material and references should be made only for the recall of material already learned.

This can be done conveniently by explaining the orators and poets. Here they must still continue in the *Aeneid* one hour daily, and the poems left over from Catullus and Horace should be completed. One should also select certain illustrious passages of Cicero such as general investigations of important questions or recollections which include praise, criticism, or some special topic like defense or class. There are always some examples of very beautiful argumentation which are properly introduced as subjects for imitation. There are also in Cicero some periodic sentences which have the utmost ornamentation and not just one kind of figure of speech and which are usefully committed to memory. In addition the very figures of speech are intermingled with the reasoning so diversely and so uniquely that unless they are taken note of, they do not usually turn up in writings.

All of these I would wish to be picked out and gathered into three books for this grade. I know indeed that those books should be disparaged which were read to us as boys, in which sentences were taken from writers without regard to order, however brief, subtle and elegant. This kind of book destroys the memory, dulls the stylistic edge, and often causes many things to be foolishly inserted into writings. But as the top orators brought some writings to the forum in Athens and in Rome, and extemporized the others with little preparation, previously outlined, as it were, so I also would wish this be done in the schools so that what it seems could not have been said by orators without having been previously composed at home, should be selected with true discernment and brought to the classroom.

It is also beneficial at this point that something from other writers be interpreted for learning's sake. The poets, historians, and even comedians who themselves are certainly poets, are midway between orators and tragic, epic, and lyric poets, but nevertheless more so in terms of structure and kinds of argument than in words and sentences. The historians, to be sure, have many poetical words and sentences, but the orators have more. Both have certain peculiarities. For the historians keep words as they were used at the times they write about, and have a certain free kind of composition more suitable for close reading than for rapid recitation. I exclude Caesar who, more like an orator than an historian, wanted to record his subjects in words of everyday speech. Therefore, him alone I admit to the sixth grade. For in that grade, especially if read between Terence and Plautus, he will provide a most beneficial pleasure. I would even also offer Sallust, though he is more usefully shifted to the fourth grade because I would prefer that they be kept on Plautine plays. In Terence there is "to turn the mind to" for "to apply oneself" and "to start" for "to begin" and "By heaven and earth!" Also in Plautus there are at times similar expressions, at times even more of them. Both freely postpone the pronouns to the ends of sentences.[16] There are other features of this kind that I indeed want the boys to note, but not to use except in a similar case or when what the teacher should demonstrate can be done with grace. The style of the orators creates another kind of speech and unfolds metaphors more bold than similes. So Catullus in the second book of Cicero's *The Orator* writes, "Fearfully as to some crag of lust, so your mind to philosophy have you applied."[17] That famous elder used the same word as Terence, but in the manner of orators in a clear simile. After Cicero, nothing is more useful than Terence. His language is pure and truly Roman. But just as the student follows an orator from the start, quite properly, so he cannot proceed without the fault of imitation. For there is here another kind of language than that of orators, which although it borrows help from all types, still wants to flow, first of all, from its own fountains as if from a very clear stream.

The teachers, therefore, will use whatever they can expound in two hours in the school. In the third hour, I would go over and repeat in full the material which is more useful and which should be suitable for writing assignments. For when the argument of a poem is being explained, Vergil is quite rightly repeated twice. Whenever the argument is taken from a letter or a debate or common places, the more useful approach is in the three books of which I have spoken. This order ought not to be changed unless the subject and time demand it. The fourth hour we give to the correction of written compositions. We ought not to regret the time consumed in this fashion, but occasionally it comes about that something should be read in place of correcting compositions). Therefore I shall with pleasure propose Caesar and Terence alternately and with commentary for the period of a month.

The Fifth Grade

The previous year about ends the instruction of pure and clear Latin and permits some respite in the presentation of rules. At this point, however, these must be repeated and applied to the Greek language. For up to the present the youngsters have been dealing with the elements of Latin as if in Rome and Latium. Now there is need to come to the experience of the Greek language whether in Rhegium or any Greek state to which Greek traders travelled and in which the teachers themselves, as it were citizens of the state which had commerce with the Greeks, were familiar with both languages. Therefore, once daily in the first months something should be introduced from the grammatical rules of the Greek language which have so much in common with Latin that learning and remembering them are easy. After six months, through the three following months of this year, the fables of Aesop—a few easy ones—will be conveniently expounded. These will be succeeded by the *Olynthiacs* of Demosthenes in the final three-month period. This should occupy one hour this year.

The work of a second book from Cicero's books *On Duties* may be undertaken, providing the three books assigned to the sixth grade have been read. For it is not impractical to leave the third until now if it could not be completed without undue haste. It is more useful in this class to work with Cicero twice daily rather than with the poets. Thus, though the third hour is designated for Vergil's *Georgics* and these should be read continuously in the first three months, yet in the following months an oration by Cicero such as the one *For the Manilian Law* or the one *For Q. Ligarius* should be interposed.

The fourth hour I leave to writing and composition, but along with this must be assigned books on rhetoric written on the ornaments of oratory which should be selected from the list that appears in Cicero's third book of *The Orator* (*De Oratore*) and in *The Orator to M. Brutus* (*Orator ad M. Brutum*). But the rules for these ornaments should be constructed and explained on the basis of Hermogenes. For expression of an idea ought to precede the method of invention[18] because the ornaments of speech are easier to learn. In the beginning, invention is provided spontaneously by the students while writing or by nature better than they can learn it from instruction. Thus a larger vocabulary should at this point be offered them and specimens of sentences should be acquired. For these provide sound, sentences, and arguments themselves and are often instructive and contain figures of speech. We may see many who in daily speech display prudence, but in the Latin and Greek languages differ very little from ignorant and unlearned men. Ignorance of material and a lack of opinions does not produce this, but rather an impoverished vocabulary. Thus with written exercises and the correction of composition will be joined usefully the analyses of tropes and figures of speech which ought to be disclosed one by one in teaching. Indeed, many and varied are the things that must be pointed out in writers.

The Fourth Grade

In the fifth year only, we must endeavor to make progress in Greek as well as in Latin literature and to join Demosthenes with Cicero, and Homer with Vergil, alternating for two hours. For the third in the first six months must be devoted as well to Greek grammar in which most likely something will still remain to be covered regarding the structure of the language, the length of syllables, and accents. Rules of rhetoric will take up the fourth hour along with style, which here begins to be more ornate and fully accords with the rules themselves. Cicero's *Divisions...*[19] excels all the rhetorical works provided they are correctly explained and memorized. But all Herennian rules which are handed down in the first book[20] in this grade are, with profit, more quickly learned before the *Divisions* are attempted. Sallust can be added after this instruction and Plautus, not for the sake of examples, which are explained in Cicero and Demosthenes in two hours, but for their history and unique type of language on which one must focus with discretion.

For often this type of language is introduced with grace. It is most elegant in an orator—like the language of Terence in Cicero which he used in such a way that it seems to have been not only ornate but also necessary. Whoever is the teacher in charge of fourth grade should teach how this should be used and should keep collected and consigned to their appropriate headings what has been read throughout these six years so that language which is common and circulated in normal usage is kept separate from poetic and historical language.

The Analysis of Orators[21]

All arts have a particular system of analysis of their own. But I would wish the art of oratory to be treated by an orator not only in such a way that he may recognize what is being done by someone in a speech which he either reads or hears and even how it was composed, but also so that he himself may achieve similar results and may keep piled up like provisions subject matter, the arrangement of facts and opinions, and the parts of these, i.e., words; also, so that he may possess a plentiful variety of topics of art like a rich and well-to-do head of household.

Therefore, there should be that well known analysis (ἀνάλυσις) of the orators: breaking up into sections an oration that has been composed and reducing it into classes, now of words, now of materials, and now of art.[22] But what is analyzed ought also to be noted by students and collected and put under headings and sections so that we may be able to find whatever strikes our mind or tongue and with these words either in Greek or in Latin be able to express it cleverly and intelligently. I mean by classes of words those which are found in the very arrangement of the sentences. For example, there are two orders of words concealed in the following sentences: *aliquem aliquid colere*: "someone cultivates something" and *aliquem amicitiam colere*: "someone cultivates friendship." Parsing these is correctly sought in accordance with the order of nature.[23] When we shall have understood the class of the words, we will easily learn where each single item should be tracked.

Moreover that division is suited to human nature by which we divide everything into those things that exist in nature and those things that do not. I mean by "exist" not only "being" (οὐσία) and things that are called "substances" (ὑφεστηκότα) but also those things that are said to be accidents, the nine categories[24] that are found in Aristotle. Moreover, rhetorical divisions[25] or restrictions of speech do not exist (in this sense). Again of those things which exist, each is either divine or natural or human and there is nothing in the universe which does not belong to one of these divisions. Whatever is divine is in truth what it is said to be, e.g. God, an angel, or heaven; or it is false and born of error, e.g. Jupiter and Juno. Anything that pertains and refers to these two, that is to say, true religion and false worship, has the same division. Natural things are either onefold such as the elements and the four natures,[26] or composite and are either endowed with sensation or lack it. Again, those lacking sensation are either generated beneath the aether and in the air itself as lightning, a thunderbolt, thunder, clouds, rain, snow, hail, or are taken from water and earth, as the sea, a river, islands, and continents. But those that have sensation are similarly divided and inhabit the air, water, or earth. This class is very wide in scope and it is not proposed to cover it all here.

I call "natural" all things that experience birth and death, except man to whom I ascribe a place of his own on account of his dignity. Therefore, those human things originate from him from whom they are named—that is from man. God bestowed on him life and for his sake brought other living things to light. Thus man and life should be kept in mind and we should include under both headings (that is *man* and *life*) both sexes, male and female. For opposites are properly joined, as, on the one hand, death is opposed to life. In addition, we separate man into body and soul and both have their own particular parts, functions, and forms which ought to be the objects of study by doctors and natural philosophers. But this living being (*animal*) that is called man and excels all others, possesses three kinds of goods just as he possesses fields and estates: soul, body, and fortune which includes justice, art, health, freedom and whatever originates from these as, for example, from justice originates law, judgment, inheritance, personal property, property of others, punishment, reward and from injustice originates murders, plunder, adultery.

For opposites, as has already been said, should always be set side by side. All have their own actions and their own effects. In the soul are thought, reasoning, memory; in the body are manner, stature, and motion. These actions are either necessary and are done naturally without recourse to reasoning as growing, wasting away, eating, drinking and others shameful to mention; or they are voluntary, as walking and sailing. Certain things precede these actions or are associated with them, as for example, place, time ability, instruments, causes. But certain things follow from all actions, namely utility and rectitude, to which can be added, but separately, ease and difficulty. Among those things that precede action are multitude, abundance, variety, paucity, and solitude; also the kinds of effects like newness, pleasantness, admiration and the like, are rightly connected with these. It is burdensome to enumerate them all at this point. I merely point out the way by which the journey, once undertaken, may be completed without too much difficulty. So, the classes of words are to be assigned according to this division.

But classes of words, in turn, are distinguished by four classes of things: substance, quantity, quality and two others which I boil down to one, namely, activity and passivity. These are terms and inventions of philosophers, but they also offer the greatest usefulness to the orator and are necessary in all arts and disciplines. Therefore, all the things that are broken up according to what is said to be in nature, are sought in these four distinct classes. But we use also those that we call accidents on the grounds that they fall under the category of the senses.

The oration and the orator are consigned to the first genus (substance). To the second (quantity) are consigned the prolix oration and the eloquent orator; to the third (quality), the sweet-sounding and ornate oration, just as we call an orator sweet-sounding and ornate; and to the last (activity/passivity), to make or speak or deliver an oration. Thus each attribute is divided into materials and the persons speaking. Each of these two is either simple, as an oration, language, and eloquence, or complex, as for example, the language of an oration, the power of eloquence, the wisdom of eloquence, or the knowledge of speaking. But all are interconnected just like antecedents, intermediates, and consequences. In this way, intimacy, friendship and benevolence differ.

The order of nature also can be maintained by a variety of actions such as beginning an oration, making and embellishing an oration and perfecting and polishing one fully. But activity and passivity also are divided into those two middle genera. For they have been divided into their classes, as when someone is making a long speech and someone else has elegant, subtle speech. One must come to opposites in a fixed order: In friendship, the first thing is to select friends; then to love; afterwards to increase; from there to confirm; from this to endure and thus flourish. Offenses do occur, and often a friend's faults happen to burst upon friends; then to annoy; then to offend; and then to rend apart the friendship and finally to separate by mortal hatred. So much for the classes of words and of subject matter. There remain other classes of art, that is of the method of speaking which we shall expound in books of rhetoric. If God will give us life, we shall publish these more fully and more perfectly in a few years. I do not see a better method than this for gaining that eloquence and purity of speech in which the ancients excel our writers. For up to the present, all are far from the goal they set for themselves. Men make judgments about a work that has been composed better than they can produce, something perfect and accomplished.

The Method of Composing Speeches in the Mind[27]

We have digressed too long from the subject we began. Therefore we must return to the fifth grade and add some things which will otherwise appear to be missing. In this grade we ought not content ourselves with skill in writing only, but something not written out should be recited from memory. After a theme has been proposed for narrating, proving, or expanding, time should be given to the pupils in the same hour in which it was to be taught for reflection, so that what they previously used to present in written form, they might now deliver orally after it has been learned through reflection and thought. We make three kinds of speeches in schools: one is written; another extempore; the third, which is in between, composed in the mind. The beginning must be made with the pen. Thereafter one rightly progresses to composing the speech in the mind.[28] Extemporaneous speeches cannot be undertaken until after a long and assiduous habit of writing and of composing speeches in the mind. Composing speeches in the mind will correctly begin just as written exercises—with familiar, everyday topics; or, if they recite in Latin or a foreign language, with things that have been interpreted in the Greek writers. Of this type are the narratives, encomia, censure, expiations and commonplaces of Homer and Demosthenes. But poetry should be presented in such a way that it is more like the forum and social gatherings than the theaters and dances. Also, among orators I desire a free tongue so that only the best things may be retained. Similar items can be changed as propriety dictates. Inferior items, because they usually occur in poorer forms or in strange vocabulary, should always be removed. This should be maintained also in writing.

Indeed, the conscientiousness of young boys should be aided by careful attention from their teachers. Just as in the early grades written themes are dictated by the teachers and are not made up and even the words are supplied individually and in many phrases, so beforehand the preceptor must explain this class of speech and he must point out what is noteworthy and what is best and what is likewise similar to Latin and what is different. For the boy will have advanced far enough if at first he correctly combines what he has heard, if his delivery is smooth, if he makes no errors, and if his utterances appear similar to the written word. After this exercise, opposing reasons ought to be made up. Demosthenes' own narration should undergo the process of composition in the mind as well as arguments which, consistent with the facts, could have been brought by neutral and by hostile critics. These ought to be given prior consideration by the teacher. For just as we hope that he who breaks a leg can walk, if he leans on another, so it is worthy of our greatest hope that the boy can correctly repeat the arguments in which the teacher has previously given him guidance.

The Third Grade

In the last year of boyhood the adolescent advances to the third grade where dialectics should be treated along with the principles of rhetoric; also, a greater ability to speak, aided by a method of making distinctions[29] ought to be developed. But it is necessary to condense the dialectics from the books of Aristotle and to give illustrations from examples of philosophers and theologians. There are in Aristotle many things that pertain not to the teaching of the art but instead to the demonstration of principles which ought to be omitted at this point. Now we have confidence in the best teacher, Aristotle, but he himself in his time had educated adversaries who were learned men whom he does not now have. Or if he does have them, they are of that class of sophists which is always censured by learned writers. Therefore we do not require the approval of the art of rhetoric but we ask for its explication—not prolix, burdensome, or obscure, but brief, easy and plain.

Among the rhetorical treatises, however, a treatise ought to be read which is sought out for the art of making distinctions, as, for example, Cicero's *Topics*. In this grade I also would want the opposing speeches of Demosthenes and Aeschines to be interpreted. But on account of their great length, they must be divided up. The oration of Demosthenes I would want to be transferred to the second grade if it cannot be completed in the third. Here the practice of composing speeches in the mind begun in the fourth grade, should be continued and whole parts of the speeches of both orators, after they have been explained and time has been given for reflection, ought to be expanded into a Latin oration from memory. That exercise is properly assigned to the younger youths when they are dismissed and they are heard after they have returned from home. One ought to take the fourth hour for this task when, depending on the time for the recitation of the material put together as a result of thought and reflection, they may read—indeed it will be useful to read the history of Sallust or Caesar. Then when these have been read, one should proceed to Livy. He is, it is true, a great writer but an observer of periods of time, therefore less like an orator than Caesar or Sallust. Thucydides pleased Livy more than Xenophon whom Caesar emulated. Sallust balanced the brevity of his materials with a distinctive use of words and with his own appropriate usage.

I do not know whether Hermogenes will properly precede Cicero's *Topics* of which I have spoken. Certainly what Hermogenes wrote about issues[30] should be read in this grade. For this will be substituted in place of the second book which is in the *Rhetorica ad Herennium*. The first book has been assigned to the fourth grade and what Herennius wrote in his fourth book I propose should be treated in the fifth grade. His third book on memory I do not want explained, for it will impede our progress. The observation of art and the principles of dialectic increase and strengthen memory more than that third book.

The Second Grade

After passing from boyhood to the assembly of adolescents and spending a year in a mature way in the third grade, a student will progress to the second grade in which he ought to find that the goal of ornate speech is the principle and beginning of the art of apt speech. But the study of related subjects must continue and be joined and bound together in close connection. Thus, what is fittingly begun in the ornate style ought to be completed in that style which ornamentation fits. Cicero, even when he knew what was apt and what was inept, learned too late what *"remos inhibere"* (to backwater) means.[31] He also taught Tiro, at a time when he was allowing his own writings to be polished, that to look after his health "faithfully" was inept.[32] For this reason the students ought to have continuous practice, but the class should be kept under supervision and the method by which it was explained should be maintained. Therefore, if the oration which Demosthenes delivered for Ctesiphon could not be made available in the third grade, it should be explained here.[33] But if explained in the third, then whatever seems suitable may be selected from other speeches.

The rules of dialectics from Aristotle about which I have already written must be abridged and made known so that adolescents study them for two years. But nevertheless, at this point, they ought to be trained more by practice than by precept. So at the same hour in which the principles are taught, a dialogue by Plato or by Cicero should be introduced in which the method of practice is illustrated and the correct system of argument is taught. Here too, Cicero's *Partitions* should be set forth to enlighten and strengthen the memory. This little book is most useful, as I previously mentioned, and ought to be retained in all the schools. But, it ought to be explained promptly. The adolescents should also proceed in the composition of speeches in the mind and in writing. Stricter judgment should be applied to the correction of written work. For already their writing will begin to appear in public and await the judgment of all grades. After the *Partitions* are learned, one must go to Cicero's *Orator* for a brief exposition of what is appropriate, what subject matter an orator ought to include, and how an oration is perfected. For in this year must be laid the foundations for that perfect work which we wish to see accomplished by the twenty-first year.

The First Grade

The fifteenth year promises freedom to the students and opens the way to the highest arts and the greatest disciplines. For after this, one ought to try to have the young men attain that kind of speech which is apt. I call "apt" whatever is literary, embellished by learning, worthy of a free man, and appropriate to the occasion and the person. This cannot be grasped in any way without knowledge of the greatest subjects and also nearly every kind of subject. And although not even the fine-sounding ornamentation of a speech is devised without benefit of the liberal teaching of the arts and philosophy, nevertheless that which perfects ornamentation is derived from apt speech. Therefore we properly take pains to acquire whatever philosophers and the most learned men profess. The road by which we reach the summit of this study we will shortly reveal. Students should therefore remain this year under the guidance of their teachers. The beginnings of greater subjects ought to be made and those things should be learned which, once the young man has achieved them, will recommend him to the public teachers.

Here then Aristotle's books *On Interpretation* (Περὶ Ἑρμηνείας) should be introduced as well as a second book of the same writer *On the World* (*De Mundo*). These two are easily mastered together in this year in an hour or so a day. The science of numbers should be taught and Mela studied. Proclus should be introduced and the elements of astrology learned. Now also Demosthenes and Homer will be interpreted—to which I add Cicero's books on oratory. Leisure must also be provided for writing and composition. The exercise of composing a speech in the mind is not to be discontinued. Finally, what is missing in the previous disciplines and those immediately preceding, and what needs to be begun, must be carefully considered in what follows.

The Festival Days and Sacred Lectures

Up to this point we have run through all the grades and have arranged in order all of boyhood, class by class! But since we have established piety as the goal of study, and have said nothing regarding sacred literature, something must also be prescribed regarding it. Therefore festival days have been instituted for listening to sacred lectures which in turn we have distributed into two parts. One day must be established separate from the public in the school itself. Then, without interruption, the entire school must be brought to a second and public session and seated side by side with the people. In public assemblies no order can be prescribed, for the particular occasion determines it. But there must be modesty, silence, and complete attention and above all, offensive behavior before the people must be avoided. For youth should present the image of honorable discipline. No small ornament is bestowed upon the citizenry by the modesty of innocence and the studiousness of boys. They dishonor the state who behave contrary to what is seemly. In the boys' school, one must see to it that before the boys come to these open sessions, they know the entire history of Christ and the apostles. Certain things must also be prescribed out of Moses, for there the boy gathers a remembrance of past deeds and antiquity, and these are useful for a knowledge of Christian doctrine. On festival days, those states which have but a one-day recess may properly add the preceding day as well. The catechism must be explained to the last grade. For the next three, this ought to be translated into Latin. For the rest, a better language, the Greek language, is more useful. Also, to the first two grades, Hebrew grammar ought to be taught, and as soon as it can possibly be done, Moses must be explained in Hebrew by way of interpretation. In this way, the first and last day must be dedicated to God. It is not permissible to put off remembrance and thought of the Divinity in the days which are in between, but it will be permitted nevertheless to reflect upon the studies of eloquence and philosophy as long as they are undertaken to illustrate religious teaching. In the afternoon hours on the last of the seven days, everyone should practice music. For the knowledge and practice of this art is worthy of a free man, and unless we learn it well as boys, we shall know it too late as adults.

Public and Free Lectures

The college of public professors is like the state of a free people in which the people itself chooses the laws by which it binds itself. In fact those who are teachers in the nine grades are, as it were, heads of the household who rule their pupils like children in what they believe to be honorable. But because law exists by which God rules the universe, nothing exists which is exempt in any way from God's law. In the same way that I call a people "free" so I also call these lectures "free," because even those lectures for youths in which there is less room for their inclinations are "free" although characterized by fixed laws.

The students who are nearest to the highest grade and to their teachers—though admittedly "nearest" by a wide gap—ought to be admitted to this assembly. For the goal of studies, less distant than before, can now be seen. Each one should from the beginning set this goal before his eyes. We have made the first and only goal of study an educated piety. That goal is without doubt carried out in many ways and permits of a division into various duties as so many parts. For it remains valid not only for theologians but also for lawyers and medical doctors, and every profession. To teach someone ignorant of religion; to defend the innocent; and to cure the sick, is the concern of charity and the Christian religion. Everyone must therefore take counsel with himself, then call upon teachers, parents, and friends, and consider in advance what kind of life he is suited for. But whatever he truly believes his nature to be suited for, he should apply all his thinking, reading, writing, and listening so as to prepare for and attain it. And he should so apply himself that he endeavors to excel others.

Depraved men practice those arts of which they are ignorant. Those who are not talented to be theologians, lawyers, medical doctors, or teachers must not be tolerated. Such behavior does not occur without a deplorable waste of acumen, of the advantages of health and of the mind. No one can excuse himself with the public who has attained less than he lays claim to. But as in theology, so also in the other disciplines, the most important thing is the mind's integrity and the fear of God. The unlearned do less harm if they are good than do the learned if they neglect virtue. Both are, however, at fault—but the unlearned less so. Nevertheless the man who still undertakes what he cannot do provides an indication of his own personal zealousness or arrogance, or foolishness or laziness. The man, therefore, who is selected for the public school and this liberal training should be as good by nature as he would wish and as conscientious as possible. He should also be of such an upright and alert spirit that he does not want to practice the art which he pursues before he has learned it and is brought with this wish into the ranks of teachers and masters.

The Nature of Public Exegesis and Private Readings

Often each field[34] has many writers, a variety of books and a multiplicity of presuppositions. A selection must be made among these. Therefore to come by chance upon books is the mark of an ill-advised man. Prudent men approach books with the best advice and the best judgment. In this matter the common saying, "No book is so bad that it does not contain some good," has deceived many. We ought to come to such books only after we have read the best—both what have great obscurity and those without which nature does not permit us to attain the object we pursue. Schools cannot teach us everything that is useful. Therefore teachers should select the necessary and best works from the best authors while the rest should be left to private studies without which the conscientious efforts of a teacher are obstructed and imperfect.

Commentaries on authors are read more profitably at home than interpreted at school. It would, for example, be a mistake if Bartholus were read by lawyers while Justinian's works were disregarded. As the sophists who did ignorantly and basely interpret Scotus and Thomas in their assemblies, so almost like them are the men who, in teaching the *Aphorisms* ('Αφορισμοί) and similar writings by Hippocrates, would explain and interpret the commentaries of Galen. Among sacred literature, except for the evangelists, the letters of the apostles, and the books of Moses and the prophets' commentaries are almost totally inappropriate. I maintain that not even Chrysostum or Basil or Gregory, who is their equal, should be read in schools of theologians. But I would entrust them to be studied at home. I have the same opinion regarding all studies of philosophy.

The poets who are arduous and hard to understand should be examined after Vergil and Homer are well understood. Since there are many kinds of poets, one must begin with the more useful. Ovid is nearly always easy and therefore should be left in the library and read at home. Yet his poem, *The Roman Calendar* (*Fasti*) is both useful and difficult. The *Metamorphoses* ought to be read complete, but at school it does hinder the curriculum. More necessary is an explanation of the Greek comedians and tragedians—not all their tragedies or comedians, but all the writers of comedy and tragedy. For there are illustrious authors like Euripides, Sophocles, and Aeschylus. If there were not so much usefulness in him that he compares to the best, I would throw Aristophanes out of school because of the famous calumnies in *The*

Clouds, invented against Socrates, the best of all philosophers. The hymns of Pindar and the odes of Horace are being properly treated and read. I judge the same regarding Vergil's *Eclogues* and Theocritus' *Idyls*, but Vergil is more appropriate for the lower grade of a boys' school. Theocritus should be included for these children. I have skipped Hesiod who should be read with the first authors and follows Homer rather well. Aratus I leave to the mathematicians together with Dionysius. Lucretius is worthwhile for philosophers, but we nevertheless hand him over to the leisure time afforded poets. In him we find the archaic forms of words and when he deals with divine and natural subjects, the construction of his sentences is remarkable. He possesses many qualities indeed which become an orator. At one time grammarians used to interpret the poets, but poets recited only their poems. Our times demand that the same person be more grammarian and poet.

Reading the historians is easy. Our writers can be understood without an interpreter. Of the Greek historians, if Thucydides, Herodotus, and Xenophon are appreciated, the rest may be studied at home. From Thucydides, the majesty of sentences and the arrangement of a full range of words; from Herodotus, charm and a fluent kind of composition; from Xenophon, sweetness and purity of speech enrich the reader. Finally, Herodotus has many qualities which you may imitate; Thucydides has more, and Xenophon has some. These three, I think, should be added to Caesar and Sallust whom I have assigned to the lower grades. Livy also needs exegesis, but some part of him should be selected. I do not expect the other three to be read in their entirety without breaks. After the individual books the introduction of new material is very often permissible.

Of the philosophers we want those subjects to be read and explained which are necessary but are not explained by the teachers of the other fields such as dialectics, ethics, politics, and physics and which are not read by the mathematicians and medical doctors. Such might be Aristotle's books *On the Soul* (*De Anima*) and *On Listening to Natural Things*;[35] Plato's *Phaedo, A History of Living Creatures, The Physical Structure of the Human Body*, and *The Powers and Kinds of Herbs*, and Plato's *Timaeus*, and on books on similar topics which can be divided up with the medical doctors for exegesis. The mathematicians cannot ignore what is in Aristotle's works *On Heaven* (*De Caelo*) and *On Earth* (*De Mundo*) because these two are helpful to the philosopher who is unable to teach everything at once, although he must know and lecture on them all. The lawyers also need not investigate all the subjects about which Justinian has written. Some should be left to the conscientiousness of the students. Lectures must be undertaken in those necessary subjects which have method and system and introduce important tools. Just as a man cannot be ignorant of custom and law, so also he cannot be ignorant of what philosophers have taught concerning morals and the state. Therefore even after a student has completed something in his own field, he can add certain material from the philosophers at a time when, in his discipline in the letters, it is necessary for the completion of the five-year curriculum. The theologian also is not free from responsibility, for he too ought to know how the state should be administered piously and how everyone should behave toward his fellow citizens and his family. Therefore it is a part of his duty to teach this when there is need.

Aristotle, Plato, and Cicero

The consideration of what to choose from the subjects which are taught is easy. For all fields have authors in whom one cannot err. Theology has two most certain and enduring kinds of writings. Among the medical doctors, Hippocrates and Galen have produced the perfect art. Among the lawyers, there is nothing better than what Justinian took care to have published. To philosophers, Aristotle has been given. Besides the exegesis of so many and such great subjects in which he covered almost everything, not only did he perfect the art which is the foundation of every other art and which they apply to all argumentation, but also he expanded the system of rhetoric by the most beautiful disclosure. Among the philosophers, Plato, the most eloquent and most productive author, supplies every kind of example of dialectics, and I do not doubt that in perfecting their art the dialecticians were greatly aided by following in Plato's footsteps. Also the orator can note most of all what he may imitate in speaking. Among wise men, the highest praise for eloquence and among the eloquent the first place for wisdom is owed this philosopher. Socrates is so eloquent in his conversations that you may believe that you have missed what we may assign. He teaches in such a way that he appears to want to learn. He concedes a point in such a way that he wins and he wins in such a way that he does not appear to have wished to do so. Therefore, after the stage of boyhood education, Plato's dialogues ought to be interpreted. The choice among the dialogues cannot be made on the basis of his full style or his doctrines, but nevertheless certain needs and the method and choice can be suited to the levels of studies and to the grades of the school. The reputation which Plato achieved among Greek philosophers is that which Cicero has won among Latin orators, namely as the wisest orator, most eloquent philosopher, clearest light of all orators, and a unique example for all learned men.

The highest praise abides with these three and, as I see it, will abide forever. Since all that they have written ought to be known, nevertheless since no one or two persons can interpret it all, a division is necessary so that each teacher may think that his concern is with what can embellish his own field. Since all cannot be read, first a selection must be made of the necessary works, then of the best. The rest are to be consigned to private studies and to the libraries.

The Distribution of Public Lectures

Teachers ought to share the duties of teaching among themselves and to distribute the tasks. If they will do this and if in the lower grades firm foundations will have been laid, we shall easily bring the remaining structure to final completion. There are, moreover, nine kinds of lecturers and teachers: One explains sacred writings. This is the first and highest kind. The second interprets rights and laws. The third kind passes on the principles of preserving and recovering health. Among these three, human life is carried on. For whatever men engage in they do it either for the sake of their souls and minds which they want to devote to God, or for the protection and production of life, or in order to protect their own property honestly and to increase it and to pass it on by hand, as it were, to their descendants. In these last few ages of ours, the men who have pursued the teaching in these three fields have been called "doctors"—a new term in this particular meaning. Each field has its own "doctors," as rhetoric had Hermetes and Hermagoras, and grammar Aristarchus. But there are some to whom the profession of these three fields is either too hard to attain or not what they wish to practice. So they follow leisure as their preference.

The fourth kind of teacher is devoted to mathematics and consumes his time in that. There is also a fifth kind of teacher, a lover of antiquity, who desires to be consulted in the reading and writing of histories for the sake both of himself and human life.

Certain excellent talents are born to enjoy and possess great power because of the strength and force of their minds. Therefore they pursue the large genus teachers of language, i.e., the genus of the poets. Some are assistants to the philosophers, namely dialecticians; others to orators, namely, rhetoricians; and some to poets and historians, namely, grammarians. This kind of teacher we have today reduced to dust and fettered with the most burdensome tasks. Now this is the lowest kind among the erudite, but once it was important in the profession. We have discussed this previously and now must explain the remaining eight.

General Policy on the Arts and All Subjects and the Number of Lectures

In these eight kinds of teachers I want to include the philosopher and the orator, both of whom seem able to lecture and expatiate on all topics. The one promises the knowledge of the world and the other, speech and truth embellished with the objects of knowledge. Since we want these two subjects to be taught and dealt with in the schools of the arts and letters of which I have spoken, their number can be reduced. For no one who has attained a perfect knowledge of any one of these subjects is ignorant of the rest. All things which occur in nature and which have a rising and a setting, are permanently and eternally interrelated by a certain bond of association. Like nature, the disciplines which treat of such things are also bound by a constant necessity, so that whoever knows one subject perfectly may say also that he is not ignorant of the others. Let us therefore reduce these eight kinds of teachers and establish a school with a smaller number of teachers. The poet will be able also to interpret the historians and we have put him in charge of grammar for the younger boys. Thus seven will daily teach on a schedule which will obviate conflicts of time and authors. They will be able to follow a path of this sort and a system so that a student may arrive at excellent learning from all the arts and letters (as much as is sufficient).

Regarding jurisprudence, medicine, and theology, there is no doubt that a student is unfit for these disciplines if, in these five years, he cannot, by spending one hour per day in the school, learn enough to obtain the rest by himself. There is no doubt or uncertainty that, once these foundations which we want constructed in the lower school have been laid down, the poet or historian can bring it about that a youth who has gone beyond adolescence, may speedily be involved with all kinds of writers without an interpreter. A greater burden has been imposed on a dialectician. For since he is an assistant to the philosopher who almost alone treats all subjects, he ought to teach the complete method of making distinctions,[36] of analyzing and judging. He must also open the way to the knowledge of those subjects which have been handed down by the greatest men, that is, the wisest men, concerning moral and life and the natural order and have been grasped through the process of learning in this life, however short it is. In this he has the rhetorician as helper, the servant of orators who must not only teach and perfect the principles of perfect speech, but must also know all those things which sustain mental acuity in subtle speech and undertake training in language suitably and honestly. No one can explain the method of making distinctions[37] better than Aristotle. Very many books of rhetoric are extant, but not to know those three by Aristotle, and the three *On the Orator* (*De Oratore*), and those of Hermogenes' *On the Forms of Speaking*[38] is but flawed knowledge. The rest which has been taught about morals and is written about nature ought to be derived from Plato and Aristotle. But the theologian is the best instructor of morals and an excellent counselor in the state. I have briefly covered what I think concerning these seven kinds of teachers. The rest I have actually established more appropriately than can be taught.

Lectures to be Heard by the Theologian, the Lawyer, the Medical Doctor and Others

Whoever wishes to know those three arts which concern human life, theology, law, and medicine, must be involved in them in such a manner that they do not lack the other arts and letters which can support these three. Thus that interpreter of God, as it were, and preacher of heavenly things, the theologian, shall not be ignorant of the knowledge of distinctions and of speaking,[39] and should be acquainted with those who have preserved the memory of antiquity and the prescribed method of establishing families and property. A lawyer is indeed unworthy of that title if he is ignorant of the things philosophers have established regarding the state and morals. He should be removed from his post if he has not learned what his ancestors have done from whom he received the laws or if he has not read the histories of all ages. And inasmuch as the Christian state must express the image of divinity, as it were, what God has desired to be committed to the monuments of literature by the writers on sacred subjects must be understood. And since many a lawyer proceeds from school to be a counselor of kings and a governor of the state, his voice must also be cultivated in the principles of rhetoric. Because he must often render a judgment regarding law, he ought to know law as well as the subjects which are imparted by dialecticians.

The medical doctor also needs to know many things to perfect his art. For unless he knows what the philosophers have explained regarding the natural order, he cannot be numbered among the great. Therefore he must learn many things from philosophers and mathematicians if he desires to run through the correct curriculum of his profession. If in the study of medicine the knowledge of making distinctions is abandoned, those things which a perfect medical doctor requires will be lacking. The advice I have given is not immoderate. One can hardly believe how great and varied are the things the human mind can cover completely in five years, once that discipline appropriate for boys is completed. I admit that to listen for six hours at a time is difficult and full of tedium, but whoever objects to four hours, I am inclined to regard as unworthy of being called a student of wisdom. Therefore, whoever wishes to be a great theologian, medical doctor, or lawyer ought to hear a teacher four hours daily in this public school of letters as he did when he attended the boys' school. He should distribute these four periods of time in such a way that he can be free in the fifth, sixth, and even seventh periods.

As for the six instructors, they should plan their time so that the topics peculiar to a particular art and not generally instructive for other students shall be read at various times when it is more useful for one group to learn one subject and for another to learn another subject. A theologian, for example, need not listen to a medical doctor teaching the cure of the eye. When, however, he teaches anatomy and makes known and puts before their eyes the parts of the human body and the functions and forms of each individual part and separates into its components, the animal in which the mind exists, as it were, in the reverse order in which it was created, then the poet and the theologian can profit by their attendance. When, for example, a book by Galen *On the Pulse* is being considered, the work can be reduced for the theologian. Similarly, when an interpreter of the law explains individual chapters in Justinian, the theologian may even be absent. But when those four books are being interpreted by which legal consultants are trained, the theologian cannot be absent without arousing the suspicion of laziness. Of all the subjects in a school, there are certain ones which do not pertain to everybody and which ought to be scheduled so that they do not interfere with the continuity of studies.

What has been said about these three professions also pertains to students who do not spend their time for required training in any profession and do not allow themselves to be confined by fixed limits, but rather are satisfied with leisure alone and the delights of letters. Yet even these students must live in such a way that the accounting of their lives and studies finds approval among friends. For the freer their lives are and the less they permit themselves to be confined to the more restricted areas of arts and letters, the more they can understand.

The Twofold Partition of Teaching in Rhetoric

A twofold way and method must be maintained in the schools. There is one way by which the whole subject is taught in general terms without undertaking discussion with opponents. The other deals with particular subjects that have their own peculiar exceptions, investigations, and explanations. There is also another partition which is especially useful to follow in schools. Sometimes a subject is taught without reference to a particular author when a teacher can do it more briefly and clearly than those who have written on the same subject. This can be done in many cases. At times a book is produced in which there is again a two-fold method of teaching. For either all things are investigated in order one by one, or else some things are omitted and only those that are necessary are disclosed. This can be done in many instances with Aristotle or Galen and many other writers who for the sake of the views of their critics had to explain matters other than the subject itself required. Such general subjects ought to be taught daily, if not for four hours, so that everyone may learn them. There should indeed always be three staff members who teach these subjects which are specialized and imprisoned, as it were, in narrow dungeons, which hold the questions about these fields and their own permanent students. In this way we shall achieve what we want—namely, that we know and maintain a harmony of all arts and letters.

Private Studies

But schools bring too few benefits if separate studies at home are not arranged. Even though no subject can be understood perfectly without an interpreter and the teacher's voice has great power to arouse the student, nevertheless, the student who undertakes no practice at home and the one who does not allow himself to be trained by a teacher, are both at the same disadvantage. Each method has its own advantages and obstacles. For the student who is instructed in a group with many others gets, as it were, a benefit, which he could scarcely achieve at home with much work and learns material in a brief lecture more accurately and more perfectly than if he should struggle through his own inquiries. But there is in the same regard the following disadvantage: Keenness of mind is repeatedly disturbed in school and the attention is distracted by outside thoughts. Although this happens even when we sit in our own library, nevertheless what is accomplished, sought out, and found there is, as it were, our very own and we embrace it as if it were our child so that it sticks more firmly in our minds.

There are many varied benefits from both systems so that if the two are not joined together, we would make little progress in letters. But in a crowd and in a public meeting, a simple task is undertaken in which careful attention and a strong memory are needed. The more private place requires care for two items: one is that he review what has been taught in school so that he may know the individual facts and integrate what has been developed and analyzed into the common total of topics. Second is that he may on his own read things which lighten the task of the teacher and by the force of these he may often finish what his teacher indicates is only an introduction. The result is that full progress and a quick ascent to the citadel of learning is made. Often it happens that, we are not present when a subject is taught, because we are prevented by illness or summoned by necessary tasks. Sometimes it is even beneficial to omit the recitation of a comedy, a speech, or a history book at a time when we have leisure for better things. Our individual conscientiousness and our library may offset the disadvantages if we achieve the same subjects without a teacher or interpreter.

Always something ought to be investigated or heard or read or argued for the student who wishes to be great. Since satiety and tedium usually occur in this strenuous exercise, the mind must be refreshed by variety and relaxed by variations, so that easy material follows hard, joyous follows sad, and new follows old; and we proceed from reading to writing, from writing to entertainment, from entertainment to learned conversation and the learned gatherings of friends.

The Practice of Debating and Declaiming

We have now prescribed how the education of boys should be established and how those last five years are to be devoted to the completion of their studies. But up to this point we have not explained the pupils' exercises which are usually undertaken in schools. There are, then, two kinds of practices: one, debating and the other declaiming. It takes but a moderate amount of work for the practice of debating to be repeated twice a month. To provide excitement, four kinds of persons should be brought together. Of these, one will respond; one will assist; a third sits on the opponents' bench and the fourth moderates the general debate. These four kinds may be reduced to two so that one includes the debaters and the other the judges. The student who states the chief points of the investigation is the only one to be questioned by those who argue against him. But inasmuch as it often happens that our mind is not quick to reply, three others ought to be added who, as it were, come as reinforcements. But the role of responding should be given out by the person who is in charge of everyone, so that no confusion arises and so that they do not become a hindrance for the one who is like the king of the banquet and gives to each one the commands that are best. One must not make a judgment before the interrogation has come back to the first debater, for he should be allowed to be questioned twice. A free discussion is what best suits this assembly, without fear or dullness. But let reverence and eagerness attend! He who was made judge should know that he sustains the role of appraiser, not of detractor. Rustic shame and fear renders null even what we have thought about and written out; but eagerness and excitement often discover extemporaneously what did not occur to us at home. The subject that is proposed for debate should be such that it has sound opinion on opposite sides: not only what can happen in hypothetical cases, but also stated cases of logical necessity often stimulate opposing opinions by which they seem to be refuted. Conclusions and argumentations that are plain, brief and simple and interrogations of the individual objections are now more useful at the beginning than continuous lengthy speeches and a multitude of arguments to which they must come after they have acquired a greater facility for debating. But in the midst of these long proofs, whether the proofs are introduced in writing or whether they arise out of the controversy itself, a brief and polished epilogue should be made which results in an intelligent debate. Brevity is most appropriate to debate and suitable for understanding and avoiding the opponents' ambushes. For the piling up of propositions is suspicious and usually practiced by the sophists. Socrates wittily ridiculed Protagoras by praising him because when questioned he could respond both briefly and at length. But the same philosopher sharply criticized those orators who "when briefly questioned, stretched out the long course of their reply" (σμικρὰ ερωτηθέντες δόλιχον κατατείνουσι τοῦ λόγου, Plato, *Prot.* 329 a-b1). So much for the practice of debating.

The exercise of declaiming must be accommodated not only to fluency in words but also to the principles of philosophy, so that the oration is not only eloquent, but also wise. There are three ways to go about this: The speeches can be made on the spur of the moment, or after some time has been given for thought, or else they may be written out at home. The first two types require a ready and prompt memory. The last can also be recited from the written copy—a practice that I cannot disapprove, particularly if the youth delivers the speech he has written and also indicates the method he followed. For in this way more benefit comes to his audience and he who will speak will apply greater conscientiousness and care to the writing. I allow the reading of poetry and festive poems which are polished and clever, for it is a noble exercise and brings great benefit also to rhetoric. So much regarding the practice of declaiming and writing without which nothing outstanding can be accomplished in the field of letters.

But we must see to it that we are not loquacious in debate and pompous, empty, unwholesome, and careless in writing. In debate, subtlety and acumen; in writing, meaning, adornment, elegance, and conscientiousness are usually praised. One must write as much as possible and debate as often as possible. We do, however, evaluate conscientiousness not by great length, but by ornament and acumen. Whatever is polished, even if it is brief, is yet praised for the work it represents; but whatever is full of errors and crude, no matter how very lengthy it may be, deserves censure. In all, we should hold to a method of argumentation so that we select whatever captures subtlety, acumen, and ornament. But in this we must see to it that we are not ignorant of the proposed subject, for what we do not know cannot be a topic for either pleasing elegance or subtle genius. What we want to treat should be thoroughly understood by us and capable of admitting all that we are eager to devise.

The Unity, Good Conduct, and Conscientiousness of Professors

In these matters, as in all other studies, the conscientiousness of the teachers ought to sustain the attention of their pupils. And although conscientiousness must be regarded as the first attribute of teachers, nevertheless, unity and good conduct are especially becoming to preceptors. Violent offenses and unbridled arrogance arise mostly from avarice and ambition. The former is wicked and the latter ignoble. Both have always been unworthy of great talents. Often envy tends to disturb studies and nothing corrupts religion more than ambition. There is no room left for charity in the person who has these two faults. But as there is eternal agreement and a firm bond among the arts themselves and the teachings which are undertaken in school, so of necessity the teachers of these arts ought to be united so that their pursuits are similar in such a college, as it were, and their counsels the same, and their wills in agreement.

When men are contorted by envy and tossed by ambition, there is no loyalty in them, and nothing perfect, and nothing that can delight anyone's virtue. If ever there were times in which religion demanded outstanding models, given the great power and the number of our adversaries, our times demand them most. Offenses should not be tolerated in those places where a stricter discipline is being established which has the most beautiful advantages flowing down, as it were, upon all people. For just as the habits of nobles mostly imitate the will and life-style of the king, so the endeavors of pupils imitate the behavior of teachers—even the most inept behavior! So, corrupt teachers do not transmit learning to future generations, but allow the stem of vices to grow roots and, as much as they can, to propagate, forever.

There should, accordingly, be agreement about studies and work. Preferences should be shared and work divided up. We must take pains not only to maintain what we ought to teach but also to be cognizant, as much as possible, of what is taught by the rest of the teachers in the classes which precede and follow our own. For what boys have previously learned, they should retain in the upper grades, and present lessons should be accommodated to those that follow. Present lessons must be taught, the past one renewed, and the future lessons anticipated—all of which have the power to motivate, to preserve, and to improve. The work of a teacher is concerned with instructing, correcting, encouraging, and cautioning. All of these are corrupted by dissension. There exist certain necessary kinds of conflict, like boyhood and truth. Erroneous ideas must be removed from the populace and teaching must be defended from ignorance and virtue from vice. But strong emotions of the spirit should be absent from every search for truth. So, philosophers justly praised Socrates whose most charming conversation with the sophists is so set up that the pursuit of truth seems to have been undertaken; that supreme politeness and humanity are manifested when he teaches, when he corrects, when he disagrees and when he laughs; that without contumely, wrath, or scurrility, he appears to have avoided vices and not to have hated the people.

Among the boys and even younger adolescents, honest competition is encouraged, for by this their industriousness is nourished and they can be bridled and guided by their preceptors when they are overheated. They are not to be rebuked if they consider it disgraceful to be defeated and glorious to excel in learning. For it is shameful never to be aroused and always to be condemned for sloth and inertia. Strong passions should not persist in youth after adolescence; yet, on the other hand, the sincerest friendships bloom from such competition. Courtroom opponents and the most prominent advocates contend harshly and shout when pleading a case. Yet when the case has been concluded and judgment rendered, they are reconciled. Just so, among more mature men, the greatest charity and benevolence exist after these boyish disagreements which were restrained by the teachers of letters. But the concerns of teachers ought to be put to use more than their controversies even if some competition will have to exist—a fact which I admit. Let their concerns be for courtesy, humanity, charity and to eschew asperity, cruelty, and hatred! Let there be an association in the school of letters like the one the poets on Helicon and Parnassus of the Muses formed with complete harmony of voices, numbers, and instruments, and of life, pursuits, and will.

I have briefly run through the advice which can be given about the education of boys and the openings of schools of letters in the present time. And while I have not opened up a road that is certain, I have at least pointed out the journey. If we enter upon it, we shall more easily attain the things that are most important.

The End

5
On the Lost Art of Speaking
(1538)

Introduction

The *Amissa* is one of the earliest works of Sturm. It was written during the first year of his residence in Strasbourg, before he began his duties as rector of the gymnasium. It is one of the few writings of Sturm not written with the concrete needs of the gymnasium in mind. It has a more theoretical character and [along with the two preceding treatises] may be considered programmatic for the later development. It offers an understanding both of Sturm's method and the principles and goals which lay at the basis of his pedagogical reforms.

The *De Amissa dicendi ratione* [*On the Lost Art of Speaking*] begins with a complaint. Nothing in his times, Sturm asserts, reminds him in the least of the flowering and creative power of ancient Rome and Athens. The great achievements of mankind were not only praised by some, but neglected, yes, even despised by others. Everywhere one sees the decline of morals, the barbaric use of language, the corruption of the nature of man and naturally, as a result, the perversion of religion. How can one improve this situation in order better to appreciate the achievements of the classical tradition? For Sturm there was only one way: the restoration of rational speech, along the lines that Cicero recommended for the education of a good orator.

The reader of this work on rhetoric by Sturm will easily spot the Ciceronian argument and themes and with patience can read the oration by Cicero which serves as his *exemplum*. A word of explanation, however, as to the roots and differentiation of the dialectical and the rhetorical traditions may be of help at least to a few. The great Aristotle differentiated pure logic and rhetoric in his *Logic* and *Posterior Analytic* on dialectic or logical argument and in his *Topics* on rhetoric. Dialectic can make its points by syllogistic argument—major premise, minor premise, and conclusion—but it does not always carry conviction. The topics are arranged by subject matter which includes the emotional overload, such as patriotism, fatherland, motherhood, and when skillfully employed by the orator convinces the hearer both by logic and emotion and moves them to action. This is a common theme among the

German humanists such as Ulrich von Hutten, who asserted that what does not move one to action is like philosophizing in the shadows. The contrast of dialectic and rhetoric is continued into the thought of Seneca, *Institutiones*, and Cicero, *De Oratore*, and other works (the *Topics* become the *Loci* or commonplaces in the Latin translation). In this treatise by Sturm one sees again the all-pervasive influence of Cicero on the northern Renaissance. It is reflected in Sturm's differentiation of *ratio* and *dicendi ratio*. Following this theme will intrigue the intellectual reader; Sturm himself served as professor of rhetoric his entire career as well as being an administrator.

Sturm uses as his example of outstanding oratory *Ciceronis Pro P. Quintio Oratio I*. It is not feasible to reproduce the oration here, but it is readily available in John Henry Freese, *Cicero: The Speeches with an English Translation, Pro Publio Quinto*, The Loeb Classical Library (Cambridge: Harvard University Press, 1961), pp. 1–109. The best and most detailed discussion of the *De Amissa dicendi ratione* is that of Marietta D. Nikolaou, *Sprache als Welterschliessung und Sprache als Norm: Ueberlegungen zu R. Agricola und J. Sturm* (Neuried: Hieronymus Verlag, 1984), pp. 73–142, plus many notes. It is the basic source of the information offered in this introduction. Nikolaou demonstrates a strong dependence of Sturm on Rudolf Agricola and spells out the nature of his critique of scholastic dialectic. Anton Schindling, *Humanistische Hochschule*, pp. 210–235, discusses Sturm's lectures on rhetoric and oratory; on pp. 236–252 Schindling discusses Sturm's lectures on Aristotelian philosophy, dialectic, ethics and physics. Of Sturm's many writings on rhetoric his most comprehensive was his *De imitatione oratoria libri tres* (Strasbourg, 1574), now made available in microfiche by the Bodleian Library, Oxford, *Renaissance Rhetoric, Key Texts, A.D. 1479–1602*, edited by James J. Murphy, University of California, Davis. An interesting aside is that Sturm's *De Amissa* was on the proscribed list, number 255, on the Spanish *Index Librorum Prohibitorum*, no doubt because of the offense it gave for its less than full appreciation of scholastic dialectic. The present translation is based upon the 1542 edition published by Sebastian Gryphius in Lyons.

On the Lost Art of Speaking

Book One
To Franciscus Frossius, Jurisconsult

It is the nature of good things, Franciscus Frossius, that they excite those who are endowed with a better mind to love them, but they are inimical to truly vicious and perverse spirits, or certainly do not seem to delight them greatly. But it is remarkable that although the power of good and evil things is contrary, since studious men differ greatly from those men who are not good, there is nevertheless much agreement among humans concerning errors. For in many instances not only are those of less dignity so employed as to oppose those who are better, but are promoted in a way that leaves no room for praising glorious things. For states and noblemen established greater rewards for military science than for political science, if this comparison may be permitted—and this is most serious—luxury, ambition and impudence are by practice and custom so accepted that the concern for frugality, integrity, and shame is of little concern. This is caused by the depraved judgment of an evil nature as well as by the weakness of good minds. For in difficult and glorious matters a method and a plan are necessary; and because all glorious results involve hardships, where such a method and plan are absent, so too are the anticipated results. So it happens that studies of the most beautiful things lie prostrate and those customarily approved by vicious natures are unanimously preferred to instruction in the praiseworthy arts. How difficult and arduous the inventive faculty of excellence is can indeed be seen from the fact that after it has been perfected and published its utility is soon corrupted. A perfectly pure religion was given to our forefathers by the Word of God, but not many years later it was so deformed and then so ruined and corrupted by licentiousness and the indulgences of vices and greed, that the place believed to be a haven and abode for Christian doctrine emerged as a seat of evil practices and as a refuge for crimes and vices. It is the nature of all good things most especially of religion that as they are easily vitiated by the cupidity and ignorance of men, so, too, the art of speaking. For when eloquence flourished, especially in Rome, in a few years it was so deformed and corrupted there that it was not restored to its ancient elegance from that time to our very own. It seemed to be deprived of its natural beauty forever among men unless some would arise who, endowed with the greatest genius, would show us the structure and method in learning that would be most like the art of the ancient Romans and Greeks. For we have lost this art almost universally. If therefore God will not send men who will discover and teach this lost art, no hope will remain that eloquence will be restored and renewed for us. And so if the greatest talents were not able to preserve it at a time when it was most wonderfully cultivated, it will be very arduous in our times to recover this lost art and to restore it as it were to its people. Therefore, Frossius, we must at this point examine the reasons that the states now lack it and that after the former age had men excelling in both learning and diligence—ours also abounds in good talents—nevertheless almost nothing complete and perfect is being learned about oratory. For though there are, as you know, throughout Germany a great many who in their everyday conversation have both a pure and graceful speaking ability, none have become more polished than the contemporaries of Ennius or Thucydides, who it is well known, engaged in elegant and dignified speech acquired by experience and natural ability rather than by a thoroughly polished art. Moreover, those who in all of Italy are best equipped to imitate the greatest and most distinguished orator prefer, it seems to me, to obtain the praise due eloquence by writing, not by speaking. But our own immediate predecessors who had a good opinion of themselves did not hesitate to imitate the best. Why then should not we, too, be able to arrive at the same goal which the ancients reached? I think we shall see how to do so if we consider the things which were confronted by the greatest men and pleased them. When Crassus, according to Cicero, deftly and accurately notes the things that an orator needs, he also cites the reason and signifies the method by which we shall obtain what we are after. Nor is it uncertain that Cicero in the speech Crassus delivered expressed his own opinion at the time of writing. For not only do individuals express their own opinions in that disputation, but also represent their age and cultural milieu. So which are the elements that Crassus and Cicero deemed important for the study of rhetoric? I shall speak, Frossius, but not as one of those with such superior talent as are heaven-sent to restore lost eloquence, but rather as one who is an eager student of this subject and does not wish what he has noted and observed and what pertains to the public benefit to remain unknown to his friends and contemporaries. I want to help our people, not gain praise for myself. But since the things that Crassus set before us are most relevant to the subject, they ought to be made known. These are: 1) the nature of the mind and its capacity for learning 2) the education and teaching of youth 3) keener observation 4) the knowledge of letters 5) the habit of daily conversation 6) the reading of good authors 7) experience 8) memory and 9) continual study. For all, however many elements there may appear to be, Crassus recalls, are subsumable under these nine headings. Thus as the poets set Apollo and Minerva above the nine Muses, so we place the orator and wise men above these nine elements, neither separating knowledge from eloquence nor on the other hand suffering discord between the heart and the tongue. Therefore to reconcile the close relationship between speech and knowledge those nine must be properly observed in accord with the precepts of Crassus and Cicero, whose opinion of them must be upheld. Which of these nine elements characteristic of their age do we lack? We see that for some years industrious and acute minds, linguists and instructors of the young, abound in all commonwealths. Rhetoricians are endowed with greater gifts than formerly. The other arts do not lack instructors. There is a very large number of orators, poets, and all kinds of writers. We see such great activity especially in Gaul, that even to those who teach it seems tremendous that the use of Latin conversation has become customary, talent restored, and the beginning of a more humane and liberal life endures right up until the hour of death. Now since we have all of those nine elements in common with those who excel us, what is the reason, Frossius, of such great unhappiness? Surely it is because we do not honor the matter sufficiently. And because we lack method and order, because we have no concern for youth, the perfection for which we look cannot but be violated. For ninety years and more there have been unpromising works for learners and the greatest abandoning of the youth. For since those who taught either pursued a faulty or a not yet erudite standard, youth lacked learned and elegant information; and those to whom God gave an outstanding genius could but note what was best when it was too late. Because while they pursued it, they did indeed acquire a great name, but from great learning, not from the art of speaking which the ancients, both Romans and Greeks, possessed. Besides, those who were able to attain that much, since the rewards offered to teachers of letters were poor, and there was a greater occasion for contempt than for praise, applied their abilities to writing, and helped youth too little by teaching. We grow old before we attain the facility of words and the art of speaking and writing, if indeed anyone did ever achieve this in the course of a lifetime. Socrates vehemently censures Gorgias Leontinus, Protagoras Abderites and the other Sophists because they were ignorant of facts in a great profession. What if Socrates were living today? He could find nobody in letters and in that philosophy now whom he could compare with those. For those men were great not because of the novelty of their profession, but so knowledgeable were they of facts that they were the admiration of the states, and to Gorgias alone not an ungilded but a golden statue was for that very reason erected by the Greeks. Thus the best constituted states established rewards not only for the military and forensic occupations, but also had a very high regard for their children, and did not encourage the teachers of letters and oratory only with emoluments but with real honors as well. States must not merely provide for genius, but as they cannot exist without the posterity of children, they must also retain teachers of letters, and maintain them in such a manner that, content with their situation in life, they do not gravitate to another profession where there are more benefits. But I do not say these things because I believe they pertain to me. For I do not include myself among the most able, and I have been treated liberally; but I want men to consider that without adequate reward, talents are rarely inspired to do things great and necessary for the commonwealth. If the task I assumed in life, carried on for many years, did not appeal to me as delightful, if I had no respect for God's choice of abode for me living among humanity for whose concerns He sent me, I would perhaps long ago have exchanged my office as a teacher for a remunerative and, according to a specious morality, a more productive occupation. But I must spend my life in letters and be content with the appointment to which my nature and God have devoted me. I must also bring benefits to our people as great as I am able to produce with diligence and zeal. It is stupid to promise it. Only a mad man believes that he has achieved it. But because that is the nature of the profession, the powers of one are inadequate and the labor of many is needed. The practice itself requires the greatest leisure, singular diligence, keen judgment, an appropriate talent, and a nature suited to it. I fear that if I try to make an original contribution, I may seem to arrogate more to myself than I can redeem either by talent or training. For although the much desired leisure has been given me in abundance and I can promise work and diligence, and although nature led me to the study of letters, I acknowledge fully and must confess that my talent is small—very small—and my judgment so tenuous that I ought not to make pronouncements on things without shame. But I am of the opinion that even the unskilled can appraise whatever is done well by those who excel in an art, and that without arrogance. For though there is a great difference in the performance of the learned from that of the unlearned, the requirements for judging are less disparate. There is this consideration: those who are high minded and who are eager for the public welfare, when they have something to contribute with respect to complex matters, whatever they may be, must publish it, if it is to be of use, and they must then be credited with having wanted to help meet the needs of the people as fully as possible. Therefore I have decided to express such a desire in an easy and humble way, and on the basis of an oration that Cicero delivered on behalf of Quintius briefly explain whatever pertains to understanding, observing and imitating it. For in this way we may learn how eloquence was lost and how the ancient custom and practice of speaking must be sought again. The form of great things, moreover, which are not themselves more easily observed, can more easily be comprehended when we have been able beforehand to determine that which fostered and perfected them.

* * * * *

The Text of M.T. Cicero's
Oration in Defence of Publius Quintius

* * * * *

We have proposed, Frossius, that the faculty of speaking consists of nine elements. They were these: the power and industry of the mind, learning from childhood, the precepts of rhetoric, knowledge of philosophy, the speech of daily conversation, reading of authors, experience, memory, continuation of studies. When I have demonstrated that we have violated nearly all of them, I shall without doubt have shown why eloquence has been lost and why our people are so unlike in speech to the perfect writers of old. At the end of my demonstration I shall also have indicated how the lost art of speaking must be restored. To speak briefly, the minds of our people have been corrupted and the philosophy of living vitiated. For though many are gifted with ready understanding during adolescence, how few remain who are not softened by self indulgence, or if able to avoid that, remain in letters and do not turn to profitable arts before they have acquired even an elementary education? I pass over those grander studies that must be learned after the elementary phase before one is led to the medics or to you lawyers. Thus the goodness of nature that must be instructed and confirmed by the precepts of philosophy is habitually abandoned either by such hastening on or by the corruption of morals. Nothing is so inimical to study as self-indulgence and softness of the spirit, even though the former furnishes too weak a defense for our morals and the latter is believed to be the very reward of virtue and is for the most part desired. But not only on these accounts are we worse, not only does a nature deformed by desires or impeded by some great affection not let us equal our forebears, not only have vices and haste led us away from the good, but also inasmuch as Latin is not so highly regarded in the city-states as formerly, and is used only by a few and that faultily, that approach is not so feasible for elementary instruction as it once was. And if it were, we have still lost it: it is now more rude and less pleasing. This being the case, speech has also been changed and conversation once pure and Roman, ornate and learned, is now impure and foreign, rude and unlearned. Roman and Greek youth once came to school and to the grammarians there better prepared than ours for learning the fundamentals and for understanding the poets and historians. First then there is in the essential business of education a dissimilarity and inconvenience, and then there is also this change in our manner of communication. Our educational efforts were thus variable, ill-defined, and tediously drawn out. For the ancient Romans the business was certain, precise, and brief. We cripple our talents with diversity, prolixity, subtlety. While the ancient method of the grammarians fails us, we are deprived of the opportunity for learned Latin conversation (though not our crude daily kind that increases daily)—but about this I will speak more fully later. These precepts of speaking and teaching are indeed difficult. For though I admit there are plenty of books on rhetoric and teachers of speaking have everything necessary for their profession, still nature resists teaching him to speak who does not know how to talk. But how few there are now or in the previous generation who had an adequate knowledge of pure Latin. And so we learn the rudiments either at a late hour or before an abundant vocabulary has been acquired; before the proper stage in learning has been arrived at the exercise is useless, and later on the purpose of the oration and its development may no longer be appropriate for our needs. For since the use of eloquence is great in all the arts, especially in theology and political science, as long as we do not possess, properly practice or cultivate rhetoric, so long too shall we not see our people produce anything that is polished in speech, elaborated by industry, or ornamented by abundance and variety. For it is unsuitable in art that artistic productions not be derived from the principles of dialectics which before our own age were despoiled and are now further obscured by poor teaching or even ignored utterly, further reducing the production of worthy things. But those ancients whom we admire and would emulate, who alone can be called orators, used both rhetoric and dialectical principles in their speaking, which was so effective that they appeared to have been born knowing those things rather than merely to have acquired them by discipline. For although studies were so divided in Greece as a result of the contentions between Socrates's followers with the Sophists, yet the philosophers incorporated many of their opponents' ideas concerning rhetoric into their own books on that subject, while those opponents, the Sophists, who were teachers of the art of oratory and were engaged in that profession exclusively, taught not a few things that they had learned from the philosophers' schools. It is therefore probable that Demosthenes was not ignorant of the things Plato taught about the art of discussion and understood them more truly than those who, after the art of speaking had been debased, gave themselves up slavishly to the Academy and the Peripatetics. There is no doubt about Cicero who reconciled eloquence with the study of wisdom. I could wish his example were followed in our own age, and that those who have made their reputation from their knowledge of letters would explain in their schools more fully those things that Aristotle taught. For although he undoubtedly wrote far more than has been handed down to us, we must content ourselves with what remains and heed his precepts. I agree that not everything that is in the logic books is complete and clear. Many unsuitable matters are interposed. However, these are so compressed and so arranged that the method we require is not obscured. It is regrettable that more effort has not been directed to this subject. Such is the nature of humans that while we avoid the base practices of former ages and do not want to appear as barbarians, yet we are negligent about some matters which it behooves us to know. We now come to the knowledge of nature of the mind and its capacity to know things; the power of memory; and the continuous nature of study, for these three are left of the nine. One must not complain that the arts are divided among themselves, and that the studies are distinct, and the medics separated from the lawyers, and that one art cannot teach the other. For we do not hold the language of Greeks inferior to Latin. And that opinion of Socrates recorded by Plato is true: "and if so, we must infer that all things are produced more plentifully and easily and are of better quality where one man does one thing which is natural for him, and does it at the right time, and leaves the rest." If Socrates wants this to be so in small, material things and separates farmers from architects, weavers from armorers, then we must observe this even more in the science of medicine and in jurisprudence. But it is a reprehensible custom that lawyers do not use eloquence and that those who would like the power of oratory do not know political science and the other arts and disciplines but that both orators and lawyers, content with their own profession, despise the others' support. For it is one thing to learn what is necessary for the purpose we have undertaken "according to nature," Socrates says, "and at the right time," another to publish the purpose undertaken and turn it to an advantage and make use of the lesson for life. Specific knowledge makes the faculty of speaking not only richer but also more illustrious. Mere facts have no light unless clear speech is added. Today the art of speaking is confused because it lacks order and method which modern authors do not have, though some of these men have nevertheless attempted to explain the arts without knowing Latin. They produce a great deal of mischief thereby. For I have no doubt, Frossius, that you pursued one course in civil prudence and are now keeping another in mind because of your extensive practice in forensic matters. Justinian's compilers were not guilty of that which subsequent lawyers and interpreters have done to contaminate and obscure their work. We cannot therefore rightly know what pertains to oratory, namely, the true scope and variety of knowledge. The defilement has robbed us of both wisdom and the memory of it. Eloquence, fixed principally by the dialecticians, sustains memory; but rude, barbarous communication destroys it. Nature's goodness and memory's record of it may suffer irreparable damage from want of proper ordering. We need a method that is at once artistic and free. Method does remain and admittedly in uninterrupted fashion amongst the special arts; but those persevering in the liberal arts are few indeed who retain that method whereby precise knowledge is joined by the power of eloquent speech. There are many astrologers, geometricians, painters and poets who, delighted with their own art, reject the teaching of other things. The medics, too, occupied in money making, having already learned their own profession, after amassing their own rewards, live so leisurely and well that they despise the study of wisdom as too laborious. The lawyers in practicing their profession and in their civic activities too, having often received their customary honors, believe that they have done their part, for profit making and preserving is their chief interest, not wisdom. Few theologians feel that eloquence is their concern. And there are those who embrace it, still such great barbarians and corrupt handling of a subject, they are not able to converse so that the fullness of expression of the oration corresponds to the dignity of the subject, for the purity of the Latin sermon should not be defiled by the strangeness of the words. For all stay with the subject itself, but many truly forego the study of eloquence. Many feel happy when all they have really done is acquire a certain volubility. But just as the splendor and ornament of oratory is necessary for all masters in the liberal arts, so is it especially for theologians. In all subjects whatsoever very few persevere so that eloquence merges with knowledge, but this is needful in order to produce what is perfect, what is desired. I speak of oratorical excellence. I wish those writers who have combined writing on useful subjects with elegance of speech might receive their due praise. But I fail to see what many see besides a speedy tongue and a diffuse audacity. Finally, I regard him as eloquent who combines the exercise of speech with the learning of philosophers; who has been

aptly and fittingly prepared in both things; who can thus furnish the substance and illustrate it. I do not see that anyone has achieved this, nor
do I believe that there is any educated man who does not admit that
freely; and yet there is a way for men to succeed. We must do what formerly the Romans, Athenians, and Asians did to gain mastery. And
though we are indeed too late, still it will prove useful for the young
and their posterity to have the way pointed out. Since those nine elements [basics] I have described have been disordered and disdained, it
is not remarkable that elegance of speech has been lost. For as the most
beautiful of choral symphonies is born of the nine different modes of
the Muses, so out of those nine elements must be produced an erudite,
accomplished mode of speech. And as all the sweetness of modulation
perishes, if some of these virgins produce the modes disagreeably and
discordantly, so unless amends are made, or their lack supplied, no well
ornamented speech meets the orator's needs. But to achieve all this we
need four kinds of people: active magistrates, parents, teachers and children. For if states do not establish rewards, teachers will be deterred,
but parents, who have the chief care of children's skills, will also fail.
Schools of letters are too destitute in Germany. This is so because fund-
ing has been taken away, not because religion has been reformed. For
as long as schools and hateful unlearned sects had reputation and
authority, as long as their misuse of church money was not considered
dishonest, there was an abundance of genius. Now after prolonged
tyrannical impiety has been exposed and people object to the criminal
misapplication of private and ecclesiastical wealth, people conclude that
their children had best live for their own advantage rather than for the
public good. Accordingly, they steer them toward the plebeian arts. I
believe good men do not approve of this subversion of religion, and that
it grieves their conscience. Others do not trouble their conscience over-
much and excuse themselves along with the great mass of people.
Though it would be well to eliminate some clerical offices, one runs the
risk of inciting public unrest. Few in our midst approve of parricide; the
very word is abhorred. Yet the ancient Romans, while still ignorant of
true, Christian piety, decreed that whoever stole or made off with sacred
objects was a parricide. They are still parricides who convert what is
sacred to specious use. Why do I say this? So that all may understand
that if sacred riches are to be preserved for their original purpose, and
entrusted to none except those of moral integrity, youth must necessarily benefit and that by re-attaching itself to the study of letters. Now
much largess once devoted to such purposes of piety has been re-
deployed. There is no room left for truth. For nothing is so inimical to
it as the criminal resort to force and nothing so agreeable as probity and

innocence. God-given potential can scarcely be stimulated to produce in view of the fact that good men are now so few. Many men potentially fit for noble endeavor are turned away out of consideration for adequate rewards. The real advantages of life are frequently misjudged, and often we embrace too late the riches of the spirit. Yet before youth can exercise wise choice, rewards must be offered them, only these must be consistent with integrity and innocence, and lead to a profession that is designed to increase the glory of Christ and not just appear to do so. If we could restore ancient learning, we would not lack for men well equipped in the civil and ecclesiastical arts. We did not, however, intend to give advice at this point, but to recall the reasons why eloquence declined, and why those few magistrates who are sensitive to these matters face an uphill struggle. Since the majority of magistrates are not eager for this struggle, and good men cannot generally prevail on their own, parents, children and teachers remain unmotivated. Parents ought to be inspired by the advantages which education can hold, and adolescents motivated by their desire for recognition. Mere worldly ambition responds to proper education and to moral discipline. In addition, there are other things which cause study to be neglected, but I prefer to pass over these now. There remains the discussion of the recovery of lost eloquence. And this is the most important problem, though the causes for the loss (of eloquence) must be removed before restoration can succeed, and that is why I wanted a title that would indicate the causes of the loss as well as the recovery from it. For this title is rather arrogant in its promise; the other is more modest. I must begin, Frossius, by saying that I believe there is a way to restore the true art of speaking to the people. We understand the causes why speech was corrupted. It is easy to see when comparing the speech *Quintiana* with our modern efforts that we have produced nothing similar to that of the ancients. Thus, we shall repeat those nine elements with which we began and hopefully we shall make progress. For it is vain to attempt that which has not been carefully considered beforehand. This is not original with me but is borne out by other authors. As I shall speak first of nature, I shall not devise any rules regarding it. For to each, heaven gives his nature. The best we can do is attempt to preserve and train it through sound discipline. The first thing to do is to protect the mind from the corruption of desire and vice. Good teaching and the imparting of wisdom do not sort well with self-indulgence and depravity. If the last are avoided, and the first promoted, excellent talent can be cultivated. The goodness of nature must be stirred up by the zeal and ardor of love in order to progress toward those ends for which good natures were born. All this must be done naturally so that the desire added is for diligence. For though nature cannot be given by friends, but is conferred together with life, youth is nevertheless encouraged by those whom it considers dear. This task pertains not only to parents, teachers and others involved either by necessity or connection, but indeed to those who care for the state as well. Children and adolescents are appealed to primarily by benevolence, praise, authority and emulation rather than by contemplation of still far off advantages. And if indeed duty is begotten by love, diligence by commendation, approbation by esteem, richness by the examples of good men, many will distinguish themselves. May this therefore serve as a second major consideration—that every effort be made to create in adolescents the burning desire to excel in letters and the opportunity thus to earn rewards and praise. But we must now come to the education of children, so that we educate properly those who have apt and suitable talent. We must remember not to overload this endeavor with a multitude of rules and precepts. It is very useful to practice forming nouns and verbs from another language and to refrain at first from excessive grammatical and philosophical disquisitions. Yet adequate explanation of the rules ought at once be joined to the instruction and always kept in view. There are three requirements: exposition of the content; observation of the method; and interpretation of vocables. First care must be taken that the matter itself should be generally known in a few words. Then the rules and the purposes to which all activity tends should be demonstrated. The contents of orations are readily gathered from narration. Yet these are often prolix and must be abridged, as when P. Quintius is brought to trial for a decision involving fame and fortune. The adversary is Sextus Nevius. He says that the day of their court appearance had been put off by Quintius. His goods had been possessed by an edict of Praetor Duvienus thirty days previously, and thus he was asking Dolabella that Quintius should give sufficient bail to remove the judgment or should give security. Quintius would rather give security and took C.A. Aquilius as judge and made a judicial wager. The opposing speaker is Q. Hortensius. M. Cicero, the patron of Quintius, denies that the goods have been possessed by the Praetor, Quintius neither owing anything nor having put off their court appearance. Then, because he could prove by the very wording of the edict that he could not gain such possession, since he was neither "One who has kept out of the way, etc.," nor "He who has left his country to go into exile." Finally, he had not possessed, because only a part of the goods was in question, whereas the edict applied to all of the goods held and possessed. Such an explanation is brief but suitable for understanding the situation. I think this method pleased Cicero, who embraced the argument of the internally conflicting orations of

Aeschines and Demosthenes with but a few comments. I should say something of the method, if it were not such a prolix subject that is more properly left to the schools and teachers to explain. I have like thoughts concerning the interpretation of words, but this pertains more to the grammarians. You can consult your books and histories. But you have explained many words to grammarians. In addition, you must know how many praetors the Romans had and what distinguished urban from provincial ones. For it was one kind that Sulla established for public cases, another of those four more ancient than these, and still another kind added by Caesar. These distinctions enlighten your understanding, which you derived from your studies. It is most useful to know that both grammarians and rhetoricians find it the right of the speaker and the Praetor, too, to grant the possession of goods and to transmit them into possession. Nor will the rhetorician grasp the power of that sentence more than a lawyer: Who then will describe for us those laws as equitable? Who establishes this? What would be fair to Quintius that would be fair to Nevius? This should be clarified by your oration: that what he believed to be equitable for another person, he should be willing to regard valid for himself. Indeed, what it means to give bail, what a mutual agreement of parties is, what bail is, what can be bound over by bail has been defined by you [lawyers]: but the grammarians have also explained it. You lawyers, however, are the authorities. It is useful to observe that often in the same book the method is not apparent in certain places, but indicated in others; in one place the opinions are obscure, but in another everything is explained. Therefore it is useful in every reading and interpretation to skim the whole book, quickly noting which things are familiar before stopping at once at the unfamiliar. At the beginning of an oration the speaker's attitude towards the subject is not clear, but later it becomes so. But whoever is dispossessed of everything needful to him by a public bailiff is at once cast off by the living and relegated in shame to a position lower than the dead. Although an honorable death often exonerates a disgraceful life, a life so disgraceful does not leave room even for an honorable death. Therefore, by Hercules, the man whose goods are possessed by edict loses his fame and honor at the same time as he loses his goods. Thus the judgment regarding the possession of goods is one of disgrace, not a pecuniary matter as is jumped bail or unpaid debts. It would take a long time to explain. Therefore we shall let it pass and come to those things that are now less in use.

6

Liberally Educated
Nobility,
for the Werter Brothers
(1549)

Introduction

This treatise is basically a reaffirmation of the educational principles
espoused in the preceding works. There is no historical evidence that
the treatise helped to elevate the Werter brothers Philip and Anthony to
great heights of noble achievement, though it was well intended. This
is a good point at which to explain that the gymnasium was dedicated
to the education of the upper class, nobility and patriarchal urban bour-
geoisie.

As to nobles, Sturm had a special relation to upper class families as
is evident from the matriculation records, Sturm's correspondence, and
his constant need for money. The *Nobiles* were well defined even in late
medieval times, but the class was changing with the cross fertilization
of noble status and bourgeois material substance, a development
addressed by historian Jack Hexter regarding the English gentry in this
century.

This is one treatise on education by Johann Sturm that was done
into quaint Tudor English and here improved in scholarly accuracy and
completeness, for good scholars do not skip. However, T.B.'s version is
so charming that we offer the title and a sample of the style:

A ritch Storehouse or Treasurie for Nobilitye and
Gentlemen, which in Latine is called *Nobilitas literata*,
written by a famous and excellent man, John Sturmius and
translated into English by T.B. Gent.
seene and allowed according to the order appointed.
Imprinted at London by Henrie Denham, dwelling in pater
noster row at the signe of the starre. Anno Domini. 1570.

This edition was dedicated "To the Right Honorable, vertuous, and my singular good Lord, Lord Philip Howard, Erle of Surrey, all felicitie and happynesse."

The preface to the friendly reader is equally splendid and especially meaningful to us as retranslators of this ancient classic. Here it is in part as published more than four centuries ago:

> Learned and most friendlye Reader: if Bookes gaine credite or discredite by their translators, I may iustly feare that this worthy worke by my euill handling shall be disgraced and be but of small account with thee. But syth that works be not accounted good, neyther are they contemned as bad for their translators or reporters, but be praised for their excellencie and goodnesse, or condemned for their base-nesse and nakednesse. I mooue not thee to lyke thys trea-tise, bicause I interpreted it, but I beseeche thee to allowe it for the goodnesse and excellent matter, plentifully flow-ing therein. But our time (alas) is so inclined, and as it were naturally bent to bestow upon barren and unhonest fruites, precious and golden names....

This treatise makes good reading when one has the historical back-ground in mind and remembers the impact Sturm's examples and writ-ings had upon sixteenth-century education and during the centuries that followed.

For bibliographical information on the *Ad Werteros fratres, Nobilitas literata. Argentorati, per Wendelinum Ribelium*, 1549, see Jean Rott, "Bibliographie des Oeuvres Imprimées de Jean Sturm (1507–1589)," in Jean Rott, *Investigationes Historicae. Églises et Société aux XVIe Siècle. Gesammelte Aufsätze zur Kirchen- und Sozialgeschichte* (Strasbourg: Librarie Oberlin, 1986), p. 348. In the same volume see also the chapter on "Jacques Sturm, Scolarque de la Haute-École (Gymnase) de la Ville de Strasbourg, 1526–1553," pp. 461–469. See also his chapter, "Le rect-eur strasbourgeois Jean Sturm et les Protestants français," *Investigationes Historicae*, vol. II, pp. 43–61.

Liberally Educated Nobility, for the Werter Brothers (1549)

For a long time, Philip, you have entreated me, and now also your brother Anthony along with you has asked me, to show you a course and a plan of studies that I regard customary for educated men, and suited to your age, family, and rank of nobility. I would gladly gratify your wish in this matter if I could include both in this small volume. For one part requires a long and varied explication in order to show what I believe the practice of learned men has been, particularly of the Greeks and the Latins. But in the other, I shall try to assist your praiseworthy and vigorous course of studies. From the one, I shall select for this treatise only as much as the matter itself and the plan seem to require. The other I shall discuss more fully at some future time when we have the leisure and when your studies demand it.

On this occasion, a decision must be made about you and your brother between whom there is little difference in age and also a great similarity in talent. Both of you have the same wish, equal capacity to learn and identical ambition which was challenged by your own will and by your love of letters, and by the diligence of your teacher, George Fabricius, whom his brother Wolfgang succeeded. He lived with you for two years, and thus repeated a threefold, and indeed, most honorable harvest: he passed his time most pleasantly in brotherly company. He was present as an example for you and he worked afresh at the pursuit of his own learning. Thus he acquired these three fruits as you yourselves observe although he appears to have been away from Beichlingo and his family not so much for his own as for your cause. For this reason, also, he seems to be active in Paris, not only to be an example to you, but also to have gone there previously for your sake.

But to return to the point from which I have somewhat digressed: I shall prescribe for you a definite period of time, definite instruction and practice, in which my discussions will be limited and in my discussions I shall give consideration to your age, to the powers of your talent, and to your capacity. I shall prescribe the course that you ought to maintain through the next triennium and what you should undertake so that when the Calends of January will have returned three times, wherever you may be, your speech will be prudent, Latin, elegant, and eloquent.

I think there is a second goal for your reflections: an educated life. About this goal you ask my advice. There is another goal, that of virtue which demands to be dealt with at some other time. Surely, if you add all virtue and the learning of letters to the nobility of your family and to your riches and resources—which you, as behooves all nobility, have already begun to do long ago—what is there which you will lack for attaining happiness and a blessed life amid these things which are within your power, as long as the gifts you possess which were given from heaven are not carried away by some fate, or force, or fraud? Yet, amid the preservation of these blessings or amid their loss, virtue, religion, the knowledge of great subjects and learning contribute the greatest possible comfort with the result that you may not be driven from a special degree of happiness—indeed you may always possess it wherever you may be. As for virtue the first elements of which must be entrusted to religion, I do not propose to give an account of it and to teach the discipline of morals. Yet, lest other men judge that virtue is not essential for an educated man or lest others think that I think this, we remember virtue, therefore, in this introduction, especially since in this part and in this program there is the greatest possible need of three virtues without which neither our advice nor your inclination will find much power: First, diligence is essential, for without it even great talents do not progress very far; then temperance in desires which is the guard of diligence and the preserver of genius and nature. Then there is constancy in both, so that whatever may be begun will be brought to completion. These virtues will be judged in the end to be true when diligence does not allow the fatigue of one's powers, when temperance does not allow ill-health, and when constancy does not allow excessive inflexibility. Not that virtues are vices, but that vices often deceive by simulating virtues. We want virtue to be happy, sound and favorable. We want the morals of a studious person to be charming, his health wholesome and his spirit flexible; nevertheless in such a way that lust is absent, softness avoided, and stubbornness has no place.

Therefore, the first two virtues that I have mentioned, which cannot be excluded from this instruction, must be suited for the strengths of the body. Constancy does indeed not only look to the goal of our studies and our life, but must also be applied in single actions that have been prudently begun. Now, indeed, inasmuch as surpassing signs of these appear in you, which I have often observed during these years, I shall admit and assist you as much as possible in this your endeavor, fully known to me, and in your study.

First, I must consider how much you have already accomplished in your study of letters, to prevent omitting or passing over anything, or offering advice in something after the subject has been prepared and completed. So then, you have mastered, as I have learned from your brother Wolfgang and have also gathered from your letters, the whole course of the Latin language which is essential for understanding writers. In this language you have acquired so great a supply and selection of words and phrases (which are the images of things and thoughts) that you are prepared by these for writing and training in style. Also the methods of making distinctions and of speaking[1] have not been altogether left out. The art of composition has always been the governing factor of this method. If indeed you have retained up to now what you first heard from me in rhetoric and dialectic and later reviewed with Sevenus, I shall require nothing in addition except annotation in reading and diligence in writing.

In Greek you have already progressed so far that no work remains with regard to the rules of language and with respect to single words and phrases. In achieving this endeavor, the work of learning is not so irksome as the thought of future writing is joyful and pleasant. I am, of course, not unaware of the fact that there are some things in these studies that you do not know, but what you do know is sufficient for my purpose and for what you ask of me. For though that famous Ulysses of Homer was πολύτροπος (much-travelled) and ἄστεα καὶ νόον ἔγνω[2] (and knew the urban customs and minds) of many men, as Homer writes, nevertheless it is not credible that in individual peoples and states he himself wanted to know all citizens and to perceive what was done in each family. Rather he wanted to learn only those things which led him to the goal he had conceived in his mind and decided upon. He did indeed never err or offend more than when he was detained too long by the love of Calypso and allowed his diligence and praises to be hidden in the obscurity of a cave.

Therefore, as it is likely that this man, whom Homer makes exceedingly wise, travelled through various countries, so we too must travel in these arts of which we have spoken, so also we ought not to stay longer in the particular precepts than is necessary to understand their words and phrases. And as he longed for his own Ithaca amidst all his labors and afflictions and hastened toward it as often as he could, so we must proceed toward the goal of our studies and our life—a goal which for the most part is set by nature in a difficult place. But of this I must speak later and consider the way we may reach it. I do not doubt that in this supply and abundance of riches, the intended for you is honest and learned. The former pertains to the discipline of morals while the latter pertains to our present instruction and brings great assistance to the former. Surely in this life I think that the happy life is that which adds holiness of morals to the antiquity of one's family and adorns the abundance of one's possessions with the elegance of learning.

I shall, therefore, divide my lessons in two parts: into the learning of subject matter which is the cultivator of the soul, and into the practice in language, both the wisdom of speech and its refinement, which when it reaches the ears of listeners declares the sweetest harmony of the mind. This harmony can be perceived by us better than the ἁρμονία (harmony) of the celestial machine that was never heard, though it was at one time taught by the Pythagoreans.

But to begin with the knowledge of a subject: I do not see what could be more suitable to you or more becoming to nobility than civil science which the Greeks call "political."[3] If you master this as you should, you will bring great adornment to your fatherland, kindred, and religion. We shall, therefore, set forth the course by which you may procure the knowledge of it—whether of science and learning or of virtue and power—as well as such skill that you can live usefully not only to others but also happily by yourselves, and may seem to have been popular among your friends, charming at home, and respected in public. The knowledge of political science is indeed taught properly in the books that Aristotle wrote about the state. But because the foundations of great cities are laid upon the approved morals of the citizens, the science of morals is rightly joined to political teachings[4] which Aristotle also taught in many books. Above all, the knowledge of history especially helps. In history we may see the different ways states rise to power, how they have been preserved, and how changed and overthrown. Moreover, it supplies to men perplexed in life many counsels and varied examples. Indeed, what study could you take up more judiciously after your instruction in speaking, making distinctions, and rhetoric?

In acquiring these very skills, the method of the Latin language must be used so that it is not contaminated by a variety of languages, or a diversity of words which individual arts and languages and individual writers use as their own in each field. They very often differ among themselves on a single subject in respect to the arrangement of the very same words and the whole style of the composition. For example, there is the historian Herodotus, of the same nationality and the same language—Greek to be sure—as also the historian Thucydides. The language of both is beautiful and ornate. Yet what a difference there is in sweetness, in seriousness, in the arrangement of words, in the construction of sentences, and as it were, in a certain transformation of clauses, phrases, periods, and finally of the whole composition! Caesar, Livy, and

Tacitus wrote the history of the same people. But what a difference among them in all the embellishments that I have already mentioned!

But more than these differences are the differences in the writings of Cicero, that have a wide variety among themselves. Write a letter in that type of speech in which the beginning of the Milonian case was constructed and you will find, nevertheless, among the inexperienced some who praise it.[5] Yet those who have true judgment will disapprove and declare that you have overstepped the rules of propriety. One must realize, therefore, that in the investigation of a subject, one may do harm by the unsuitability of the words and language when one supplies material for dealing with strange subjects. Not that these men were not Latin and others not Greek, but for the reason that, just as the whole people (horse and foot), in the senate, in the forum, at home, whether Greeks or Romans do not wear the same clothes, so, in different subjects which must be dealt with in an oration, they do not apply the same kind of speaking, or the same form of speech. I praise a man for seeing Rome. I approve that you heard Cratippus in Athens. I tolerate and praise you along with others for being called Atticus. But I do not praise you for wearing a Greek mantle in Rome. I regard it as a mark of levity and a testimony to stupidity. So they all together with all the others are good for learning, but each in his own style, because each of them had something appropriate to his own individuality that suited him best and that each could do becomingly and in his own right.

Now with regard to the study of the greatest subject of all, namely God, religion, piety, charity, and the others virtues as well as outstanding morals and the salvation of mankind: What is more godly and more essential than what Moses, the prophets, and the Apostles wrote? Yet these can be made more beautiful if due care and purity of speech and of the Latin language are observed and the Roman tongue and Latin eloquence are not corrupted with Hebrew-isms that in Hebrew are agreeable but in another language offend the ears and often cover up the light of the subject with darkness. Thucydides, then, Herodotus, Xenophon, Polybius, the man from Halicarnassus,[6] and Herodian of the Greeks should be read. And all of them should be accurately comprehended, so that your judgment may be strengthened, your memory broadened, and your learning of subjects increased. Of prime importance are the things which were first handed down divinely to the Jews and then the same things explained more clearly after the death of Christ. But, in this way: as the mind itself ought to emerge and remain pure and undefiled through the reading of these works and by meditation upon them, so I would wish that the tongue be aided, not impeded by them. It is not ungodly, particularly in our age, that the purity, refinement, and elegance of mind and speech are the same. How much more is the fullness of speech becoming to the teachings of Christ than the immense building of temples! Not that I take no delight in these, but I am more delighted with the other kind of beauty and regard it as more becoming. As an image of God painted by the greatest painter delights us more than one by an inexperienced artist, and as the statue of Jupiter hewn by Polyclitus affects us more than those by other sculptors, so also when religion and ceremonies have an eloquent expositor, they are taught more intelligently and explained more brilliantly. They do not allow the love and fear of God that have been divinely aroused in us to be dismissed or to grow faint.

Now on to political science which most befits the nobility: The writers are most helpful whose books about the state and morals are outstanding; also historians, both Greek and Latin, indeed also interpreters of other languages, if any time remains or the times demand it. Truly, before all in importance are the authors of our religion, both teachers and historians. Since we call "political science" what is named by the Greeks πολιτική (political) and it includes τήν νομικήν (the law) as no small part of itself, we should again and again get to know those famous monuments of Plato *On the Laws* and the two books of Cicero on the same subject. When these are rightly understood, they will readily demonstrate what must be decided and how one must answer whenever a question arises about other matters which lawyers have compiled and set in order. So that you may not be disturbed by the large number of readings or be impeded by the variety of languages and the complex treatment of themes, I shall, before I come to training in speech, show you the way I believe you must go in order to reach your proposed goal. Therefore, I shall divide this whole plan into three periods: one of listening, another of reading, and the third of discussion.[7] If you apply this method to these three and adhere to the plan I shall prescribe, you shall reach the goal toward which you are striving. There will also be enough time daily after the individual activities, for relaxation of the mind, refreshment of energies, and the strengthening of your health. I want great care to be taken for your health because in a sound body the mind thrives more and apprehends more keenly, sees farther, and retains more carefully what it has traversed in its learning, understanding, and discussions.

I shall therefore return to what I proposed for the first period, namely to the time of listening. In this, there are two kinds of persons, for we also use teachers. As Marcus Cicero, the son, heard Cratippus in Athens, so we also use readers. In a letter to Atticus, the father Cicero, mourns over the death of his slave, Sositheus, a genial reader as he calls him.[8] Writers difficult to understand and authors of hard subject matter must be learned from others whom they today call "readers," teachers of language, and schoolmasters. Such works among the philosophers are Plato's *Gorgias* and *Protagoras* and many other of his discourses, and Aristotle's first books on the state and on morals. Among the historians, Thucydides; among the poets, Lucan, for he also makes a citizen and a civilian intelligent and wise. Among the orators, Demosthenes and Cicero, not because their meaning is obscure, but because their art lies hidden. The light of their thoughts through the fullness of their composition affects the sharpness of the mind as the sun affects the sharpness of vision. You can read Caesar's *Commentaries* by yourselves, also Xenophon's *Cyrus*, Herodian's *Caesars*[9] and Polybius. The task of the reader is to review what we have heard from these and from others and what we have read by ourselves. It is also frequently helpful before we read something for a reader to read it aloud, and if something is not clear to have him explain it in a few words and later have it repeated by us in reading and discussion.

Up to this point we have shown what our teachers should explain, what our private readers should read aloud, and what we ourselves should be reading. Now let us put off[10] the questions as to what system is to be followed, what selection is to be made, and what limit is to be observed.

The best possible teacher to be chosen is the one who professes the art he teaches and has practiced it for a long time. It is a pernicious thing in schools of letters (*gymnasia*) to have a man for teacher and learner at one and the same time, and for teachers to begin teaching before they learn. This has been too common in my day. Nevertheless, I do not deny that many possess excellent talent. They, even while they are learning, are better able to teach than some others who have long before both learned and taught the same subject. We are, however, speaking about the present time when a choice of two men has been given us. Then we may always prefer the most learned and experienced. But if the contrary occurs, we shall follow the example of great leaders and famous emperors who ordinarily favor a valiant recruit to a cowardly veteran. However, in the choice of two or more, one must consider not only their learning, but also the method of teaching and skill in explaining. Here one must, moreover, observe the learner's strengths, his capacity, and his learning. When I was in Paris, Peter Danes and James Tusan achieved the same purpose, though by different methods, so that they were heard by many. Both of them covered many lines in an hour. Tusan examined them according to the rules of grammarians. Danes was interpreting Demosthenes as much as he could and as far as that language (Greek) allows, in a way that Demosthenes seemed to be a Roman molded by Cicero's words and sentence forms. Accordingly the more learned scholars gladly heard the latter, whereas the former had those for his students who wanted to be taught the fundamentals of the language by a learned schoolmaster. It is evidence of good judgment, a mark of great learning, and a sign of diligence and sincere industry, not to dwell longer on a subject than is necessary and not to skip over what must be explained in the subject matter, the words, the art, or the comparison with other writers. So much regarding the teacher.

Now to take up the order and choice you must make and the method and way that you ought to follow in your reading and listening. At this point I must recall to your memory the goal of your studies: An honorable life associated with a knowledge of important learning and a polished style, as well as speech and language beautified by the brilliance not only of words but also of subject matter. Inasmuch as you understand in no small degree the basic arts of speech, the rules of the two languages (Latin and Greek) and the differences between them, with which the knowledge of words and of subject matter is connected (especially because words are the images of subjects), from this time on, you must undertake the study of both languages at the same time. To this same purpose, I must address my treatise.

We shall, therefore, divide the day into two periods: one includes the hours before noon and the second the hours after noon. All the time before noon we assign to Cicero and composition. The time which remains we assign to the other writers from whom the learning of the arts and letters can be acquired. Not that these other writers did not achieve excellence and extraordinary praise for their speech among learned and erudite men, or that Cicero did not teach the most important subjects repeated as a result of his zeal for wisdom; but while each is aided by the other, nevertheless I judge that Cicero must always be imitated first wherever there is an occasion for an example.

I must make this distinction so that it may be understood to whom it is at times permissible to digress and from whom it is not permissible to depart. Inasmuch as you want me in this course for your teacher, as it were, you ought to make up your mind that there are some things that are permissible, to which I permit you to turn. But there are some that are not permissible; if you turn aside from these precepts, I shall regard you as unmindful of the benefit you have received from me—and this is an impious breach of morals. Although at first I demanded only temperance, diligence, and constancy of you, I nevertheless do not want you to neglect the other virtues. As far I am concerned, I earnestly request your faithfulness and the remembrance of my counsels. I consider this to be a sure sign of gratitude. If you do not believe that I give counsels that are true, my treatise will have little authority with you.

Since, therefore, a body politic is a society and fellowship of people among themselves and no society is more widespread or is scattered through so many tribes and nations secretly with incredible power and strength, than the society of Christians which is called the church to which Jesus, the eternal Son of the true God to whom has been given a name of Royal Majesty and who is called the Christ and has summoned all mankind from every part of the globe, since, therefore, this is the true society, it is necessary that political science also chiefly rest upon the doctrine of Christ and God and that a Christian man most of all trust in this doctrine because it is prepared for the celestial society and agrees with celestial laws and the government of God.

The philosophers have investigated this and they could not discover it. If Minos of Crete or Lycurgus of Lacedaemon or Solon of Athens had possessed this, they would have left their fellow citizens more blessed than we see they did leave them. Plato's Socrates, Plato himself, and Aristotle failed in respect to the perfection of this knowledge. I do not say this, however, because they did not write well and gloriously. They did write very well, for the most part, considerably more, more precisely, in a great number of fields. But I say it because they did not know of that Divinity through which they could have called men to heavenly concord and could have brought their fellow citizens to the goal that they brought forth in their books: namely happiness and a life content with itself. If these things are really true, as they certainly are, we must consider that there are some things that we must read throughout our whole life and that there are some things that it suffices to have read once, if only our memory may not fail, and some which must be re-examined at specific times. This system you must always observe and never allow or permit yourselves to be seduced or forced from it, if you wish to continue in the constancy you promised.

Therefore, religion and reflection on it must always be observed. Often the most famous people and the wisest and best of men, after having performed acts of glory and having achieved at sometime the highest honors in administering the affairs of state, have abandoned their office, compelled either by sickness or age, but were not dissuaded from virtue, religion, or the sacred observances of their fathers. I believe that Cicero, and other noble orators,[11] did not always agree, on account of their age, to plead courses in court. Yet, they resolved never to forsake an honorable life, but always to give thought to something, and as much as they could to write what would profit their fellow citizens and what would be appropriate to a full explication in Latin of the study of religion and wisdom. Therefore, if religion is to be cultivated throughout our whole life and particularly at its end, and if the pen should not be dropped from the hand of a wise man, we ought always to know those writers whose speech we wish to imitate and by whom we would be instructed in virtue, religion, and wisdom. Now if this cannot be denied, it is proper for a wise man to dwell with the sacred writers and for an eloquent man to dwell with the works of Cicero and to end their lives there. Religion sanctifies human society and eloquence makes it pleasant and both together make it wholesome. To the study of religion I add the discipline or morals and all political science and histories. I hold that a wise man ought to end his life in these. These are the sort of things that I consider must always be read and studied.

Now what needs to be read only once is discerned in the following way: Whatever is of this class has the characteristic that it is either not worth reading because of absurdities or it does not need repeating because of its brevity or even easiness. Of these two, whatever is absurd ought to avoided. The class that is short and easy to understand and remember, must be adapted to further the goal that we proposed in our various studies. It is chiefly to be used when the mind, wearied by more serious tasks, has turned to relaxation. In this process of refreshing oneself, it is timely to use a reader whose voice is somewhat trained, clear, and distinct so that he can easily be understood and so that he does not by his expression produce aversion rather than pleasure which should be provided at a time of leisure and relaxation.

There remains the third class, which consists of those writers who are sometimes to be reread. This class is best done at two times: One of these has an honorable necessity. For the other, a reason must be given to a studious man. It often happens that the writing and reading of histories may be interrupted for some time, while we write something about religion or produce a work on some part of the state or when we work on a poem. Once this is completed, if we resolve to finish the history of a period of time or of some war, we must return to the expositor or the events whose account we intend to follow in the events to be communicated, and whom we most desire to imitate. If after the completion of this work it seems best to write a philosophical dialogue, you must return to the author from which you digressed and whose steps you decided to follow.[12]

Inasmuch as we have designated three years for the execution of my counsel, I shall next proceed to them. First I shall enumerate what we must achieve in this time. In the Latin language we must know all of Cicero, Caesar's *Commentaries*, Sallust and Vergil. When we have time to spare in this study, we should interpose something from Plautus, Terence, Varro, Lucretius, and others who can be easily understood and are pleasant to learn. Of the Greek authors we must read Xenophon's *Education of Cyrus* and *Commentaries* on Socrates,[13] also Herodotus, Thucydides, Demosthenes, and Aristotle's books on morals and on the state, also Homer and Hesiod. When we can take a recess from them, we must sometimes visit Theocritus, Pindar, and Euripides, Sophocles, and any other philosophers, historians, or poets who may delight us. But whenever we study for knowledge and understanding, we must always apply the rules of logic that spy out the truth.[14] The teachers and schoolmasters of geometry, cosmography, and astronomy must also be heard to the extent that the goal of our studies requires it. Out of all of these we must gather the material for composition. This must be sharpened daily since its nature is such that is dulled by leisure and interruptions. Through practice, however, and by constant ploughing, as it were, it becomes brighter and sharper just as a plowshare becomes more shining. You see the burden I have decided to lay on your shoulders. If you bear it until the Calends of January three years hence, we shall achieve our desire, namely that your speech shall be wise and eloquent and the sound of your tongue and of your mind will agree. This I think is sweeter than any other harmony. I have named for you quite plentifully, yet perhaps not distinctly or fully enough, the authors you must read and understand. I shall, therefore, discuss briefly this plan before I give you my opinion on observation, imitation, and composition, so that you may know the time each one is to be read and you may also understand the way you must go to be able to understand through your reading all these authors whom I have assigned, within the time I have set.

First, therefore, we must observe that old and noble precept (which we do very seldom) to take the most serious account of time and that this account stand firm for us and that we ourselves stand firm in diligent and continued reading and listening. If we heed this rule, we must chiefly shun three kinds of vices: The first is intemperance in eating and drinking. The second is untimely association with a circle of friends and the selection of idle persons. The last vice is promenading about. This brings so much evil that even the industrious and intelligent are wont to be drawn to sloth by the perverse habit of wandering about, as it were. Writers on farming also teach us this lesson when they forbid a gadabout to be an overseer. Yet the eye of the master as well as of the rich overseer feeds the horse, and walking about the works makes the workers do more. Since his habit often deceives the imprudent, it must ever and ever be diligently avoided, lest the sweetness of roving about makes us disregard time, deceives us in our concern for study, softens good natures, and by a false habit drives good resolutions out of the minds and thoughts of studious men. Neither the fame of the Peripatetics dissuades me nor does my own habit move me from my opinion—for I am by nature a rover. The Peripatetics sauntered about while they were disputing, but we are giving rules for reading. As for myself, I would have attained more and also would have produced more if I had been more in the habit of sitting. For that reason I censure walks and promenades while reading. There are other times for health and relaxation. In meditating or discussing or conferring with one another, I allow it, provided they are in moderation, so that after a small walk and in a short time we may again go back to reading. However, in a library, I do not disapprove of being engaged in searching among books and standing at a desk. An erect posture is conducive to some people's health. In bringing together authors and comparing many passages, we have to go from place to place. Yet just as we require moderation in food and drink and in associations with acquaintances, so here also, we believe, we must do this in a way that allows due consideration to what is necessary and what is tolerable—the one being measured by the rule of usefulness, the other by the rule of pleasure. Whatever is done with profit in our reading, we do not reject.

Now that I have shown you these three vices, let us see what must be done next. Perhaps we should consider whether you can complete all the authors I have named, in these three years, even if you avoid these three vices and in which periods of time this can be done. The periods of time must be distinguished since men measure every action not only by what is done, but also by the space of time in which it was done. Let a start be made with religion. To it we assign the first and the last hour of the day. There is no doubt that in these two hours we are able to understand and to remember much that adds to the learning of religion and a Christian life, particularly since our writing acquires for itself a great deal from the sacred writers. This should result in making better Latin from good Latin and in either translating Greek so that the Latin language remains pure, or handling and polishing it so that something excellent may appear, though where it was taken from may not be noticed; if something is apparent, it stands out as more beautiful and erudite. These three times, I say of reading and writing have been able to supply even mediocre minds with varied material on religion and doctrine, if they join diligence with unfailing attendance. The remaining hours before noon I assign to the books of Cicero and composition. These can without doubt all be read and understood in a triennium.

If this is granted, then it is also true that in the afternoon hours as much can be learned by other writers, Greek as well as Latin, in addition to the books that shall be recited by the reader, of whom we have spoken before. There this triennium will contribute a great store of religious knowledge and in Cicero not the least part of his philosophy, many examples, many accounts of his times that are learned thoroughly from his letters and orations, beside every kind of opinion, counsel, deeds, and sayings. All of this can be done by work in the morning that is not either great or unpleasant if a plan and method is followed.

The afternoon studies will offer a great many things indeed out of Aristotle, Plato, Demosthenes, Xenophon, Herodotus, Thucydides, Homer, Hesiod, Euripides, Sophocles, Pindar, and other Greek orators and poets; also out of Latin as Caesar, Sallust, Cato, Vergil, Lucretius, Catullus, and Horace. And although you add none other to these, you readily perceive how much learning and variety can be gathered from these. Yet I forbid no writer to be omitted without tasting something of him, running over a part of his writings, and diligently observing some things in him, but indeed in a way that our concern for time is observed, and the plan of a triennium is adhered to, as well as the goal of our studies which we have determined. For this reason I have not named all writers, and I do not bid you to read them all. But neither do I forbid you to know the ones I have not named. Plautus is a true Roman poet and Ovid by nature a prolific and charming one. Each Pliny is most useful. Livy is a grand historian and Tacitus a true reporter. As for those who wrote about agriculture, architecture, and the military science, who would deny that a learned and educated man should know them? But my prescription is for three years and is appropriate to your age and family and strengths. I am writing this work for your sake. In it I am considering what kind of nobleman I wish to be educated for the councils of emperors and kings and the care of the state. Nevertheless I have no doubt that if you succeed in remembering in part what you should understand in part—namely from the sacred writings, from all of Cicero, from the better orations of Demosthenes, from the books of Aristotle and of Plato regarding the republic and the laws, and from those writers whom I just before briefly indicated, among whom I even allow some things to be omitted if time presses—nevertheless, I say, if you with care and reason achieve only these things, I doubt not that you will be welcome to every learned gathering and to every educated assembly and to every wise council, no less than Cotta and Sulpicius, the pleasant and happy auditors of Scaevola, Crassus, and Antonius at their three discourses on an orator, and as Cicero enjoyed the presence of the young man Triarius at the disputation he had with Torquatus about the limits of good.[15]

But now it is time to come to the method of reading and writing that is the foremost part of our present instruction. Nearly everyone knows who are chiefly to be read and what one should read with profit. But in the first place few know how one must read and secondly there is a difference of opinion. For as that famous man says, "As many opinions as there are heads."[16] I shall give my opinion in my own way and with my own judgment, thinking nothing to be my own if anything in this has been appropriated by others, and leaving to everyone his own judgment. I am counseling you and not binding others to these precepts. In reading, moreover, the same plan ought to be closely followed as in writing and speaking, so that the first concern is for subject matter, the second for words. In writing and composing, the first thing of all to be thought of is what we wish to teach or defend or communicate, then, by which methods we wish to attain it. Thus in reading you must first take the parts in hand one by one for learning, judging, and weighing, so that nothing shall escape your understanding. Without understanding all is but a fleeting memory, an uncertain observation, a false imitation. It is true indeed that in the ancient writers, passages of great difficulty and obscurity often occur that cannot be understood, or do not equal the labor. Such in my opinion should be passed over. I recall that when as an adolescent at home in Louvain I read Cicero's Roscian oration[17] for myself, I passed over to the allegory of the Servillian Lake. But when I interpreted it publicly in Paris, I did so as well as I could after consulting Budeus. But at that time I also remember having given the advice to my audience that in such difficulties they should do what good plowmen do in sowing and reaping when they bypass the thick brambles, the deep roots of trees, and the rugged stones at the time of plowing and harvesting, if the cost exceeds the value of the crop. They should also mark the passage which for the present cannot be learned with profit. Nevertheless as the plowmen remove the stones that can be removed profitably, and dig up the stumps of trees, and root out the brambles, so let it be worth the trouble for students to stay with the sentences that can be understood even if they are difficult, particularly if they shed light on the rest that would be obscure without them. Thus the first task of reading consists in these two points. The next regards the order and arrangement. The third concerns the treatment of the subject matter. We note not only what subjects are to be placed at the beginning as in a battle line or a procession, what are reserved for the end, and what are fitted into the middle; we observe not only what subjects are enumerated, what are briefly run through, and how often some things are repeated; but also we note with what kind of words and forms of sentences this is done and by which method and way. The whole method of understanding, imitating, writing, and speaking is based on these observations. For this method we must provide three kinds of topics,[18] one of topics, these textbooks are called books of commonplaces; another of words, and a third of rules and examples that display the precepts of the art. The places for subject matter and for words are almost identical. Their differences I have shown in other books. The passages on art are taken from the same sources from which we have drawn the precepts that have been taught best and most perfectly of all by Aristotle and Cicero. This entire method is ἀναλυτικά (analytical). You have often heard from me about it. One must begin it in the early years, be trained in it, and constantly progress, if we want to follow those who obtained glory for learning among the Greeks and the Romans and who were regarded as wise in the administration of the state; not only rhetoricians, orators, and philosophers, but also consuls, emperors, and kings who have been honored no less by their reputation for learning than by the glory of their deeds. For this reason the barbarous custom and coarse opinion of many of our nobility must be censured. There are many who think that they are not sufficiently regarded as soldierly and warlike if they appear skillful in letters, and who are ashamed of learning but not of their morals. The morals of some are such that I am ashamed to mention them. How much more laudable it is in an illustrious home to have noblemen whose class, life and learning are in agreement and who by virtue of examples of a distinguished life taken from their own forebears or better families, are themselves an example for their posterity and who rouse other mortals to similar virtue! Did any greater obstacle bar the road of Alcibiades, an Athenian noble, to true glory than his failure to obey the counsel and precepts of Socrates? Formerly in the same state, Pericles assumed, by reason of his eloquence and learning, the greatest part of whatever fame and reputation he achieved. The new tyranny of C. Julius Caesar was detested. Nevertheless his *Commentaries* reduced the unpopularity and the censure by nobles. In them, his military prowess shines forth, made known not so much by his deeds as by his distinguished literary monuments.

But to return to the point from which I digressed: We must have the three kinds of volumes of which I have spoken, namely of subjects, words, and art. And though many commentaries of Latin are already in the hands of men, some men have endeavored to collect and to fill in commonplaces on every sort of topic. It is nevertheless helpful for the memory and for completing one's task, for each to have commonplaces collected by himself and to add or subtract or to change something in the findings of others. Inasmuch as I have often spoken and written at other times regarding places of words that are almost the same as storage places for topics, there is no need to repeat the same things here. The places of art are taken from the very precepts of the rhetoricians, as for example concerning the parts of an oration and the kind of cases, of arguments, of embellishments, and periods. Since the observation of these belongs to the second task of reading of which I just began to speak a little before and the occasions for reading, observing, and taking notes ought to be connected and continuous, let us explain the method of observing and taking notes a little more fully. This method begins with taking note and ends with comparison. I call taking note[19] γνῶσις του ὑποκειμένου πράγματος καὶ ἐργασίας (knowledge of the underlying subject matter and treatment) and comparison[20] ἡ τῶν ἄλλων συζήτησις (the examination of the others). For first we must consider what is said and how it is said. Then, inasmuch as the same subject often has a different kind of treatment for the sake of embellishment, the subjects before us are to be compared with others that have either been composed by the same author or put together by other writers. After this bipartite study, one must go to taking notes. What has been noted and understood must be assigned to places of art and a notebook. They are to be separated, as it were, in their cubicles. Again there are three methods of note-taking, namely, one when we write out complete passages; another when we briefly summarize the same passages in a few words which are called ἀποσημείωσις (abstract); another when we delineate all the members[21] with drawings which for the purpose of teaching I usually call ἀποσχηματισμός (schematism). So that the σχηματισμοί (sketches) may pertain to the authors, let our drawings be called ἀποσχηματισμοί (schematisms). This method was not invented by us but was once taken over in Greece and Italy by the dialecticians and the teachers of rhetoric. The Aristotelians distinguish kinds of conclusions and contrary propositions by drawings, and the rhetoricians name their periods δίκωλος (two-legged), ἰσόπλευρος (equal sided) and ἰσοσκελής (with equal legs). The Greeks also speak of προσοικοδομήσεις (constructions) of writers and orators. Antonius makes mention of the construction of a history in the second book of *On the Orator*.[22] For all these things can be sketched like real buildings, so that foundations appear, the roofs extend, the entrances are seen, the rooms separated, and the doors, windows, columns, and the other parts skillfully set before the eyes and the whole structure becomes apparent. In this kind of a structure of words, in the case of Albucius and Crassus, Lucilius and Scaevola have noted,

> What a charmingly composed speech, like all the little tesserae in the tightly fitted floor, and with a mosaic with its pattern of wavy lines. I have a son-in-law Crassus, lest you be inclined to speak in an inflated style.[23]

Let us then sketch the first sentence of three members by Cicero: "*Quae res in civitate duae plurimum possunt*" (which two things have the most power in a state). Member one consists of fourteen syllables. Another follows, also stated in as many syllables, "*hae contra nos ambae faciunt in hoc tempore*" (these both work against us at this time). The third is shorter, reduced to ten syllables, "*summa gratia et eloquentia*" (greatest grace and eloquence).[24] Hermogenes noted this kind of sentence with an erect ἰσοσκελές (isosceles) triangle.

But since the short member sometimes placed first, sometimes put in the middle, as may seem agreeable to mind and ear, it may also be sketched with three lines, two of equal length, the third shorter.

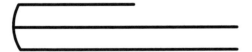

The same method can be used in combinations of two and four members, also in longer periods of which you have heard in rhetorical works. It would not be difficult for me to produce many examples if the publishers would permit it and this were the place for it. We shall have to return to this device at another time. For the present it suffices to show you this method from afar, as it were, particularly since you at some time will learn similar things from me.

Not only sentences and periodic sentences may be sketched in this way, but also the other treatment of orators that they call ἐργασία (treatment [of a topic]). This summer I expounded Vergil's *Eclogues* for you and showed you the beauty of style in the verses about the sad and unfortunate Meliboeus. How is it handled and by what method is it constructed?

> *"Tityre tu patulae recubans sub tegmine fagi,*
> *Sylvestrem tenui musam mediatris..."*

("Tityrus, as you recline under the cover of a spreading beech and practice country songs on a slender shepherd's pipe...") He sings of the happiness of Tityrus in two verses, but he laments about himself in a verse and a half:

> *"Nos patriae fines et dulcia linquimus arva:*
> *Nos patriam fugimus."*

("We are leaving the boundaries of my fatherland and its sweet fields; we are fleeing my fatherland.") Then he returns to the happiness of Tityrus, completes the verse he began and adds a whole line.

> *"tu Tityre lentus in umbra*
> *Formosam resonare doces Amarillida silvas."*

("But you, Tityrus relaxing in the shade teach the woods to echo back the beauty of Amaryllis.")[25]

This treatment has the form of a circle, for as in words so also in subjects there is κύκλος (circle) and ἐργασία κυκλοειδής (circular treatment). Therefore those who were following the mathematicians note this with a circle, but also this figure can be applied:

Meliboeus begins with Tityrus and ends with him. But perhaps someone will ask of what use this method may be, inasmuch as it is prolix, almost infinite, and free to writers. I shall respond to the last point first. It is not free because it must satisfy the ears of the hearers and the judgment of the learned and must be appropriate to the subject matter itself. Then, though there are infinite examples—for many are extant, a great number has perished, and many new ones may be invented—nevertheless this very treatment is bound by fixed classes, as for instance the very comparison of which we are speaking. This is either of similar things or of opposites or of things that differ in some points. Furthermore, both parts are either shortened or enlarged alike, or one part more than another, or the first part is again repeated at the end, as for example we see at the beginning of Vergil. It is not necessary for an architect to view and know all buildings everywhere, but it suffices for him to have surveyed some of the better structures in each class for imitation; so also a writer should select a few from among all whom he may emulate and with whom he may wish to compete. The usefulness of this method lies in the following: In the first place, the subject may be better understood and so be retained longer in the memory. Next, the observation of a work of art produces pleasure, from which constancy and an appetite are born while reading the writings of others. The opposites of constancy and appetite are the vices levity and satiety and there is nothing more harmful than levity and satiety for studies. Finally, this diligence gives much aid to judgment and often taking note of the art in an easy place brings out the things hidden in the more difficult places. Thus Tityrus in his reply[26] in his first line speaks of God and leisure:

"O Meliboee Deus nobis haec otia fecit."

("O Meliboeus, a god has created this state of leisure for us.") Thereupon he gives the reason in two lines and promises sacrifices:

"Namque erit mihi semper Deus: illius aram
Saepe tener nostris ob ovilibus imbuet agnus."

("For he will always be a god to me and often his altar will be stained by the blood of a tender lamb from our fold.") In the final two lines he returns again to his leisure state which he recalls and explains:

"Ille meas errare boves, ut cerneis, et ipsum
Ludere, quae vellem, calamo permisit agreste."

("As you see, he has allowed my cattle to roam while I play the music I wish on my rustic reed-pipe.")

Therefore all these five verses can be depicted with lines, so that the very structure of the work will appear.

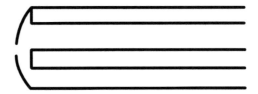

There is another advantage in this method that, first of all, consists of taking notes which I have called ἀποσημειώσεις (abstracts) and second, those *aposchematisms* because in the way just shown, one perceives how the different classes of speaking differ from each other and by which methods we may discern it. For how will a judgment be made as to how the three beginnings of Vergil's works differ from each other, namely of his *Eclogues, Georgics,* and the *Aeneid?* The first has been carefully put together by this comparison—a thing that fits the shepherd's song. The second is developed to a modest[27] partition, which befits rustic economy and agriculture. The third is embellished by a sweeping period sentence as heroic dignity required.[28] These three can be distinguished by lines as well as by the vocabulary of the art. Therefore this method has also the advantage that those which differ but slightly can still show very clearly just how they differ. For these two lines have the same feet, as they are called:

Tityre tu patulae recubans sub tegmine fagi,

(Tityrus, as you recline under the cover of a spreading beech) and

Protenus aeger ago, hanc etiam vix Tityre duco.[29]

(Although I am sick, I drive <the goats> further, but O Tityrus, this she-goat I can scarcely drag on.) But they differ both in the combination of words and letters and in harmony, from which the meter is born. This is understood by the following method:

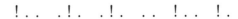

For the first foot and the fifth are consonant. The stress of the word is on the first syllable, that is, on the third syllable from the end. The second and third feet have the stress in the middle. But the second line, *Protenus aeger...* is measured with the same number of feet. Yet it differs with regard to the stress and the arrangement of the letters:

! . .   ! . !   !!.   . !   ! . .   ! .

For the second and the third heroic measures have two sharp stresses, and the third has a contraction of vowels,[30] and the two spondees are more emphatic so that this verse is more serious in tone just as it is sadder than the first in content.[31]

These are examples from the poets, but because I interpreted and pointed out these things for you last summer, I wanted to use examples from your most recent notes. Next, we ought to pursue the same method in the orators and the historians, for all writers have many things in common among themselves. If I should say, *"Vir sapiens semper homestatem sequitur, et pro ea mortem libenter oppetit; stultus rebus honestis voluptatem anteponit, quam sapiens non sensum titillationibus, sed virtute atque honestate metitur."* ("A wise man always strives after honorableness and gladly suffers death for it; the stupid prefers pleasure to honor, which the wise does not measure with the titillations of the senses but with virtue and honorableness."), this is a philosophical kind of speech, but structured in imitation of the example of poetry. Without this art or method or observation, or whatever you want to call it, it will be either hard or impossible to understand. It differs also from Vergil's verses in the class and nature of its words, but in form it is almost identical. Thus two togas that are sewed after the same pattern may differ; but one is green and of a livelier color, the other black and more austere, and one is shortened by an ell of cloth, more or less, according to the judgment of the tailor. To observe these things and to arrange them in their proper places provides great advantages in using them and changing them, and gives rise to pleasure in learning. Though it may be varied and diversified, still by devoting daily one hour with diligence, if neither a teacher nor talent is lacking, it is wonderful how much a man's industry can achieve in one trimester. In consideration of the circumstances of your life and birth, I advise you to devote your labor at first chiefly to the orations of Cicero and Demosthenes, then to Cicero's philosophical and historical books. But also his letters, should immediately from the very beginning be taken in hand. Amidst all these we must at frequent intervals also turn to the poets, but sparingly and not too long at a time until our composition becomes both fluent and meet for an orator. Antonius in Cicero[32] pleases me. He trained diligently and constantly in civil cases and the law-courts. He amused himself with history and he read the philosophers but did not follow them because of their narrow and concise disputations. He abstained utterly from the poets as if they had written in another language. But Antonius concealed his studies as well as his art of speaking. When he says that he does not understand the philosophers and stays away from the poets, he intimates what ought to be followed in imitating and what should be avoided in the case of an orator whose oration ought to find approval among the people. I write you this so that you may see on what you ought to bestow your greatest labor so as to reach the goal that you have set.

But inasmuch as all observation and all note taking of examples has been prepared for composition and is directed toward writing and the remaining exercises, we must now speak of that method of writing we ought to follow. In this method, this is taught first: that you think about the argument which Aristotle calls τὸ ὑποκείμενον πρᾶγμα (the underlying subject). It should be a subject that we can fully understand. For it is no more possible for us to express something in writing the nature of which we do not fully understand than for a painter to paint what he has never seen or heard of—as for example the shield of Ajax, the armor of Achilles, or the honorable meeting and the gifts of Diomedes and Glaucus. Therefore, let this be the first precept: that the nature of the subject be fully known. From this follows the second: a choice must be made in subjects so that in the beginning of the training those subjects are selected which are easily understood and not too prolix to handle. For in prolixity and obscurity, particularly for the beginner, irksome annoyance is to be feared, from which an aversion arises to this training which we want to be joyful and happy, not sad and abject. For as he does not sing well who sings reluctantly, so also he who writes with aversion does not write as gracefully as he who writes when his enthusiasm is aroused. Therefore in the beginning, let the pen be applied to known subjects not to prolix and obscure ones. To these two precepts a related one has been added, namely, that the subjects be set forth briefly. For I want the measure of diligence to be judged by the lines of writing, not be the general nature of the subject matter, as for example the treatment of something brief, either a letter, a short story, or an argument, a comparison and a likeness, and similar brief topics. Here the precept is properly given to devote the first year to Cicero, from whom we may supply the material for composition. We should not assign whole orations for imitating him, but at first some briefer sections that have either an essential or a notable passage. By "essential" I mean that which must always be used, and by "notable" I mean that which is recommended on its own merit, because it is rarely introduced on account of its conspicuous elegance and is concealed in lighter subjects.

We have, therefore, assigned Cicero's books to the first year for both reading and writing. As for the other writers, both Greek and Latin, it is enough throughout this time to know them only by reading. This year should be given over only to the rhetoric of orators. We may give the other two years also to historical and poetical exercises, but sparingly, so that the first and principal training is not impeded, and we may not appear imprudently to infect the mouth and voice of the speaker in the senate and in the court with the strange exercises of historians or the language of poets. Those shall more easily and more surely achieve all this who are connected with a guide and teacher. Since there are few teachers who can do this, we must see to it that an unlearned and inexperienced teacher is not acquired instead of one who is learned and well trained.

So much regarding composition and practice in writing with which the ancients connected practice and declamation before civil and forensic court actions. But since all of these are undertaken in vain without imitation, we must now speak about it. And here we can ask these questions: What is imitation? Which authors are to serve for an example to imitate? Ought only one serve as an example, or many? What is to be imitated and how? Finally, at what time should training in imitation begin? I shall give you my opinion about all of this but briefly. For it is not appropriate to discuss all these matters extensively in this small book and in the counsel given you. I am not teaching you what all imitators ought to do, but only the way you ought to proceed. For you are separated by the nobility of your family and your mode of life from other learned men whose sole purpose is to apply themselves to philosophy.

I call imitation μιμητική (the mimetic art) in which there is ζῆλος (emulation), zeal and love of achieving what is praiseworthy and admirable in the speech of another. This is indeed the method to express in your own language the things that are praiseworthy and illustrious in another's language, the treatment and forms of speaking which the Greeks call εἴδη (forms) and ἰδέας (ideas). Therefore, we want art to be in this method so that nothing is done contrary to what is becoming—which must always be nourished with the greatest care—as well as science of the whole subject and of all subjects, not just of some one subject or of a part of one. For who praises the painter who can paint only a person's hands but no other parts and who can draw only human heads but does not know how to present other animate beings with appropriate colors and shadows?" This method requires no small art or tenuous knowledge, but in this learning one must master what all kinds of speech demand and to what all imitation must be directed. From this is known what we should look for in the second place, namely who should best be imitated and whom we ought to have for an example to emulate. For the man who ought to arouse us the most to strive for his virtues is the one in whom these virtues appear and stand out as the most numerous and most artful. Not that the ornamentation must be applied in a manner that everyone understands. I am speaking of you and imitators who can discern these forms of speaking and their embellishments which others cannot. But inasmuch as among the Latin writers, those ancient Romans whose language was wholesome, voluble, and ornate, there is no one who has given us all these ἰδέας (ideas) of speech which ought to be observed more properly than Cicero, and since both the writers of his time and also those who wrote in subsequent years granted him first place in eloquence, who would doubt that he ought to be placed among the examples in the front line of the troops, as it were? There is no form either of rhetorical eloquence, of philosophical discourse, or of daily conversation that he has either not completely expressed or has not left such a pattern of a part of it that even an ordinary craftsman cannot fail to understand how the rest must be formed. Therefore let this be given and set down as a sure principle: in Latin there is no example more certain or more excellent than this writer. But let him not be the only one. Let us indeed look at other glorious examples. If I were asked the question whether all subjects have been handed down by Cicero in his writings and whether all of them are still extant for the people to this day, I am asked what cannot be known and what should not be asked at all. For we lack his books *On the Republic* that all the grammarians knew.[33] We do not have any histories written by him. He also wrote nothing on the subjects on which Varro wrote *On Agriculture* or Pliny, *The Natural History*, Vegetius, *On Warfare*, and Vitruvius *On Architecture*. Indeed, how many writings there are among the Greek philosophers, physicians, writers of histories, that Cicero did not touch! But we are speaking about the science of imitating which alone makes a perfect craftsman and which is the directress of composition, though composition itself is called the maker and teacher of speaking. I permit all writers and everything written to be read, but with method and judgment. Although we may consider that a great deal of important and excellent material can be gathered from other writers, indeed also words can be collected, as well as that composition of which we are speaking, the imitator of each best example can provide choice and introduce forms that are suited to the subjects themselves, yet the types and the propriety of these forms are never observed better than in Cicero's works. I must confess, however, and gladly do so, that there are some things in Demosthenes the like of which you may not easily find in Cicero. And in Plato's dialogues there are many notable and divine things worthy of imitation, but their image, although often sketched by Cicero, nevertheless was sometimes not sharply drawn. Then also, who would gainsay that if verses are to be composed, one should imitate a poet? Thus if history is to be written, one should also select a historian with whom to vie, and we must try to come as near to his image as possible. What then follow? The order of imitating is the same as that of reading. Our prime task must be assigned to Cicero, and whatever is lacking in him, search for it elsewhere. First learn Cicero and train yourself first in him and as long as you make progress do not repent of your example. Previously I made mention of comparison that the Greeks call συζήτησις (joint inquiry) and σύγκρισις (comparison) which is a most useful method of study. Who would deny that the same embellishments of many subjects often derive from Cicero and Demosthenes alike, but that there is often also a difference? Who would not consider it praiseworthy when you find in others what is good and singular, to note it, to refer it to the places of art and of imitation that I have mentioned; there to sketch the handling, to judge the author, and briefly copy the subject that is being handled? Since therefore our question concerns the Latin language and our purpose is to polish and adorn the voice and speech of a nobleman, and inasmuch as priority is always assigned to Cicero and no one else has expressed such a variety of speaking with supreme elegance and adornment of speech as this writer, who will deny that he is worthy not to be passed over as long as excellent subjects are being learned, of which we were previously ignorant and as long as we find in him what we desire? But it would be foolish not to take from others, if one may, what Cicero lacks. But if you are instructed by his powers of speech, his resources, and riches and then come upon others, it will not be difficult to note what you lack and what you need. After your palate has been well sated with these most salubrious fountains of eloquence, there will be less danger amid the drinks from other authors, that they will be corrupted by a distorted taste. As one therefore usefully proceeds from Demosthenes, a brawny orator, to Isocrates, polished and well groomed, or properly joins them together at the same time, so I do not only permit you to shift from Cicero to Demosthenes, but also counsel you to digress at intervals and urge you often to compare them with each other. If we purpose to write history I recommend that we employ another kind of speech, as Cicero himself judged it should be done. For in history, speech is "diffuse and drawn out," as Antonius says,[34] gently and evenly flowing forth. But in court and at the bar, there is harshness as well as barbed sentences. Hence history, as it is observed in the best authors, demands another kind of speech. Nevertheless, to attain this, Cicero who was equally competent, perhaps more so than Sallust, Caesar, or Livy, will provide great resources and will supply a well-honed judgment, so that you may not only do the same, but sometimes even do it better. In Livy, as Quintilian writes,[35] Polio sensed Patavinity. This he would not have discerned, if he had not learned from the better writers what is Roman and what is Patavian. Whoever has had his mouth wetted with Cicero's waters can with the same taste sense that foreign, so to speak, accent in Livy which Polio sensed. So much then regarding the question which asks who is the most important author to imitate and what others beside him? Cicero, first of all, and beside him whoever is the best in his genre.

Next we should indicate what is to be imitated and by what method it is to be done. Although this part is lengthy and runs through all precepts of eloquence, we shall reduce it to just a few points. For every deliberation of this kind begins with the one main heading and is at once divided into two sections. For we ought first to consider to what the argument pertains that we have undertaken to develop. Then we must see what treatment of the subject matter it demands and what embellishment of the subject and of words it requires. This is the reason why I extended the definition of imitation[36] to include the handling of the subject matter and the class of speaking. And it is not unclear that if we intend to write a dialogue and to present people conversing with each other, we should not look for a pattern to follow in Cicero's orations, but rather in his *Tusculan Disputations* or the *Academica* or in his similar dialogues. So if we are to write an oration, comedy, tragedy, or satire, it is obvious to what we ought to turn our eyes and what our mind ought to observe. Accordingly this study begins with the argument and divides into two parts. The argument I have repeatedly termed τὸ ὑποκείμενον πρᾶγμα (the underlying subject), others call it ὑπόθεσις (hypothesis). We may call the kind of speech ἰδέα (form) and the handling, in our judgement, sometimes μέθοδος (treatment), sometimes ἐργασία (handling), not because that very method of treatment is related to the forms of speaking (for each has its own treatment of subject matter), but we properly call the treatment of subject matter the embellishment of elocution and of the form, especially because each subject requires appropriate and suitable embellishment. An argument must be selected, and in its selection we ought to follow the advice of Horace who prescribes,

Sumere materiam nostris qui scribimus aequam
Viribus et versare diu quid ferre recusent,
Quid valeant humeri.[37]

(...take a subject equal to the strengths of us who write and meditate for a long time on what our shoulders refuse to bear and what they are strong enough to bear.) Our strengths indeed are aided greatly by diligence. Those who are less able in talent or learning ought to couple their diligence with the example and aid of the best orators and writers. It happens that the appraisal of one's strengths may be achieved on the basis of three criteria: talent, knowledge, and diligence. Whoever is endowed with a keen wit and has added learning to it as an attendant and leader, if he brings diligence to bear and vigorous training and application of self, it must be a great thing that he would not be able to achieve by writing and polishing. We cannot wholly explicate this part of our deliberation before we learn about the time for imitation.

Inasmuch as one's strengths, talent, and learning have been mentioned, we shall briefly set forth the last point as to when imitation ought to be taught. This is to be determined not so much by age as by one's strength. As therefore Aristotle excludes boys from his ethics, so I also keep away from this ingenious plan not only boys, but also men who have not mastered the precepts of speaking, have acquired no learning of subjects, and do not strive with ardent zeal to make their speech as like as possible to the best and most highly praised. In my opinion, Aristotle kept adolescents away from his teaching because they possessed neither a steady practice in exercising the will nor moral judgment. Thus we too admit to this study and method of imitation the φιλορήτωρ (the lover of rhetoric) with ardent zeal and whose heart has been schooled in some learning of letters. But until the ignorant have been educated and the slothful have been stirred up, I relegate them to the teachers of the other arts who can cope with them. Accordingly when the mind and heart are thus put in readiness and instructed, that is the most appropriate time for the experience. Though I do not demand detailed learning but am content with your moderate skill, there are nevertheless, three times for this exercise: one when we are learning it, which is the first time. The second is when we have learned it, which is the middle stage; and the third and last, when we know it perfectly. For we ought to be learning this art as long as we have not mastered it and are not producing what can be published, as both worthy to be heard by all and agreeable to the educated. After we have achieved the knowledge of this method and of the most possible subjects, just as an actor well trained for acting in secondary roles is rightly admitted to leading roles to be seen on stage, so even your speech, after it has been polished by this means, will not dread the opinions of the general public or fear the judgments of learned men. As for the third time, that of having reached perfection, though it is desirable and is to be striven for so that we have no need for an example, nevertheless I really do not know whether anyone has ever attained it. For in view of the great variety and excellence of philosophers, orators, historians, and poets, there will always be something that we have either not read before or in learning have not always given our attention to. It is difficult to read and understand everything. To remember everything has been denied to almost all mortals.

Yet we must strive and go on as far as we can. It is shameful to stand still on the path to virtue, praise, and glory, when one may proceed, especially since the later labors are very often easier and more joyful than the first. It is also true that although you cannot be equal or superior to the most perfect, it is still honorable and commendable to contend with them in many things, and even to do something better when we can, and to add or take away or change something in what we have found or in the examples that we imitate and to try always to build something that is more excellent. Imitation ought to be free and not servile. We wish that an imitator would not always follow in the footsteps of another, but as often as possible and as many times as possible when he is able, if he can do so becomingly, outrun the one ahead. Therefore until a young man is imbued with some measure of learning and has learned the rhetoricians' art or speaking, and has heard a teacher of dialectic, I shall not admit him to this school. I leave him to the grammarians whose lessons and prescribed materials he will trace like lines drawn by other men. But after someone has mastered these, if he has talent and is imbued with love and zeal for eloquence, as you are, this school shall be open to him and we shall test how much this method and practice can do.

At the beginning of this study we shall with the greatest diligence read the writer whom we regard as the best in each language. In doing this we shall consider what he says, then in what order, then with what type of speech, and what treatment. Of these the first pertains to invention. Order refers to arrangement; the type of speech to its form. The treatment is what decides most of all the form itself and includes the ornamentation of the speech, the elaboration of sentences and arguments, also the structure, combinations, and numbers of the sentences and periods. The differences among themselves of all these topics that have been taught in art is here observed and, as it were, sketched and painted and stored away in the notebook that I mentioned, so that it is at hand whenever we need it and we are able to see in what footsteps we must follow in each subject we have undertaken.

Therefore the following is the first occasion for diligence: by way of an example, to observe and to note what things that art has taught us. Nor ought we to wait until we know everything and our book is full, but from the very beginning, as soon as a copy is made and a note taken, we ought to take up the pen and produce something similar. At this point the rule is laid down regarding the material and argument, namely, that we start with the easiest and do not burden our work with obscurity, but lighten it with ease. Therefore, in regard to letters, in the beginning we should select the shorter ones for imitation. In regard to orations, as also in the longer letters and in philosophical discourses, some short part like the conclusion of an argument or an analogy or a comparison, a short narrative, a commonplace, a general opinion, or a contradiction.

These things pertain less to the material than to the types[38] of which we shall now speak. Here indeed the rule applies: each in its own class. For as a historian imitates a historical writer, a satirist Horace, or Persius, and a tragedian imitates Euripides or Sophocles, so inasmuch as the language of the market place, the speech of philosophers, and colloquial conversation differ greatly, here, too, the example must match each one of these in its own class. But it is hard to judge what kind each is and ought to be.

Next therefore, briefly as I began, I speak of the method of imitation. Here we must first consider what is capable of imitation and what is forbidden to be imitated. I mean by "capable of imitation" what we can follow and express by imitating. The Greeks called it μιμητόν (mimetic).[39] From this can be understood what ἀμίμητόν (inimitable) is. To begin with and take up things that are not capable of imitation is indeed very foolish, but there are two classes of these: One is not capable of imitation by its nature; the other is not capable of imitation at certain times. Quintilian denies that talent, invention, power, and facility can be imitated. What he writes is true since these things are born in us and the natures of others are not ours. They can neither be imparted nor taught by art, even though they appear in our example. Hence these do not naturally pertain to imitation, although they do shine forth in our imitation, and as a result of our training, also our natural faculties are aroused, refined, and strengthened. But the class that is not capable of imitation by its nature does not belong to this method of ours. These are talents of others, not our own. There are also certain works of others so composed that they are beyond the reach of our powers. Thus Pindar appeared to Horace:

Pindarum quisquis studet aemulari,
Iuli, certatis ope Daedalea
Nititur pennis, vitreo daturus
    Nomina ponto.[40]

(Whoever desires to rival Pindar, Julius, soars with wings fastened with wax by the art of Daedalus, doomed to give his name to the sea.) He also gives the reason:

Monte decurrens velut amnis, imbres
Quem super notas alvere ripas,
Fervet, immensusque; ruit profundo
    Pindarus ore.[41]

(Like a river running down a mountain which rains have raised over its wonted banks, it seethes and is immeasurable, so Pindar rushes on with deep utterance.) Horace believes that Pindar's majesty and luxuriance, and grandeur, if one may call it that, is ἀμίμητον (inimitable). But although there are certain works by great authors that should not be touched at first because they are beyond our reach, they are nevertheless made easier in the course of time. It is not given to the beginner to compose an entire oration or indeed any whole work. Nor would I advise it, if it were. Time will assist ability and give facility. Therefore, let the first endeavor be devoted to the easier parts of works and to smaller portions. Then little by little one may progress to the larger and more difficult works and finally to an entire work. Not even in regard to the most perfect works is despair to be permitted. For either we shall obtain what we wish or we shall take from them many precious items so as to compose the things that have been adapted naturally to our own industry, as Horace also admits to have done:

Ego, inquit, apis Matinae
    More modoque
Grata carpentia thyma per laborem
Plurimum circa nemus, uvidique
Tyburis ripas, operosa parvus
    Carmina pango.[42]

(I, he says, after the method and manner of the bee from Mt. Matinas as it seizes pleasing thyme amid its toils around the grove and the banks of the dewy Tiber, I a humble man, compose laborious poems.) This modesty is praiseworthy in Horace since he gives the first prize to Pindar and encourages Julius Antonius[43] to a greater lyric. For the imitator must avoid arrogance more than anything. It is the companion of levity and folly. Yet Horace did not despair, for in many ways he is equal to Pindar and often even vies with Pindar in a modest way and also with praise. Because an infelicitous imitation is ridiculous, he talks about himself modestly and prudently warns others not to try to undertake anything that exceeds their powers if they want it to come to light and be judged by learned men.

At home, we ought to attempt and try everything, even to stay with the same topics as long as we are making progress. The beginning of this study ought, however, to be devoted to the lighter, yet necessary things. I mean by "necessary" that which is used not rarely but everywhere. There are things of this class that I mentioned previously in which one ought to see what is worthy of imitation. Whatever is worthy of praise is either apparent or hidden. One class we designate with the Greek word φαινόμενον (apparent), the other κεκρυμμένον (hidden). I name things apparent, as well as the arrangement of the devised subject matter and the structure. There are hidden things; in an orator of amiable morals there are signs of this: advice not expressed in words; arguments and opinions omitted which could have been stated; even ornamentation omitted which could have been used. These are of such great importance that he who misses them while searching will produce nothing outstanding. For just as it is a matter of virtue to undertake what is good and worthy of praise as well as to avoid the things that are bad, and just as virtue itself is at times not seen but is understood, so the duty of the imitator is accomplished by considering what is openly shown and plainly spoken, and what is omitted and concealed. An imitator, therefore, must have trained eyes. First because the hidden things are not seen unless they are dug up. Then because the very things that we have said are apparent are frequently so woven together by writers that they can be sensed only by a sharp-sighted teacher and artist. Therefore, at the beginning this art requires the help of a teacher, if one can be had, who may give us materials, indicate what is to be imitated, teach, correct and show how similar subjects must be concealed by contrasting elements.

Whoever wants to be a good imitator ought to be a good concealer of his art as well. To use the same features in an example for all purposes is childish. For though it is artistic to follow the Venus Anadyomene of Apelles or the Satyr of Protogenes, and to use the same colors, lines, and shadows and to do nothing different from them, still it is more excellent to express in a picture of Apollo or of Achilles the same art that Apelles showed in the picture of Priam or of Asclepius and to achieve this completely from the example of Apelles. Therefore, let Priam be attempted so that the similarity may not be obvious and, if it should be obvious, let it be done in a way that seems to have been done as a result of conscientiousness. This is also the way of learned men. This must, however, be done when the effort is laudable, and the elegance is similar, not in the same, but in diverse subjects, and not so much in the type, as in the treatment.

There are many orations of Demosthenes and many of Cicero; yet in the orations of Cicero, even in the *Philippics*, the very title of which proclaims, as it were, the example, contrast in the same kind of speaking has been sought and similarity hidden, although he imitates Demosthenes. What a difference there is between the sayings and doings of Aeneas in Vergil and the words and deeds of Ulysses in Homer! What is often as similar as the kind of speech of both poets! Yet what a striking difference in this great similarity! How much variety, although Ulysses is not mentioned nearly so much as Vergil's Aeneas! Nevertheless it is pleasant at times to have the imitation appear and be perceived. I do not dislike the beginning of Bembo's book. Bembo: "O Teupolus, my father..." which he made after the example which Cicero uses in his book *Brutus*.[44] For as Cicero, hearing of the death of Hortensius, conceived sorrow of mind deeper than anyone would have supposed, so his father Bembo when the report of the death of the Duke of Urbines reached the senate of Venice, conceived a truly deep sorrow. He uses these words and like Cicero, Bembo includes the cause of his sorrow. As Cicero's grief increased in writing, so also Bembo's grief increases. Whether Bembus for some reason wanted the similarity to be recognized or whether he thought that this could not be detected, in reading this personally, I conceived happiness instead of the grief that he and his father conceived, and as I thought of it, I remembered to think about this method of mine. Nevertheless, the imitator must conceal every likeness that is praised only when equal fame follows the writer but one cannot detect by what means, in what places and examples, this has been done. The method of concealment consists in three things: addition, subtraction, and alteration. In alteration there are conjunction, figuration, substitution, and transformation of words, sentences, clauses, and periods. Of these three, what addition and subtraction are is understood well enough by themselves. The Greeks call the one πρόσθεσις (addition) and the other ἀφαίρεσις (subtraction). Often a word, or a clause, is cut and the sentence arrived at by these, whether through subtraction or addition creates a new form or image, as it were, of speech. To illustrate: Cicero says, "I conceived a sorrow of mind deeper than anyone supposed." Bembus says, "I conceived a truly deep sorrow." These two are rarely used without the others, but without these imitation is childish.

Alteration I call ἀλλοίωσις, one part of which is συζυγία (joined together/conjunction) or σύνθεσις (combination/synthesis) which consists in different arrangements of words and subjects and is accomplished by placing either before or after or between, words, clauses, subjects and other things that are necessary. Figuration is, in Greek, σχηματισμός. It occurs mostly in genders, numbers, and cases. Variety in these brings pleasure and prevents boredom.[45] But as in composing, so also in concealing and altering, one must do what is becoming and what is suitably ornamented.

Substitution is called κατάλλαξις (exchange). Here a word or topic serves in place of another.[46] In words it is called συνωνυμία (synonymity); in topics it is called a different argument. That is, sentences and speeches pertain to the same point, even as there are συναιτία (accessories) in the things done and συλλογισμοί (syllogisms) in the conclusions of many arguments.

What the Greeks call μετασκευή (modification), I call transformation. This includes all ornamentation of speech, the metaphors and tropes of words as well as the ornamentation of speech. These metaphors and tropes can often accomplish the same thing and therefore change may occur. Nor is there anything in which an imitator may glory more than in the exchanging subjects and words and in combining them. In these techniques diversity and variety are demanded, and therefore transformation has μεταβολή (change) added to it which dispels boredom and is generally the chief cause of every delight. The following is the distinction between μεταβολή and μετασκευή (modification): the latter creates a work with diverse features, the former creates a work with varied features. There is indeed nothing more pleasant and agreeable to the ear than the same things often expressed in other words and everywhere a diversity of ornamentation and a variety of periods, and measure in their clauses everywhere different through their intervals. These are the things that conceal art and similitude, and though they seem but trifles, yet they alone affect what the ears of learned men expect. Their power is not understood unless we learn it through usage and practice.

One must also bear in mind that no concealment is worthy of praise unless it substitutes something equal or better, or if it appears worse, that it nevertheless does not happen without some intent and reason. Who does not see that Vergil's periodic sentence *Arma virumque cano...* (I sing of arms and a man) was formed after the likeness of

Homer? But there is still a distinction. Homer calls Achilles by name and briefly prays the Muses to recall his wrath and the evil it inflicted on the Greeks. Vergil does not mention Aeneas' name, but develops with more words what he has set about. Thus if we do not want to concede superiority to Vergil, we must—if the Greeks will permit us to do so—nevertheless admit that his exordium is brilliant and equal to Homer's. It is sometimes honorable to yield if what we propose demands it. For to continue with the example that I used before, who would deny that this is fuller and more rhythmical: *opinione ommium maiorem animo cepi dolorem* (I conceived a sorrow deeper than anyone supposed)? Yet the other also is unassuming and suited to its present subject: *Magnum sane dolorem cepit* (He conceived a truly deep sorrow).

Now let me return to the subject. In the place of what we imitate we must always substitute something better or as good or something which for some special reason, is less elevated. We must think that those three points are truly observed whenever they not only cover the traces but also add ornamentation. Whatever is artistic ought also to be elegant and harmonious. The three points that I mentioned previously produce a greater measure of power and ornament than the inexperienced think. Arrangement (*figuratio*) is almost among the least in effect, but is it not most pleasant in the comparison of Vergil?

> *Tityre tu patulae recubans sub tegmine fagi,*
> *Sylvestrem tenui musam meditaris avena:*
> *Nos patriae fines, et dulcia linquimus arva:*
> *Nos patriam fugimus, tu Tityre lentus in umbra*
> *Formosam resonare doces Amaryllida sylvas.*[47]

(Tityrus, as you recline under the cover of a spreading beech and practice country songs on a slender shepherd's pipe, we are leaving the boundaries of my fatherland and its sweet fields; we are fleeing my fatherland. But you Tityrus, relaxing in the shade teach the woods to echo back the beauty of Amaryllis.) What is shorter than *tu Tityre* and *nos fugimus*? How much charm this change of numbers has! Here Tityrus too, as is usual in bucolic verses, imitates the same harmony, but without haughtiness—as behooves a shepherd friend—and invidious rivalry:

> *O Meliboee Deus nobis haec otia fecit,*
> *Namque erit ille mihi semper Deus, illius aram*
> *Saepe tener nostris ab ovilibus imbuet agnus.*[48]

(O Meliboeus, a God has created this state of leisure for us. For he will always be a god to me and often his altar will be stained by the blood of a tender lamb from our fold.) Similarly he has changed the number: *Nobis fecit*, (He has created for us) *mihi semper erit* (to me he will always be) and *a nostris ovilibus imbuet* (from our folds <a lamb> will imbue). As therefore, when we write without an example, this kind is elegant, so it is also elegant when we do have a design to follow, and it conceals what we do not want to be recognized as imitated by us. There is no need to discuss all the points that we have previously set forth, for you have heard them in part from me and in part they are understood by themselves and are not for this occasion. I shall nevertheless give an example of transformation. There is an elegant repetition of sentences by Theocritus which the Greeks call [ἀντιμεταβολή] (transposition):

αἴκα τῖνος ἔλῃ κεραὸν τράγον, αἴγα τὺ λαψῇ·
αἴκα δ' αἶγα λάθῃ τῆνος γέρας, ἐς τὲ καταρρεῖ
ἀ χίμαρος· χιμάρω δὲ καλὸν κρέας, ἔστε κ' ἀμέλξῃς.[49]

(If he chooses the horned goat, you will take the she-goat. And if he takes the she-goat as a prize, the kid falls to you. The meat of a goat is sweet before you milk her.) For this repetition Vergil uses the circle of which I spoke previously. Does Vergil use other words for those that Theocritus used? Who can deny that these serve as an example? Does anyone then say that Vergil does not use either the same ornamentation or the same words since he did not wish the traces to be recognized by the inexperienced? But why *Non equidem invideo*[50] (indeed I do not envy) since also Theocritus writes κοὔτοι τοι φθονέω[51] (and I do not envy you)? Because he wanted it to be known whom he imitated, but not how he imitated to be noticed. Someone may perhaps deny that this is imitation since the same features are not in both. To him I say that imitation is not of the identical but of the similar, and that which is similar ought to be diverse but still related and this relationship ought to be judged on the basis of the explicit purpose and form of the speech. Thus in the verses of the bucolic song the purpose is sweetness and for that reason Thyrsis, according to Theocritus, praises the song of the shepherd Aepolis[52] and says ἀδὺ τὸ ψιθύρισμα (sweet whispering) and soon afterward ἀδὺ δὲ κὰι τὺ συρίσδες (sweet pipings).[53] In like manner, Vergil, for the sake of pleasure and sweetness, as Theocritus repeats his ἀδύ (sweet) and uses the repetition of which we spoke in his *nos patriae fines and nos patriam fugimus*, and in place of the repetition he enclosed the sentences as it were in a circular orb.

The beginning of Homer is known: μῆνιν ἄειδε θέα (Sing, Goddess, of the wrath). It is thoroughly Homeric: grave, ornate, and meet for the intended work. But Vergil's *Arma virumque cano* (I sing of arms and a man) has neither smaller nor fewer virtues. Also fully heroic and in the great dissimilarity there is an artful similarity in the gravity and ornamentation concealed by the methods of which I have spoken. As Homer shows the wrath of Achilles, so Vergil describes Aeneas with more words and particular characteristics, so that there is variety in the roles and likeness in the handling that ought to be suited to the purpose, namely gravity. So he has embraced many great matters within a narrow compass, but Vergil balances also that sweetness of Homer's letters and voices and the sound of the poetic words that are characteristic of the Greek language with very beautiful arrangement (*figuratio*): *Arma virumque, Italiam, Laviniaque littora, terris lactatus et alto* (arms and a man, Italy, Lavinian shores, tossed on land and sea), and both numbers are thrice knit together. In the verse *vi superum saevae memorem Iunonis ob iram*, (by the force of the gods above, on account of the relentless wrath of Juno) not only numbers are joined but also the sequence of cases is changed. In that clause *genus unde Latinum, Albanique patre, atque altae moenbia Troiae*[54] (whence the Latin race, the Alban fathers, and the lofty walls of Troy), what distinction of gender, numbers, and words! Finally, that clause *Musa mihi causas memora* (Muse, recall for me the reasons) differs in regard to arrangement from the Homeric invocation while in magnitude it is equal to the beginning of Homer except for these distinguished traits: it not only inquires, but also laments, wonder, and applauds. Therefore the imitation of the resemblances is concealed by arrangement, changes, addition, and variation. Vergil separated the statement of the theme from the invocation and interchanged the persons and subjects. He recounted more things and that is addition. But the variety of words, gender, cases, and numbers—all things are resonant and this is apt for gravity, so that elegance does not stand in the way of gravity and gravity does not impede elegance. Therefore likeness ought to be concealed amid dissimilar things and it ought to be done in the way I showed. After we have selected whom we want to imitate and what subject we want to relate, our first consideration ought to be a genre. To the purpose and form of the genre both the subject matter and the words and their arrangement and variety must be related.

But a teacher is necessary, for without art the stealthy image of an imitator is not perceived. This practice also calls for much experience and only a few acquire it. Sallust is a noble historian and Quintilian's testimony regarding his brevity is known,[55] but how many are there who know how that was achieved? Dionysius of Halicarnassus writes that in Thucydides the weaving together of words is beautiful but not sweet, whereas in Xenophon, on the contrary, it is sweet but not beautiful. But the composition of Herodotus, he says, is both ἡδεῖα καὶ καλή (sweet and good). It is a matter of keen judgment and experience of a clear eye, as it were, to see where delight lies and how beauty differs from sweetness. Not that there is but a little difference between virtue and pleasure, but rather, since in speech, elegance and sweetness are not easily separated, art is therefore necessary; there is need of a teacher, and training is required. Vergil's *Georgics* are said to be perfect but his *Aeneid* not polished. I would, however, wish that some expert on poets were given me who could point this out and show this to me whenever there is need. But about this, I shall speak some other time.

Now to our purpose regarding the form of speech of which we must put the image before our eyes while we are working and composing. To this we must fittingly apply our pen, like a hand, and words and their ornamentation like colors, shadows, and lights. I call suitability in ornamentation among the first things to be necessary in imitation in which two criteria must especially be observed: namely aptness and moderation. It is aptness when subject matter and words match. It is moderation when amid appropriate subjects nothing is lacking, nothing is left out. Thus in the beginning of Homer's *Iliad* nothing is lacking and in the exordium of Vergil's *Aeneid* there is no superabundance, even though it is more comprehensive than Homer's. Aptness is considered to lie in emotions, morals, and nature. Among these (emotions, morals, nature) I mean by nature whatever does not concern people, such as herbs, trees, gems, gardens, estates, villas. These are expressed and described by a certain kind of speech that is idiomatic to them. Morals and emotions pertain to poets and orators when they express their own morals and those of their characters, as they stir up the minds of their audience or[56] readers to wrath, hatred, love and mercy. Out of these three come three kinds of diction from Aristotle's third book of rhetoric: ἡ παθητικὴ λέξις καὶ ἡ ἠθικὴ καὶ ἡ ἀνάλογος τοῖς πράγμασι (emotive diction, moral diction, and diction suited to the subject matter).[57] Aristotle, greatest teacher of the art, has shown of what sort these ought to be and likewise are. Also in this passage on ornamentation, it is prescribed that we should not imitate only the likeness of the form, as if only the skin, but that the blood and veins and sinews and muscles should stand forth and be seen. Therefore we must strive for our speech to be beautiful, prudent, and sound. Of these, beauty is a matter of elegance; prudence an aspect of the subject matter; and soundness a matter of nature and adornment so that the form itself is natural and becoming. For the Venus of Apelles rising out of the sea was doubtless sprinkled with some foam of the sea, but in a way that the foam makes the form of the goddess even more lovely. But as Apelles left some parts unadorned, so the writer and the imitator must do likewise. He must consider not how much something can be embellished but how much is becoming. Unless this happens, his speech will of necessity be pompous, inflated and inept. Thus they give good advice who say that Homer's Minerva ought to be imitated. She often changed Ulysses into various forms, sometimes with a wave of her wand making him wrinkled, small, and deformed, φτωχῷ λευγαλέῳ ἐναλίγκιον, ἠδὲ γέροντι[58] (like a poor, wretched old man), but sometimes μείζονα τ' εἰσιδίειν[59] καὶ πάσσονα θῆκεν ἰδέσθαι[60] (she made him larger to look at and mightier to see) and κὰδ δὲ κάρητος -- οὔλας ἧκε κόμας ὑακινθίνῳ ἄνθει ὁμοίας[61] (and down from his head she let thick hair flow like the bloom of a hyacinth). This also an orator must do. He must not always go out in a silken and costly garment, but often also in a worn, ordinary, and everyday suit.

Now that notice has been taken of adornment, we must bring things together and arrange them, get a store of words, and we ought to follow the counsel we have given you so that nothing is done or set in order without a reason and yet in a way that the general public does not perceive it. For as it is desirable to have our speech please all men, and as that should be our chief endeavor, so must we likewise guard mainly against having our art, imitation, and similitude become apparent.

So much now regarding composition and imitation concerning which it was decided not to cover everything, for example, how to translate from Greek to Latin and by which methods to change poetic verses into prose, so that it does not appear to have been a poem; also how one must comment upon and how one must begin and complete a declamation. All these things are properly undertaken only after we have had a great deal of practice in the things I have talked about. But regarding these another time. For the present this will suffice for your studies, especially since I am still with you. Therefore we ought again to return to this course from the beginning and come back to that broad reading and writing I spoke of. Reading is of two kinds, namely one kind that sets an example to imitate, the other for learning. Of these the first requires a longer span of time, so that whatever is latent in the example can be brought out. The other requires a rapid review, notetaking, and remembering a multitude of varied subjects. This must be done in the manner I presented at the beginning. There is then no doubt that all of Cicero can be read for understanding during the hours before noon within the period of three years. It is clear that very many things can be learned from him for imitation. The others that are left over we shall offer in the years to follow. As for the other authors, who would deny that more can be achieved from the ones I named before, such as orators, historians, philosophers, and poets, so that this triennium can provide us with beautiful speech and prudence in a variety of subjects? If now you achieve these two, you can serve as an example for the men of your rank. Indeed, after military virtue, which is a matter of knowledge and fortitude, what behooves a man of nobility more or agrees more with an ancient lineage than approved morals, a cultured mind, a wise tongue, a remembrance of all antiquity, and a knowledge of all public affairs? Were not Contarini, Bembo, and Sadoleto shining lights in the College of Cardinals? What a great ornament was the Bishop of Atrebat at the imperial court! Is not France honored by reason of Cardinal Du Bellay and now also Cardinal Guise and the Bishop of Mâcon? Is not Julius Pflug, my patron and host, an ornament of Saxony? What a great name and commendation Jakob Sturm and Christoph von Carlowitz achieved by virtue of their learning![62] All of these were great men of nobility. Nevertheless, their very nobility, illustrious enough in itself, was rendered even more renowned by their learning. If our Germany and the families of princely men were governed by such men, we would not have to fear any dangerous revolutions, barbarous custom, or any deformity of church and religion. Therefore in writing these things to you, I encourage all men of nobility in these studies which, though they behoove all classes of men, certainly are fit for men of nobility above all, who, the more they exceed other classes in glory, ought also to excel with more and greater virtues.

At The Press of Wendelius Rihelius, Strasbourg, 1549.

7
On the Education of Princes
(1551)

Introduction

The advice of intellectuals, the thinkers, to princes, the doers, is an old tradition dating from classical times, a major production during the late medieval and Renaissance periods, which continued into the Reformation era. You have here a piece of advice by the "Rector perpetuus" of the Strasbourg Gymnasium to Duke William of Cleves (1516–1592), whose wife was expecting and so we date this treatise to conform to the usual nine months in late 1551. The baby, however, turned out to be Princess Anna, a girl, but the ideas reflect the values of the age. Sturm was an advocate of classical culture and Ciceronian rhetoric, but wished to apply the wisdom of the ancient ages to the cultural problems of his age and of our own, for Sturm looked ahead to what lay ahead. Sturm was a Christian humanist with a religiosity which was not very consequential or effective. This treatise was very ecumenical, directed to a Catholic prince and in praise of a very excellent Catholic teacher, Conrad Heresbach.

This essay is in reality a tribute to Heresbach, another renowned educator of the sixteenth century. He attended the University of Cologne where in 1515 he became a Master of Arts, entered the juristic faculty, and later visited various French universities. In July 1521 he accepted a possession as professor of Greek at the University of Freiburg. He went on to Ferrara, a degree mill and favorite haunt of German students, and six months later received a doctorate in law. But alongside his legal courses he was involved in the theological questions of the day and went on to study Hebrew at the University of Padua. He then returned to the University of Freiburg, but soon accepted his first gainful employment as a tutor to the hereditary Prince of Cleves, who was a most enthusiastic admirer of Erasmus and his *Philosophia Christi*. In 1523 Heresbach began his work as a tutor to the young prince. With this background it is easier to understand Sturm's adulation for both Heresbach and the prince. Apart from teaching and tutoring, Heresbach gained recognition as a prolific publisher of significant classical and pedagogical writings, helping to establish a Renaissance tradition of learned excellence in the classroom still reflected in our contemporary academic culture: there is no logical distinction between good teaching and good research.

This treatise is merely ancillary to Sturm's basic essays on education, but it represents the specific application of his educational ideas to the ruling class, the aristocracy, an interesting application of ideas developed in an urban bourgeois setting. This treatise reflects Sturm's basic educational ideas and it was reprinted in eight editions by the year 1600 and was thought of as a "Golden Booklet" among the educational writings of the time.

Sturm reminds Duke William of Cleves of his tutor Conrad Heresbach and his classical studies. Duke William was a hero to humanists, including Erasmus, who dedicated two treatises on education to him. Sturm underlines the values represented by Heresbach, felicity, prudence, diligence, faith, erudition, religion, and moderation. For a prince the most important subject is history, the experience of rulers and peoples through the ages. The teacher is a "creator," for he molds the mind and character of the ruler. Consider the examples of Lysias and Epaminondas, Seneca and Nero, Scaevola and Marc Antony, Cassiodorus and Theodoric, Aristotle and Alexander.

The basic and very excellent book regarding the *De educatione principis* (1551) is that of Bruno Singer, *Die Fürstenspiegel in Deutschland im Zeitalter des Humanismus und der Reformation. Bibliographische Grundlagen und ausgewählte Interpretationen: Jakob Wimpfeling, Wolfgang Seidel, Johann Sturm, Urban Rieger* (München: Wilhelm Fink Verlag, 1981), reflected in this introduction. For Heresbach see the *Allgemeine Deutsche Biographie* (Leipzig: Verlag von Duncker & Humblot, 1880), XII, 103-105.

On the Education of Princes
(1551)

To the most illustrious Prince William, Duke of Jülich, Cleves, Count of Mark and Ravensberg, Lord in Rauenstein, Johann Sturm's *Most illustrious Prince.*

The most desirable thing in this life is the natural union of a good appearance with a healthy body. It is also a splendid thing to be most nobly born and a member of a very ancient family. And these good things are all the more excellent when mental acumen and talents are nature's gifts to those so born. But to be well taught, reared, and learned is very laudable, for without that, natural ability often tends to be unconscious, weakened, hindered, and produces nothing outstanding. Since the strength and form of your body declines with living, the praise of your origins would not greatly outlive you, except for the probity of your character and display of your mind's keenness, those two things we all love and admire in you.

However, these two attributes would be incapable of developing their potential without family training and discipline. In this very important matter your father, the very best of princes, and your very wise mother were splendid models. Your eyes see nothing, your ears hear nothing, and your mind knows nothing that is foreign to the virtue of great men, to the religion of Christians, to the trustworthiness and honesty of all men. Learned men believe that your good fortune is partly due to the fact that as a young adolescent you were entrusted to Conrad Heresbach for instruction. He is credited with prudence, diligence, optimism, learning, religion and moderation. When these six virtues are found in the teacher and preceptor, and are passed on by the parents, he can produce only what is noble and excellent.

It is wise to consider how great it is to be able to teach a prince's son whose parents want him to be their heir. The people expect that he will govern the state well, salutarily, moderately, wisely. Although people who are useful, honorable, worthy citizens of the fatherland are often born to families not in public life, how much more fitting is this teaching for noble families! If they preside with so much authority, esteem and honors, so should they outshine all others in learning, virtue, and morals.

Therefore, it is the business of the teacher and preceptor of morals to consider above all what a great task he has undertaken. He must take into consideration the expectations of the parents, of the fatherland, and of all good men as well as of the erudite. For it behooves all associations of literate people that noble families should be taught correctly and well so that the Aristotelian education given to philosophers, which so nourished Alexander, can be applied not only to a state governed by philosophers, but that the magistrates and the princes of the state and kings can be instructed and reared in those wise customs that human life and the nature of man require.

It is uncertain, therefore, which of the two has accomplished more in their lives! Aristotle, who instructed and refined, or Alexander, who inherited the supreme authority from his father Philip, and bore it with that knowledge which he received from Aristotle so that all envy of the father passed to the son. Although Greece had nothing to offer him at first, he so enlarged his father's authority that he was made the ruler of nearly all men and earned a glorious surname and was called Alexander the Great, not only because of his power and good fortune, but also because of his philosophical knowledge of ruling and governing. Aristotle did not undertake such labors and concerns for the sake of money or fame, which philosophers wholly spurn. Aristotle gave top priority to what he thought pertained to the wisdom and duty of a learned man. What a great thing personal discipline is, especially for rulers, when they are not only informed and taught by their parents but are also trusted by the people. Aristotle himself experienced similar care from Plato and he from Socrates, whose disciples they were, who well formed them in wisdom. Though they were commoners[1] they nevertheless because of their teaching increased the profits, praise and glory of the fatherland.

The first virtue, then, of the master or the teacher or preceptor is to dispose the mind to the magnitude of the task, so that he does his duty praiseworthily, which when well done will not fail.[2] As a second requirement we expect diligence, for without diligence nothing great and brilliant has been able to be accomplished. This diligence made Anthony, Crassus, Cicero and such orators what they were, those whom we read and recognize. This made Ulysses appear a rarity to Minerva,[3] as Sophocles expresses it:

> Always, oh son of Laertes, I see you
> Trying to forestall the treacheries of the enemies.

For diligence searches out everything most wisely and probes all hidden things and follows all the tracks of everything as when hunting, so that nothing is hidden from the learned or concealed by nature or hides somewhere carelessly neglected so that it is not examined.

But the teacher's diligence is divided into three parts. The first part is recognition of that which is already known; the second is speaking of what has been neglected; the third is reflection on how one can best instruct the pupil, so that with minimal labor and without difficulty he obtains whatever is necessary for him in terms of practice, wisdom, learning and life. For in our day what misfortune or rather misery was set before boys, how much that was not necessary, useless, bad, barbarous, ill assorted, without rhyme or reason.

Nevertheless, we have received from others good and even excellent things and have provided others ourselves. Careful management requires that these things be brought together and treated according to their nature, order, necessity, usefulness, method, facility, so that our provision (of speech) is not only copious, but suitable, diverse, well arranged, explained. Nevertheless we must retain these things so that the pupils learn them, for we do not read for ourselves, but for the students. All kinds of writings must be sampled, so that we preserve and prepare well that food which we feel to be healthful for young stomachs, so that when the time comes we shall serve it up well preserved and well cooked. When these two things have been done, discussion should follow as to how we should present this and in what order teach these things to others. Precautions should be made to include Faith, which should be valued for its usefulness and for the learner's growth. For there are many, not careful of their own students, whose energy is nevertheless expended on ostentation, which is wrong. It is quite right for us to require carefulness here. Therefore, whoever teaches others should be learning himself. He who seeks his own pleasure and not the advantage of others and he who seeks approval in the recollections of children by reciting Latin and Greek verses settles for a few hours' wages and does not wish for the rewards of those hidden riches and resources he alone wants to possess.

The fourth place we have given over to erudition, and the fifth to religion, although religion should have first place and erudition should be very close to that. But it has been my intention to set these things forth in this order. Therefore, this teacher must be wise and learned in the arts, and in many other disciplines, too, a wise and learned education so very different from the first kind I spoke of earlier; one which is universal and by artistic skill forms the centerpiece of every discourse. This is truly the wisdom of all learned men without which those first three virtues in the education of children cannot excel, except in the vulgar and plebeian. This is truly something singular, refined, and admirable. It is wont to emerge in men of genius.

Thus, the teacher of such a young prince should be like Conrad Heresbach was, or better yet, as he is now, with a perfected course of letters, the use of many teaching aids, consummate judgment, amiable gravity, grave gentleness, so that teaching should be seen not only to have attained perfection, but also an acceptable elegance of morals. For there is a ridiculous teaching in arrogance, pedantry, fastidiousness, levity. Moreover, it is possible that there can be learned people in whom the motions of the mind are of these kinds. For in every generation there are some who are inept such as the orators Erucius, Curtius, Mamercus;[4] poets such as Marcius, Zoilus,[5] and Charilius; senators such as Valgula, Asellius,[6] Mancius; and emperors and dukes such as Thersitas, Glaucius,[7]—whose crimes were not reviled so much as their ineptitude laughed at!

They, however, were usually amiably inept, as one reads of Scipio and Laelius.[8] For relaxation they were in the habit of collecting oyster and sea-shells for Caietas and Larentus. Concerning Archimedes, the most learned mathematician, it has been reported that he discovered in the bathtub how to calculate the amounts of pure gold a thief had taken from a total sum of gold. He leaped out of the water, ran home naked and cried aloud in Greek: Eureka! I have found it! In the same way we are able to bear the ineptitude of men and they at times serve useful purposes, as we shall soon demonstrate. But no one looks at the fastidious, the soothsayers, the arrogant, the brawlers, the peevish and finally, the inept, except to laugh, ridicule, or bewail the cause of letters.

For this reason we require of the teacher sound erudition, knowledge of many other great things, principally of antiquity and political science, without which only rarely have governors and men who are princes of Republics been able to exist. Plato derived so much learning and knowledge of things from the thought of Socrates that he committed the Republic to philosophers, something for which I nevertheless have little desire. For after Socrates there have been far too many inept philosophers. Antiquity held the knowledge of civics to be so important that when Numa Pompilius[9] understood little of political affairs, they gave him the nymph Egeria as an advisor and Homer gave Ulysses Minerva, by whom he was taught daily. Concerning antiquity and history there is no doubt but that they contain examples from all the republics of teaching and of life. Ulysses in place of histories, which in his time did not exist, learned about the flaws of many peoples' customs.

For he saw the customs of many men's cities according to Horace, which is the same reason Homer gave Nestor[10] three lifetimes which furnished him with the memory of so many great events.

We may give up fables because there is no history more ancient than that of Moses and none has more authority. The patriarchs learned in their long lives many useful, necessary, and remarkable things. But afterwards God shortened the life of sinful men to a brief span. He gave them historical writing to record their lifetime and that enduring experience by which humankind lives, and gave them Moses and the Prophets from whom mortals might also learn many things.

But if the memory of antiquity attaches to any kind of man it is to magistrates, kings and princes regnant. For them and their position it is necessary that they possess not only will and genius, but also the knowledge and recollection of examples to be deliberated, judged, provided or avoided in all the functions of their reign.

Therefore, the teacher who should educate the children of princes and especially instruct their young minds so that when they grow up to rule the Republic, wisdom and practice are seen to dwell in them as adults. As adults they should hold the histories of all periods, peoples and individuals of primary importance.

But in all these matters it is necessary to remember this, that I do not only recommend history, for there are many other excellent subjects to be learned. Nevertheless, history should be among the first subjects a youth should learn. The teacher, if he can, should know everything and from all he should select what is suitable for the age and abilities of the students, that which pertains to the plan of teaching, about which I shall speak later with moderation.

Now I shall write about a fifth subject, that of religion, which alone embraces all other virtues combined into one. For as soon as religion occupies the mind of someone, then all the other virtues suddenly burst out and necessarily pour forth. It is therefore clear that even if Stoical dogma should be obscure, nevertheless, it would be understood in religion. They said that if they have one virtue, they would not only pursue but actually have all of them.

Here I call religion piety and also the knowledge of the divinity that while this is partly an appendage to teaching, it is partly a singular virtue of man, lighting a fire of divine love in man. So just as some require that an orator be a good man, I require of a teacher that he be religious, not through some special profession in life, but according to the common duty of all Christians, desiring religion in all men, that they fear, love, venerate, implore, pray, supplicate God, and that without any false superstition, but with understanding. For there can be no true religion in the ignorance of God. This is why we desire such a preceptor for the young prince, from whose mouth he will draw as from a fountain the salubrious and heavenly waters of life.

For not only religion but also superstition is set with the deepest roots. Superstition permits itself to be taught less than religion, for it has often grown roots that cannot be torn out of the minds of men. God wished to teach us this in earnest with monstrous examples from many ages so that we would believe it to be true. Thus many nations have adored the sun and the moon and worthy human beings have been made gods and godlike with names such as Flora, Robigus, Lympha, Bonus Eventus.[11] For even animals have been held to be gods, by the Egyptians, for example. They had keenness of mind, opposite to that which then prevailed, and they claimed for themselves the invention of letters and the arts, so how could they root out the errors of those times and that monstrous superstition of their opinions, how could they stick by what they were clinging to?

Socrates, held to be the wisest man in all Greece, nevertheless was caught in these same errors concerning the gods and took his own demon to be the divine will. M. Varro[12] celebrated as the most learned—see what he prays for in the first of his books on agriculture: "I also beseech Lympha and Good Fortune." Is this anything else than words of a prayer of divinity? For this reason it can be concluded that he believed these gods existed. Because all agriculture, he says, is arid and miserable without water, for that reason Lympha must be worshipped as a god? Oh dialectician! Because, he says, without success and a good outcome there is frustration, not cultivation, is that proving a point or being silly? I can excuse Ajax for whipping cows,[13] in place of men, but I cannot pardon Varro for worshipping Lympha. For he was a great man in the state, well read, a good writer, a person of experience and practice who saw that the Egyptians were insane to worship the crocodile, but did not perceive that he himself was raving with his Lympha.

Such is the force of education, custom, and persuasion in falsehood that those with the keenest eyesight are blind, the wisest do not have a clue, the most acute show themselves fools. The Jews, because of these horrible errors, did not allow themselves to be led by the understanding of Moses, and hid from the prophets and from a suffering God. I also do not understand the Mohammedans who would rather err in a particular way of worshipping God than venerating vain gods. But how can we praise Numa Pompilius, though he was held to be most learned, holy, and knowledgeable about religions, he celebrated his Egeria and commended that vanity to his people? In this consummate king did not this base blemish inhere, so that it seems to us that his whole religion was vain?

And so I return to my Jews whom I shall seem to have left someplace in civic matters, because I excuse the worship of a vain and false divinity. They seem not to have been deprived of all sense of divinity when they predicted such great calamities and the ruination of the whole population, when they confessed how very long they would be chastised with these evils. But they could not open their eyes so that they could see, just as those who are oppressed by Ephialtes[14] perceive evil, but when it happens are not able fully to grasp it in a time of sleep.

The Jews have such great faith in their religion that if they can, and if some powerful, false and seditious Messiah would arise, they would yield to no men of any other religion, and believed the whole world was created and established just for them. They wiped out other mortals with fires and murder. And so, what is more, their true religion is not only grave and holy, but also false, hard, morose, stubborn and cruel.

What shall we say concerning the Turk? whose example can teach us only one thing, not to prove the truth of religion with good success, nor with the severity of discipline, nor with the advance of time. For how many years now have they ruled, held to their religion, and fought for their law? With what constant faith of the whole people and obedience to a tyrant, with what ceremonies and institutions, false indeed, fictional and foolish, but nevertheless harsh and rigid discipline? Moreover, with how great and of what sort of success? In a corner of the world one mass of people joined with an audacious man who now rules in Africa, occupies a large part of Europe, holds all of Asia in his rule and power. Moreover, he is called by our monarchs not Lord, but The Great Lord in the embassies. Would it be any wonder to believe that he succeeded his ancestors and that the rule over all peoples was given to those ancestors, as if into their hands, by God? So without a bad conscience he (i.e., the Turk) has for so many years conquered, harassed, slaughtered, and destroyed thousands of people.

It is so important that the prince who protects his religion be well instructed, not with the sword, but with that teaching, whatever it be, in which he was nourished. Always one should make provision so that nothing false, either the evil of the times, or the ignorance of men, or the fraud of the godless creeps in, especially since we can be instructed by the examples of the past and of its peoples. For what was more glorious for the Athenians than when the teaching of all disciplines flourished? What was more sacred to them than the founders of their state, Neptune and Minerva?[15] What could be greater for those persuaded that these were gods although they were only fictions and the vain names of an impious religion? This opinion that these two (Neptune, Minerva) were gods was as compelling to their wise men, mathematicians and philosophers who very diligently inquired as to how a circle can be squared, as the proposition that they must fight to protect them and the fatherland. But the squaring of the circle did not bring philosophy to a peak as the ax and hatchet, with which the round and circular trunk is easily squared, did for architecture.

The Athenians are greatly to be marveled at. For they were more ignorant in those things they believed they knew than in those which they confessed they did not know. They worshipped at a shrine to the unknown god; because they did not know Him, they named Him that. If the philosophers had inquired and found out that this One was called Jesus and given the cognomen Christ, or if the magistrates had realized the implications of their ancestors establishing a shrine without face, shape, and name, they would perhaps have been milder in their judgment of Socrates, who, when he followed his demon, was accused of worshipping new gods and thinking evil of the gods of the fathers.

I therefore pardon the magistrates of our times and of our religion who are severe in defending their religion. For if it is necessary to maintain religion with force, and if the Romans were able to do it for Jupiter Capitolinus and for the hero Romulus, if Athens for Minerva, if the Egyptians for a cat and a crocodile, why shouldn't a similar severity be maintained on behalf of the Christians' religion? For they have not only established themselves for fifteen hundred years, confirmed arguments and reasons, and explained miracles, but also acknowledged the precedents of the patriarchs and the pronouncements of the prophets set in motion so many centuries earlier. I truly forgive those magistrates, but with groaning and tears and a prayer that they will have better intellectual judgment.

If austerity were all that was required in religion, the greatest austerity was that of the Roman emperors; if multi-facetedness, then the Egyptians'; if honor, what more than the Roman religion, than the cushioned couches of the gods[16] at urban ceremonials? Constancy? What more constant than the Turkish religion? the King of Tunis? or the King of the Numidians, who is like Caesar? A host of celestial martyrs reveals that even in false religions there was reverence, constancy, and gravity for which spiritual beliefs martyrs were seized and put to torture. If, as we see, those who erred nevertheless agreed in their error, persuaded by their religion, why do we not hold our breath a little and consider that our savagery is displeasing to God or that the judges err, or that the theologians, or customs err, or that those who suffer punishments are more blessed than those who condemn?[17]

The magistrates and princes must think again and again who are they to lead the accused persons to flames and to tortures? For it is not the executioner's sword that glitters and slashes their necks, but the sword of the prince. It is not the executioner's hand that lights the funeral pyre and incites the flame, but the right hand of the prince. Just as the iniquitous judgment does not pertain to the lictors[18] and hangmen but to the magistrates, to whom, if they judge badly, the guilt must be charged in the celestial judgment.

Therefore the young prince should learn from this preceptor, on whom we rely, true religion, which he should protect with his sword, so that he not only governs his people, but is able to do it justly and piously. For ignorance does not excuse magistrates. Ignorance might excuse the King of the Numidians, the Persians, or the Turks. Not tradition, (which also deceives the Jews) and on which they sat for such a long time, as did the Greeks, as did the Greeks and Romans, both very ancient religions. Not that the Christian is not certain, but we demand not only the Christian religion, but that it be pure and uncorrupted. For us nothing must be more sincere than religion. But nothing is more easily corrupted by the addition of superstition. It is therefore the duty of good and learned men to battle against impious ceremonies and against false doctrine and to meet death and tortures for the sake of pure, sincere, and sound religion.

For it is not as in the republic of Plato and Aristotle that some bad laws are to be borne and tolerated, so that no perilous uprising occurs. Among Christian people one must reject irreligious ceremony and godless prayer and opinion against the precepts of Christ and of God. It is right to be faithful and just, even if the whole world collapses. So blessed are those truly heavenly spirits who in our time have suffered for the purity of religion, have poured out their blood and I do not know whether they have done it less bravely than the first martyrs of the church. For they suffered the same rule of judicial men for the belief that Christ is God's son and partakes of the same divinity as the Father.

Since this doctrine had been corrupted, and ceremonies vitiated, godless laws have entered the church. They believed it had to be reformed. It is the duty of the Christian prince to see to it that with these aims no bodily injury is done to them. It is necessary that he be well instructed from boyhood in the precepts of the Christian religion, so that he nurtures justice, defends religion, which is already very badly tarnished, and does not allow it to be stained.

8
Concerning the English Nobility
(1551)

Introduction

The day of April 4, 1550, marked the inception of a most remarkable epistolary exchange and friendship between Roger Ascham in England and Johann Sturm in Strasbourg. The theologian Martin Bucer, who had subscribed to the Wittenberg Concord with Martin Luther, was forced to flee as the Habsburg Catholic forces moved in on Strasbourg. He left for England and at the University of Cambridge became a spiritual counselor and father figure for Roger Ascham. Ascham for two years was tutor to Princess Elizabeth and the noted author of *The Scholemaster*, one of the two most noted English treatises on education in the sixteenth century. On that date Roger Ascham wrote his first letter to Sturm, in a most elegant Latin, discussing the interconnection of logic and rhetoric and the importance of eloquence for men of achievement. Ascham tells that he has read all that Sturm has published and written, even in manuscript. He urges Sturm to complete and publish his commentary on Aristotle's rhetoric, for Aristotle fails to provide examples by way of illustrating his abstract precepts.

Much of Ascham's letter displays the well-known and well-deserved inferiority complex of English intellectuals of that day compared with Continental, stridently asserting that the English are able to hold their own in classical studies. Ascham is quite confident about Cambridge, but fears that Oxford is in a state of decadence, so far as Greek and Latin studies are concerned. Like Sturm, who pumped up the *nobiles*, Ascham declares that the English aristocracy have a great zeal for learning, the king, the Brandons, the daughters of Thomas More, and Princess Elizabeth. Sturm was a busy administrator, but in the late summer he sent his response to Ascham via Bucer's wife, who was on her way to join her husband in Cambridge.

Sturm had Ascham's letter in praise of Princess Elizabeth and the English nobility published as an inspiration to the German nobility along with his own letter or treatise under the title *Epistolae Duae de*

Nobilitate Anglicana, along with Sturm's *De Educatione Princium* in Conrad Heresbach's *De laudibus Graecarum literarum oratio* (Strasbourg, 1551), presented here in translation.

The major work on Ascham is that of Lawrence V. Ryan, *Roger Ascham* (Stanford: Stanford University Press, 1963), especially pp. 116–118, *et passim* on Sturm. Ascham in *The Scholemaster* reflected Sturm's influence and he even named a son for Johann Sturm, who, however, died before his fifth birthday. The edition of Sturm's *De Nobilitate Anglicana* used here was made available by the Huntington Library, San Marino, California. Ascham's writings are to be found in an old edition done by the Rev. D. John Allen Giles, *The Whole Works of Roger Ascham, Now First Collected and Revised, with a Life of the Author* (London: John Russell Smith, Soho Square, 1865), the letter in Roman print, pp. 180–193. See also, Roger Ascham, *Letters of Roger Ascham* (New York: Peter Lang, 1989).

Concerning the English Nobility (1551)

Johann Sturm sends cordial greetings to Roger Ascham

See, my Ascham, what your letter has accomplished! In my little book which I composed *On the Periods of Orators*,[1] I have made a dedication to your Elizabeth so that, since she can reweave this most skillful and precious web of the orator, she may also make a judgment about this little work which was composed at night from fine as well as thick thread. For I suppose that the loom of Homer's Penelope correctly can be compared with the poets' lines and the orators' sentences—both of which not only ought to be compared but also should be taken apart, further transformed, and the stitches removed as often as they appear to warrant correction.

Certainly when it comes to youth and the feminine sex—girls especially, what can be more virtuous an occupation? What skill is more noble? What habit is more agreeable than the habit of writing and of composition and of making an oration that is pure, elegant, complete and accomplished? For this we struggle and strive. Since you are a learned and good man, and deserving of that glorious title "Evangelical" all of which does not merely appear but indeed shines forth in your letter, I think that in your letter there were no false additions to the virtue and praises of the young princess and of the royal line. But what more desirable occurrence can befall mortals than that from out of the princely families and from the nobility geniuses of both sexes arise to whom the study of letters is agreeable, who cherish them, who learn them thoroughly, and who follow the teaching of letters, of nature, and of the arts. Therefore, the English are more blessed in this kind of good men than are the Germans among whom there are very few of the nobility who think that the distinction of literary studies has anything to do with their class. Yet, there in England, very many men, all nobles, are either struggling to become learned in letters, or if they appreciate them too late, they think, nevertheless, that learning bears upon themselves and their families. For this reason there is ground for hope that Germany may strive assiduously to claim the praise that heretofore Italy always arrogated to itself (and after Italy, France). England then may claim abundant praise. Such a home as the masters of speech and of wisdom had at Athens and at Rome, two cities about which you write, is like that which has now been made in England, so that your people may even match the grace and glory of those whose virtues they imitate.

But to come around to you, my Ascham. I do not know whom to congratulate more: you to whom God has given such a student or Princess Elizabeth to whom He gave such a teacher and artist. Assuredly I congratulate you both and rejoice and judge those two years fortunate when you taught her and she learned. Now I also am happy about your leisure which King Edward has kindly and graciously and generously granted to you. For the methods of our studies require active leisure and leisurable activity. To the public we seem to be at leisure when we are at work, and we seem to be working when we are at leisure. Other men, when they are hunting, fishing, or building, seem to be busy with work. Scholars, when they read, write, or discuss, are regarded as unemployed. Although scholars are engaged upon a life that involves anxiety and worry in their work, it is not from fear of dangers or from vexation at work, but from taking up and meditating upon the most important spiritual subjects. But since the highest leisure has been granted you, the most delightful and abundant fruit will come to me, for you promise me in your letter, many and frequent letters. These I eagerly await, not only because of your affection for me, but also particularly because of my teaching and the two arts in which I, for many years, have been concerned: the art of disputation and the art of speaking. Both of us wish to be dialecticians and rhetoricians. You are indeed, but I struggle and strive to be. Undoubtedly, without the resource of eloquence, the profession of the dialectician is unintelligible and base. This same eloquence without the art of disputation is puffed up and swollen, wanders aimlessly, and accomplishes nothing by method or reason and nothing skillfully. Thus your judgment and mine are the same. We want the same thing, follow the same thing, strive for the same thing. Indeed the same thing must be undertaken by all who desire to live a life of letters and to acquire praise through learning.

But let me return to your letter. It was a great delight to me both on account of the expression of your good will toward me and then because it reported many details about your kingdom which has for many ages been considered always most noble and well defended. It reported about the king from whom the hope for religion, mercy, and prudence is seen as clear and certain; about William Paget with whose excellence and restraint of judgment and courteousness I became thoroughly acquainted five years ago at Caletus; about Cheke and Smith of whom many have made mention to me; about John Mason whom our Montius salutes with great good will, and often praises to me as often as I remember Paget; about Haddon your vice-chancellor whom you compare with your superiors; about your nobility and those who set forth to France with your three envoys; finally about Princess Elizabeth, a subject on which your treatment was more extensive than on the rest and on which I needed more details for my reading. This all, I say, has been very delightful. But where you attribute to me so much that I could by no means acknowledge it, there you "strike shame" into me, to use Horace's words,[2] because I cannot excel in knowledge and judgment such as you have attributed to me. But when you ask me to translate into Latin and explicate the *Phaedo* of Plato and the books of Aristotle *On the Soul*[3] and Aristotle's rhetorical works and similarly to translate the rival orations of Demosthenes and Aeschines,[4] to publish about the method of eloquence and oratory in Latin, I shrink—not so much from the work which must be undertaken as from the presumption in undertaking the work and the suspicion of temerity and arrogance in publishing. This calls me back to active duty, as it were, in the program that I entered upon last year. For I decided to explicate Aristotle's books on rhetoric with a continuous dialogue among men of differing opinions and I have given a part of this work to a copyist. But I have changed my mind. First, for the reason that I have already proposed, and next because certain other things kept interrupting, which discouraged me from what I had begun. Nevertheless, I am thinking of resuming them this winter and completing what has been begun, if life and God will grant the power. I am translating the orations of Aeschines and Demosthenes for my students, but in such a way that I am busier explaining them than I am translating them. It satisfies me if I explain the meaning[5] and the significance and force of the words.[6] The rest of the task is taken up with showing the artistry so that they may understand constructing arguments,[7] so that they may examine divisions and partitions, also arrangement, types of arguments, forms of conclusions, the embellishment of sentences, the ornamentation of general questions, proof by elimination of specific cases, enlarging upon both, and in every case, types of periods, and the sequence and rhythms of the beginning, middle, and final parts of periodic sentences.

You ought to be content with having doubled my winter's work—both you and Bucer who, it seems, has been encouraging you! As for the *Phaedo* and Aristotle's books *On the Soul*, some other time—when there is leisure and if I live long enough and shall still be able. Whether or not I have noted in the *Gorgias*[8] certain topics that have to do with the school of dialecticians, I can indeed in the *Phaedo* work out something that makes a continuous speech and which does not bother the mind and ears of learned men. And whether or not I understand rhetoric and can perhaps in some measure bring forth books into the light, I shall be able, by arguing and by writing, to maintain that most important debate about life, about death, about the immortality of souls, about how good men approach death, about the eternal rewards of distinguished men, and about the eternity of nature.

Nevertheless, you have quite unnerved me by the fact that you ask me for books about the Latin language. I promised them some few years ago, but I clearly confess that even if I had the talent, nevertheless, I could not in terms of opportunity, as Bucer has often heard from me. How much midnight oil work of this sort burns, for how brief a time, after comprehending the precepts, you get the opportunity to grasp something by thinking and to be able to express this in Latin in a speech, so that it is not only pure but elegant, ornate, and graceful and so that you have examples ready and what subjects there are and by what embellishments of words and sentences they are to be polished, and that you have these all not only brought together, but also divided by topics and arranged in order. Although I have such a work, only begun in its design, but explained and thoroughly thought out in its argument, nevertheless, because of the lack of means, I let it lie with other works unfinished until I am rebuked. Though if our gymnasium rebukes me sufficiently, yet, since it may rebuke me, but does not force me, I think that I will do enough for men, if I am not indolent in the rest of my duties.

Now, to turn to what you are writing about Augustine: I praise your judgment and in this section of your letter I am delighted by your humanity and love. I really regard this theologian most highly above the others because of his learning. He teaches everything. He draws conclusions accurately. He refutes subtly without making errors in stating premises, in classification, in argumentation or in his solutions. But, when I exhort my students to the stylistic ornamentation of a speech, not only do I take into account the teaching of content, but also its embellishment and treatment. As a result I think that those men of old[9] were better in speaking, but that Augustine was better in learning, although they too were learned and must be esteemed as learned and liberally educated.

For indeed, even in teaching Latin and Greek, one must be on guard diligently not to place writers inferior in speaking ahead of Cicero and Demosthenes and other better writers because of their treatment of the subject matter. The very name of knowledge and wisdom is pleasing and agreeable to everybody. But the subject matter itself is not only most desirable but very advantageous as well. For no one can write anything, no one can speak or say what is excellent who has acquired the skills and discipline but has not acquired knowledge of subject matter. Therefore, a man who is endowed with this judgment and depends on meager resources, should, I think, not be considered in the ranks of the eloquent, or of the fluent Latin orators or writers or artists. His speech is merely inflated verbiage. I think he is not only inept as an author but also stupid as a man.

Therefore, even if a most preeminent man, such as Longolius, Sadoleto, Bembo, Naugerius or anyone else, whether he is Italian, French, or German, has striven after words and their embellishment, but has neglected subject matter—which, however, these men did least of all—even if he were someone, I do not judge him praiseworthy. For what shall I say about Budé, a man of excellent learning? Nevertheless we love him and defend him and admire him, just as those whom I have named. Nevertheless there are some to whom he in some books seems to strive after words more than substance. Therefore I think that the man who believes that the embellishment of an oration is based upon words, not content, must not be placed among the best writers or orators, but among the worst. But this must be the prime consideration so that one may not choose whatever one wishes at all times: whether there is some distinction in times, ages, and abilities. The Greeks proposed that Homer should be taught to their adolescents. This could be done without trouble because at the same time almost with their mothers' milk the boys drank in their native speech. The Roman grammarians taught Vergil in their schools. No problems resulted from this for the same reason. Similarly, the Romans translated Homer from the start. It was not unsuitable in a foreign language and Latin was the language spoken then by all the citizens of Rome. The Greeks could do the same, if this language had been pleasing to them.

But what use to the formation of the language and to its purity will a boy derive from Cato's distichs, from Aquinas, Gerson, or Cocca? I have named but a few. Besides these, very many others can be considered to be from the same flock and are more outstanding than others. Yet, I am not willing for them to be read, not because I censure them, but because they are not suitable for what we intend. But let us add also to these the barbarous crowd of grammarians, dialecticians, medical doctors, theologians and philosophers to whom shabby usage has been preferable to pure, and crabbed usage to practical.[10] A great part of this is preserved up to now in the colleges of sophists of our century. This part fights savagely for its barbarity as though for another Palladium.[11] What a graceful flock! What religious harmony[12] in which it is glorious to be conquered and most disgraceful to conquer! What can the state of affairs of learning and of religion be in such ugliness of speech, language, and rhetoric! Who among them will not be despised if one should perceive the sound of their speech, the deformity of their words, the baseness of their sentences, the ineptitude of their opinions, the obstinacy of their minds, their unworthy usage and their foreign ways? They have imposed barbarity on the noble disposition. They have corrupted the arts and disciplines. They have sullied histories, religion, and ceremonies not only with their rotted kind of speech but also with their ignorant opinions that are removed from all consensus concerning doctrine that they have made unintelligible by their squabbling and have defiled by defending.

Are these men to be placed before boys and are the minds of youths to be imbued with their writings so that in our city-states crude ideas are heard instead of pure, barbarities for Latin, obscurities for clarity, and disconnected for ordered thoughts? Because we are making decisions in bad times, why not retain the same course of study even in its less perfect and less complete form?

But the study of language (*studium verborum*) has always been held to be the more important of subjects. Clearly the obligation to be eloquent is the first subject to take up after the study of language. For it is a mistake to speak what is either inane or stupid. Nevertheless, seeing that both wisdom and elegant speech are required from orators, let us separate these two that cling together, each joined to the other by its nature. Wisdom demands that what you say must be true, or probable, or certain, or insightful, or teachable, or complete in form. Why should it be elegant (*ornatus*)? So as to be meaningful, sonorous, full, harmonious, decorative, and clear. But if wisdom should demand that I have no reason for embellishment, then I am perfectly content with purity of style and would not affect further ornamentation. I would let myself be free of a great amount of work, of immense cares and vigils of long duration. If however it should demand that I neglect purity of style, certainly I would never comply with that kind of wisdom, however foresighted it might be.

But if one were to respond that it is important and thoughtful in terms of teaching—indeed also excellent for it—to combine eloquence and a method of speaking and to teach both of these from among the best authors rather than from authors of lesser rank and that these tasks are best taken up with consummate authors, then I shall follow the advice of wisdom like a divinely given oracle. Those authors, therefore, which I wish to have explicated to boys first and to be read first in practice and drill are those who have combined eloquence with learning and not those who are content with learning, or despise eloquence or have not been able to aspire to it. The nearer any author gets to perfection, the more it is agreed that he excels in style and arrangement[13] and is preferred for examples.

The following question has bothered me: Why have I preferred Chrysostom to Augustine? Not because Augustine is not wiser or not so skilled in speaking as Chrysostom, but because he is less skilled in speaking than Chrysostom and nevertheless is learned and erudite. I have accorded to Chrysostom first place for his style and his language[14] but not for learning and genius, although I prefer many others to this very Chrysostom. For in the pursuit of speaking one ought to avoid barbarities and always to prefer better speakers to good ones.

Perhaps I shall seem to trust too little in your brilliance, I who plead this case so anxiously. Nonetheless, because I think it is of great importance to decide in what sequence each author may be read, it has seemed best here to explain to you my opinion to which I think you are not hostile. I did all this more freely because you say in your letter that the name of peace is sweet and that the subject itself is salutary. I know the passage where Cicero says the same and expresses it in the same words. I have tried to express the form of his passage so as to play a game of rhetoricians with you.[15] Unless you take care, I shall jest again with an example taken from not far away from here, before I repeat what I wish about Princess Elizabeth and why I wish it. For I cannot forget that she also united the arts of speaking with the learning of the important subjects on which you write. She cultivates this training that especially graces her sex but which nevertheless lies spurned by all. But she thinks correctly for herself. For if the shape of a young maiden's body is pleasing, why shouldn't her speech be modest, chaste, pure, and beautiful? The other tasks of maidens, spinning, weaving, or embroidery, are common to the nobility and to ordinary families, and often we see women of low birth performing them with more artistry than noble women. We see however that elegance of speech wishes to live in the homes of nobility and with excellent families and just as with clothing and ornaments, so too with the charm of speech, noblemen are distinguished from commoners. Besides these very things such as expensive clothing, gems, rings, and the other ornaments are only a matter of fortune and often abound in inferior natures. Elegance of speech and beauty of language cannot be separated from the beauty of the mind and this is the mark of excelling talent and of a noble nature, while the conspicuous signs and ornaments of riches at home are merely adornments. Speech truly requires artistry and after it has once been heard, often flies to foreign peoples and nations and is deemed by them to be worthy of admiration. All the more reason then that I approve of Princess Elizabeth's industry. She will bring it to pass that the nobility of unmarried girls and women is to be valued not only for the antiquity of their family but also for the elegance of their learning and speech.

Therefore, I have appropriately sent her this little book. In publishing books, it is absurd to address those who are ignorant of what is written or who do not greatly love the same subjects. Since a book cannot speak freely for itself, since it is inarticulate, please be the intercessor with her as often as it will err and please be the recommender where it does not err. In each case please be the patron especially to King Edward, to whom I am also sending a copy, so that it will be protected with a threefold patronage: first, yours to Princess Elizabeth and next hers, to her brother Edward. If he wishes, on his own authority, to be the highest patron, who could be more propitious for my little book? As for me, I very much wish to please England, for I love the people for their religion and on account of the fame of such a great king in our time. I hope that the king may be able to guard, defend, and keep firm the religion that he learned in his early years and the council he has established with harmonious opinions, so that he may not be attacked. To be sure, this pertains to God and His providence and His will. Indeed it remains that what could not be established without disturbance, cannot be kept without fear of perils. It cannot be corrected and embellished by the dispensations of ecclesiastical monies and by the discipline of morals, the teaching of religion, by the sanctity of the courts, and by the confirmation and dignity of the orders. But now there is less fear, thanks to the constancy of the council which has made it firm through edicts. Moreover, that it may endure as long as the kingdom and religion require it and that the king may not be injured by any outrageous behavior must be prayed for with the most sincere prayers to God the Father of all mortals and to Christ, the Savior of all men. In this matter also those who are involved in the royal council must be praised. The king must be encouraged toward constancy and magnanimity so that the council may not repent its decree and the king may weary of the perils which seem to threaten. Therefore, not only must praise for piety, religion, and learning be given to those who were the authors of such an excellent improvement, but also for the courage of those who did not fear those perils which, thanks to prudence, they foresaw were about to come, but because of religion they condemned.

O Sacred Council, which has placed honesty and religion ahead of practical matters and the life of ease. Men seem to have been born there so that they might renew the name of England and so that in this kingdom the cornerstone of the church may again take its proper place and be a refuge not only for those who must be taken in and protected, but also in short order must be sent forth and ordained as angels and messengers of peace, of learning, and of dignity in the Christian republic. In regard to impiety, the status of republics is unstable, but in religion a firm status is usually hoped for. Indeed no change of governments is to be feared except after contempt and disrespect for religion. A republic of men who in the disgracefulness of their life fear the purity and holiness of religion and learning is an unstable republic. But those who uphold, foster and defend them can change the republic into no other status except the divine and heavenly status in which lies perpetual and eternal happiness. For in this life, not only kings and princes and magistrates are transitory and short-lived, but even cities themselves and republics and kingdoms flourish and are illustrious but for a moment and then are perceived as fallen to ruins and demolished.

Is not this blessedness of eternity the appointed goal of good men in all ranks of life? Their rewards have been founded in this blessedness. Were they not, what wise man would wish to devote himself to the hardest labors and highest perils for his country and seek death for his religion? Therefore, very prudent men have wisely consulted one another. They have recovered that without which no republic can be stable and which they ought to hope for posterity. They themselves achieved this at their own peril and with peril they preferred to accept the responsibility for the religion and piety of the fatherland rather than to hand it on to posterity without risk. This praise is more admirable than any triumph whatsoever and is not comparable to the slaughter of enemies. It shines with piety and religion. It has required not the blood of enemies but the piety of its own citizens. It has not strived for revolutions, but has restored what was lost.

Afterwards there was the decree concerning religion. Peace with the kingdom of France was established, laws of morals and of life were promulgated. The secondary schools (*gymnasia*) of men of letters were improved. The light of truth and the illumination of the Gospels have once again reappeared. The words of good men will never be silent about these as long as there will be men for whom religion is precious and for whom the memory of brave men is pleasant. Although the praise for this deed, or rather for its wisdom, belongs for by far the most part to his most serene majesty King Edward, if the parliament had not taken heed at one and the same time to support his prudence, to increase his dignity, confirm his desire and zeal for religion, and seek and demand the same thing, he would have undertaken with greater peril what he has established and decreed. Therefore, all the ranks of the kingdom must be congratulated: the king, because he obtained what he wished with the assenting opinions of all in the council; the council, because it wished the same thing as the king and it knew that nothing more holy could be achieved; the people, because, since the authority of the king and the senate interceded, it seemed enacted by the voice of the Republic, not by a popular uprising, it being the case that the nobler part of the people longed for it. All ranks must be congratulated because in this meeting of minds there was no apathy to be dreaded, but peace and harmony flourished again and true religion is again cherished. May the voice of the Gospel sound forth vigorously and the rule of Christ have the highest authority in England.

This advantage, indeed, this glory of the kingdom should remove fear from the minds of all and should arouse the king up to increase this glory and to exhort the parliament to courage and to arouse the people to charity and respect so that the authority of the king, the advice of the parliament and the opinions of the people may stand as a bulwark against deceit, snares and the power of the common enemy of God by whom we cannot be conquered so long as we remain constant. For if we must die, mortal life will be exchanged with the immortal. If we shall live, what is more excellent than to bring back the heavenly life into this life on account of religion?

I have been carried away longer, my Ascham, than I was intending. I was animated by your letter in which it was more pleasing to me to learn the praises of the king and his sister even though I had heard them before from many others, than to accept Gaius Caesar whom I had not seen before like this on coins. Nevertheless, the gift was pleasing since it was sent by you and was ancient and because his portrait can be compared with the most brave, most skilled, and most fortunate emperors in the glory of war.

Farewell. At Strasbourg. September 9, 1550.

9
For the Lauingen School
(1565)

Introduction

By the mid-sixties other and more strident voices were being heard regarding educational planning and the education of the young. Johann Marbach, for example, an orthodox Lutheran educated in Wittenberg, developed a plan for the Hornbach Gymnasium in 1558 that called for the students to spend their final two years at the Strasbourg Gymnasium. By then a controversy naturally had developed regarding Sturm's Academy and curriculum. Given his often self-induced difficulties at home, it is remarkable that Sturm continued to be taken so seriously in other parts of the Empire as the premier educator at an exemplary institution of learning. Sturm offered his advice and provided plans for a great many reformed and humanistic schools, but the most elaborate of these was the very thorough and detailed organizational and curricular plan for the Gymnasium in Lauingen on the Danube in the principality of Pfalz-Neuburg. The Count of the Palatinate Wolfgang, who since 1559 was also ruler of Pfalz-Neuburg, planned the school as a Protestant counterweight to the university of the Bishop of Augsburg in Dillingen. In 1562 he could begin classes at Lauingen. In 1564 the Count Palatine invited Johann Sturm to work out the organization of the school in Lauingen, about the same time as the Jesuits were arriving in Dillingen. This development was not unrelated to the experience the Count Palatine Wolfgang had benefited from with the founding of the academy in Hornbach. Sturm came to Lauingen in 1564 and with the help of local teachers worked out statutes for the school that naturally reflected the decades long experience of the Strasbourg Academy. In 1565 Sturm published the plan of studies under the title *Scholae Lauinganae*, which largely repeated his well-known pedagogical principles. Sturm hoped that the educational model he had developed would continue to serve as a pattern for educational institutions in the future, as indeed it did into the present century. A humanistic gymnasium continues to flourish in Lauingen, with a new set of buildings and under new auspices, to this very day.

For the nearly definitive account of the gymnasia of Hornbach and Lauingen, see Anton Schindling, *Humanistische Hochschule und Freie Reichsstadt: Gymnasium und Akademie in Strassburg, 1538–1621*, pp. 34–44. For the text, available in both the Stanford University and in the Concordia Seminary, St. Louis, libraries, see Reinhold Vorbaum, *Die evangelischen Schulordnungen des sechzehnten Jahrhunderts* (Gütersloh: Druck und Verlag von C. Bertelsmann, 1860), pp. 723–745. See also K. Reissinger, *Dokumente zur Geschichte der humanistischen Schulen im Gebiet der Bayerischen Pfalz*, 2 vols., *Monumenta Germaniae Paedagogica*, vols. 47 and 49 (Berlin, 1910 and 1911), vol. II, pp. 51–96. Lauingen's most famous son was Albertus Magnus, b. 1193, who with his brother Heinrich, joined the Dominican order, and was active in the monasteries of Cologne, Hildesheim, Freiburg, Regensburg and Strasbourg. His association as teacher and brother to Thomas Aquinas in Paris and Cologne is well known. The gymnasium to which Johann Sturm addressed his advice naturally changed in character with the subsequent militarily induced recatholization of Lauingen, the proud ducal city on the Danube. Two items of special relevance and interest are Matthias Simon, *Evangelische Kirchengeschichte Bayerns* (Nuremberg: Selbstverlag des Verfassers, 1952) and, a little something in English, Claus-Peter Clasen, "The Anabaptists at Lauingen: A Forgotten Congregation," *Mennonite Quarterly Review*, 42, no. 2 (April, 1968), pp. 144–48.

For the Lauingen School
(1565)

To the princes of the most illustrious family of the Rhenish Palatinate, dukes of Bavaria, and counts of Welden: Lord Philipp Ludwig and Lord John, most famous sons of Duke Wolfgang, the preface of Johann Sturm.

When in the month of December I was in Neuburg in Bavaria, you proved to us your industry and the faithfulness and the diligence of your preceptor Peter Agricola. I admired you for so many things and so many different things. You were able to respond from memory, and that in such a circle and assembly of learned men. For you knew the grammatical precepts of the Latins and the Greeks, together with individual examples. I perceived that I could propose no Latin writing to you that you were not able to interpret correctly. Concerning religion and its principles you responded in such a way that I do not know whether your memory or piety itself and religious feeling should be admired more. You recalled so well current history and the memory of antiquity from the beginning of the world up to our age and the last emperor, that at no place did your memory falter. What shall I say concerning the rules of dialectic and rhetoric? In these things I perceived that nothing essential was unknown to you. What of arithmetic, concerning which you responded in the morning hours? What of the following day, when what was proposed to you in German apparel, you suddenly returned with a Roman garment, ornate and like a toga. What of the French language which you read, interpreted, and unexpectedly wrote?

I wonder, then, how it is that two brothers, youths, dukes of Bavaria, in the presence of their father and mother (whose great love is wont to indulge their children in such a way and in such a court in the neighing of horses and hunting of hounds, the clashing of arms, even in the arena of gladiators) at the same time can do all things: to ride horseback, to hunt, to contend with a gladiator and never to surrender to him, and nevertheless can understand such great things in the curriculum of letters. Thinking about these things I perceived two other good qualities that are part of your nature and genius and partly pertain to faith and service of your teacher, Agricola.

I attribute first place in these advances of yours to a father's care and concern for your education. For I remember that when I was a

youth, nothing held me to the study of letters and the duty of persever-
ance more than the hope and expectation of my father, Wilhelm Sturm,
and the daily prayers of my mother. I believe you have the same sense
of paternal love and piety that I had and that you sensed the secret joy
of your own father, which hidden tears did not betray. So when you
were asked about so many and such great things, you responded in
such a manner that those who were present approved of and admired
your industry. And they acknowledged and praised the faithfulness and
diligence of the preceptor. The will, hope, and expectation of the father
has great force in a youth endowed with excellent morals. It is very necessary that what with the daily signs and prayers of the parents is hoped
for, can be seen in the children. Not only in these prayers of the father
are you able to see how many advantages the teaching of letters brings,
but also in the establishing of the schools of Lauingen. For, not content
with the Hornbach gymnasium, which demands great expenditures
every day, and increases expenditure still further, to the arts of discourse, to teachers of grammar, dialectic and rhetoric, he adds as well
theologians, jurisconsults, natural philosophers, and mathematicians.

Should I speak of this, your father's liberality as piety? Certainly I
even dare to compare both piety and liberality with military virtue, or
prefer them to the bravery of famous men. For why should I not do this?
With Charles the Great we see the glory of battles that he waged in Gaul,
Aquitaine, Italy, Spain, Saxony, Sarmatia, and Pannonia, among foreign
peoples and nations both on land and sea. The future would have been
less brilliant if it had not been illuminated by the study of religion and
the patronage of letters. He himself was similarly both learned and
devoted to the refinement of education and taste, so that he could recall
the language of the forefathers to the rules of the grammarians. He
offered great rewards to learned men. He wished to have Alberus, the
Englishman, an erudite man, be with him and he did not leave him, but
after some years became more erudite than his tutor. He sent Albinus,
the Scot, a man of letters, to Insubria (in the neighborhood of Milan)
and preferred him to the play of letters of Ticinus. He sent Clement the
Scot, equal to Albinus, also very learned, to Paris. He endowed stipends
for youths and founded a college, which admitted children other than
those of noblemen, for he truly wished that students be chosen also
from the common people who were not sons of the wealthy. He was so
pleased that he wished to be present at the examination of those youths.
For not only the information of the preceptors was tested in them, but
truly also practical application, which was tested either with an unexpected piece of writing, or with a surprise declamation, a thought-out
oration, or the composition of verses, of which the Emperor himself was

able to explain the meaning. And he spoke, if what the historians relate is true:

In the testing of Paris, how great is the honest praise of poor youths? Arise, o youths, continue as you began, to receive the greatest rewards of your industry, you who have followed my authority. I shall choose bishops from among you and shall appoint high priests from your midst. This honor shall be given as you are gathered here at my right hand and seen by all. How much severity, truly, is in this condemnation of nobility? I shall make an example for you of my severity and of your idleness, youths truly anointed for war and pleasure, who strive for the riches of your parents, believe firmly in nobility, and despise the authority of your Caesar and the majesty of the Emperor. These poor and needy shall be placed before you in honors and also preferred to you in rewards. I call God as my witness that there can be no return for you to honors and no rewards extended to you before you come back to the path of virtue, diligence, and respect.

Who would not compare this discipline of the schools with the fortified camps of the Emperor himself? For the discipline of soldiers often disappears with the soldiers themselves and with emperors; but at schools and gymnasia, and at schools of letters, once good instructional discipline has been established, it is set up once and for all. As long as their usefulness is felt and perceived, so long will the recorded tradition of learned men who have gone forth from schools of this kind exist. That one emperor had so many and such great virtues must be admired, but one must admire especially the fact that he did not consider deeds and arms to be sufficient glory, limited only to an armed camp unless he also armed men in the colleges of the learned against barbarity and bad morals. He armed them, I say, with laws, morals, precepts, arts, doctrines, disciplines, with rewards and honors. For this purpose letters are preferable to arms, because from the discipline of arms no one can know the arts and learned disciplines, but truly from the monuments of letters many famous leaders and emperors have arisen. An excellent emperor for whom in all honesty nothing was enough! For he was not content with this or that college of his prefect Clement, but he also called Waldo from Swabia, a man of outstanding reputation, as is worthy of belief, and made him superintendent for the college, one which lay on the plain of St. Denis, which was a journey of two hours from the

city of Paris, either because he wished them to be nearer to those Diony-
sians in Paris, or because he thought it was too remote and that those
schools should not be separated by the hours of the day. And he
selected twelve Augustinians or Jeromians according to the number of
provinces which, having been captured in war, were subject to the
Frankish imperium. And if God willed that his wish would be fulfilled
in those times, what else do you think would have been done than that
he would found schools in the provinces for each famous governor?

I recommend similar counsel to the very courageous and brilliant
prince, your father, who founded at Hornbach that college of masters
and students situated on this side of the Rhine. So he has added this one
at Lauingen on the Danube of better construction, more expensive, and
more richly provided for students and masters. Consequently, this will
shine forth as a brilliant jewel in the heart of Aaron among the virtues
of your father. This I was allowed by the councils and I adorned it both
with teachers and doctors and prescribed the authors. I intend to make
known the principle of teaching which the preceptor of the arts should
follow. There can be no doubt that within a few years the youths will
have made incredible progress. And although our schools in Strasbourg
have been built with these same foundations of the preceptors, nay
rather, these of Lauingen have been derived from them, nevertheless
these foundations of yours, which I am sending you now, have certain
fountains gushing forth that I shall divert from yours to our meadows in
opposite parts, so that each gymnasium may seem to arise, the one from
the other, and to stand at the very beginnings.

But I do not wish this to be praise only of the father, although it
would be appropriate for him. I wish to add you to this glorious inheritance and to surround that which has been established with authority
and stands till now safe and sound with the father. Consider that these
matters are not only his concern but yours also. With your father present
you can profess yourselves openly as helpers, while God grants to your
father and to you to see this light. Eberhard the First, Prince of Württemberg, the first of his family to be called a duke, received that most illustrious title of great dignity from the emperor, dignified because he had
indeed founded the college of arts and the academy at Tübingen, and
added to the claim of dignity the testimony of piety, religion, and
humanity as well. These are adorned in the highest degree with learning. Therefore, if anyone calls him most illustrious Prince and most venerable Duke, he will be addressing him aptly. It is truly worthy of the
very highest praise that children, heirs, and nephews perpetuate this
paternal and ancestral praise. Nothing about Duke Ulrich pleases me
more than that because of the constancy of his councilors, he also

shows this benignity to human beings who received his patrimony. Of his own free will he from the very beginning summoned learned men to himself—Philipp Melanchthon, Ambrose Blaurer, Erhard Schnepff, Simon Grynaeus, Joachim Camerarius—and by their counsel established this college with regulations and stipends so that it seems to yield in will and desire neither to the Academy of Plato, the Lyceum of Aristotle, nor the Stoa of Zeno. This paternal and ancestral praise the most illustrious prince, Duke Christopher, so enlarged with benevolence, devotion, and liberality that the name of the father seems to detract from Eberhard, the grandfather, so that he should really be called the father of this academy. I exhort you by that done by this prince so that in what the father prudently and praiseworthily has established, you become your father's helpers, so that it is secured by him, while he still lives, and by you. And truly for that reason I have given you these praises for industry and diligence, as we judged them at Neuburg, so that you will always want them to be yours, you being determined to be constant in all these things that were admirably established by your father, a most illustrious man and a very brave prince. First, therefore, I certainly commend the schools themselves to your authority and benevolence, and next, the teachers whom your father has chosen: Simon Ostermann, director of the gymnasium and capable rector, a man well approved for his judgment, counsel, diligence, seriousness, teaching, and memory; Celestin the theologian, a defender of the true and ancient teaching of Martin Luther, erudite in Greek letters and not at all uncultivated in Hebrew, and a man diligent with regard to the written memorials of the fathers; also, Cyprian Leovitius, mathematician, who has grasped all the loftiest principles in this discipline, but of whom many greater things must be expected; Martin Roland, physician, a natural philosopher at this lyceum of yours, for whose diligence, teaching, industry, and modesty I give testimony; and I give freely and I give true testimony, and I commit them to your care. And I recommend all the others to you whom you have and those whom you will add to them, the reverend and brilliant man, Doctor Johannes Sebastian Pfauser, imperial orator and the superintendent of the churches in the province of Lauingen; and Conrad Laetus, jurisconsult, an eloquent man, your father's counselor, a most illustrious prince (who are not a very small part of this gymnasium and do not need my recommendation, since their virtue, teaching and worth in the republic easily recommend them to you).

But what need do you have for me to exhort you? You have Peter Agricola who has a heart of delightful sincerity, diligence, zeal, industry and learning as another parent in this life; surely the tutor of that humanity that is in you, of the intelligence, knowledge, memory, the excellence of which virtues you proved to us when we were in Neuburg. But it is now time that we say something about these schools, how they ought to be distinguished for buildings and for teachers, what plan of teaching ought to be established, which authors should be explained, what should be the preceptors in teaching and of students in learning, and, lastly, what kinds of exercises should be arranged for in this gymnasium.

* * * * *

[There follow then dedicatory poems by John Frederick Celestinus, M. Wenceslaus Caldenstein, Martinus Rulandus Frising, and two citations from Charlemagne and Louis the Pious on the founding of schools.]

Schools of Lauingen

Schools of philosophers are the best and most beautiful arsenals of the republic. Philosophy is the study of wisdom, of which religion is the most excellent part. All human beings should be desirous of religion and for it if they wish to enjoy eternal life after this one, but especially learned men who wish to help human society by their example. The Greeks call the science of religion theology, which shows what piety accomplishes; what is learned by the precepts of divine doctrine; and what kind of life God has put before our eyes in the prophets and apostles.

　　Beyond this benefit that God conferred on mankind, which is truly heavenly and divine, he bestowed other things together with knowledge concerning them, something truly necessary in this life: not only so that men should merely endure, but that they should more gratefully cherish their civic intercourse. For what is more necessary after the cultivation of religion than that their very own hearth and home be an ancestral residence? And so all our private needs are abundantly supplied by the divinity, God-given and in such matters a good preparation, amplification and preservation of these things is known by the Greek word "Economics," whose vestiges are still visible from our first parents and the patriarchs, the knowledge of which was described by the Greeks and by learned Latins.

　　To the head of the household belong necessary fruits, herds of oxen, droves of cattle and of horses, and additional troops of asses.

Accordingly, husbandmen must be provided and shepherds must be hired and it is necessary to trust essential things to them. The Greeks called the study of such knowledge Georgics. The Latins called it agriculture, the conception of which should be embraced and ought to be practiced with industry. It was known by the Greek Xenophon and by the Roman Cato as well as by Varro.

Ethics

These two arts are necessary, to which must be added the grace of honesty and beauty. The knowledge of morals, which the Socratic philosophers call ethics—for which early Greek writers, those men who lived before the light of the Gospel, furnished incomplete precepts—is perfected by the teaching of the apostles and theologians. But even our first parents from the time of Adam on and also the patriarchs up to Moses, David, and the prophets handed on to posterity the excellent precepts of this teaching. They provided examples both for living and for establishing the practice not only of this private teaching of morals and religion, endowed with singular beauty, but also of the public establishment of the body politic, about which I shall shortly propose suggestions. Notwithstanding, these are also admirable subjects that are disputed and taught in the writings of the Socratics, that is, of the Academicians and of the Peripatetics, acutely by Aristotle, ornately by Plato, concerning the greatest good, virtues and vices, and wicked movements of men's souls. Hence the books of Aristotle concerning mortals; hence the various brilliant dialogues of Plato and his discourses; hence the books of Marcus Tullius (Cicero) *On Duties*, derived from the fountains of the four virtues; hence the *Tusculan Disputations*; hence the disputations of that Academy and the excellent disputation concerning the limits of good and evil.

Politics

But because individual households cannot exist by themselves, and human beings need one another for assistance and support, and because life is not lived by individuals or by a few people, but by many and by all, God also gave public usefulness to all things used amongst men that are either necessary for living or are convenient for living pleasantly. And he separated the various kinds of men (according to their usefulness) for cultivation of the land, for city states, for governance and empire. At the same time, he also gave with these very things those gifts that are necessary for rulers and governors: reason for administering the republic, of which our first father at the beginning and again after the deluge of the world, Moses and the books of the prophets opened up the fountains. But their streams were dispersed thence to the ancestral home of Greece in its various city states. Their most impressive achievements truly were the Athenian Academy and the Lyceum and the Stoa itself, in which the philosophers published books and discoursed concerning civil knowledge, which was known as the political art and was so explained by these authors that this one seemed to comprehend all the arts.

To this art pertain the discourse of Plato on *The Republic* and *The Laws*, as well as that of brilliant Aristotle that are called the *Politics*. Also parts of this are the books of Cicero concerning *Laws*, from the precepts of which the excellent laws of the Roman consuls were derived, as well as the praetors' edicts, the princes' commands, and the responses of those skilled in the law, which is spoken of as jurisprudence and is called νομική by the Greeks, the bride of the civil science we call politics.

These four things that we call the arts and the subject matter of these arts are divine benefits given by God, and revealed to our fathers, and have been handed on to us by a continuous law. The first of these is of sanctity; the second is of household and estate; the third of virtue; and the fourth of the human power which God gives to the magistrates, whatever kind these may be, either overseers of states, or governors of kingdoms, or rulers of empires. For one must believe that princes have been divinely established for human society. For all power is from God and has been handed down by God to him who wields the sword of justice, the governor of the republic.

The Law

But the head of the household as manager must know the following. This civic knowledge requires jurisconsults, the art of which is called νομική, whose principle and origin have been taken from the two tables of the law which Moses received from God and brought to the people and promulgated, more holy by far than those twelve tablets of the Roman Septemvirs, also by far more pure than those of Lycurgus among the Spartans, or of Solon among the Athenian tablets of the law ἄξονες, for that is how those two legislators named the tables of their laws. From these the Romans created their own laws and promulgated them to their own citizens, conquered peoples, and other tribes and nations. These have now been explained by many other laws and their authority enlarged by the laws of jurisconsults who wisely defend them. And the magistrates hold fast to them in the better republics. Ever since we have kings and princes, men of Christian name, many of whom wage wars for religion and no less for hearths and homes, and most of all for positions of power. And our kings and emperors also are not lacking zeal. Where there are states of this kind, we commend the study of theology also to them. And we concede that civic knowledge, which we call political, embraces all the arts and doctrines, and it defends and amplifies them. The best authors have followed in this opinion, not only Aristotelians, but also sacred writers among whom is Paul the Apostle, whose law is everlasting. All power is from God, and in him is soul and spirit. It is necessary that he rule in some way with his superior power.

Medicine

Therefore, just as we include those skilled in law and their teaching within the official duties of cities and states, so also the doctors of medicine. For Greece needed the help of Hippocrates during a plague, and it was necessary for Galen to follow the Roman army and camps. Likewise, those two Homeric characters, Podalyrius and Machaon, were well known; and Homer himself preferred a doctor to many other citizens. And in Holy Writ it is related that a doctor is not given, but created, for the cure of diseases and the necessity of medicine.

War or Strategy. The Art of the Military and of Governing

And since the sword of the magistrate is given and granted by God, yes, handed on and entrusted, not only should it be used at home against their crimes, but also in the marketplace it can often defend against force and injuries, because the law of kings and emperors is supreme. They should use the sword justly and employ it skillfully. Justice is handed on in laws. Military knowledge is comprehended by theory, which the Greek authors named Polemice (πολεμική), because of the nature of war, and generalship (στρατηγή), on account of the commander and army. The Latins name it from soldiers' "military science," not only because a soldier (*miles*) is necessary for waging war, but also because it must be enlarged by the exercise, labor, and use of soldiers and perfect military discipline.

Architecture

But the private and domestic matters of individuals are closed in by the walls of the paternal house. All citizens are truly defended on land by the ramparts of walls; at sea by the fleet, which requires workers and experts for correct proportions. These masters the Latins called architects, imitating the Greeks, among whom there were architects whose knowledge of architecture was inherited from the Athenians.

Arts of Natural Philosophy

The arts that we have proposed above require exercises, labors, and great exertions, and they are engaged in by a large part of the population. However, there are others that seem to be more leisurely and quieter, but nevertheless are opposed to leisureliness and very seriously so to idleness, and are cultivated by nothing more than by industry and languish more swiftly due to nothing more than to sloth. They love diligence; they summon up industry. They are remote from loud noise and tumult; not from labor and vigils.

Those Pythagoreans, who called themselves philosophers, appropriated these arts to themselves and they wished to be known and seen as natural philosophers. One of these arts deals with things which grow up and perish, which are created and destroyed, concerning those things which are put in motion in the air, as are thunderbolts, flashes of lightning, peals of thunder, rains, snows, winds, lands and fields, movements, comets, portents of heaven; and also those which lie hidden in the lands, as do gems and stones, metals, plants and herbs, shrubs and fruits, animals, and their parts; first of all, certainly, man; and the elements of all these things, which they first wished to be called physiology, to which the teachings of the mathematicians are related.

Mathematical Arts

Their teaching consists of certain beginnings, progressions, and ends, the arguments and conclusions of which are called demonstrations (ἀποδείξις), certain, firm, and lasting confirmations set before the eyes which can in no way be refuted. Among these one is the art of enumeration called arithmetic, because its material is numbers, in which there is a diversified order, which requires a multiple consideration by adding, subtracting, multiplying, dividing, and comparing. Although the knowledge teaching of individual things is certain, nevertheless, various cases and conversions of numbers exist. It is a necessary art in human society, necessary for all fathers of families, but perfect knowledge of it is not equally necessary for the unlearned and for the erudite man. For the moneylender uses a number in one way, but the mathematician uses it in another.

Astronomy

Most of all the astronomer uses the help of this art. His art is not only called astronomic, but he calls it astronomy. He wishes it to be seen as law (νόμος = law), because it is quite equally a science, and the profession of this science should be certain. And they themselves are certain, the perpetual rising and setting of the constellations, and the near connections and the intervening spaces, the courses of the sun and moon, lights and eclipses. Yes indeed, those who understand this art perfectly wish to be certain, not uncertain.

Astrology and Prognostication

Astrologers, foretellers of future events (the which art is called prognostication or προγνωστική), are able not only to predict those things we have named such as the rising and setting of the constellations and stars, eclipses of the moon and sun, but also sterility and famines, humor and good health, tempests and floods, healthfulness of years and plagues.

Geometry

To geometry pertain certain dimensions of bodies, the consideration of spaces, the observation of figures, how long or short a certain thing is, how high or low, when considered by itself or brought together with others. It is the duty of geometry to see and to understand this. That this science is useful can be understood in one Archimedes, whose industry and more nearly, whose art, enabled the people of Syracuse to defend the city, when they had to fight against the slaughter by Marcellus's army. To such an extent the art also has its own oracles and genius and may be seen to fight with its own power, not only with cleverness, but also with strength.

To these arts which are more leisurely and indeed, more liberal, for knowledge is of the free and the good (ἐλευθέρων γὰρ ἀγαθὸυ), to these teachings, I say, music has been added also as a cause of pleasure, which as a science of numbering judges concerning numbers. So it demonstrates certain and perpetual precepts concerning the variety of sounds and voices, dissimilitude, harmony, spaces and time. And it considers with admirable variety in these things what should be sharp, what low, what intermediate, what long, what short, what moderate.

Arts of Logic

These are the arts which we have recounted whose home is in the schools of the philosophers, which we have spoken of as arsenals of the republic. The maid-servants of all these, which lie hidden in every kind of thing are called logic. Therefore, because they pertain to precepts of a discourse or oration, without them a mathematician could never teach his subjects, nor could a jurisconsult defend his laws, and the theologian without these would be able to show nothing very clearly to the people, nor protect the church against heretics.

Grammar

All of these three things are necessary in a republic: one is purity, a second truth, a third is eloquence. For the duty of the grammarian is to recommend precepts of pure speech, as if rules.

Dialectic

Dialecticians distinguish true from false conclusions and explain the kinds of argumentations, by which necessary things are separated from the merely probable, permanent things from transitory, pure things from corrupted ones.

Rhetoric

But rhetoricians adorn this truth more splendidly, defend it more bravely, commend it more delightfully. They bring it about that by this skill men surpass other living beings. By the very same skill one man excels over another man, so that no discovery or work of man seems to be more admirable than well expressed and eloquent prudence, or prudent and wise eloquence.

These are the principal arts of humanity that we call liberal, a vocable of the Aristotelians, as befit free and honorable men, so that having been instructed by these arts, they follow liberty through the good peace of laws and the charitable deeds of their lords. Since they served freely, they preserved themselves in liberty.

All these things have been handed down in the monuments of letters and were lucidly explained. They rest quietly under the protection of philosophy, from which they direct arms and fortifications against a variety of things—against the perturbations of minds and for their tranquillity; against falsehood and for truth; against hunger, fasting, and poverty, and for a sufficiency; against plague and for good health; against the violence and perils of wars and for hearth and home; against fraud and injury and for law and liberty; in short, against misery and for good fortune.

For what purpose, these being as ordinary and as numerous as they are, should we point out the end for which schools are established? How the teachers of letters must hasten towards it, and the goal we propose to which they should aspire, and the banner that the school administrators hold high, which they will direct in a straight line. Nor should they allow the keenness of their eyes to be distracted from it, no matter how often they teach the students. For there is nothing read or taught that should not be of such an art or should not be referred to art.

But the arts must not be taught in the order that I have related. The true principle must be taken from that which seems to be the least of all and whose appearance seems to be the least, but which truly has the greatest understanding, and that is called grammar (philology). It holds the key and opens the door of the halls of academe and of the palace of the philosophers. For it is given to no one to look upon the Academy of Plato, the Lyceum of Aristotle, or the Stoa of Zeno unless he is an expert in this discipline.

Now, since we have what comes first, the fountain and streams to which the teachers of the schools should refer everything from the first class to the last, the means should also be explored, and these from the beginning to the last things.

Good Order in Teaching

Therefore, this is a work of order. And since the humane studies are liberal, it is necessary for the order to be open and elegant, which the Greeks call discipline (εὐτοξιαν). But we call it good because it does not weary with prolixity nor obscure with brevity, but delights with pleasantness. Fastidiousness does not threaten the industry of students. In short, it puts better things ahead of worse things so that the young person is not only taught in short order, in a brief, easy, and pleasant way, and the teacher himself is not only quickly understood, but is truly very much loved as well. Thus, we give the first hours of the day and subjects for discussion to the grammarian who puts out the fundamentals of pure speech; second place to the dialectician and rhetorician. The one transmits the rules of truth; the other explains the riches of speaking, as far as the nature and the skill of the students allow. For what is said in the schools of the rhetoricians is well known: the wise orator governs his audience's ears if he wishes to rule their minds. The same must be done with all doctors of philosophy, first of all those three who teach speech, so that they do not prolong what is to be enjoyed, which would vex the language of a tender age with bitterness and would offend the stomach with crudity.

Nor does it move me that it has been said: The roots of letters are bitter, but the fruits are sweet. For I am entirely of the opinion (and the thing is itself obvious) that there is nothing bitter in letters if they are easily understood. I am not able to praise a physician who is not able to conceal and to correct healthfully with more pleasant ingredients the loathsomeness of seeds, roots, and medicines. Although that defect should be ascribed not so much to men as to the times themselves, which repeatedly have an influence by authority rather than by truth. Defending the vices of ancient authority is tyranny, not teaching.

Defects of the Time and of Custom

Therefore, in founding schools and correcting defects one must first see what defect lies in the times. For custom can be a very large part either of good or bad things. What barbarity was entrenched more than fifty years ago in the schools of the grammarians, dialecticians, rhetoricians, jurisconsults, and doctors! How much frightful impiousness in the semblance of religious piety! In all these things many and great are the remains. Whatever new vices creep in, if they take root, our descendants will observe the evils, both more pernicious and more lasting than we thought, of which, however, the age was the most evil. It is not necessary to illustrate these things with examples, for they manifest themselves in the great sorrow of many prudent men. Nor can examples be given that would not offend.

Evils & Virtues of Parents

But the good teacher should not only consider the times, which may be good or bad, but those vices that may be in the boys. There are many who are strong in memory, but truly are able to understand slowly what must be committed to memory. Many have a lively talent for understanding, but are weak in memory and are poorly endowed. Others, because of laziness, abhor studies, which is the worst kind. Some relax their industry because of close friends or household tutors, and allow themselves to be corrupted. Others there are who are more delighted with things other than the study of letters. Some are quickly tired out, but follow many subjects for a brief period of time. Others are able to sustain labor, but do not wish to work according to their ability.

Desirable qualities of the Preceptor.

You should weep for Telephus or Peleus,
if you are able to weep.

All of these evils must be noted and corrected by the good teacher and the skilled instructor, but in a good manner, and with an appealing method. The most important principle of teaching is what the teacher wishes the student to be, such as he himself is seen to be. In this regard even the parents at home are at fault, so much so that often youths who are by nature good are contaminated by the blemishes of the parents. But in the teacher and professor the vices stand out conspicuously, as do the virtues.

Therefore they should appear and be visible in the teacher. Vigils, labors, readings, and writings should be carried on in the sight of all the youths. He should daily bring something to his students, as a good father to his sons, by which he revives and nourishes their young minds. He should consider how voraciously fledglings should take food, how diligently the parents should bring it, how frequently and how continuously they should fly away, how precisely they should guard against fasting and hunger, rain and wind, hostile beasts, and other misfortunes can befall these small creatures.

But nature impels wild animals to their normal activities, which for men are done more by reason, and for that reason must be more energetically worked for, lest they should be excelled by brute beasts.

Two Virtues of the Preceptor

Truly there are two main things that we expect of a teacher of letters: diligence and method. The Greeks call the one the love of labor (φιλοπονίαμ), and the other method (μὲθοδομ), without which those evils that we have described above cannot be corrected. I am not forgetful of teaching, for it is not a question of remembering. For who is the teacher? Not one who is not erudite in those subjects that he has undertaken to teach to others.

Concerning Classes

But with a good gymnasium founded, the method of teaching must be introduced, and the crowd of pupils must be parceled out; and it is a multitude with fixed levels of abilities, which they call classes, curias, or tribes, according to the example of very many people using their own terms. Among them we call those first who have reached the pinnacle of learning, and we give to them the name first curia, class, or tribe. Indeed, we give second, third, fourth, and fifth class to those who in truth take their place among the second and third classes, etc. For just as there are sodalities and societies of schoolfellows, there are also colleges of scholars and schoolfellows who are associates in the very same discipline.

Concerning the Fifth Class

Therefore it seems good with respect to time to divide the College of Lauingen into five parts and to put into the fifth grade those who are unable to read, who cannot by themselves learn anything. These are the cradle of our home and household; among them lies our heir and comrade. The peasant has hope in the seed he has planted. The head of the household rejoices at the whimpering infant in the cradle, to be educated sweetly by the mother and nurse, and he expects the heir to be what he hopes for!

1. Love of the preceptor

But the good schoolmaster, as a second parent as well as the creator of a new nature, delights in the youthful stammer, and has his school for a cradle. He should hold the little boy as an infant son to whom he should give the food of learning. He should nourish him healthfully. He should influence him pleasantly. He should soak beforehand what he must eat. Nothing should be eaten which would be harmful to the stomach nor should he with some crude food develop peevishness in the child. Therefore, as soon as the boy has begun his sixth year, he should take him on his lap like a nursemaid: foster, care for, educate, and make him learned. He should consider his school to be a mother's lap. He should give him milk. He should clean him. He should revive him. He should protect him with bandages. He should clothe him. He should involve him in a philosophical manner.

2. Easy things pertaining to the arts

He should, therefore, from the very beginning, pay attention to that which we have proposed as the division of the arts and should not divert his eyes from it, but should not approach its mysteries, or wish the boy to rise too high. Nor should a man be changed by lost mental power into a brutish animal or as Actaeon into an antlered stag, so that arrogance appears without genius, a heart without strength of character.[1] The wings of Daedalus are harmful.[2] The teacher must proceed to serious, difficult, and arduous things at the right time. It is enough if he stimulates the boy, so long as he does this correctly.

3. Catechism

This youth, therefore, if he has learned how to pray to God at home, if he holds to the confession of the universal church, if he can recite from memory both tables of the law in his native language, need not be burdened with the Latin or Greek catechism. His youthful industry must be relieved and liberated from every oppressive weight. It is enough if what he has received at home is not forgotten in this school. It suffices if he prays piously in his native language, for his paternal language is equally pleasing to God, and these are the things that we wish the youth to learn.

4. Letters and their pronunciation

At the very outset, therefore, the forms of letters should be set before this little boy, so that, whatever of this could be done, he would know how to pronounce the Roman language; nor should his intonations sound strange. For his race (i.e., his fellow countrymen) also has a language that is not perceived to be either different or foreign.[3] I have observed crude Spaniards become learned Louvainians in one or two years recite songs and a fluent oration with more erudition and a more pleasing intonation than others who had recently arrived. And the students of Louvain themselves, and the Belgians, from the Spanish usage and vocal sound produced better and smoother speech.

5. Division of Letters

Nor does it seem in this beginning to be an obscure division of letters that should be handed on, which this age is not able to understand or which can be and should be understood as such by them. By means of this method progress in learning and in listening is made, and the class-times are divided; which divisions can and should be indicated.

6. Inflexions of nouns and verbs

For this reason the teacher must always lead from the letters learned to the inflexions of nouns, in which the order of cases and inflexions must be held fast and the variety of the final syllables must be observed. Nor is it proper to change the boys' nouns and verbs very much. But the teacher should also think otherwise about what must be read and what must be changed. He should hold to Pliny's advice concerning readings. In the conjugation of verbs and the declensions of nouns we really should follow Quintilian, who wanted boys to know first how to decline nouns and conjugate verbs. This learning of youth must be prepared by daily and constant exercise and usage, not by explanation of the art in the manner of mathematicians and dialecticians. For the job of the mathematician is one thing, but that of the grammarian is another at this age and at this beginning level, at which all obscurity must be avoided as also the teacher's prolixity.

7. Vocables

Then from that beginning the teacher should hold to the two-fold aim of these arts that we have set forth above. The first is the three-fold art of pure, true, and pleasant speech. The second has to do with those teachings which concern things, whether pertaining to ethics or to nature, and from those by means of skill to search out words and by them to think in an orderly fashion and to apportion them amongst the students.

Thus, when the child first enters the *gymnasium*, he should see himself entering a foreign state, unknown not only as to customs and institutions, but even in truth as to language and speech, so that upon entering the city, let him have a guide who will point out the city's mysteries to strangers and courteously entertain the visitor.

8. Noteworthy vocables

Therefore simple vocables should be set forth in this class and their inflections learned from the very beginning, by which the boy must be enriched. But he should not be burdened by these riches, rather tested by this silver and gold and improved by these better expressions. For the gifts and rewards of the host should be gentlemanly, not barbaric or sordid. The beginning of eloquence is the delight of words; really, delight in the very best things. Therefore Latin words should be from that age in which Roman citizens spoke best; from the consuls and governors up to the death of Cicero, at whose demise eloquence itself can be seen to have settled into the grave.

Thus Roman and Latin words ought to be selected and proposed which are not barbarous and foreign, but of everyday use, pertaining to those things used and enjoyed and daily observed by men's senses. We call that language and that writing the better sort not that which is rare and unique (for what is rare is seldom used), but what is commonly used and was used every day by Roman citizens. First of all, to be sure, the new freedom of our age must be avoided, and that new mixture of words without choice of language, devoid of accuracy concerning antiquity, and likewise, of any auditory discrimination. For although a youth is not able to judge (not even Roman or Athenian children were able to do so) what is Latin and what is barbarian, yet when nursemaids were wont to speak to them they used those words which Romulus and Remus used and which the consuls and praetors used; not what the inhabitants of southern Italy and of Reggio Emilia had brought into the city; still less what the Gauls, Aquitanians, or Celts brought in. Let me be nourished as Cornelia, mother of the Gracchi, nourished her babes while they were in swaddling clothes and in their cradle—by her own, not a stranger's milk, and nourished more abundantly and more healthfully. From out that mouth let the sound of language also be received, as wholesome words; that is, real Latin, not foreign language, not new nor insolent nor produced in the schools of barbarians.

Supply of words

A supply of words is acquired by the weak student, but let him not be over-burdened or oppressed. Let him rather be enriched, if only by good things or by single words set forth individually each day. But language is not distributive; truth is diverse. Neither is it useful for citizens to have just one kind of merchandise. It would be a great thing if someone had not his small portion only but a part of everything. In that manner God created all living things. In that manner he formed man. In that manner he established the world. It is useful, fitting, and right to follow a leader like God, creator of the universe. In business matters, in the sale of goods and merchandise, exchanges are made. Adolescents exchange and adapt vocabulary items amongst themselves. One must be compared to another as to his industry and style in remembering and his freedom in communicating.

Therefore on the very same day one boy who occupies the first place in one class knows what God is, another knows what the world is; a third what heaven is, and a fourth what fire is; a fifth knows what air is, a sixth knows what water is; a seventh boy knows what earth is; while an eighth, what an animal is; a ninth, what a man is, and a tenth, what a beast is. This same method should be retained in other classes, whether these vocabulary words are retained as the beginning of discipline, or whether living things can be selected from their distinguishing traits and by their pronunciation. First one should ask, what virtue and vice are; second, what prudence is; third, what justice and injustice are; fourth, what bravery and cowardice are; fifth, what temperance and intemperance are. This plan must be followed, for a few days continuously. On the first day, ten students from the decurions (groups of 10 students = one decurion) will bring to class all kinds of goods purchased by the teacher from a retailer whose business has been licensed by the laws and undertaken by the state. Rewards ought to be conferred to distinguish this kind of abundant profit and honest gain.

The first duty of the teacher is diligence

First the utmost diligence is required of the teacher, then knowledge, and last, method. On no day should diligence be lacking when he does not teach or review these things and daily spin these threads. He must also be diligent in keeping notes as to what words he shall be giving to whom and on which day to which classes. It is a matter of knowledge which vocabulary to choose from approved authors and what kinds of things to include and what kinds of ideas to separate and if he should or should not be able to make a Latin word from a German word. Nevertheless, he should be able to explain that briefly in a few words so that he may respond according to the definitions of the philosophers and of those writers from whose works of art and writings the words themselves are taken. In this way the task of teaching will be lighter and he will not be heavily weighed down, if he has access to the best authors, from which he moves on. This is true in military matters to Vegetius and to the historians; in medicine to Cornelius Celsus; also to Cicero on the parts of the human body; for agriculture to Cato and Varro; for law to the books of the Pandects; in theology to the sacred books, first to those of Lactantius and Jerome. Many things can also be culled from Cicero when appropriate and natural, then changed and translated and altered and skillfully embellished and shaped, even words which have amplified meanings, which in our religion are capable of being elucidated. But since in all these things method is necessary, moderation and reason are required. Method is first and foremost that order that we wish to establish and follow. Secondly, do not hasten on more quickly than the abilities of the students allow. Third, help speed on whoever is capable of help. Review not only the present day's work, but also that of the last few days. That may be done first by questions from the teacher on all the decurions' activities—in a clear voice, so that the rest of the class (even those in the rear) may hear. Just as in music it happens that everyone sings and listens at the same time, so even here in this arena ought this to be done, so that everyone is at the same time either doing battle or watching. On this occasion all the boys should either be asking questions and answering, or listening to those who are responding and asking questions. It is a great misfortune and a poor method to prick up the ears of just one boy and not all ears by such questioning and responding.

By this good method the class and teacher should be governed. If he has assigned a certain word to anyone, he should necessarily require that he use it in many sentences. If indeed from among those things that were assigned to others some boy called upon should answer correctly, that boy should be encouraged by praise so that he receives the reward of his industry and the commendation of his teacher. The others will be made better by this one's example.

Interrogations concerning vocables

But not only should the schoolmaster question, but also the student should question the teacher in the teacher's presence, and before the teacher gets to school and afterwards when school is out. For the decurions must also be brought together, where one will try to surpass the other and test the soldiers of another war-tent. This could be done more regularly if the teacher were present; but nevertheless, if the teacher is absent, the pupils' industry must be tested. It is useful and an old custom in the schools of Paris for students to devote one hour in the morning and another in the afternoon in the main hall of each school wherein the masters dwell so that they may hold disputations with one another and discuss those things which on that same day or on the previous one they have been listening to and been made acquainted with by the teacher.

Genera with their species

It would also aid the memory if some intermediate kind of the same sort of question could be applied, a servant or handmaiden, as it were, so that equity could be placed next to justice; gratitude and faith be joined with friendship; and wisdom be placed at the right side of prudence, with providence at the left side and custom that has been formed from the experience of everyday things and the memory of things gone by and of great deeds. In this way, the middling sort of student is taught by his companions if he loses his way in the middle of class.

The substance of vocables in a game

It is extraordinary how understanding is clarified and memory established. In this manner are the facts of language formed, so that those things that do not fall under any one particular meaning, then principally in those cases do the senses move with some enthusiasm. It is as if in a game a cook comes out from the kitchen with her helpers and brings her utensils and sets out her victuals and sustenance as for sale. She makes known how much she estimates each one of them is worth. If an architect should produce his stock of tools, rocks, woods, fragments of stone, pebbles, sand, and blueprints, why should not a school of letters serve as the stage for such a pleasant spectacle?

It is also a good idea to provide something by way of change sometimes, so that minds wonderfully tired may relax. Whatever things one must really demand from memory—and they are many—those should be assigned to the morning hours. Whatever things must be reviewed may more comfortably be consigned to the afternoon exercises.

Limits should be placed on what vocabulary items are demanded from a youth by way of memorization. Let the boys who are reading and know how to form their letters be taken notice of by the school's headmaster. It is as it were a remarkable kindness by the decurions who display outstanding industry and by their example make the rest of their fellow students more eager to compete because all to a man demand that this opportunity be given to them too.

Thus, in this class the greatest task is reading and modulating the voice. The second is the bringing together of words, the choice of which is the beginning of eloquence. The third pertains to writers, about whom we must now speak. About these it is cautioned that whatever is long be avoided at the start. Nothing here ought to be long except the quiet of the night, of which this age ought not to be defrauded, and honest enjoyment. But the amount of enjoyment must be judged by its utility. Meanwhile, it is useful to be refreshed, since studies are aided by enjoyment and bodily health requires it.

Observation of the teacher and gravity and moderation in punishing.

However much I desire the students' joy, sometimes the severity of sticks and whips is desirable and necessary. Orbiliuses [Orbilius was a Roman grammarian] are the plagues of schools; but we wish to have Catos, really charming, while we cultivate virtue, and duty is not abandoned. Even laughter occasionally seemed appropriate to Cato. He could not be sad in his delight at virtue.

But this concerns the severity of teachers, while I had begun to speak about the writings and books that the students in this grade are using. So, as I was saying, I am removing from this school and from this class and sending on to the upper grades even the shorter speeches of Cicero, and likewise the philosophical books and whatever pertains to them.

I will certainly allow sentences that are comprehended by individual clauses. "Parsimony is a great source of income."[4] Then those things that are disposed of by pairs, for example: adulation, which is at first agreeable, but whose end leads to bitter results. These are followed by sentences of three clauses, and even four. I allow longer circumlocutions which the Greeks call πνεῦματα and τάσεις and καγαφοράς but after an interval of time has elapsed, and the foundations of declensions and conjugations have been laid, when there will be no verb left which the youth is not able to inflect and when he will have acquired a certain store of vocabulary items.

But these prolix amplifications of words and sentences are more suitable for the higher grades, already confirmed in the habit of inflecting, and after the rules of the grammarians have been handed on, youth will begin to speak Latin correctly.

Subjects in longer periods (sentences)

For I do not wish these sentences to concern only morals, goodness, religion, and other virtues, nor to contain only the contrary vices, but also other kinds of words which belong to the same kind of things, and refer to them, so that they are like the parts of buildings; various movements of the human body or living beings; the actions of living things and of men; the world and its parts; a house and its foundations, roofs, walls, and other principal parts, kinds of food and drink; agriculture and agricultural tasks; estates and everything peculiar to estates; literary studies and their practical applications of whatever kind, such as are found in the speeches which Cicero gave for the poet Archia, excellent examples of the usefulness and pleasantness of letters.

That which I prescribe for nouns, I do likewise take as the case for verbs: what common root have they in which they are contained. Just so actions exist by reason of bodily movements—remaining seated; going and coming back; going out and turning back; advancing and falling back; so too in the movements of the mind—to be excited and to be perturbed; to be aggrieved and to be made cheerful; to lament mournfully and to be excited by pity and anger; to hate. But the nouns and verbs in speeches should take priority and the beginning should be made in this class from nouns.

Moreover, it is also useful in this class that one other letter be completed as an example of all those rules that are handed down from the grammarians in that section that is called syntax. For even if the scope and behavior of all these words pertaining to things and their activities are natural, teachers have examples of their own. But this pertains to teachability. In one written selection and on one page all kinds of things can be contemplated.

Concerning the Fourth Class

After the boy will have been educated in this school for one year by means of exercises in these things that we have discussed we wish him to advance to the next grade in which he will become more learned. Not only will he learn to speak, but he will also know in what manner and for what reason something can be said, and what categories of things are those which he has learned from the first teacher.

1. Memory of those things that he has learned

Therefore, the teacher who receives this youth from the hand and bosom of another should know the customs and mores of the state, that is, of the class, from which the student has progressed. To retain these things and not to change anything of them; also to take care that nothing of those things that he has learned is forgotten, and what he has been taught in the family should likewise here be diligently retained, so that portions of reality can be kept and preserved. And may there be an increase in works and talents! The same precepts should therefore be maintained; the same books; the same rewards; the same method of inquiry, the same method for gathering resources, and the same means for gathering facts and vocabulary.

2. Etymologies

Here, accordingly, the grammarians hand down the same classification which they call ἐτυμολογικὴμ, things which should be demonstrated, what the chief portions of an oration are, and what things and how many of them fall to it, or what would belong in a certain oration, and the part of speech which must be considered in which the principal parts are inflexions and types of nouns and verbs. Examples of every-thing which the youth has learned about nature and language should be included including those drawn from the daily word-diaries or journals.

3. Examples of teachers

Not from other books, not even out of those from which he has been taught before he received instruction, so that the youth will understand as many things as his first teachers presented, and so he sees what from all that his new teacher is taking up is review and what he is adding on his own.

4. Syntax

To this portion of grammar that which is called συντακτική should be added. In these I want the same things to be retained as in the former, as examples taken from earliest childhood and from the first instruction.

At each point I desire brevity and clarity, both when they are set forth in books, then again in the teacher's work. For he is like a tribune and prefect of this class, both by way of explaining the reason why the verb is singular; and in such cases what is to be done and after which pattern. By repetition and by doubling in the same hour and by repeti-tion and review in the days that follow, and by going back over what is done at a given time (it may be after an interval of several days) the same will be attained and accomplished, so that the boy may under-stand more quickly whatever he will be taught and not be overwhelmed nor debilitated by the growing abundance, but made firmer by memory.

5. Care and diction and Latinity

The teacher will also observe what Valla, Linacre, Cardinal Adrian, Budé, and the dictionaries relate pertaining to these two parts of gram-mar. But he ought to demonstrate without these authors and their books and even without the things said which words are Latin and which bar-barous and which of the words and their sequences are pure and which are impure and which kinds of words are for things and which for speaking were used by Cicero in the age of Varro, and what was added in the manner of Pliny and in the time of Quintilian. He should also understand even without the interpretation of these books what is long-standing when it is spoken. Otherwise, they sense what was less usual and was really contrary to practice. A boy knows Latin when it is said, "Come to me as soon and as quickly as possible." But it is barbarous if it is said: "as soon as possible Cicero returned to the city from Cilicia.[5] It greeted him there and he was embraced in the middle of the Forum." They say that whoever really wanted to speak Latin came back to the city as soon as possible. However these things may be, and whatever unique nature they possess, disputations should derive from one or another situation. But to explain these is by no means necessary and it is long-winded. They can be taught better. By no means everything of this sort ought to be given to this class. Certain things must be left for the next highest grade. If someone is having difficulties he will not be able to move forward (pass) from this class.

6. What books and authors are to be explained in this class

And even the rules and precepts of grammar for this class are now taken from books and authors amongst whom no one is better than Cicero; first because he has explained the things; then because of his abundance; but especially because of the purity of (his) Roman speech. He will be forever an example even for these things of which he did not himself treat in his books. Things may not be similar nor the same but have a similar treatment and polish. But even a large number of diverse things concerning contrary matters fall under the same form and type in arranging, arguing, proving, and elaborating.

But because in the next lowest class this is often done, not everything we choose in the first year can be completed, either because of the slowness of ability, or because of the difficulties of the times. Then war and disease and various changes are accustomed to assert themselves. We wish to keep in our hands if only in adolescence that book of sentences and examples; and because in that other class one was not able to, in this class we want explanations to be completed. It is often the case that these are run through in the higher grades; however, here it is necessary to recall to mind the better explanations.

Thereafter in this manner from the lower grade the boy will ascend to the higher well provided with a supply of words and of forms whose various meanings can be expressed and by whose examples the most important teachings of the schoolmaster he will be capable of.

7. Augmenting vocabulary and everyday meanings

Even from this place I want the boy to set forth and with him to carry various examples of sentences, arguments, conclusions, decorations all covered in one book. He will be helped by these in the next grade. There he will be made acquainted with the principles of rhetoric, and will use that same rhetoric book. During that time they will be provided with whatever they lack. Whoever is in charge will guide the student. For whatever the boy really learned before he ought to recall and review from his teacher. For how long has the youth not understood sufficiently what he has learned, or not well enough to extend or to join it all together and to get something more out of Cicero from this book. As soon as the boy shall feel the force of it, he will make progress, so that his word diary will be increased and the forms of his sentences will overflow and these same examples that he will have as a guide by which he will untangle definitions and partitions, rules and precepts and advice.

To this book we want added the sixth book of accusations against Verres which is filled with various matters pertaining to narration.[6] For seeing that we are placing this foundation for Latin speech, in the first grade the boys should know separate words. Let them take up conjunctions to the extent that it is within their power and let them make sentences and begin to speak about these same short sentences. Demanding, ordering, questioning, choosing, deprecating—in this manner they somewhat accustom themselves to copious speech—not by precepts but by examples, the first practice of which is narration. For even if the perfection of skill be to narrate and to explain something well, still it is very difficult to argue about obscure subjects. For this reason I will make narrating explain. And what can be more praiseworthy in a boy than a narration made of pure speech, of smooth sentences, and clear understanding? Of this skill nearly everyone gives six examples about which we speak in the accusation against Verres. This can be recited from memory, too. It is not without use. And indeed, boys are helped by memory. The teacher's restraint is used not only in interpreting, but also in repeating, and not before memory shall be wearied, before a thing be well learned and repeated and indeed several times recalled to the understanding.

These exercises will be properly cultivated from several selections of Cicero's letters from which the boy may possess something that can be properly imitated in producing letters, whence he begins to be accustomed to borrow his own writing style. About the former enough has already been expounded here.

At first let the youth understand and accept as true the teacher's useful exercises in style that have been set before him. And indeed, even genius has been sharpened, memory helped, the store of vocabulary increased and purified, the various forms of sentences supplied and also speaking skill, which he may carry off by himself. In this way he will produce swiftness from slowness and wit from dullness. He will conquer natural hindrances by an excellent mind, to which moreover, nothing comes with difficulty, nothing proves arduous; and this not only in those things that are seen, but even those which are not seen he may penetrate. There is nothing concealed by darkness that cannot be brought thence into the light, so that it may be seen and understood. Herein there is no judge, for fear of condemnation is compatible with this style. He will not fear Aristarchus.[7]

It must be confessed, however, that we old people recall from our own adolescence that these matters were full of trouble and loathesomeness for us. But that happened because of the unskillfulness and sloth of our teachers. Difficult matters must be explained by the teacher's industry. Thus, he will consider himself again and again as the builder of style, and will accept nothing that would prove damaging to this youthful estate, nor would a teacher himself do anything like damage. If such things might be so managed by the director then he will be the ideal guide.

Let therefore this be the first rule and that which the teacher accomplishes: that every day the boy writes something. Every day he brings something together and composes because soon he will be able to draw upon it by himself and speak of the poet Horace. Never indeed have I thought of skipping this exercise on alternate weeks or even one single time in a month, but rather, daily as I have promised, something has been written, and the students' diligence, facility, and skill must be helped by the teacher's industry.

It is an easy thing to propose short arguments, a thing that it is customary to do in the native tongue and in daily speech and not badly. The youth does not have anything to discover but only to be translated. But here are two problems that must be avoided. The first is (the possibility) that they are made prolix by circumlocution of words. Those youth cannot follow by any certain understanding. Of their writing style I say nothing. The other is that they are not shown words and sentence structure in the native tongue because it is then visualized in the ancestral language. Students want the Latin language to be translated after the usage of their native tongue. That will corrupt the purity of speech.

However, Latin and Roman sentence structure inherited Persian treasure, Phoenician missiles, Gallic arms and Greek phalanxes. The Roman boy proceeds to ornate Latin by his discourse, dress, insight, and knows Verres to be reprehensible, and the Greek toga and royal purple were seen in the house of harlots.

In this manner a comprehensive vocabulary was quickly learned. Let it be displayed in short clauses, or in short sentences, or let it be bound in groups of two or spun out in groups of three, or drawn out and freed to make complete sentences. But at first single and double exercises are more agreeable. That which takes a more prolix expression can be accomplished at intervals by the author.

Vocabulary and sentence structure are not enough. By questioning one tests also how much the boy will be able to set down beforehand with pen and pencil. Similarly an infant's belly is not harmed by prechewed food, rather this is healthy. For whatever reason, that which is anticipated cannot be useful for the learner. The same reason prevails in writing exercises as in singing. In writing it is the same as in music. What can the student hope to sing before he has been taught by a singer or has been helped by the prescience of the teacher. Thus, let this exercise be taken up and begun and completed at this age in the class. This exercise is in another way affected by the state. We, moreover, aid in the process almost from the cradle.

The very ease of style helps the consideration of those things that the boy has learned in this fifth grade. It is almost like an infant's cradle, from out of which he brings nouns and verbs and many facts to adapt to his argument, repeatedly to recall the same to the boy's mind and greatly contribute to his capacity and skill.

We anticipate enough fluency of expression at this stage to pursue science, for which we wish that our teacher bring to these exercises someone with readiness.

This achieves truly liberal and erudite knowledge so that the kind of letter should be produced that is liberal, keen, serious, natural—not only with words, but also with rich ideas, which the youth will obtain by the repeated use of the pen. Moreover, either a singular ability unites with this knowledge, or if it does not immediately freely follow these things, nevertheless the youth will not satisfy himself, unless he accomplishes similar things, and he will try so that he accomplishes it. He does not give up before he arrives at the point of knowledge which the teacher sees fit to determine.

He even turns out a letter like any of Cicero's short ones, or part of a letter or argument, by no means long; or a little story or elaboration of medium length to be translated verbatim into German. Let the boy propose it and translate it into Latin speech, all of this negotiated by the boy and not by the teacher. Indeed, let him feel that he is educated by Cicero himself. Everything, moreover, of this sort ought to be done in school openly in the presence of the teacher so that he does not get it from some more learned fellow student and so that he does not copy it out of Cicero. And let the teacher skillfully teach him by keeping tight the reins.

In this class also it is profitable to translate the catechism from the native tongue into Latin and to respond in Latin, on the grounds that in the fifth grade he will have pronounced in German, for which reason let the last book be learned by heart. The teacher will take pains so that purity may be retained in Latin speech. It is not the case that beautiful language is pleasing in Germany. In Latin ugliness causes disgust.

It is also necessary to remember two things. First, let the teacher speak in Latin; that is, so the words he uses are both natural and common. As for the native tongue, do not have recourse to it except if it be necessary, when a word from our language can be translated more graphically, and when some new word is encountered.

Oh! Telephus or Peleus: If strength comes to me,
I must grieve for you.

The second thing that we enjoin is of the sort that can be seen by the teacher, as when a pupil wishes to and does love literature so that he be admired and given counsel, and that he be inspired by example and encouraged, and so that he may exercise his pen and compose something by himself or recite some meditation, so that in the morning he awakens and is not seen without a book, not even outdoors. His self-control at food and at drink, his refinement, and his fastidious manners are conspicuous in this student.

Concerning the Third Class

We nourish youth on this Latin milk to this point, just as the Cornelii adhered to the profitability of the Sempronian Law.[8] In the third year a moderate change is indeed made in the approach to food, and it must raise up a youth stronger in the poets and sons of Greece so that he may become accustomed to such sport. For such among the older fellows at school and among his own age-mates are not forsaken, or forgotten. Nor may those from the two lower grades whom he has heard, learned, needed, talked to and written of be forgotten.

1. The accent of a syllable

To the higher precepts of grammar are thus added in this poetical spot metrical verse or meter, which are called *feet* by most people, after the forms of poetry. In this matter see Vergil's *Bucolica*; these are explained in the books of the *Aeneid*. Here some of Horace's *Odes* or letters—now this, now that, or a speech of one of the satirists added to the same poets and on account of religion, nearly the same sort of poem as the hymns of Prudentius, and may be listened to and sung.[9] But for holy exercise others are advised for the space remaining.

2. Greek grammar

Here, too, the inflection of Greek nouns and verbs is begun. These are taken from the examples of Greek writers, and the circle of orators such as Demosthenes, Aeschines, Isocrates.[10] Of the philosophers, Plato, Plutarch, and Aristotle have been collected and brought forth in the presence of all. In this matter the philosophical books of Cicero and also his speeches can be refreshed by reciting and by translating, adding in Latin writing that will not previously have been seen, and expanding the store of words and things, so that before the precepts of rhetoric and dialectic they are taught by example, to which precepts they have more distinctly progressed.

3. Figures of syntax and of tropes and of rhetorical figures of speech

In this manner the teacher shall venture to add to grammatical inflections modes of rhetorical speech, that is, tropes of words and things; ornamentations which are called figures of speech, a kind of precept, but by illustrious examples which were formerly learned and enjoined, to be memorized by adolescents as shall have been agreed upon here in this manner.

4. Short letters of St. Paul

On feast days and on the days preceding them some letter of Paul's and something of the gospel stories based on some writings of Nazianzen; of the Greek sacrificial banquets; and of holy offerings must be tasted and chewed more healthfully by the tongue and more perfectly drawn out by the mind.

5. The pen to be more diligently sharpened

The pen (should be used) in a manner like it was in the last class. Indeed, it must be with more diligence drawn out and exercised daily with no interruption of even a day's interval. But let the teacher be present, so that it is he who reminds, he who inspires, he who gives counsel, and he who helps, which things be almost likewise the association of effort, so that the youth is not ashamed to strive because the teacher does not arouse annoyance.

In this manner the school year must be centered upon the boy's industry. Nor will there be some who finish the course before that time because that happens very rarely.

6. The memory of those things that he had learned in the last class

But as to the beginning of this school: as soon as the boy has entered this *gymnasium* he ought to know and memorize everything his two school teachers will have taught him nor tolerate that his memory of them fails, nor forget anything. All of it is necessary. In this way what is necessary, what is emphasized they retain in part for a long time. Moreover, what they daily encounter, they cannot forget. But some things are naturally more difficult and they are those to which they are not accustomed. Here the teacher will be tested by his industry. By this sort of thing the test will be made. Moreover, it is excellent if the boys are tested. If it is a standard of measurement it will be retained. What is proved in this building is kept, for that which is settled is not only for the good of the establishment but wherever there is something corrupted or neglected or lacking in historical precedent.

For this decadence of the structure in the memory of the adolescent is forgetfulness. That forgetfulness must be removed by the teacher, indeed, daily—and by daily questioning. In this way not only will memory be brought to its height in two years' time, but also made reliable. Just as greedy noblemen's families protect their property, so in the same way diligent pupils must retain their knowledge; and in the same way those (noblemen) do not neglect their palaces and pots of silver, in such a way the students of letters must conserve their copybooks which are almost like granaries of letters for this kind of culture.

7. Provision for things that are added

Moreover, that is only one of your jobs as a teacher; to watch over, retain, and preserve those things that have been taught. Another is to watch, consider, and even to comment upon those things that must be added from the previous classes, and those things that are left over and not in proper sequence.

8. Not changing precepts nor rules nor any of their vocabulary

There is also a third task: not to let the preceding definitions, partitions, and their terms, still less their meanings change. Fluency is to be followed in all things. As long as that old and hoary falsehood is active let your industry and diligence be produced. It is as difficult as it is beautiful.

Falsehood, too, will display itself as long as it may. By that same token, the roots of literature are bitter. These two opinions are not mere cover-ups for the teacher's laziness. It may be that the boy will be hindered unless you praise him. If youth does not meet up with anything arduous, nothing impassable, mistakes appear. The disgrace is to think that these grammarians are a difficult undertaking. In Greek and in Latin the native tongue is learned according to the degree that young people make use of it beforehand. By this, skill is recalled to the schools of our own age. I will think us arrived at this point if we have no unwilling teachers and if by their industry they help young people's industry.

Concerning the Second Class

The second class is of a stronger age and will require beginning exercises and nearly military rigor plus an ideal gladiatorial field. With respect to the dialectical (logical) comparisons and to the rhetorical battles, (these are required) not because one ought to meet with adversaries, or because one may be able to, but because these two disciplines can be begun by precepts and exercise. For to this class one ought to convey in speech the Latin nouns, verbs, particles, and also the supply of conjunctions and all the variations. None of the precepts of the grammarians are necessary, the examples of whom are not abundant and whose usage is preserved.

In the language of the Greeks is so much vocabulary and doctrine. How much could one by the teacher's diligence and suitable industry attain in one year! Similarly the poets' teachings must be grasped by rules. That is really demanded first of all so that poetical words of the orators and their ornaments can be distinguished. For not only is it possible to accumulate all words which are of one kind, but also to select (them). Word selection is the beginning of eloquence, since it is not enough to anticipate what is not sufficiently observed. One must be observed before one starts doing. It is however necessary to have a supply of words and to be able to have made a choice amongst them.

And in this class must be completed whatever may be seen to be lacking. The Greek and Latin writers are to be explained, along with the poets, then the orators, and also books of the philosophers and of the historians. Terence may also be added to these, and several of the fables of Plautus.[11] No better way of reasoning can be known than these two authors' friendly and domestic relations and they themselves are almost daily to be spoken in these schools among the young people for which reason we anticipate getting to that place where after daily exercise we shall teach the whole school.

Two ways of teaching

By means of these authors, explanations must be speedily brought together and all unnecessary delay must be avoided. But my two Romans are seen to have had two ways of teaching, of which one was quick and speedy; whether of brevity and even of speed, what had been true of the poets? They recited their songs and verses which did not consist only in reading and speaking, but also in meaning, whether pointed or obscure or of skillful construction, and they put them in order according to their value.

Just so was the method of poets when they were teaching their comical stories and tragic poems to actors. Such had been the case among poets not merely to set a price on their stories for aediles and magistrates, but also to teach the meanings of comic and tragic verse and also of language and the meaning of obscure ornamentation and of authorities. But all of this was done speedily so that it could be practiced beforehand and everything prepared.[12]

The other way was that of the school displayed by Juvenal in his first *Satire*.[13]

> Must I forever listen without responding
> To the harsh insults of Codrus's *Theseus*?[14]
> And will he have recited once again to me
> Without impunity that kind of Roman drama?
> Those verses? without fear of retribution?

Will Telephus so hugely waste my day? Or
Even when the margins of the book are filled
To overflowing and the back as well? Why
Has not Orestes not yet brought the thing
To an end?

This plan in some one or other hour of a day and in some book and in obscurity I allow. But yet in such a way so that by means of this itinerary we may depart on a great long journey. I do not also praise Juvenal's master, Cordus, whose pupil will have annoyed him rather than have taught him the prolixity of a dictator. First this method rather than that other of Juvenal, for it is more fruitful. Often too it is useful for the boy to translate literally rather than change the meaning freely, or to explain by pluralities, or to draw things together for conciseness. In that way the teacher does not lead, he whose quick reason is so very suitable.

Rhetorical precepts and their division

The daytime hours I certainly separate in this order: The first I allot for the teaching of rhetoric; certainly the teachings of Herennius, in which writer not only are there useful precepts, but also pure speech.[15] But this same hour may if you prefer also be replaced alternatively with fundamentals of dialectic using Aristotle's definitions, partitions, and rules which by the skilled and diligent *magister* are easily drawn together in whatever order they will be chosen. For that matter, Aristotle's are not translated into Latin but are in Greek, whose native powers shall be retained by this method, and whose translation will not be poisoned by the language of youth. And when he (i.e., the pupil) shall be led to the *Organum* of Aristotle, he shall not be transported to a land not his own because he will think that he has remained in his own, and as in Herennius's Latin speech, so in these Greek orations that philosophy will be elegantly preserved. Really, in the precepts of Herennius I concede that there is that which is skillful and is appointed and distinguished. But more briefly, and on the other hand, if these boys will be annoyed by this I do not approve. Other things are more necessary: attentiveness to arrangement; annotation of arguments and their handling; propositions and reasons and concluding perception and the comprehension of deliberation. They will make of memory a support. It is sufficiently great if they are necessary or illustrious and committed to memory as examples. The remaining four hours I grant to whichever of the writers' language—Greek or Latin. The truth of the matter is that in so turning one thing must be guarded against: that the Greek skill in speech not overtake the skill of Latin speech and take precedence over it.

The explanation of good authors which have something hidden in them

For both are necessary, the Latin tongue, however, has a wider use; although that of Greece also extends to things and actions of men in our century and in our Europe. They really will be explained by the authors. These may not be very numerous among them. Some may be understood by themselves, without the work of teachers and without the grammarians' or rhetoricians' commentaries. But by which art and body of knowledge are they kept hidden from sight, and from which examples can they be readily grasped so that the student will feel he is being helped by the teacher?

Of style

This daily stylistic exercise must be persevered in, and to dare something more praiseworthy is fitting, and to give space to deliberation. An argument is put forth almost at the same moment it is run down by an opposite saying. But it will be given grace by adolescents, whether it be a commonplace or an elaboration or an argument or a practice of oratorical ornamentation or a written narrative. He will recite whether he carries it home or whether he completes it in the hour in which it was assigned. And if it belongs to the thing, only with a domestic exercise or even with higher exercises it should be finished in the schools. Because in the fifth class we have already introduced this, it must all be retained by the students in the upper class. And we want it to be observed by the teachers. So let it be stored in journals and diaries and let it be enriched by daily reading and listening and writing, so that students may more abundantly learn, and the master, like a good steward, may daily view his family's wealth increase. And the primary school teacher, like a diligent lord of the manner, may be able to acquaint himself with all of the rural laborers' interests.

Of the First Class

After this we come, as it were, to the highest class, which occupies a privileged place—a group of students about to graduate. To this class and tribe, nonetheless (and to this group alone), by virtue of its superior position, not yet in the Senate, or in the Forum, or in the Courts of Law, but in relation to public schools, and according to those who are called public teachers. The order (ἔπαγγελια) of these are the arts that we call Physics, Mathematics, Ethics. But up to this point the year must be reserved for that boyhood discipline that is even more important for the adolescent, which they call logic, λογικάς. Purity of speech, truth of argument, ornateness of discourse—toward this end we desire a higher degree of speech, as far as possible fit for the intellects of masters and of doctors.

1. Dialectic and rhetoric must be completed

Wherefore in this highest class one may leave off the fundamentals that are called slavish exercises. Such must all be set in order and must be explained more practically; more usefully, I say, in terms of what I perceive as useful for the adolescent, not for the self-esteem of the master, who then in the final analysis is judged a fine teacher when many students learn. The teacher is the best judge of time and everything may be seen as superfluous which is too wordy. One should always keep Horace's precept in view: whatsoever you teach, let it be brief. Nothing, moreover, is too brief and short which is adequate to the intellect and to knowing.

2. Latin and Greek authors must be explained

But these things have been received beforehand by dialectic and by rhetoric and the upper class has already had this kind of thing. I allot one hour daily to this. The remaining hours are to be divided between the Latin and Greek authors, starting with the orators. I allow, however, during these hours whenever it is seen as useful and as the progress of youth may require, three of Cicero's books—*On Friendship; On Old Age*, and *On Official Duty*. For these orations are enriching, and those concerning the orator contribute to the precepts of speaking, of ornate oratory, and of the knowledge of things.

3. The plan for explaining this

In that kind of explanation by writers, truly one must not hold to the kind of reasoning of boys, but rather to that done by the teacher. If this adolescent class recites by this superior approach to periphrase, let them interpret it. Similarly with Latin periphrasis if they desire. If they do not so desire, let them recite back singly in Latin those portions from the

Greek. Somewhere by means of language they will reflect on the literal meaning of words, when the seriousness of things and the power of discourse shall require. But neither periphrases nor anything else is exclusively pursued. They are really only a means of establishing the beginning of the whole. The teacher will explain all kinds of narrations, all kinds of questions, all commonplaces and amplifications. The teacher will explain only the more obscure passages. He will give examples for such passages; he will point out eminent ornaments; he will remind them of laws and historical events. In this fashion he sets in motion and in this way dwells on the subject and also in this manner will hasten sometimes in months, sometimes in weeks the first book or first oration towards completion. These things really will be remarked upon and referred to chiefly in the students' journals, where they will be shown. In this fashion they ought all to be noted. Whenever it shall be necessary, they might be demonstrated. These things shall be committed to memory. Let it be made known and anticipated in advance, if they are able to, by the boys.

4. The use of diaries and journals

If they are not able to explain, let them return to their journals, which books are the custodians of memory and its companions and helpers. Such is the use that a zealous adolescent makes of his journal. Just as the diligent head of a family puts money into a strongbox, and just as this head of the family is delighted each day equally by his old and his new money, so is it fitting that the literature and teaching of the learned is perceived with delight. They are not compared in the same way. But they are certainly compared every day. Yet things of antiquity ought to be diligently guarded. Nothing must be neglected in this dimension because it pertains to God, to nature, to art and to humanity in what is a quadripartite organization whose starting point is from the lowest class. Observation and resolve concerns all the teachers in the school. In such a way diaries and journals are brought to completion.

5. Practice of style here. Three things that must always be kept in mind

Here more important stylistic exercises are begun—commentary, declamation, translation—and of these the school master will not as yet think of himself as a judge of such as are done, but rather as an assistant, and he will pursue in all three things the things that are of constant service:

brevity, clarity, information. Out of that which is accomplished what we will require is one simple thing: a total knowledge.

Concerning the Public Teachers

While in this lower school adolescents are being educated, they live, as it were, under the rod where, enclosed by private walls, they are tamed by the teacher's hand, to be taught by him to endure, not because of his power, but because of his desire. But he also extracts judgment from the teacher. Educated from these as if in court and in the Senate, as if in the market place and in the law-court: so-called public places. And to theologians religion is handed down. And to physicists, the very mysteries of nature; and to ethics teachers and lawyers, too, the customs of human society; and to dialecticians, all perfected truth. To rhetoricians, eloquence itself.

Theologians

For what reason is one led to the theologian? This will have been learned in catechism class. The separate commonplaces will by more difficult questions be recognized. Paul's Epistles and those of the evangelists may be attempted. The psalms may be practiced and requested daily. But of the exercises presently, now truly of them only those pertaining to religion concern us. You will have partaken, therefore, in a lower place; of these which we have called classes (*curia*) and tribes (*tribus*) the youth in which are all of middling ability and they will accept anything as it comes from the interpreter. From the theologian greater things may be expected. He will explain more difficult books and the more obscure passages of the Apostles and of the Prophets. He will apply the Fathers' doctrine. He will show the succession of Christian assemblies, their corruptions, changes, disagreements, friendships, warlike and peaceful times, their battlefields when fighting for their countries and their apostles and prophets, and will make connections between them and in all of this he will point out (that) which is true and probable. This person will be an inquisitor and a moderator in disputations so that in these questions and answers agreements may be reached about religious doctrine. For the same thing may or may not be seen in the same way by everyone. Besides, just at that time where there are contrary opinions amongst them do they defend dogma. Moreover, by debating the speeches of Cicero, the art of reasoning is most excellently handed down. From Plato comes sharp and brief questioning, although even this writer would often digress (by making the digressions longer he wastes space). Then at the place where he broke off suddenly he is allowed to wander off, or like Gorgias or Protagoras or Socrates, he will show how he was able to bring it off by eloquent praise in a tedious argument. So, for that reason, because the Sophists were trying this, they might have been able to do the same thing. One could of one's own accord, if one wanted, do the same.

Physicians and Mathematicians

Whoever really wants to be a physicist let him begin young. Likewise, may all the others whom we wish to learn stay in class. But all those who want to become doctors must wish to be seen as both learned and well trained, and must wish so to be. They must know those books of Aristotle on physics and also on measurement. These teachers must prepare themselves in arithmetic, not only so they are acquainted with it, but also practiced in it, and in astronomy are not contented by the spheres of Proclus, but inquire of higher authorities, and ascend to the peaks of Ptolemy, Archimedes, and Theon without neglecting the basic groundwork. And the situation of the whole earth and of earth's descriptions, and also of peoples and of nations: let them be acquainted with fields and the fruits of the fields; (with) merchandise, customs, laws, surpluses and shortages; with salubrities and maladies, with rivers and springs as well. And in other living beings whose nature is in some way admirable.

And we desire that they know these writers and teach all of them to adolescents and young people; and likewise we desire mathematics and physics teachers to teach them so that their teachings may be kept in the classroom. Brevity, clarity, memory—by whose simple and fulsome teaching we have been said to be accomplished.

Now whatever we have said of mathematical knowledge, the same we feel goes for music, to the extent, however, that what we wish to be taught be practiced daily.

Ethics, Politics, Law

We are held fast under the law of knowledge, the first of whose books has been proposed by us. Not only those which are called ethical books by Aristotle but also political (books) about public knowledge—all laws these, as many as there are the science of law. And, moreover, in this legal abundance the good and diligent teacher ought to devote his attention only to what is necessary; not to the unnecessary; he should follow what is rare by what is frequent; what is extraordinary by what is ordinary; what is obscure and abstruse with what is distinguished by him as nevertheless useful and clearly preferred. Not only is the adolescent indebted to the teacher for lessons regarding life and the society of men and obliged to learn, but he learns to teach himself by reading these writers and to help along the teachers' lessons. In like manner the beginning soldier who not only wished to be trained by the master, but even for himself and the master and so many others he strives to keep at work. And therefore this beginner learns, and is prepared to struggle. Similarly, this student wants to listen in the public school. He is a lazy fellow who has nothing of his own prowess, it is said. Thus the teacher's labor is bi-partite: one part is centered on teaching, so let him teach the things that are of the most importance. The other part of teaching lies in admonishing, so let him advise what the student ought to read at home.

The students' task is also two-fold. First he must learn from the teacher what he (the teacher) has grasped. The second, that he teaches himself at home. Let him always have something that he may read at home. Let him always have something he will be able to comment upon, something that he may write. Because by the art of preparation he will increase in ability.

Dialecticians

The same thing is to be done with dialectic by the teacher and by the student. One is teaching in school, the other is at home reading so that he may do his duty. The one is helped by the other's power in everything that is handed down in Aristotle's *Organum*. We want this book to be used forever by dialecticians in school so that young people may read, teachers may explain, and all may follow in these matters and in the things that pertain to disputations that are contained in a communion of liberal arts.

Rhetoricians

The business of rhetoric in these public exercises is to teach all the arts, to know everything that has been taught about rational speaking by Aristotle, Hermogenes, and all of the Greek writers. But Cicero is the first on whom to hold fast. This teacher ought to be the first undertaken in the emulation of reason, foremost among the excellent writers, he of whom we speak as M. Tullius Cicero. But in the same way did he follow behind Demosthenes; nor was the latter far from following after Isocrates, who was outstanding before him. And, moreover, we do not wish speech to bear only the shape of eloquence, but also of maturity, even as that well-proportioned philosophy that comes from the Academy and Lyceum. Xenophon and Plutarch, Polybius, Thucydides, and Herodotus have much that will be able to help these teachers of rhetoric and oratory. In reading and in explaining these, write down the propositions completely. The chief point in all this is that in speaking the lessons are recalled to memory as if by calculation. And from these examples may be shown by means of the authors; not each one in one and the same way, but out of one many diverse ways; and material things demonstrate how these forms may be applied, or how these forms can be described. Not very many things under investigation can be received by speaking figuratively; in imitation itself it is necessary that that which is required in every function should be suitably manifest.

To this teacher we concede every kind of discussion. He can enjoin whatever kind of proposition may be executed and achieved in art, in medicine, in agriculture, in architecture which speaking about history might require, and to which property belongs that kind of embellishment, to which author that kind of subject. This approach will have been pointed out by Plato and introduced by Socrates by way of discussion. This precept may be capable of being calmly taught and by philosophical speech rather than by dialogue—by what is acute, brief, and closely questioned. In such does Plato abound. But I have even proceeded by means of ordinary discourse, as is found in Aristotle's account of living species and in many other books. And Cicero in his book on public service gave an even fuller account in his discussion in which students do not find the contradictions given in the introductory sections.

On Daily Exercises

As it shall be for teachers in the regular classes, so too will it be for the public teachers, who, if they shall do their duty in the way we prescribe, will be able to lead their students together; for to be led to what is beneficial is also glorious, pious, and religious, learned, and eloquent, which end(s) we have established for our students.

The chief discipline in teaching adolescents is daily drill; it is inimical to the lazy, the enemy of the unskilled, and to all the expounders of difficulty. This kind of exercise is really not unexceptional, but in our gymnasium ten exercises are especially important: psalms, recitations, speeches, written work, declamations, disputations, conversations, demonstrations, dramatic readings, and games. Daily reading and explaining matter is, notwithstanding, the daily business of this exercise.

Seeing whereas that business pertains to the teachers, we maintain this duty for each of the ten years of student life.

On Psalms

Because even though we hold religion prime by sacred song and by recitation we give assemblies the foremost importance. And in the first grade we have taught singing so that instruction begins to teach before class begins. Some complex psalms and some written in a straight line are sung to accompaniment by the adolescents. All the voices together, each with the same movement of tongue and in the same space of time undertake not only the verse, but also its meaning, and as well as all its verses and at the same time begin and move forward and then stop simultaneously, and pause often submitting neither to diversion nor preventing what is discerning. One ought to sing intelligently what is to be sung, so that God's law can be known, the recollection of discipline be promoted, and ability be enhanced, as often is the case when it must be measured by performance.

This duty must be performed thrice daily: in the morning when they come into the school; at mid-day when they have returned home, and before the evening meal when the daily work is finished. A number of psalms must be sung to accompaniment weekly by each one. The brevity and prolixity of each must be appraised, so that by the third month everyone in this school is singing and every year they wish to sing four times. Three therefore must be sung and three invoked; what is requested is that what is pious and holy must be referred to the contents of the psalm, and that is the theologian's job. These prayers must be completed and guarded in this school.

Exercises for Daily Recitation

I call recitations that which the Greeks called repetitions (ἀναγνώσεις), whence ἀναγνωσαὶ after which the readers of the church were named. These are introduced at lunch and at dinner, and consist of the following: the books of Kings, Genesis, and several of the Evangiles. More difficult certainly are the books of the Apostles and Prophets whose works diligent theologians have to be able to explain and to teach rather than to recite because it is pleasing.

Let him who recites in a hall read first to himself what another reads aloud so that he may be able to read without any hindrance and to pronounce more intelligibly; so that his sentences may be suitably distinguished and not only his voice but also his body language should contribute something, as with all things as are said to be suitable.

It is also useful in those psalms that are played weekly to explain the words in Latin, Greek, and Hebrew. For it is necessary that the readers of these be more knowledgeable and recite these more carefully and the students are almost reverently committed to this duty.

On Orations

Orations we call ὁμιλίας, which at Strasbourg we hold after dinner before which adolescents are accustomed to go back to their rooms and lie down. These are brief, but serious, and either written down or carefully prepared and learned by heart so that the message appears as holy writ and a work of piety, even as the keenness of dialecticians and also of truth and is as elegant and as embellished as rhetoric. These kinds of examples are taken from Augustine as it is this doctor adolescents seek eagerly to pursue, first for purity of speech, then for clarity of meaning; so that not only are adolescents seen as interpreters and reciters of that author, but even the imitators and rivals.

On Writings

Three-fold writing

I want writing to be a daily affair and the hands and ears of students I never want to be lacking a written composition or a pen, or minus a pack of paper. For the task of writing is three-fold. The most elementary is that in which the child becomes nicely accustomed to the writing of an elegant hand, which is accomplished about the time he is attending the fourth grade. We will have ascertained this very thing so far as the advantage of custom leads not only to literary study but also to the practice of public service in the magistracy and in the limits to which the counsel of reason can be properly observed. Yes indeed, in the matter of public service it can be seen (that) to the republic belong learned men and distinguished writing.

Diaries should be kept faithfully

Another kind of writing is diaries and journals, of which we have spoken, and of language and things, opinions and authority and the examples of each of their specifics, that which will be important in schools of dialectic and rhetoric. Their books must be carefully saved; for their skill is revealed to the teacher by the things in these books, which are learned through daily notation. They are carried hidden in the minds of the boys. They are witnesses of diligence. These are the custodians of memory, the defenders against critics of both boys and teachers.

The third kind (of writing) is stylistic, which we daily wish to be sharpened and from day to day more and more greatly to shine, whether it be the whole or some part of orations and declamations; whether somewhat remarkable arguments or enlargements; whether charming epigrams and well-constituted letters, or whether it be somewhat heroic narrative. By these kinds of daily commentaries, which ought to be described as journals and shown to teachers and to their aides and often examined by the director of the student.

The Daily Exercises of Declamations

Speeches that are wholly intelligible are in truth rhetorical exercises (μελέται), but the most elegant words for things come from the Greek. They are indisputably earnest and profound. I do not know why Latin speeches are to be called pleasing, unless possibly because the first service of speaking out loud used to be permitted the inexpert, or because it was by no means menacing in this way to employ those with loud shouting voices to be speakers, seeing as how in the forum they could orate on serious matters, and in this way the oratorical voice was not only begun, but taught various things such as speaking softly, teaching tranquilly, exclaiming strongly. Useful speakers are acknowledged by everyone, but they are few. They praise him who is acknowledged and they make use of him and cherish him.

First, then, comes the duty of the preceptor and of the director whom the Rector appoints. And let him see to it that the practice of declaiming not be left off, and that continual declamations are held, so that you go with the times, equal to the rank of debater by turns. In declamations likewise the same evidence ought to exist as in public addresses: knowledge, custom, eloquence.

Arguments can be made as long as possible if they are such things as move the spirits of those who listen to them and make a close approach to the truth. The preacher must be chosen if it is possible to do so who has somewhere reached a certain discernment in these matters and wisdom as well, and will defend these Latin pursuits. How wonderful it is that the use of Latin speech is so practical, and as much so for the praise of studies and of letters as of character. If you are not able to achieve it (i.e., Latin speech), in its stead may be substituted contrary behavior, such as persuasion and discouragement, praise and vituperation, accusation and repulsion. But another approach is more suitable, and tends towards the truth and towards the material prosperity of the republic and towards the glory of literary disputation.

Disputations

In order that the exercise of declaiming may extend as far as rhetoric, (then) as disputing is to dialectic, dialectic must in the highest degree accommodate the practice and use of this habit of disputation. From this come many good things and many warnings. Many vices have crept into this practice, but this is not the place to pursue those problems, which, moreover, can be corrected if questions are chosen which are useful for living; if rules of logic are maintained; if jealousy, ill-will, and irascibility are prevented—which vices are gravely punished and shunned by whatever means, as is shown by Plato and the speeches of Cicero.

In like manner it is taught in the higher type of oration that in this way of speaking nothing should be done in a mediocre fashion; not only should the debater or orator not reveal his plan but also the moderator and teacher should not reveal it.

Conversations

We want youth—all of them, including those harbored in the lowest grades—to have Latin conversations. We do not want teachers speaking to them in the native tongue, nor will it be necessary. At the same time that the boy enters school, let him have a master who teaches him Latin vocabulary items, and inflections of nouns and verbs, and let him commit these to memory. This practice must be retained even more in the upper grades and must be praised and must be confirmed by the rules and guarded by severity and by punishment.

In school, then, the schoolmaster teaches. We want quiet. When boys enter school, when they play, when they walk together, when they are coming on the way to school, their speech should be Latin or Greek. Let no one come here if he is going impudently to stray in this matter. But these conversations are free, for adolescents, having returned home, have some discussion amongst themselves. It is equally useful and laudable as I have said to practice in Latin. But in a certain way conversations are necessary and are advisable in school and at lunch and at dinner, so that they are educated in school, by questions and answers. In this way the boys have entertainment; even the lowest classes— which calls into question vocabulary items. Then is productivity brought all the way down from the highest to the beginning grades and distributed from the whole to the lowest members. This will be an easy plan if there is a moderator presiding. No path leads to error which has a guide, no problem if the guide is an orator.

Demonstrations

I call demonstrations not only the proofs (ἀποδείξεις) of the mathematicians but also the expositions (εὐδείξεις) of the grammarians. There are two kinds of things that are translated by vocabulary. One of these has been noted or is daily observed by the eye, as with bread, wine, house, roof, wall, goose, duck, capon, which are seen daily. But the other kind is obscure and unknown because there is a need for disclosure and demonstration. So it is with the seven planets and the Pleiades and cynosura (the north pole's constellation!) up in the sky and in the muscular tissue of man, the crystalline color in the eye, the nerves inside the head. Many herbs need to be identified and all of the parts of herbs and plants; similarly with gems and stones. Many qualifications are not recognized or seen. There is no skill which has not had its director. If that which is taught in school is useful and necessary, its usage will be preserved. This must by no means be neglected. We must use a switch to drive away ignorance in enlarging our resources and skills, in conserving what is in our memory, in the facility and in the renewal of genius, in the avoidance of disdain; because nothing is more pernicious in this discipline of youth.

On Comedies and Tragedies

Comedies and tragedies are not gladly explained by many teachers. Indeed these necessary genre have been neglected in another way. Notwithstanding, many penalties accrue from this, and I want youth to recite from memory. These skills will be attained if in an individual group of ten students (the famous decurion) particular stories are set forth and their characters who say little without difficulty are performed. The first roles require more work from the actors. These things must be carried out. They (the roles or characters) can be divided into two or three and begun in groups to be learned by heart. It should be disposed of by everybody so that they are introduced to this gradually every day, or by repeated performances by adolescent minds. The object of this work is not to tire them nor overwhelm them. In a few months a large portion of stories will be able to be introduced into schools by this method without explanation by teachers and minus the scorn of students. What privately seemed obscure will be seen and understood.

That is made clear either by acting and by habit or by the brief explanation of the teacher or by conversation and the connections made amongst the youth themselves.

It is, however, the duty of teachers to know those stories thoroughly that the pupils are doing and to draw out from the authors and historians to be explained the passages in which something is either obscure or corrupt, or acute and erudite, different or contrary. It is hard, but it is nevertheless true and wonderful, with a little help from a learned and industrious teacher how many things and how much a pupil can comprehend.

Games

All the above exercises should be held with games. For such is the nature of men that they seek pastimes in the movement of the body rather than in the exercise of the mind. And so dice, die, and quoits are sought for, races and dances are desired. Hunting, fishing, swimming delight, and "gladiators" offer much more recreation than teachers so. Nor am I so rigid that I would not wish the minds of the youths to be refreshed by games of this sort. But we ought to follow Cicero, who wished us to use jests and games, with slumbers and rest periods, and then indeed after that satisfaction was given with grave and serious studies. And so it must be played so that the game is honorable and moderate, so that the soul is not carried away with desire and that perils are avoided. There are many things of this dangerous kind in fighting, swimming, fishing, and hunting. It is, however, a characteristic of our schools to teach the Latin language in the games. So when the times of the games have been set, the moderator should be present, so that more suitable and more useful games are chosen, to set goals for the races, for running and jumping, also to pitch a camp, to lead a troup, to command an army, to appoint leaders, centurions, decurions; to make the legions ready, and to separate them into cohorts. That is liberal, useful, and delightful.

It is also honorable to make descriptions of buildings, gardens, and pleasant estates. Get out of cities to view the fields and gardens, to dig out plants, to ask their names, to taste them and to share them. Nor can there be any doubt about the pleasure and utility that this method of play has. To do these things and to seek other similar kinds of amusements is useful, honest, delightful, and necessary. For the spirits of men fatigued by serious studies wish to be refreshed. But finally repose must be praised, both pleasure and recreation, which maintains itself within the boundaries of modesty and propriety.

Laws of the Lauingen School[16]

Wolfgang, by the grace of God Count of the Rhenish
Palatinate, Duke of Bavaria, & Count of Welden

Concerning the office of a prince we are not uninformed. When rightly
established, it takes care that the people shall not want for anything, and
then that schools be established: training schools of virtue, good morals,
piety, knowledge and religion. And seeing that we are adding to the
Hornbach gymnasium the Lauingen school, and are in the act of building up these places of residence and providing them with masters and
with a choice of school governors and a designated Rector, we want the
men of each of these two gymnasia to be restrained by laws and that
the Rector, Vice-Rector, public teachers, classroom teachers, the classes
themselves, the pupils of the schools and foreigners, guests of the citizenry, may be seen to have the greatest amount first of religion, next of
morals, and then of correct knowledge.

Concerning the Rector and Vice-Rector and the Professors'
Duties at Lauingen

1. Concerning the Rector and those given him as staff, for all that
they exist it is nonetheless the Rector who is the first in authority by virtue of his knowledge, diligence, moderation, humanity, seriousness.
2. In order that the preceptors, masters and everyone perform their
daily task, these same people will be closely watched.
3. The teachers will be the first to arrive at school at the sound of
the bell and the last to leave.
4. These same teachers will follow the Rector's regulations for the
method of teaching which is backed up by the school board's authority,
and they will not, between teaching, speak ostentatiously against them,
or by intentional digressions stray from the subject matter; rather, they
will adapt to the ingeniousness of men and in general serve through the
practice of knowledge. A final consideration is the brief amount of time
that we have at our disposal.
5. Of clothing, food, drink, vigilance, diligence, and home reading,
even of home writing, of the frequency of attending church assemblies
and of piety there are many examples. The examples set by overseers
and masters are lost while those set by adolescents' wit are preserved.

6. Drink-loving teachers either devote themselves to the school or are ejected from it. They are a sign of spoiled discipline.

7. In reproving and punishing adolescent carelessness and inactivity, firmness should be far removed from cruelty, censuring far from reviling.

8. As for adolescents who are not naturally well suited to literary study, the Rector and governors of the gymnasium, the parents, we the faculty and the other protectors to whom such things pertain must in time come to a decision. Those who do not with time bear fruit might be beyond recovery and admitted to other walks of life, at any point where an irreparable damage is about to overwhelm the student.

The Laws of the College

Concerning the college we really feel this way: that we have established it in this fashion and we wish it to be just this way, so that first, the serious discipline of religion and of morals, then of knowledge is cherished.

1. Prayers before midday and in the afternoon are attended by each individual at certain times and places.

2. No adolescent is to be admitted nor retained in whom there is no indication of modesty and diligence.

3. Those who are to be admitted are to be named by the controller. They shall pay for three months' maintenance and so on for the following months.

4. No one will be admitted to the school without giving surety. The situation of everyone sent to us will be taken into consideration.

5. Unusual fees and related expenses will be provided for by the parents. Students who withdraw early from the college will be liable to fee settlements. All pedagogical customs will be complied with.

6. He who does not bear with pedagogical discipline will be punished. He who does not listen to the rules is to be chastised, fined, and punished by the director.

7. Anyone who injures another will be held responsible for their injury.

8. Anyone who has a place in the school and wants a dormitory room to be saved for him may be absent from meals until his room and board (i.e., elsewhere) terminate.

9. Students must go to church services twice on festival days, and that decorously. They must listen earnestly to assembly programs. Without their reading from the *Book of Psalms* or the *New Testament* at home, they cannot remember and review the gist of the assembly.

10. Daily drills and exercises are to be attended to. No one is excused from these.

11. Latin speech is prescribed for everyone everywhere. All scholars must attend classes. Other schools do not enforce this. No loud shouts, no singing, no walking around, no noise making or din of any kind. Whoever shall offend by reason of his offenses will pay the penalty in just measure.

12. In this school no student can do anything without a teacher's approval; no teacher without the Scholarchs' permission.

13. One and all will dress in a creditable manner. In dress, the customs of the city are respected by the establishment of the school, and they permit nothing else pertaining to dress outside the home.

14. No one will leave the school grounds, no one of any rank nor emanate from them, no one from any place without the consent and thorough knowledge of a teacher; in winter particularly is this not allowed.

15. At dinner, lunch and breakfast, in every gathering, speech must be about wholesome, chaste, and profitable things. The Latin similarly must be modest, respectful, gentlemanly; neither capricious nor contentious. At dinner and at lunchtime, so that there be no lack of conversational material, something memorized might be requested for recitation. No one may despise the exercises of the school without punishment.

16. Quarrels, injuries, and infamous acts are unsuitable from everyone in the student body. Who does otherwise, will be restrained and subject to supervision.

17. Whoever the author of discord may be, if he does not desist, he will be expelled from school.

18. Weapons, swords, and daggers may not be worn. Whoever gets arms into his possession must give them over to school authorities for safekeeping.

19. Whoever by force attacks or threatens another with arms is to be ejected from school. Whoever does the same thing without arms will pay for the offense.

20. The evil deeds and habits of groups of companions everyone must flee. Whoever encourages these is to be punished.

21. No one without the permission of a supervisor may approach an inn, tavern, or public entertainment.

22. No one from the outside may be brought into the school or into a dormitory without an important reason, and probably, no one will be permitted to remain after 9 o'clock in winter or 9:30 in summer. After these hours they must go. Everyone should, before going to sleep, call upon, propitiate, and praise God.

23. The door of the school will be closed in winter before dinner, in summer, whenever the teacher shall be seen closing it. No one may go out after that time.

24. Why shouldn't the teacher make the rounds, entering into every student bedroom to inspect on a weekly basis, neglecting nothing; the doors to these very rooms being opened, they may be entered upon by knocking by whomever undertakes to make this visit.

25. As soon as anyone gets up he will make his bed with his bedspread over it, smoothed down and prepared for daytime. The room will be cleansed like a sauna, with all filth removed to the dung-heap, and every item put in its place.

26. Fellow students and dormitory companions must devote their time to study while in the dormitory, not to chatting, or walking around, and not to make a hindrance of noise making.

27. As to neighboring dormitory rooms, no one without reason may go into or hold meetings nor sit with one another nor permit any room to be damaged. Whoever does such things may with good cause be punished by a teacher.

28. Whoever cannot be judged to be doing his duty may be asked to leave and find some other kind of life. And everyone will comply with these laws that follow from and are in accordance with knowledge, discipline, and religion.

Laws of the Congregation

Religion is the first end of studies, of the knowledge of God, and also of His divine works. This same religion and knowledge is taught and perfected by eloquence; but one must distinguish between the two in this manner: that while knowledge may be necessary, ornate eloquence is helped by these two disciplines nevertheless, and by good law in which this distinction is made. For laws without discipline can accomplish little. Discipline, indeed, discovered the laws by itself, so wisely agreed upon. It is, therefore, up to the Rector of a school of letters to establish, and the schoolmasters to agree, since this is God's will. The teachers, indeed, have many professional reasons for supporting these, and they ought to do so, not only diligently, but eagerly, and avidly. For this is God's will in the first place. After that, the Rector's. Finally, it will require a great deal of Christian charity from everybody. How much may be proposed by a Christian society!

But it is the practice of teachers and masters of letters to adhere to the laws themselves even if nobody else does. Adolescents, in truth, and boys of whatever sort must be ruled and protected by that rein that is the law. Without law all one can do is wish, not effect, and do that superfluously. Wherefore, they do great moral works who wish to comply with and work within the laws that are preserved by authorities.

1. Someone may ask what happens if they are not present during established hours, either at school or in church assemblages. They must be corrected by whipping unless they are excused by their parents, or the master of their household takes them home. The boy in question is committing a sin of the will, he is not inspired by weakness.

2. Whoever comes in after the established hour ought to be punished in a reasonable way. That is the judgment of the Rector, of the Visitors, and of the teachers, all the moreso if he is three times admitted late in the course of one week.

3. He who is careless about listening attentively, who doesn't review his reading, who when questioned cannot answer, who in other respects is neglectful of the discipline of a good student, for his errors, faults, inclinations and age should be punished. For strong medicine will be provided for this disease by the severity of the switch. By no means will words alone provide a sensible remedy.

4. He who does not listen diligently, who thinks of other things, who is a trifler, who writes down others' work, will be a doodler and will read everything else but what is taught. This kind of fault is punished very little by threatening and rebuke. The firmness of discipline can heal the defects of these natures.

5. Those who are delighted by harmful things, whose speech is quarrelsome, who bind up their fists for fighting, who go off and fight somewhere, who swear, who scorn their teachers, who go about irreverently, who either stare at or chide those worthy of respect so that their elders, or the authorities, or men of authority or virtue, when they meet such in public places do not remain modestly and as is fitting in studies of letters. Good and serious thought ought to change them.

6. Whose conversation is employed with anything but Latin, who are shameless, I find shameful; for faults of this sort they are with good reason to be punished.

7. One may turn against the teachers and bear away false complaints to his parents or tutors or to relatives or to friends or to his intimates and to good men. And although what he says is untrue, and although it is against the teachers and against the authorities and is unpleasant, because he is at home his lies arouse his folks. Instead of his serious misdeeds, he castigates the hardness of the whip, or else it is the protective environment of the school which confines him so; or whatever there is good in firmness might be better.

8. He is not one of the decurions (class monitors); in observing and calling to account the whip must be used; it cannot be morally amiss in this case. Otherwise this could be permanently corrupting and he could set new fellow students a bad example, or draw others towards a fellowship of vice and ruin the school's discipline.

Foreign Students Upon Entering Into the Duties of Students

1. Whoever is sent to school from elsewhere, let no citizen detain you without the consent of the Rector and Vice Rector.
2. Let no one separate you from your host, or change your residence without their will or permission.
3. It is a destructive thing to be amongst intemperate companions and to live without moderation. It is harmful to be among the greedy. In either case, the laws are shunned.
4. You may not wear military dress, nothing effeminate, nothing lewd, nothing that goes counter to good and honest, manly custom.
5. Do not bring books with you. Do not procure new clothing. Do not accept money on loan without the consent and wishes of the Rector, Vice Rector, teachers and of those to whom the youths have been committed. Townsmen who sell things by lending you money are not allowed by municipal law to prosecute before the law.
6. In psalm-singing assemblies there is danger, especially among students who live with townspeople. At the right time one may sing, listen, and prophesy.
7. Those same companions from town ought to attend the public gatherings held at school on feast days.
8. Without permission of the Rector and the school authorities, no one in the Prince's school and no one among the townspeople is given leisure for dueling matches, musical performances, or leaping contests.
9. All foreign students within the school and lodging with townspeople, having committed themselves to living in such a manner, must by the end of the third month obtain testimony from parents, patrons, relatives, friends and tutors and send it in.
10. If, among the townsmen and the students any dispute or controversy arises which is in all cases to be guarded against, do not rashly and privately seek vengeance. Rather should it be carefully reviewed in the presence of the Rector, or alternatively, turned over to the city Magistrate or Council assembled, and their opinions respectfully awaited.

10
Classical Letters
(1565)

Introduction

In the *Classical Letters*, twenty-four highly stylized epistles, Johann Sturm explains the teaching plan and strategy written to Duke Albrecht of Prussia, to the Strasbourg scholarchs, to the preceptors, professors, and other scholars. As Anton Schindling has observed, these introductions to gymnasium studies are very much in line with his *The Correct Opening of Schools of Letters*. Consistency may well have been one of Sturm's faults, but his pedagogical influence continued to expand even in politically difficult times. By 1565 times had changed, Luther's death, the Smalkald War, the aggressiveness and triumphs of the Catholic forces and the Habsburgs, with Strasbourg in a vulnerable spot between Austria and the Spanish Netherlands. Polarization within Strasbourg affected Sturm's gymnasium or Academy as well.

Sturm was constantly consulted on educational matters, but also on interstate, not yet international, matters. For proper compensation in 1552 he informed and advised Henry II, the King of France, on conditions in the Empire and on the other hand offered political intelligence, along with the political agent Cardinal de Granvelle to the King of Denmark. His correspondence was always fascinating and, like Calvin, he enjoyed an exchange with Cardinal Sadoleto, though the letters reveal the great difference between Sturm and Calvin in terms of theological depth. Sturm was also personally involved in reform efforts outside of Strasbourg. In 1542 and 1543, for example, he accompanied Bucer to Cologne, where the archbishop had summoned Bucer to help to reform his diocese. With the help of the moderate Bishop of Strasbourg, Erasmus of Limbourg, he was spared the return of his Gymnasium buildings to the Dominicans and Catholic rites.

No need to rehearse in detail the political events that transformed the power configuration in the Empire with all its resulting fall-out on Strasbourg, a story well known and often told. The polarization in the Empire was reflected in the rise of Dr. Johannes Marbach, a staunch Lutheran, in Strasbourg. He served as superintendent of the Strasbourg church and became the professor of theology and visitor of the Academy. Marbach received a bad press from the older French Calvinist historians, but he was the man of the hour. He resented the flaccid nature of Sturm's Erasmian Christian humanist theology. Change was underway, but Sturm persisted in advocating his traditional educational ideas. In that very year, 1565, he did his plan for the school at Lauingen and the letters that he included in the *Epistolae Classicae* reflect the struggles of the time. With Marbach's support, the Emperor's privilege transformed the Academy into an institution administered as a gymnasium by the director, authorized to grant degrees of bachelor and master of arts. This was an important step in the direction of establishing the University of Strasbourg. The letters reflect Sturm's adoration of Cicero, appreciation of physical education, references to his many editions of texts, and the controversies underway. Despite his philosophical and theological shallowness, as a pedagogue Sturm was among the best of the leading educators of the century.

See the precise pages of Anton Schindling, *Humanistische Hochschule und Freie Reichsstadt: Gymnasium und Akademie in Strassburg 1538–1621* (Wiesbaden, 1977), pp. 38–40. The great Sturm scholar and master of the Strasbourg archives Jean Rott, editor and translator into French of the *Classicae Epistolae*, has an excellent and comprehensive introduction, pp. vii-xxxi, *Jean Sturm Classicae Epistolae sive Scholae Argentinenses Restitutae* (Paris: Librairie E. Droz and Strasbourg: Éditions Fides, 1938). Jean Rott, "Bibliographie des Oeuvres Imprimées du Recteur Strasbourgeois Jean Sturm (1507–1589)," *Investigationes Historicae: Églises et Société au XVIe Siècle; Gesammelte Aufsätze zur Kirchen- und Sozialgeschichte*, II (Strasbourg: Librairie Oberlin, 1986), pp. 471–559, on page 361 gives a list of the reprint editions of the *Classicae Epistolae*. On Sturm's pedagogical editions of texts, see Johannes Ficker, "Erste Lehr- und Lernbücher des höheren Unterrichts in Strassburg (1534–1542)," in the *Festschrift für Heinrich Wallau* (Strasbourg, 1912). We have decided not to annotate this chapter because the French edition of *The Epistolae Classicae* edited by Jean Rott provides such detailed and precise documentation.

Classical Letters
(1565)

1. 1565, March 30. Strasbourg.
    Sturm to Albert, Duke of Prussia.

> To the illustrious Prince and Nobleman, My Lord Albert,
> Margrave of Brandenburg, Duke of Prussia, of Stettin, of
> Pomerania, of Cassubia and of Wendes, Burgrave of
> Nuremburg and Prince of (the Isle of) Rügen, Johann Sturm
> sends his respectful greetings.

The young people whom it pleased you to entrust to us last year, we
wished to encircle with loyalty and aid by our earnestness, as the rank
and virtue of so great and valorous a Prince obliges; but in the middle
of our studies the plague interrupted us, so that, in order not to expose
all our youngsters to a cruel death, we found ourselves constrained to
send them away and to suspend our classes. That is why we thought it
was our duty to wait until they received from our Scholarchs the travel
provisions they needed, and why Conrad Dasypodius, Vice-Rector,
accompanied them and left them with the people in Frankfurt, so that
they could care for their health and their studies and leave them in want
of no necessity. Although we were obligated to render such service to
all our students, we were nonetheless very happy to have been
entrusted thus by such a great Prince with Fabian, Baron of Dohna, and
Christopher, son of the very noble Gaspard Nostitz, chamberlain and
counselor, and of the two sons of the most wise Balthasar Gans, Frederick and Albert, and that by a Prince, by a Duke, Duke Albert, I mean,
healthy and vigorous in old age, and laden with all kinds of praise for
his princely virtues by so many and by such learned men.

   Moreover, what I find reassuring for our religion in these critical
times is not only the arrival to power of many good princes, who in the
Empire have taken the place of those deceased, but especially the presence of those of the older generation—and there are few left—among
whom you occupy the first rank. Last autumn I was visiting Christopher,
Count of Oldenburg, my host, my protector, my father. I was greatly
cheered by the kindnesses with which this prince overwhelmed me, as
well as by his vigorous old age, his venerable white hair and his courageous soldier's spirit, still ready to expose himself to the perils of death

for religion's sake. Thinking of this man, I seem to see as well the venerable man who is Albert Duke of Prussia, shining and resplendent with many virtues and, at his side, his son Albert Frederick, his father's image, whom all good men fervently wish to see inherit not only such immense wealth, but also the most sacred virtues to guide his actions. This Prince (i.e., Duke Albert) is loved and honored by his people; he names to churches pastors capable and well paid; he founds schools and generously endows this holy Zion, this royal mountain, I mean, this literary school, this academy of the most eminent learned men; he makes it possible for the sons of so many of his subjects to have spiritual nourishment. The son of such a Prince, Albert Frederick—a young man full of good prospects, I am one of those who are convinced of it—is for God an object of solicitude, so that he may outlive his father and walk in his footsteps and, by his virtue, keep alive his memory. Often great and glittering personal attributes produce acts of slight significance. For myself, in any case, the recommendation given me in placing in my care the youngsters just cited is an example of those virtues which Joachim Camerarius and George Sabinus attribute to you in their books. For our part, we treat these young people and those who come to us from Prussia as our dear children, just as long as we are deemed competent and our discipline and instruction seem suitable for their spirit.

Just what is our method of procedure in our schools, our way of instructing children and of shaping their youth, I have set out in several letters that I am sending to you, illustrious Prince, so that thanks to the protection of your authority and your greatness, these principles may be sheltered from the malevolent (if any there be), and thus, if this method pleases you, the Academy of Koenigsberg may profit by it, if it approves, or may indicate what it finds needing revision. I wish indeed that my studies and my labors profit other people and not merely those in Strasbourg. And I rejoice especially at my age—I'm nearly sixty—when I hear of the reform or the founding of schools. Also, the fame of Koenigsberg has gratified me these several years; as for the Academy of Rostock, if it sings the praises of your son-in-law, the great Prince Duke Johann Albert of Mecklenburg, it delights me because I love that Duke for his literary culture and his learning and his rare virtue, and especially because I hope to see the study of letters spread not only in cities and in states, but also with time to the future generations of humanity.

That these studies are being cultivated as well among the papists I am pleased and gladdened, and I congratulate the Cardinal of Augsburg for having founded at very great expense, it seems, the Jesuit college. The archbishops of Mainz and Trier are doing the same, someone told me: it will be all to the good if they tolerate the wholesome and pure doctrine of the Evangile. It is proper that the resources of the churches have been allocated as much for public utility and needs as for authority and dignity. Because the Prince-Bishops do not possess merely their own goods, but other abundant resources; the chapters provide to each canon everything he needs in order to live, and that honorably, and the other priests and ministers of the faith have their large revenues, and nowhere is there a lack of hospitals or hospices. All that comes their way by right, if they profess good doctrine, and without exciting jealousy, they could maintain an influence and a larger, more assured and more lasting influence than that they now enjoy, but which is every day diminishing. And who would not praise the metropolitans and the patriarchs? But in defending one individual only, they do not cease endangering their dignity; and they prefer to be clients of the Pope and of the Bishop of Rome than of the Emperor and the Empire, and to be rather the sworn ministers of the Pope of Rome than of the free Princes of the Empire. They are endowed with many and remarkable qualities: I know them and esteem them and I rejoice at their virtues; but because of them, I suffer to see them all through the fault of their oath and of their religion, powerless abundantly to spread their fruit. However, these institutions stimulate me as much as did Bembo and Sadoleto whilst they were living, but even more so the schools of our magistrates. Upon my return from Neuburg in Bavaria, the poor students' house at Tübingen, adjoining the college, filled me with joy. More than one hundred young people specially chosen are, I believe, being maintained by the Prince under the good rules and under the fine direction of Samuel Heyland: in groups of two or of four, they have bedrooms and heated study rooms nearby, hygienic because vast and airy, beautifully constructed, pleasant, a monument forever to the memory of that great Prince.

But enough digressions; I turn once more to your young people: upon their return (from Frankfurt) and along with any others who might come from your duchy, we will surround them all with love, protection, care, and concern as their own parents and friends would do. But, since our experience has taught us that young people, and especially those who are a bit more advanced in age, obey regulations all the less the farther they are from home, it is the very young who are the best subjects for instruction; on the other hand, distance from their homeland presents fewer inconveniences, thanks to the recommendations and wishes expressed by the princes and magistrates, if one provides for the strict issuing of report cards, not just annually, but on a trimestrial basis. Not less than distance, long intervals of time breed negligence, disenchantment with studies, and cause youngsters to forget the limits which decency and modesty impose to the extent of making them no longer regard the wishes of their parents and of their family. The limits placed on eyes and ears, more than those placed on the spirit and heart, have the power to command respect for discipline and regulations. We are more fearful of the unsheathed sword than of that hidden in the scabbard, and two days passed in the expectancy of death make a greater impression on such unfortunate mortals than does a demise awaited many long years; that is why an old man in good health often fears God less than a young man ailing. The oftener a young man sees himself obliged to ask for a report from his teachers, the likelier he is to muse on the bad consequences which negligence and a dissolute life entail, and on how much an honest and studious life bring profit, joy, and respect.

Most illustrious Prince, may God give you an obedient and upright people; youth who are hardworking and cultivated; a son who is sensitive to his father's wishes, the wishes of decent mankind, our hope and our expectation. May He protect him, increase his prospects, and preserve his mother as his father in good health, in all security, in every happiness, and in prosperity for many long years to come.

Strasbourg, March 30, 1565

* * * * *

2.   End of March, 1565. Strasbourg.
     Sturm to the Scholarchs.

> To the noble and illustrious men Henry of Müllenheim, Charles Mieg, Frederick of Gottesheim, Scholarchs; former Stetmeister, former Ammeister, members of the Council of Thirteen, Johann Sturm dedicates this preface.

The Jesuits' name is brand new, and it is the clever invention of an ingenious man intended to ensure the support of many people and cities, of foreign populations, even of emperors and kings. The man who invented it wished to win the approval of the Pope then living, and to control access to a superior dignity and even to the papacy, and achieved this, thanks to this new order of monks of which he claimed authorship and leadership, even when he was still of an inferior station in the ecclesiastical hierarchy. However, more than any of the other monastic communities, if it were necessary to praise any, this order would deserve praise. Because that which neither the excellent and pious Johann Reuchlin of Pforzheim, nor the eloquent and learned Erasmus of Rotterdam, nor even before these Alexander Regius and Rudolph Agricola could obtain from the theologians and monks, i.e., that they at least permit good scholarship if they did not wish themselves to cultivate it—this the Jesuits undertook on their own impulse. They teach languages, (and) the rules of dialectic. They explain to their students in so far as it is possible rhetoric, do it so well indeed that the fewer there are of those schools we call academies as compared to these new schools being introduced into the cities, the greater are the numbers of people from whom they gain gratitude and favor.

I rejoice over this work for two reasons: first because the Jesuits support us and cultivate literary studies, the object of all our labor and our great passion. In fact, I have seen the authors they read, the exercises they do, and their method of teaching is so close to our own that it would appear to be derived from ours. So let us not worry ourselves any longer that Bembo, Sadoleto, Contarini, Pole, and many other savants and distinguished people have amongst us many friends and disciples, to whom they have given arms not against us, whom they have defended, but against idolatry which, along with us, they have energetically attacked. And here is my second reason for joy: they oblige us to have greater zeal and vigilance, for fear that they will appear to be working harder and preparing more learned and literary men than we.

In three places in Bavaria and in Swabia, high schools are found close together, two in Ingolstadt, the former university and the Jesuit college; in Lauingen the school of our own faith and in Dillingen that of the Jesuits. I earnestly wish that emulation may prove for these schools a stimulus and that it will tend towards the same objective: knowledge and eloquence; but the schools of Lauingen surely defend a better cause and, if they continue to apply in the education of their youth the method begun last winter, they will not let themselves be outstripped by the Jesuits. In fact, at Lauingen they use the same pedagogy that I began twenty-eight years ago and are following the same path I have been smoothing out ever since so that it might be made level and straight, without any rough spots, detours, or hazards. I have not even allowed for pleasant bypaths that threaten to impede the course of study. I undertook this work for three reasons, of which one was provided me by the Scholarch Pierre Sturm, brother of Jacques Sturm, a year before he died; I mention him to honor his memory. Because while consoling me on the occasion of my mourning, and seeing that I was apt to follow his advice, he begged me to perfect whatever might seem deficient in this institution so well started by me, since I had recommended to the Senate not the creation of our school (the idea of founding it was the Senate's own) but of its organization in that spirit. The other reason was indicated to me by the kindness of our Senate and its resolve to sustain this enterprise and to serve well not only its own fellow citizens, but also foreign nations and peoples. And the last reason: the reputation of our schools, in full flower for nearly thirty years, will surpass itself in the future, will undoubtedly spread its fruit better and more abundantly than men have ever seen up until now, if we persevere in the way we have pledged.

That is why and to fulfill Pierre Sturm's request and obey the Senate's will and for the good name of our city which adds to that of our Academy, I have completed that which you see here done: by means of twenty letters I have regrouped the classes, redistributed the work, determined the exercises, and published a teaching method which seemed to me to attain very nearly if not completely the full possession of the language of the Greeks and of the Latins, at least a certain facility and custom of its use, and that not only for the great profit, but further for the great glory, of the Senate and of our Republic. For although our city exercises its charity widely every day in caring for foreigners, in sheltering indigents, in the hospital, in nourishing citizens, and in the house of St. Mark, still I know not how it is that the glory of our schools seems more pleasing to God and produces fruits more wholesome and sweeter when it comes to education and religion. In any case, the wealth of the church has been garnered for this purpose.

Although there are three kinds of thefts, one which prejudices private wealth, one public wealth, and the third ecclesiastical wealth, so misappropriation of public property is considered a more odious crime than mere theft of private and sacrilegious thievery more so than misappropriation of public funds, with the sacrilegious man considered more detestable than the misuser of public wealth.

The Romans punished theft by a four-fold fine; the misappropriator was exiled after restitution of the diverted sum; but sacrilege was always left to God's punishment, and God punished very severely even those who looted the gods' temples and never left a sacrilege unpunished. If the testimonies of historians have faithfully related all such facts, the Romans considered as a parricide he who had stolen or carried off a sacred object left in a sanctuary. This law was so ancient that by Cicero's time the wording of the text had become archaic, although its vigor and authority still held in the memory of good citizens. As for myself, I rejoice often at the notion that our Republic is aware of all that it receives and spends and that it has not in respect of its resources soiled its hands in parricide.

So up until now the reserves of the Chapter of Saint-Thomas have not been touched; and we who administer them and who, in accord with the laws of the ancient church, have taken upon us the duties of the dead, we diminish them not, but add to them and withdraw in our turn only enough to keep the temples from lacking preachers and the schools instructors. Moreover, things have been so well planned and calculated that not even one miserly economy, cunning or underhanded, could succeed in draining anything from the Chapter's revenue based on cartularies, charters, and fees in cash and in kind. And since I am an official as well of this Chapter, I recommend first to your benevolent protectiveness that you preserve with us this treasure of letters and of religion against violence, injustice, and barbarism; next, to prevent any modification after my death of the enterprise which for more than twenty-eight years has procured so many advantages for the churches, schools, civic bodies, royal courts, embassies (and) diets in all those places where learned men with much experience, educated in our school, still live. And you will be faithful to this method, if you follow my advice; and you will not authorize any changes in the choice of books and authors if you wish to avoid those evils which barbarism and a poorly conceived education usually breed.

Finally, if the teachers do their duty, for as long as they do so, do not let them lack anything and take care of their children, too, so that the faithfulness and zeal which the parents have demonstrated in their work does not impoverish their children. and since Sevenus, having served many years as teacher of the first class, and so well that no one surpassed him in dedication or in learning, to which many of his former students who have become distinguished men will attest, I recommend to your generosity the cause of his children, for whom I am tutor and whom I must loyally protect as if they were my own children. Also, I must fulfill my duty as a father to them: as for you, I earnestly call on your aid on their behalf, considering you as their grandparents and family.

* * * * *

3.   February 26, 1565. Strasbourg.
     Johann Sturm to Abraham Feis, Teacher of the Tenth Class.

What farmers habitually do in watching with the greatest care over trees
just planted or grafted by their own hand for their posterity, rather than
over those they got from their forebears, this same duty is incumbent on
the good teacher in our school in the smallest children's class, for which
you were engaged, dear Abraham. This teacher must regard his pupils
as his plants and graftings, which he received from no other school,
whom no strange hand has ever trained, and whose cultivation will
leave for the master a most pleasing recollection and the most abundant
fruit.

You receive, dear Feis, from their parents' hands these young boys,
almost babes, still lacking in instruction and even in good manners, so
much so that it is from you they receive the first moral training and
instruction in arts and letters, of which you begin to lay for them at this
age the first foundations. Now, for maturity and old age, for all subsequent living, the foundations of education and instruction are for everyone begun in childhood and in youth, and a double duty is imposed:
for you, to teach; for them, to learn. They must learn the forms of letters,
not certainly by a subtle or obscure analysis and definition, but by visual
and sensory means, by pronunciation and linguistic exercises. One must
in fact eliminate during the first few years everything obscure and difficult to grasp. Just as milk and light food are most suited to the delicate
stomach of a child, so is instruction that is pleasant and easy for him to
assimilate.

To this observation in every one of these letters I add almost immediately reading and the articulation of the written sentence. But it seems
preferable to me—and I have personal experience—to begin with the
inflections of nouns and verbs rather than by the parts of the catechism,
first because it is not necessary to teach them the Latin catechism if they
know it in German. It's but parrot's language, not that of men, such Latin
or Greek uncomprehended by the speaker. He calls well upon God
who calls upon him in his native tongue. And too, one must see to it
that they do not forget what they learned at home with respect to the
catechism. As for any omissions, their parents must make them up at
home and you at school, in the time given over for such things.

One must lead the child to declensions and to conjugations at the
same time as he is learning his letters. Because, from the fact that the
same word changes case and gender, that the first syllables remain and
that the latter ones change, not haphazardly, but according to rules, the
teacher derives two advantages: the child learns without difficulty how
to read and how to register in his memory that which he needs to retain
and that which is necessary in order that the instructional edifice be solidly established. We have said that in your class you must lay the foun-

dations for studies as on a rock; your class must be so to speak a nursery for the finest trees, which you'll not see rooted in soil nor standing in gardens nor orchards, but at the bar and in the senate (and) the courts of kings, and bearing abundant fruits of wisdom. One can scarcely imagine to what extent the memory of the benefits he received in early life is anchored in the memory of the learned man. Of my mother, Gertrude, and of my father, Wilhelm Sturm, and of my paternal grandfather Jakob Sturm, and of my maternal grandfather Conrad Hulsen and his wife, Eva, my grandmother, and of her mother, my great-grandmother, all of whom I knew and remember, the fondest and sweetest memory has remained; but in truth, the picture I have kept of Johann of Neuburg, my first teacher, of Jakob of Blumenthal, of Antoine Dalber, of Gerard Episcopius, whose student I was in my home town and whom I so love, is such that it would be the greatest joy for me to be able to express my thanks to their children and grandchildren. As for Arnold of Eynatten, whose courses I followed at Liège and at the College of St. Jerome, I love him so much that I am tied to him from the depths of my being. What praise for Socrates to have had Plato as a disciple; what praise for Plato to have been Aristotle's teacher; but these cultured men, before having been led before Socrates, probably did not have less affection for their first masters than we for ours.

That's what I wanted to say to you, dear Abraham, so that fulfilling your duty as the industrious schoolteacher of this class you do not regret this use of your talents, of which we are aware, myself and those who, with me, hired you for our school.

Strasbourg, the 26th of February

* * * * *

4.   February 26, 1565. Strasbourg.
     Johann Sturm to Heinrich Schirner, Teacher of the Ninth
Class.

I am sending you, Heinrich, the letter that I am writing today to Abraham, because I want you too to think about the things that I am asking him to ponder. In fact, your pupils are not much more advanced than his; that is, they are, but they are also much alike. Abraham begins teaching declensions and conjugations, and you carry it further; he has pupils working on certain kinds of endings, and you those for all words, all cases, and all tenses; he sends them to you still stammering and hesitating, and you manage to give them such solidity that they can decline every word except those which are invariable.

But besides these exercises on endings it is necessary to strive ceaselessly to get them to expand their vocabularies of everyday objects that impinge upon human awareness. Let nothing that can be seen in the human body, nothing of cattle, nothing that is in the kitchen, in the wine cellar, in the granary, or that can be brought to the daily meal, nothing that can be seen in the garden, no fruit or tree, nothing in school that is of any utility, nor in the library, or used in church, or having to do with the weather—nothing that does not affect the human senses in daily life be something your pupils cannot say in Latin, at least in so far as the Latin words exist.

The way to arrive at this I have shown you: let everyone be quiet; let only one answer you, and that in a firm, clear voice in order to be understood by everyone. You too must take pains that your voice may be clearly heard. To your questions the pupil must answer from a spot some distance off, not only so that the others understand the question and the answer, but also so that they remember it as a result of hearing it repeated. The greatest defect in teachers is to speak into the ear of the pupil they are questioning.

Every day you will give every pupil a set number of words, all different, all pertaining however to the same category of objects. It is not necessary that a student know all the words on the same day; but that the whole class knows all the words, and every individual knows his own list. Just as with respect to commodities and money amongst citizens, there ought to be at school an exchange of verbs and nouns. We'll get to that point if you ask questions, as you've seen me do, if the pupils ask questions amongst themselves, if you proceed as I have done, if you review frequently with them what has been already learned, especially the difficult things, if gender is presented with all its species, if the whole is followed by all its parts, if in a small school room almost the whole world is contained. For if geographers can clearly enclose the position of countries and cities, of mountains and forests, oceans and rivers and lakes and even many living creatures, if they can do that for certain kinds of things, why could not we do it for everything that exists, for species and their many forms? It does not take so much ingenuity nor even much work; but the work of one single year prefigures all that will be needed in a lifetime.

This method, I wrote down twenty-seven years ago, but as far as I can see, it has not been understood; now I want to see it understood, adopted, applied, and kept in the schools, if my advice is followed. How do we imagine the young Romans and young Greeks were able so quickly to acquire the arts of expression? It is because at home, almost from the cradle, at their mother's breast, they learned how to make sounds; it is because their nurses carried them in their arms, still babbling, as long as befit their development, and corrected them as their powers grew; it is because their servants taught them words and played with them, not only in order to amuse them, but also to exercise their Latin. This advantage was strengthened by daily intercourse with comrades their own age, wherein games and conversation brought new, unknown objects to their homes and the words needed to express them.

This method of learning no longer exists in our period and for your youth. There are no parents in our houses, no servants, friends, citizens, or magistrates speaking Latin. This public and widespread calamity must be corrected by the inventiveness of schoolteachers and by the method I have just been urging; if I can achieve this in your class among children who are seven years old, surely the teachers in the upper grades will obtain the same and even greater results than those I ask for, those which are indispensable to their grade.

That which I have asked of Abraham, I ask of you as well: do not grow weary, and do not evaluate your work in such a way that it seems unworthy of your learning, but rather, judge according to its usefulness to the community whose good citizens must be taught. I admit that you could be useful and adept at teaching the upper classes, and one day you will be given one, perhaps before long. But right now we need you in our arena as a pugilist against barbarian gladiators who by their negligence spoil Latin purity and, out of envy, will not permit it to go forth. But go forth it will to those youngsters whom you are guiding, and it will flourish in the upper classes and bear the most beautiful fruit in public and judicial life, in city government and in the counsel hall, and in the temples and churches of Christ, everywhere in the Christian Republic.

Farewell,
Strasbourg, the 26th of February

* * * * *

5. Johann Sturm to Mathias Huebner, Professor of the Eighth
Class

What your work is, what you must teach your pupils and what method you must use in your teaching you can see for yourself, my dear Mathias, set out in the book that I wrote twenty-seven years ago, "On the Schools." I have of late drafted a book on the Lauingen School, which may also be useful; since the same system that I recommended at the start must, it seems to me, be maintained in secondary schools or academies of this type. In fact I can find nothing better, and in my opinion no one can find anything better, provided that it is well understood and that capable schoolmasters are found which up until now have been scarce.

Furthermore, in recent days I have begun an inspection of Henry Schirner, the master of the ninth class, and I expect to continue through all the grades so that I do not appear merely a theoretical writer, but a man of action, too, and so that I do not neglect any of the resources offered by nature, already utilized and elaborated by the philosophers and rhetoricians, both Greek and Latin, and which will win for us the approval of our own philosophers and cultivated people and help us rediscover the art (lost by us) of ancient Greeks and Latins in teaching, oration, discussion, writing, and speaking. But this concerns the upper classes of our school, and I am still along with you amongst the smallest. But they are such that we cannot arrive with our young pupils at the upper grades if we do not begin with the lower, and if we do not blaze a trail towards the summit. In this program I will help you as well as Henry, not only by my advice, but yet with my labor, just so long as your zeal helps in the realization of my goal.

You will have thus to watch yourself with the greatest care and incessantly so that the children do not lose the memory of what they learned in the ninth. Of what such knowledge consists one can check by the books of examples and in the daily notebooks. You will not let them neglect these books, blaming severely each student who does not take care to keep them up. They are the witnesses of their zeal, the guardians of their memory, they indicate what the children have gained from their work and their master's care, they reveal what must be added next. What I ask of you I recommend as well to the teacher of the upper grades: to save faithfully these books and notebooks just like the sacred fire of the Vestals was not allowed to die.

The child who rises from the lower class into yours must know examples of all the inflections and how to decline all the nouns and conjugate all the verbs, but he has acquired this skill rather from habit and exercise than from theoretical reasoning, as at Rome the Latin children and at Athens the little Greeks learned to speak with their parents, their family, their friends and acquaintances before learning from grammarians why it was necessary to speak as they did.

He must also possess all the kinds of simple sentences and of complex ones composed of two, three, or four members, and which the Greeks call periods, which explain whatever concerns life, manners, and study. But since these sentences cannot be so numerous that they include all the verbs and names of common objects, the child must have a store of terms touching these questions, grouped according to gender and kind, the whole and its parts, analogies, opposites, clear characteristics, causes, effects, all those things about which he will sense the meaning only from a certain distance, but of which he will acquire by memory the use, so that each time he needs any of these, he will have them at hand, drawing them out from his store room.

But this abundance of words and this ease of expression will not be entirely attainable in this grade and by these little pupils because of their age, of the great number of ideas, of the novelty of the instruction, and of the shortness of the working hours. Also, you will have to add whatever it seems to you they are still lacking. In the other class the pupil will have learned what a message is, and what a letter is, what it means to write, receive, answer. With you he will learn what it means to send a message, to write a letter, to receive what a friend or relative will have written. There (in the other or former class) he will have learned the largest possible number of nouns and many verbs. But you will have to add still others. There he will learn many individual words that you will have to classify.

This first acquisition of words you will complete in so far as is possible, and to these sentences that the child will have learned with Henry, you will add others that seem lacking in order to round out the notebooks and daily journals and to develop his memory and knowledge at the same time as the richness of his vocabulary.

In all these things consider this word of Quintilian not as a piece of advice but as a rule: "Let the children know before they decline and conjugate." Because although that is the concern of Abraham and Henry, nonetheless, it is up to them to begin and up to you to perfect. In fact, as amongst mathematicians conclusions that derive from principles are considered superior to those which follow from simple facts, so your work promises a deeper understanding. For just as there is a difference between the teaching of parents and that of the schoolmaster and of the grammarian, so is there established a distance between you and them.

In fact, you deal with all the richness and variety of the language and of style in the eight parts of speech; you prescribe to each of these parts their definitions and divisions; you lay down the basis for the declensions of nouns; you draw to their attention their gender; you do the same for the verbs and you follow the same method for the other parts of speech. All these results you will obtain if you choose what is essential, discard the superfluous, avoid obscurity, stress clarity, explain by appropriate examples, selecting from what the children have learned, calling frequently upon their experience and letting nothing escape their memory, observing the method of questions and answers prescribed for Henry.

Beyond these classifications, divisions, and inflections, beyond these grammar rules, these notebooks and daily journals and this sentence review, you will explain my selection of Cicero's letters: one must hurry on to reading without omitting anything essential, and slow down enough so that we study what is needful; and as we take it upon us to teach each child certain words (different from his neighbors') all relating to the same subject, we must do likewise for these letters. We must submit not to each child, but to each decurion or group of ten one or two letters so that they can explain them word by word. You must interpret them to them so they may connect each word to its grammatical function. In this way they will be able to learn more things, and you will be able to acquit yourself of the task that we lay on you and which is your own.

I do not ask of you yet any composition exercises. You will do your duty especially during the first six months if you vary the modes of expression and whole groups of propositions by substituting the genders, cases, modes, tenses, persons, verbs and nouns of different or same meaning, of the same kind of ideas, and adapt them to the usage and current forms of speech. In such manner you teach them how to speak. It is not, however, without usefulness to try some composition during the latter months, just as one lets children handle a sword, unsheathe it and walk with it in public in order that the teacher of the next grade, like a good gladiator, not receive them complete novices.

But of all that, I will speak to you in action when I visit your class. It is enough for now that I prescribe something for the ninth class, for I enable you to make progress too, your pupils learning that as well and adding those other ideas that you will have to teach them in your class, to which your pupils will have to devote themselves.

Farewell,
Strasbourg, in the month of March

* * * * *

6.   1565 March, Strasbourg
     Johann Sturm to Theobald Lingelsheim, Teacher of the
     Seventh Class

If, as I hope, I can continue the organization of classes that I began to review in the last few days, we will deliver to you at the autumn promotions, Theobald Lingelsheim, boys well formed and prepared for conjugations, declensions, and answers. You may then question them on parts of speech and their divisions, or on the declensions of nouns or on genders, on verb conjugations including tense, mode, numbers and all their inflections, on whatever indeed you find it well to quiz them. And you must do this as well on that which teachers must teach them, and on whatever pupils must know of that knowledge indispensable for understanding the other parts of speech. One will already have provided them with a moderate number of words, divided up and distributed in such a way that they possess in fact a knowledge appropriate to the divisions of the liberal arts and to the distribution of all human knowledge.

After the instruction dispensed by three schoolmasters, your duty, Lingelsheim, consists of not letting the students forget these notions, but to reinforce them by your actions and by continual exercises, adding others that are especially suited to your class and that are particular to it, such as the connection of (Latin) sentences which the Greeks call syntax. This I do not wish to be too weighted down with rules, but brief, clear in its expression, and accessible by examples taken from Latin works, especially from Cicero, like our syntax written by Theophilus Goll. Oblige your pupils to retain these rules and their usage through a daily analysis of Cicero's letters and from illustrated texts in the sentence miscellany and by review of material learned in the lower grades.

To make progress in the career that you are pursuing and whose limits and goals lie before you in this your stadium, you will have to assign each child every session a letter or a part of one if the whole is too long, or a rather long sentence or two shorter ones so that he can explain them word for word. But one must repeat these exercises often and change the pupils and the texts given to each in order that everyone can seem to have answered without hesitation and all to have studied the same texts.

The way to arrive the most speedily you will learn from the instructions that I have given in the lower grades; but you will be able to progress more easily, especially in the last months, because capacity grows according to the increase in vocabulary, and as theoretical understanding grows, and practical daily exercise, which usually outdistances theory, develops. It is one of Pliny's precepts I would like you to make them read much in order to make reading habitual.

You must commit to the child's own hand stylistic exercises, and it is in this grade that one must form the young pugilist new to the handling of the pen. You will do what the gladiators do: by movements of the torso and limbs, by steps forward and backward, by leaps, varied postures, they do not cease to give examples until their fencing pupil begins to do the same. Musicians do likewise and sing for their pupil until he is capable of joining in or singing alone.

You will assign then to each pupil a subject on which to write, a sketch one may call it, on some topic you have thought up. It ought to be taken from daily life and be comprehensible as to action, characters, place, and time. But this sketch must not be too long. You might describe it briefly or, especially at the start, outline in detail the points to develop. Gradually it will be necessary to proceed to sentences of two, three, or four clauses. In these sentences you will suggest names of objects; you will classify them; and you will indicate the manner of expression, not only orally, but also in writing on the blackboard. Further, you will repeat in front of them once, twice, several times the summary that you will have composed, just as the gladiator and singing master must do, so that the child uses his hand and his pen, but always according to the voice and careful instructions of the teacher.

This exercise must be practiced daily, sometimes again later in the day, but in such a way that it causes no ill will. Nothing is more wearisome than composition exercises, and in our day nothing has so harmed our young people in school than overly long texts with which their teachers have not helped them. Here lie two inconveniences; one is that no help has been given, and the other that (the pupil) is weighed down by this burden. These subjects you must not draw only from events of the last two days, but you must call to attention also that which they learned in the lower grades. From thence you will draw forth the nouns, verbs, and expressions. One can never repeat frequently enough that which has not been thoroughly understood, noted, and anchored in the memory.

Here again is an advantage of this method which consists in refreshing the memory: since the pupils carry about in this little community the words they have learned in the three lower classes, divided into types, they will be able in this written exercise and in composition practice to grasp without difficulty in one sole group of words all the things of the same sort. To keep you in line with this method, I shall point out the term that the Greeks use for it: the art of remembering, which makes it necessary to review what has been taught and learned, what they still call in rhetoric "rejuvenation." It is in fact a sort of renewal of the memory and of things learned, this repetition, this review. Consider too that the daily notebooks of the pupils are memory helps, but it is your duty to exercise them every day until they remember.

Along with the composition exercises too, on holidays or on the night before, goes the translation of the catechism from the maternal tongue into Latin with that facility of which we have already spoken. You will read the text out loud in front of them and the pupil will follow mentally and through writing. In this area you will make sure that you do not use any but Latin words and turns of phrase, except in those cases where our religion has peculiar terms that, due to the authority of the Church, must be kept, so that they appear not only particular but also sacrosanct. Such words include terms like "trinity," "unity," "sacrament," "baptism," "evangelist," "apostle," "bishop," "deacon," "the keys of the kingdom," and so on. However, one might illustrate them with definitions, synonyms and epithets of which I will speak to you personally.

Giving the children another catechism than that which they learned in the lower grades (Bucer's) I cannot at all approve. Those who press for this, what are they doing if not wasting time, neglecting more important questions and troubling these youngsters with superfluous work, which, far from developing the memory, sidetracks them with great suffering and for no profit.

If you heed my advice, Lingelsheim, you will perform your duty conscientiously as a teacher, and as you have already proved during long years your conscience and zeal, I will praise you still more if you conform yourself to my views.

Farewell.
Strasbourg, in this month of March.

* * * * *

7.   1565 March. Strasbourg.
     Johann Sturm to Martin Malleolus, Teacher of the Sixth
     Class.

Please dear Malleolus, turn all your attention first to the counsels I have given the teachers of the lower grades so that you can give the same attention to facility, clarity, purity and abundance in your teaching, your questions and your exercises. For, despite the diversity of your instruction, you cannot but follow the same path and method. Next, think about the variety and scope of the knowledge that the pupils bring to you in the sixth class from the lower grades, the which you will easily understand if you attend the examinations that precede the promotions from one grade to the next. It is the case that the master of the upper grade receives the young pupils who arrive fresh from the hands of the examiners, given over to his confidence and zeal.

In the third place, it is your duty to see to it that they retain what they have learned: the authors and daily notetaking, the rules and the vocabulary, and every time the occasion presents itself—and it's a useful exercise—to recall to their mind by questions especially the material that seems most difficult or most necessary. Because one can hardly review enough that which the student does not retain well. This maxim applied to the domestic scene must also have its place at school: "To save what one has acquired is no less an advantage than its acquisition."

After the three points there is a fourth that plays an important role in your task: think what you must add to their knowledge. Among such things are the longer letters of Cicero. You will give each one at first a section, each of differing content, which they will translate into their mother tongue. Then to each group or decurion (i.e., a group of ten students) you will give several letters written in different periods and treating of a variety of subjects. You will do the same for anthologies of poems; the leader of the first decurion will try to learn from you or from a student in one of the upper grades, or by asking his tutor, and with the help of one of these learn Bishop Ambrose's hymn.

> "Come, o Redeemer of the world,
> Show us the Virgin's son..."

So in the same way the leader of the second decurion cites Martial's epigram:

> "What it is that makes life happiest

O happy Martial lies here…"

While the third decurion leader presents this ode of Horace:

"You will fare better, O Lycinius,
If you do not head for the open sea."

One must do likewise for a large number of poems when several groups of ten are drawn together as in your class. Let them do the translation for you first and answer all the questions, and let them elicit answers from their classmates in a clear voice so that the whole group can understand. You will do the same sort of thing from the book of examples, whether it be a matter of translation or explanation, or recital from memory.

As the objective is achieving a rich vocabulary, one should eschew the lazy way out which is simply giving to each pupil one or two words to learn. Let each master for himself the expressions and words concerning one subject such as those pertaining to heaven, the elements, the house, warfare and armies, the wine cellar, the barn, the kitchen, the Senate and Counsel, public life and the courts. But it is not necessary to exhaust all these subjects. One must leave some words for the upper grades to learn and choose only those which are appropriate to their grade and age.

You know that stylistic exercise is at once the craftsman, the artist, and the instructor of speech. You will begin to polish it just where Lingelsheim stopped with them. You will proceed with the same method, but the composition exercises can be a little longer, though without many parts and still less, many sentences. Although these sentences may be made up of words from but one subject area and not from all (for that is impossible), they should yet permit of variety. Their style must be Attic in its purity, its finesse and its clarity.

You will follow the study of the Latin catechism during the weekend and on holidays. There are certain letters of St. Jerome's that are valuable for their religious sentiment, their propriety and their instruction and which are nice to read on Protestant feast days.

That is what you will have to undertake and complete and for your activity, your loyalty, your scrupulous care for your pupils, you will be able to count upon my good will, my love and my devotion to you and to expect from me tangible support.

Farewell. Strasbourg.

* * * * *

8. 1565, March. Strasbourg.
    Johann Sturm to Jonas Bitner, Teacher of the Fifth Class

Since we have arrived in our inspection through the last class as far as yours, Jonas Bitner, and have achieved what we wished for amongst the younger students, for the rest if we do not achieve our ends it will be due either to the fact that I have failed where you are concerned or that you have failed me in the accomplishing of our task.

We bring to you boys not yet formed, but well drilled in the grammatical rules of the Latin language. For everything that one sees in the heavens and in the air, all which the waters offer us daily, that the earth dispenses, that one grows in gardens, teaches in temples, notes in mankind, observes amongst the animals, deals with in the Counsel and at the bar, finds with regard to human intercourse, all that changes with locale, time, age amongst the sexes, the professions and actions which attach to them, of all that there is nothing which they do not know how to name in Latin and explain by a Latin verb. I am speaking of daily events of which each bears the knowledge of his class in his mother tongue, or that he learns with age and the passing of years. Let us suppose that they acquire these ideas fairly well in the lower grades, while learning the inflections. I see no risks that could follow from this so long as they are active and laziness does not hinder them.

But why am I telling you all that, you whose good will, activity, care, conscience I have experienced, and why to all the others whom I know to have the same qualities? But we all need to know what the pupils are learning in each grade and by what method they are taught, what the exercises of the various sections are, and what fund of knowledge all the pupils possess, what each individual knows or ought to know in his class, and the ideas that every pupil must acquire. For a great number of things are reserved for the upper grades and have to be. In your class you will have them learn unfamiliar things and call them by unfamiliar words.

In fact, they have not yet learned anything about poetry. Now you will dare initiate them in this art and show them the quantity of syllables long, short and common; the number and kinds of feet; the different varieties of verses and poems and hold up for their inspection samples of all those things. You will set out for them too the Greek maxims on virtues and vices, on the manners and life of men, on public affairs. Vergil's *Eclogues* are useful for your little troupe. They must learn who were the nine goddesses of the poets, the Graces, the "Parcae," the Naiads, the Hamadryads, Parnassus, Helicon and everything drawn back to these sources, not hesitating to read to them the "Cato" or the "Laelius" by Cicero. The muses love these kinds of listeners and orators and poets recite their works to each other and both are useful to philosophers and historians. You will be able to unify these exercises, since your pupils bring to you from the sixth grade the first elements of Greek, a grammatical foundation on which you will have to build.

You will have to look carefully at their journals, not only at the start of this new kind of instruction, but also during the subsequent years and review their daily notebooks in order to repeat these ideas and add to them what they could not acquire due to their age and the shortcomings of their teachers. Let each pupil explain each passage where homonyms and related words are hiding, conserving the order not only of the different sciences, but also of nature. Here is how you will be able to proceed in this explanation of authors. When they return to their rooms after your class they take back daily a well-understood eclogue of Vergil. The same must be done for the exercise book. In their memory drills they do not all have to read the same piece, but the whole class together will read everything that made up the day's work. You will have to go as quickly as may be, changing roles in the question period and after a certain lapse of time or interruption review the same texts.

What I told you concerning the Greek exercise book holds true for the poetry anthology in which all kinds of verse is to be found and examples of many subjects that will have to be imitated in their poetic composition.

You will now have to exercise them in style, refining it, polishing it increasingly as the children learn more words, rules, and examples than they had in the lower classes. They will have to begin writing verse in the last months of the year without having any assigned subject, being aided only by prose translations so that they are not obliged to think up sentences, not to choose the words, but only to group them. However, it is not a bad idea to have them replace the poetic words sometimes by those which an orator or historian would use, which is a procedure for testing the degree to which a young man has applied himself, and for getting him to notice how the orator differs from the poet. To translate into German a passage from a speech and then translate it back again into Latin increases their facility in elocution, sharpens their wit and enables them to find not only in yourself but in the orator as well a corrector and a schoolmaster.

I have briefly laid down for you what, in my opinion, you must undertake, elaborate and achieve; these points are in need of a longer explanation and require a guide who can show the way. But you will have in me a companion, a supporter and a friend along the way in the application of this method.

Farewell.
Strasbourg, in the month of March

* * * * *

9.   1565, March. Strasbourg.
Johann Sturm to Lawrence Engler, Teacher of the fourth grade.

Yesterday, o Engler, I wrote to Bitner a letter in which you will take note of the knowledge that the children bring to him from the lower grades and to which he will have to add, and from whence you will see for yourself what your task is to be in this same class. For although I want to present you with children who know the rules of Latin and of Greek grammar, and who are furnished with a choice of many words and who know countless examples from the poets as well as the orators, especially the latter, I expect you to do considerably more to make these youngsters really cultivated.

Your first duty is to see to it that the children listen to, translate, and understand as many texts as possible, recite many from memory, not only those they learned previously, but also those which you assign daily. The lessons that I suggest are largely chosen according to the youngster's capacity and do not surpass it. This standard results not only from the quantity and quality of the written matter, but also from the fine method and from wise proportioning, the method I indicated for the teachers of the lower grades. For I want you to follow along the same path, and adhere to the same goal, but not to the same concerns. I want to see my soldiers happy under their knapsacks, with each one helping to lighten the load of the other.

I give to you and assign to you amongst the miscellany of examples that which contain the longest sentences, specimens of argumentation and development. To these I join the sixth speech against Varro which contains almost all kinds of narration. You will complete as well whatever remains in the poetry book, and you will from the Horace collection of epistles and satires choose those which seem appropriate to you. To these Latin authors you will add the book of Greek examples in which are found in abundance the ideas and expressions, together with the raiment and trim with which they may be decked out.

I do not need to remind you of that which in your capacity as father to one of the older classes you ought not to forget for one moment: that is, that the children must never neglect that which they have learned in the smaller classes from the teachers who have given their young plantings such vigor: the rules of grammar, their collections of and classifications of words, the authors they have learned to know, their notebooks and daily class notes.

One must guard and continually place upon the anvil that what the blacksmith has made so that whenever he finds it necessary to retouch it he will not also have to fashion it afresh.

I urge upon you most earnestly to attend to style. You will augment the work done on this in the lower grades as shall seem possible to you to do. And although the youngsters by their own skill can attain to very much, still it is useful, even necessary in certain cases, that you give them some stylistic examples orally, or in writing, and that sometimes you go over it with them, when there is an error in what you entrusted to them.

You will share out between yourself and Jonas (Bitner) the Epistles of Paul for holidays and the prior evening. I mean the shorter ones. The longer I am saving for the three upper grades. In explaining them, do not regard what the theologians said in their commentaries, but rather what the Romans were doing when Paul wrote to them, and the same for the Corinthians, Galatians, Philippians, Ephesians, and what Timothy and Titus read to their churches in the letters that were addressed to them. What they got out of them reading them why shouldn't you obtain explaining them, not by means of a learned commentary, but by the transposition and rhythm of the words? It's one thing to annotate a text by means of a commentary, and another thing to teach a pupil. One must press on, never slacken, when one has entered upon one's career and is in the stadium.

Farewell, dear Engler.
Strasbourg, in the month of March.

* * * * *

10. 1565, March. Strasbourg.
Johann Sturm to Michael Bosch, Teacher of the Third Class.

I think I have reached Mount Helicon and see nearby the assembled muses, when coming from the lower class I arrive in yours. For I hope that you may be the interpreter not only of orators and historians but of poets as well, and that beside your spring the voices of the muses and the poets as well as those of orators, far from drying up, swell into a concert. You know indeed that both these two kinds of writers have cadences that the Greeks call rhythms, and that everything connected with the orators is eurythmic. These cadences should be observed by the children in prose, too. Titus Livius begins with an epic verse:

> "Facturusne operae pretium sim (...), nec (...) scio, nec si..."
> [*Praefatio T. Livi, Ab Urbe Condita*, opening lines, *Facturnusne operae pretium sim si a primordio Urrbis res populi Romani perscripserim nec satis nec scio nec, si sciam, dicere ausim...*
> "If I am doing something worth the effort, if I write the history of the Roman people comprehensively from the founding of the city I do not rightly know, and if I knew I probably would not dare to say."]

And our Caesar, in saying: "Gallia est omnis," why did he not add: "omnis Gallia divisa," but for the fact that harmony achieved through word order was his aim? One must not go too far for fear that someone will not cite these verses from the satiric poet, Juvenal:

> "Exceeded so oft by the *Thebaïd* of Codrus [actually the *Theseid* of Cordus] an Orestes who has written even on the reverse side of the page and not finished even yet..."

One must be wakeful in torchlight and hasten towards the finish line and the prize of victory. You will not let the children forget what they have acquired from the lowest grades until yours wherever books, authors, daily notes, rules are concerned, and you will explain to them examples of exordiums, oratorical partitions, narratives, digressions, general themes and lofty development. You will teach them also the ideas that are enhanced and about oratorical style, that is, about tropes, metaphor, periphrase, of which they will be able to bring in many examples from the lower grades. But you will add your own which you will explain to them, taken from the example manual I spoke to you about and from the authors assigned your class.

It does not displease me at all to see you place in their hands the Rhetoric by Herennius or that which I edited several years ago; but that which I explained concerning stylistic configurations from the treatise by Hermogenes requires an experience and knowledge more profound. One must leave that to Hertel, and it is the province of the teachers of the public classes that sit atop our Parnassus and form its crown.

The speech to the Court for Cluentius contains, so Quintilian says, examples of all the possible varieties of narration. This speech you will explain so that the children can understand it and observe the passages worthy of imitating when they know the rhetoricians. Or else, if it seems too wordy (for you will often have to change your teaching techniques according to the human situation and the capacities of the children), you will be able to substitute for it another speech.

Moreover, from the anthology of Greek examples, you will choose as well the best speeches of Demosthenes which will permit you not only to study the different varieties of oratory, but also to assess the abilities of your students. For often one gets further with a lighter load than with a heavier, and we accomplish that which we pursue: Do not let a moment pass which is not fruitful and strive for victory.

In the poetry anthology, you will not find much left to explain. If nothing at all remains to be done, you will add the first book of Homer, either the *Iliad* or, if you prefer, the *Odyssey*, for with this poet everything is pleasing, I do not know why, moreso than the purity, force, and gravity of the other poets. And he who will have learned to know this poet, will be able to sojourn amongst the others, as if Homer had come to chat with Aeschylus, Sophocles and Euripides. What do you think? Would Homer have admired those poets more than they him? You understand I think just why I write that and whenever you wish and as often as you wish we can talk about this together.

Holidays make necessary the holy books, the Epistles of Paul which I wish to see read and re-read and understood in the five upper grades, in such manner that they are known by heart in their entirety or at least insofar as the most important passages are concerned. These should be noted in their daily journals, so that you know what the youngsters have learned and what account they may give of knowledge solidly established by you during your question periods.

Any advice on the subject of style which I make is superfluous, since you must always exercise, refine and polish it. But with you the young man will have to undertake more. He will translate the exordium or narrative or argument, a commonplace or a development from a Greek author into Latin or vice versa. He will try to do the same for the poets and historians. In the poems of Horace or of Pindar, it is praiseworthy to translate not only literally, but in the different rhythmic forms as well. It is worthwhile to compose many new poems, to write many letters. As for exordiums, narratives and discussions of general topics, if they are not able to draft them by themselves, you can at least give them the theme, parts, ornamentations, periphrases and sketch out for them the general rhetorical traits, until they know the rules thoroughly, and make the same sort of comments for the book of stylistic examples.

As for the comedies of Plautus and Terence, it is better for them not to have you repeat them for them, but to learn them for themselves, sharing out the roles and work, performing them and competing with the upper grades for recognition. I would hope as a matter of fact that as soon as possible, all the comedies of these two poets might be performed in the four upper grades. Why couldn't one do this in the space of just one year? One year, what am I talking about? Why wouldn't six months be enough for 20 sections? When I was in the adolescent class at Liège, I played the role of Geta in Phormion by Terence, in front of the Church of St. Martin, without ever having learned it from a teacher or a comrade, but I was myself actor and poet. That was three years before the Peasants' War, and I was still young, almost a child. I played the part so well and studied the comedy so hard that I still believe I got the maximum amount of profit from the exercise. But at that period one could not as easily find teachers, nor teaching methods, nor the knowledge of languages which one encounters today and especially in our school.

I would ask of you more earnestly to follow my advice if I thought it necessary; but I do not think I have to, for I know your zeal will not fail you as you take up this duty, nor me in the expectation that you will accomplish your task.

Farewell.
Strasbourg, in March.

* * * * *

11. 1565, March. Strasbourg.
Johann Sturm to Johann Reinhard, Professor of the Second
Class.

What I have written in the past few days to the teachers of the other eight classes I suppose you have read, my dear Reinhard. Now, since I have progressed from the lowest class as far as yours, I perceive not too far off, but still at a certain distance, the assembled Muses. I am close enough to hear and understand what language they sing and what they sing of. I see their leader Apollo playing the zither, his own invention; Atlanta's eloquent grandson, Mercury; and Minerva holding the citadel of science and of wisdom. I can catch a glimpse of the nine Muses themselves and of one of the Graces with her two sisters and the other nymphs; see as well the blossoming laurels from which we will shortly pluck the berries and strip the branches and garlands, rewards for the zeal and labor of those in our group who seem to merit them.

But since in this band you preside over the games and will distribute the rewards to the young soldiers of this force, you must decide how great and of what sort are their accomplishments, what battles they have won, what progress they have made in the lower classes, what languages and what dialects they have learned in their period of enlistment in this foreign service and what kinds of arms and skirmishes they have known, what manners and what institutions they have seen; when you know all that, you will judge easily, if I know you, dear Reinhard, what remains for you to teach.

You will no longer have to translate the orators and Greek poets word for word for them: that is their task; yours, while they are thus engaged, is to replace the poets' words with those of orators, or combine the one with the other, intertwining for clarity's sake, the text of a story or of a fable, pointing out particularly brilliant embellishments and noting estimable passages, making students record those in their daily journals as in a book of recipes.

One must proceed in the same fashion for the Latin authors, comparing the words and modes of thought with those of the Greeks, noting and recording in their lists the oratorical and poetic ornamentation.

You will place in your students' hands the instrument of wisdom and you will show them of what it consists and how they ought to use it. I am referring to dialectic, that which no sage has ever neglected and without which no literary monument that is illustrious, eternal and pleasing has ever been created. Although the rules of invention are naturally anterior to the rules of taste, still I would prefer that you begin with the critical considerations rather than with the topical.

To this you will join by way of accompaniment, rhetoric, so that they march side by side. It is advisable to acquaint the students with Herennius's treatise, or it may be, Cornificius's, as it is probable, or Cicero's which is similar as to methods of invention, words and expressions: he is a good rhetoric teacher, clear and brief. But you will illustrate this book with technical Greek terms and you will explain it using examples, which they can give you many of from the lower classes, and every day the Greek and Latin authors which you will be explaining will provide new ones for them. This method you know, must be followed for dialectical works as well, but you will divide the rivulets of dialectic from the abundant waters of eloquence, so that each genre may be studied individually, dialectic short and lively, eloquence ornate and expansive.

You will then be able rapidly to explain the Olynthians and the Philippics and turning to them, have the children write down in their notebooks of the usage of rhetoric rules which they will have to learn. You must do the same for Cicero's speeches, the choice of which I leave up to you and the students whose preferences one ought frequently to follow.

As for the stylistic exercises, I recommend them for all of you alike from the seventh class on, every day and without interruption. As for your work in this composition, you will observe in my letters to Bosch and to Lawrence Engler; they have almost the same method, but you will carry it to a higher plane and you will strive to obtain greater results, not only with regard to style, but also with respect to emulation. Because it is incredible what man can achieve through effort, imitation, rivalry and that if he thinks nothing impossible where there is genius and industry.

They will make speeches in which they will recite from the text or from memory; the Latin orators were allowed to do the same—I think the Greeks as well—in the curia and forum.

For holidays we reserve for your class and for the first Paul's Epistle to the Romans; I would like everyone to know it and to recite it by heart at each of your examinations. For in fact it is a relaxation to undertake this kind of reading on holidays and to set up this kind of memorization contest amongst the youngsters.

I recommend to you the comedies of Terence and of Plautus which they begin to perform in the third class; but your actors will be obliged to bring daily to the stage a larger skill and after several months add a comedy by Aristophanes and a tragedy by Euripides or Sophocles. You will study these with them during the first months, but if later they enact others, they will confront the stage and the competition at their own risk and peril and with their own defenses: we hope indeed that our tragedians and our comedians will be self taught as soon as they can attain a certain level.

You will do your duty as a good professor and a good master if you so comport yourself, and you will surely do so; you have performed in fact and you do perform the task as a calm, devoted and learned teacher.

Farewell.
Strasbourg, this month of March.

* * * * *

12. 1565, March. Strasbourg.
     Johann Sturm to Theophilus Goll, Teacher of the First
     Grade.

Goll, for some years already, my speaking has made you wiser. You know the customs of our gymnasium and what I expect of all of you. The letters I have written to your colleagues will be instructive for you as well, and this one likewise. What kinds of students Reinhard turns over to you, or ought to turn over to you, you can see. Your task will be to add what is lacking.

Since we must fashion and mold these children according to the same rules and the same method, you will finish what remains to be done in so far as dialectic and rhetoric is concerned, not to perfection, like Aristotle's disciples and some of the Greek rhetoricians, because that we leave up to Hertel, but deftly by this method which is right for us and which, while not clarifying all the points brought up by Aristotle, comprises nonetheless all the categories and all the parts not only of Aristotle but also of Hermogenes and Cicero.

Thus it is those rules that you will teach and of which you will demonstrate the use made by Demosthenes and Cicero touching their decorative flourishes, and modes of thought. This you will do not only for the simple cases easily recognizable by anyone with a minimum amount of training in this method, but also for the hidden and subtle examples, which emerged from the schools of rhetoricians and logicians, seemingly without much savor, but which nonetheless prove their own virtue, like those medicines that affect the taste in a particular way and act quite otherwise in order to restore health.

To these orators you will join the poets: that which remains to be read in Vergil, that which you wish to add from Homer. For these writers, too, mold not only speech, but the spirit as well and are laden with many enjoyable oratorical touches. I think for my part that all the flourishes and all the lessons of the orators can be collected in Homer, so much so that, even in the absence of all rhetoric, one could reconstruct and reconstitute it with the help of this source.

Thucydides, the Greek historian, will rightfully be explained in your class and one could add Sallust here too. But for these authors, I want the students' own work to be your support so that they bring from home to your class what they have read, what understood, and what they will demonstrate in other words, in another language.

But it is up to you to give to each student his task, so that all do not bring to market the same merchandise, but each his own. I want your youngsters to create a great commerce by bringing from many different places many diverse things to exchange amongst themselves, not of course things they have spent money on, but things they have labored on, which have cost them an effort in memorizing and have required zeal. I suggested this procedure from the lower grades on. For I wish there to be for everyone the same method, the same pedagogy, so their beginning, progress and success will match in a manner that is wise, ingenious and delightful.

The actors of comedies and tragedies must be as was Roscius, knowing their trade better than those in the lower grades, so that the theater need not stand idle for a single week, the urge to attend need not languish, the performance of one day surpasses that of the night before, and the last actors to appear are more able than the first and more pleasing to the public.

I urge, too, a more thorough practice in composition and speaking. Everything must be conformable to the rules of the art, whether it be a question of written compositions or of expositions made after a period of reflection, or a mixture of these two, whether it be in verse and of poetry or of prose.

One could also do a few exercises on holidays. That is, they could explain to you themselves one of Paul's Epistles, or else they could develop a famous passage as the rhetoricians for you are permitted to do this at school and this method is not just a little useful for sermons and speeches. In fact, one does not teach the holy scriptures, one reads them. The advantages and the arms that eloquence gives help the theologian above all, but the legal expert and the practicing lawyer too and no less the senator, which is what happened in our city in the person of Jakob Sturm and of Martin Herlin. Herlin, however, was naturally a gifted speaker; Jakob Sturm aside from his natural gifts, studied letters and was formed by them. Our legists, Ludwig Gremp and Bernhard Botzheim, have proved indeed of what help the orator can be for the man of law and in law. Our Senate has besides recognized the services that the school renders to it, and men do not lack who, by their example, can give encouragement to their fellow citizens, men whose spirit and whose speech have been formed by literature.

But why tell you all that? But because these are birds of Attica, of your Athenian city and of your Minerva, I have hoped that mine would fly to you too, to prove to you that often the same thoughts inspire me that occupy you so delightfully, especially, it seems to me, right now. For here we are, freed not only of fear of the plague, but of this cruel scourge itself, and the way back opens up to us the arena and the career that truly makes the years shorter for me as well the months and days.

Farewell.
Strasbourg, in the month of March.

* * * * *

13. 1565. March. Strasbourg.
Johann Sturm to Johann Marbach, Doctor of Theology

I believe that I have finished a large part of the work that I was speaking of several days ago when explaining my ideas on the organization and reform of our school. I have written to the various classroom teachers and have explained to them what I perceive the functions and daily work of each to be. I hope that they will do their duty, and the more excellent they are, the more I see them interested and persuaded by this method. I know that many people think that this is among those things that are scarcely realizable, and for that reason I have put my energy to the test and the method too, in order to find out what burdens the ninth grade students might hoist, carry and bear on their shoulders at the tender age of seven. Everything is going well. I realized that none of my instructions will be unfeasible in the upper grades. I have the impression that of all generations ours will make the closest approach to that admirable oratorical skill of the ancients and will be best able to imitate that abundance of the Latin and Greek scholars and of that famous period when Plato (and up until Cratippus) flourished, from Demosthenes down through Cicero, whose death marked at the same time the loss of liberty itself and the glory of eloquence.

Now, I think I have introduced into our school four things that were especially lacking: an abundant vocabulary; grammatical, logical, and rhetorical progress more perceptible than I have ever before noted; similar and simultaneous progress in the expounding and translation of the orators, historians, and poets; and daily usage of the Latin language. In order to make the pupils conversant with these things I have, one might say, recalled Plautus, Terence and Cicero from Hades. As for writing, exposition, public speaking and conversational ability, which were in vogue at Athens and at Rome in those halcyon days, it seems to me that our teachers not only attempt but achieve these. If you are smiling, permit me, I beg of you, to hope. To hope? What am I saying! Let me rejoice in the spectacle and at the theater of such great activity and exercises. If you fear that I will not realize what I propose to do, be of good cheer: at least we shall achieve more than we have done in all the years gone by. The tenth and the ninth grade classes have made me see more clearly what the upper classes can accomplish.

You will see in the coming months, as will Melchior Specker and J. Glocker. In our theology course, keep Moses, the prophets, the evangelists, the apostles and in order to explain them, the authority of the Fathers of the church, before which all those hostile to our doctrine must incline. But it is scarcely necessary nor useful to read the Fathers in class as long there remains to be read some material of one of the four sorts of writing I just mentioned. And there will always be. Experience itself has taught our generation what evils have crept into the academies and into the churches during past centuries as a result of the compendia of sentences, and of summaries that had chased the best writers from their place; such were the inventions of an ignorant laziness, fit advocate for its own despicableness. Our age possesses better commentaries and better methods of teaching which have no need for an intermediary or of a glossator, and the church finds in such men a sure protection against the corruption of doctrine and against idolatry. And thus, let us fight for religion and letters, and watch that only those authors mentioned above have their place at school.

I urge you to apply then the kinds of exercises that I have described in *The Lauingen School*, so that we might introduce them in the boarding school that is under your care as it is under mine, and that we neglect nothing that is mentioned there and which can be applied to our school and to our scholastic family. That which must be done at school, I am asking you to practice as well in our public lecture classes and to initiate group discussions there, especially in the school of theology, where two or three students should be assigned a prophet, a psalm, an evangelist, an apostle, an epistle, a part of doctrine, a controversy, a father, a commentary by one of our theologians. These they will read and prepare together and they should be able to answer questions put to them on these subjects. How many fine results we shall owe to this method will be apparent shortly in disputation and will be proven in theological oratory and in the sermons which, since these are your province and that of the other theologians, doubtless you must have a profound interest in. But of all that we will speak again earnestly in public and in the teachers' meetings of our gymnasium and in the faculty council.

Farewell.
Strasbourg, in this month of March.

* * * * *

14. 1565. March. Strasbourg.
Johann Sturm to Lawrence Tuppius, Doctor of Law and Jurisconsult.

Even though there is no need to warn nor to exhort you, Lawrence Tuppius, for I have no doubts concerning your knowledge, nor your zeal, still, so that our successors may know after our death what method we all followed, I have thought it well to write you a few lines to encourage you and to ask that you help us by your activity, your interest and your advice in the education of youth. I will not point out to you that which you know yourself, what path you ought to follow in explaining the *Institutes*, which passages you ought to skim and which of the rest you ought to spend more time on, what are the customs we follow in the court, and in trials, what laws have been allowed to fall into desuetude by the customs and institutions of our religion and of our Empire, what profit one can derive from abrogated texts. I do not recommend to you and I do not show you which passages of the *Pandects* you will be able to add to your *Institutes*, and I do not point out those which are well known, frequently cited and of current use in trials; for it is up to you to know these things and indeed you do know them and deal with them daily, as do others of your colleagues who are doctors and masters in our public courses.

But there is something in our present circumstances, and in view of your concern for me and your zeal for our schools, I am asking and would like to get from you your assiduous cooperation in our debating and in our oratorical exercises and as soon as you can. For it is necessary to make haste, and right from the beginning, now that all the classes in the school have been resumed, when the epidemic has been vanquished, and the number of auditors and of pupils is quite high. This work we are asking you to do comprises two things: first, send us from the classroom benches debaters, and determine to which one of them you will give first rating, to which the second, and to which the third. And in order to do that without delay and rapidly, I am asking you to hand out those chapters of the laws that are most often applied, not only from the *Institutes*, but also those preserved in the *Pandects*. Let each one get a different text so that in a short time many have been submitted to discussion, after having been read and re-read at home, prepared and understood by means of commentaries, in the choice of which your students will be guided by your will and judgment. In this way they will themselves learn much in a very short time. In debates they will understand how to treat many matters, and the enthusiasm of all our students will be ignited.

Your task will consist in the second place of increasing the number of those who speak and of putting at their disposal not only the resources of the law, when they require these from you, but also of current topics in our era and in our procedures. For although the cases treated by our speakers may be fictitious, I nevertheless want them to approach reality as nearly as possible. I know that there are various kinds of subjects for this exercise. One is poetic; for example, the dispute between Ajax and Ulysses for possession of arms, or the quarrel between Agamemnon and Achilles. It is no useless exercise to develop in the oratorical manner Homer's contradictory speeches. But as these are mythical subjects, they are less stirring to an audience, though useful to whoever wishes to practice on them. The other type of subject is drawn from history. To persuade Sulla to give up his dictatorship; to advise Augustus to abdicate his imperial rule; to transpose into oratorical style Cato's harangue and his adversary's, written down by Titus Livius in a historical one.

It is an excellent exercise to deal with these matters, who denies it? But they are remote from our own period and thus less interesting. Our period engages the interest of the spirit. Thus I would wish that speakers be aided by our theologians and by you, our legal experts. The city court offers numerous cases in which you intervene sometimes as defense counsel. I think that it will be very useful for you to mention these cases briefly and suggest to each of the speakers arguments from both sides, so that the young people may write more willingly and more easily and make themselves brandish with all the force of eloquence and grace in their good solid way the arrows that you put into their hands, ready to be launched. For if the legal experts aided Lucius Crassus and Mark Anthony and those eminent orators, and if those had had the practice of finding in actual cases really sought out a master who, as Cicero said in the second book of *The Orator*, "Give them these javelins fitted out with thongs" following Antony's phrase, why do we not renew the same custom in our schools and at our recitations? But as these will be real cases and since perhaps the parties to them would not want to be named, we will follow the example of Martial, who in a biting epigram both vehement and insulting, uses an imaginary name. We will do the same and will have our Earinus, our Attalus and our Gellius who will be unable either to cry out or to be annoyed by these invectives, while we will be able to plead these cases and correct such manners quite comfortably. You will excuse me for writing you, as I said earlier, not in order to give you instruction, but to ask of you and beg of you to collaborate, to associate yourself with and to participate in our exercises with a willing heart.

> Farewell, dear Tuppius.
> Strasbourg, in this month of March.

* * * * *

15. 1565, before March 30. Strasbourg.
      Johann Sturm to Michael Beuther, Doctor of Law,
Jurisconsult and History Teacher.

I greet you, dear Beuther; even if you were here, I would write you the same letter. At the very moment that I decided to take up my pen, our friend, Doctor Eusebius Hedio dropped by, the son of Caspar Hedio who was a preacher in our own cathedral, a man of humane spirit and of an admirable goodness beloved by his fellow citizens, even those of the opposite party. He told me that in 1550, when you were studying law at Poitiers, you had begun to write historical pieces and that the one who had gotten you started on this business was Philipp Melanchthon, the father of most educated men. What he told me interested me and greatly gladdened me as well because of the close ties that bind us together in our tasks. Because I hope that you will become one of us and that you will not refuse the position of historian. And so I write as if you were one of our own, just as I have written to all the classroom teachers having engaged with each in letter form upon a consideration of the organization of our school.

I am absolutely convinced that you will join us; even if by some misfortune our wish were not realized, he who will teach the history course for us will know by this letter what he will have to do and what his task will be. But we won't hire anyone who will be unwilling to exercise what we are told you possess to such a large measure: the knowledge of Greek and of Latin, of all periods of history as the literary monuments of the Hebrews, Greeks and Romans have set forth. But in you is something grander still, which is the science of law which we would hope for in a historian, but which we cannot expect to command, in view of the small number of those who have been able to acquire both a historical education and the practice and theory of the law as well. That is why if you did come to us you could, as Titus Pomponius Atticus did for the Romans, preserve and note for our youth the facts of all times and like Atticus, condense in one small volume as well the story of all those events or else publish your historical pieces which would be like rendering the same service. You could do that and you could choose amongst the historians that which you would explain not indeed as a translator, but as a historian, criticizing what is fallacious, untangling the truth, severe towards the vices of the magistracy, decided against the crimes of evil doers, bearing praise for the virtues of good men. You could set down the chronological order of events, set down the description of places and of battles, make understandable the introduction and presentation of resolutions, facts and events. You could show causes omitted or included by historians and you could distinguish between the vocabulary and flourishes that characterize the historical style and that of orators and of poets.

To the advantages of this two-fold task you could add a third: you could either lay out whole subject areas for our students, proposing topics of special study and to be given both orally and by written exercise, or else you could provide them at their request examples about which they might debate and on which they could do research of their own to write up.

As a legal expert you could also work with our own jurisconsult giving him whatever help he needs, and getting in return any help you might need, but for a better cause than those of which the comic character spoke. Such are the profits that our school could gather from your coming and which we will ask of whoever is to be our history teacher.

But you will come, you will stay, you will be one of us, and between ourselves, we will cultivate friendship and will live happily from literature and by it.

Farewell.
Strasbourg, in the month of March.

* * * * *

16. 1565, March. Strasbourg.
Johann Sturm to Jakob Schegk, Teacher of Physical Sciences and of Medicine.

"Look to nature, it goes by at a gallop." You must excuse me for speaking about nature to a naturalist. I am not able not to give you encouragement, to exhort you, to beg of you to join us. You know all my arguments and I cling to them; I trust that your wife will make no objection.

You will lecture on Galen whenever you choose, and when you wish on Aristotle's books about physics. We only require one hour per day, unless you yourself wish to add a second. Along with your ordinary work, you will give us a hand in our common tasks and you will help the classroom teachers select and share out words and expressions that are relative to your art. This work will only last one year and it is minimal because practically everyone is prepared and there is no longer any need for searching out afresh what has already been found and classified. To indicate the elements, set out the parts of the human body and their functions, make known drugs and explain each detail is but a game, especially for you, a great doctor.

Pardon me if I seem to be giving instructions, as if you were already one of us, or if I seem to insist, as if you were refusing to come. I beg of you to consider joining us: you will not regret it. I am importunate because I like you, but also because it is in the interest of our Gymnasium to urge you. I am hoping to build a school that no one will be able to fault, unless he be one of those who fault everything while yet imposing no more effort on the faculty than before, but with much greater productivity of the fruit of their labor, and while we procure the students' joy. I would like you to help in this beginning. Even if you do not share my desire, I would wish at any rate that my second desire be realized, which is that you stay safe and sound, happy and prosperous. I beg that in exchange for this last wish, you give in to my first one, which is to see you amongst us and to live with us a safe and tranquil life.

Farewell.
Strasbourg, in this month of March.

* * * * *

17. 1565, March. Strasbourg.
Johann Sturm to Conrad Dasypodius, Mathematician.

Conrad, your father, Peter Dasypodius, not only gave innumerable proofs of his gravity and constancy, but especially in the administration of the school never abandoned our Gymnasium program, unable to tolerate any change of authors or of books, of method or instructional procedure. Herlin did likewise, and both were very learned, the one your father, and the other your mathematics teacher. You have succeeded both and have become one of the three administrators of our school, named as Visitor by the Scholarchs. I am glad to see that you are at an age that will enable you to perform these duties for a long while and are full of determination to follow in the footsteps of your father and guard our regulations and to maintain the class organization and not to circumvent the prescribed program.

When our Senate began this Gymnasium in 1538, although I was much younger then, yet, not being able to count upon a long life, I used to console myself by thinking that doubtless after my death, Capito, Bucer, Hedio, Bedrot and Sevenus would by their authority defend the selection of authors, the order of classes and the teaching method already adopted in the event that there should be people who would prefer their own ideas to those already established. But all of them have already met with death, and I am the sole survivor of all my former colleagues. Though I used to think that I had not long to live then, I know now that I will never double the number of years that I have already attained. So I confide to you and to other colleagues to whom health, vigor and age promise a longer life, the care of defending our organization, which I do not desert.

Because this school plan of Lauingen which I just authorized for publication a few days ago and the letters that I have written to the classroom teachers and to the professors of the public courses have not strayed from the path which I traced in the book concerning the correct way to open a public school. My only object in this work (i.e., on the Lauingen school) is that the children make even greater progress in a shorter number of years. I believe I have achieved that, and you can see what the pupils are doing in the ninth. As for the upper grades, the matter is even more apparent. Continue on in this way then, dear Conrad, as you have set out to do, supporting me and the other classroom teachers as well. Let us create an enterprise which men of our times can approve and which posterity may praise.

You will have to explain the elements of geography this year—the *Sphere of Proclus*, the *Phenomena of Aratus*, Euclid, arithmetic, Aristotle's treatise on the world, for whoever wrote this book it contains very useful notions. I am not prescribing the way you should teach. You are familiar with my method and you will have done enough this year if you can accomplish all this. And you will do so, I am sure, for from this beginning I see that you will achieve the whole and that you have no wish to brush aside a single line.

In your capacity as Visitor and as Vice Rector, you will support your colleagues and see to it from day to day that the schoolmasters do not set aside their work, that the pupils keep up their journals, that they perform their work precisely; it is necessary that their daily work be strictly comparable to their capacity. Let the ten types of exercises be the object of vigilant care, for these contribute to the formation of manners as well as to instruction; but let everything be done according to their capacity, as the poet says, without burdening them or bothering them too much. For you see what the muses can accomplish day and night and with what gentleness, if we believe the poets: one muse alone dictated the whole *Iliad* to Homer: "Goddess sing about Pelide's anger" and the whole *Odyssey*: "Muse, tell me the names of the heroes...." It would be extraordinary if that same muse were not also the inspirational source of many other poets, the same chorus of these goddesses having been invoked by all the Greek and Latin bards. And the same muse dictated to Vergil, too: "Muse recite again the causes...." While Hesiod invoked them all: "Muses of Pierides..."; and Vergil again: "Muses of Sicily, let us sing of somewhat greater deeds...." What is the meaning of these fables and of these purely imaginary stories? There exists in us, though mortals, a natural energy or rather a divine force and power, to which nothing is impossible, nothing remains inaccessible, as Vergil said while rambling through the world of nature, exploring it, taking it all in, if one uses reason and restraint "all is possible in so far as our capacity is concerned and without exhausting ourselves, without causing displeasure." For this natural power needs to be supported, not effaced. And then it is important to call upon the muses, that is to say, to follow Nature and not to outstrip her by some exhausting route. Nature permeates all natural things, and as the poet says: "everything is full of Jupiter the god."

It is marvelous that things that our senses cannot even count, nor grasp, our spirit can nevertheless embrace, like the whole world, the sky, the seas, land. How many things astronomy taught you! What a variety of knowledge cosmography offers! Did Euclid describe the finite or the infinite? Euclid's problems and mathematicians' axioms are finite, but how many propositions one can deduce from them that have not been dealt with by the doctors!

Many mortals and learned men know many things, moreover, they know most of them from nature without ever being aware that they do in fact know them and never realize it until things impinge on their consciousness. So then concerning the subject Theophrastus Paracelsus. New doctors affirm that he was able to detect in advance the virtues and efficaciousness of no matter what type of plant, even if unseen and unknown to him before; the first look was enough, even though he had never seen the substance before, though he had never touched nor chewed it. As for knowing if our program is in the realm of the unrealizable, we will all know very soon, and during the last few days in the ninth grade, and in your presence, and you having spent yesterday and the day before in the tenth grade, we have made the experiment. It is not necessary to wait for a year. A year did I say? Not six months, nor even three. This very month, this week, yesterday showed you how much we can expect to achieve each day, teaching us and the children, while learning of how much work and their talent may be capable, with the help of their teachers, of gathering and garnering in just one year.

Farewell.
Strasbourg, in this month of March.

* * * * *

18. 1565, March. Strasbourg.
Johann Sturm to Leonard Hertel, Professor of Aristotle's Dialectics and Visitor.

The Scholarchs who were set up from the start of our school have given me three collaborators who, in my absence and whenever I am busy, must inspect the classes. I can also call upon them whenever I have any problems with instruction, discipline or when I must reach a decision in any particularly serious case. The first such were Hedio, doctor of theology; Jacob Bedrot, commentator on Greek; and Christian Herlin, mathematician. They gave us all names; they were called Visitors and I was called Rector, terms borrowed from other schools. The title Rector, it is true, seemed to me too pompous, although it came from the Roman who had always detested teachers and monarchs; but the term Visitor never seemed to me to reflect the dignity of your task, nor seemed adequate for it. For, although it suggests friendship (we visit our friends when we wish to calm our spirits) it still suggests more the notion of pleasure and joy than of study and concern.

And yet your work is incessant and your task austere, or rather absorbing and heavy, consisting not only in reprimanding young people, but also in warning teachers; in giving them advice; in pointing out to them their duties; in examining, questioning, and teaching young people when it is necessary. But since this term is received and used in other schools called academies and here as well, it is necessary to keep it, not only because you must daily visit all the classes, but especially because this term implying an idea of pleasure, assures by its very being good conduct, gravity, and authority to your labor and duties. In Greece in matters of religion there was also an inspector, but his functions were honorific.

These three men were the first visitors and prefects of our school, chosen in 1538 by the Scholarchs Jakob Sturm, then Stettmeister, Nicolas Knips, then Ammeister and Senator, and Jakob Meier, member of the Council of Thirteen for military affairs. But the plague took Jakob Bedrot off in 1541; Christopher Caerlin succeeded him and he died in the eighth year of his office, having for successor our colleague at the Gymnasium, Peter Dasypodius. Hedio, whom we lost in 1552, was succeeded by our colleague, Doctor Johann Marbach. Peter Dasypodius lived until 1559 and we replaced him by Gerard Sevenus, a very learned grammarian, who died of the quartan fever before Herlin's death. Conrad Dasypodius replaced him. Herlin filled his position for several years with much zeal and loyalty, but his death followed closely that of Sevenus. He died just one year after him in 1562. And now it is up to you to perform the role of Visitor as successor and son-in-law of Sevenus and as a relative of George Nessel. Our Tuppius succeeded this learned jurisconsult when he died. Nessel was such a good and illustrious man; if only he had lived longer.

I am writing you about them all in order to remind ourselves of their memory and to honor it; but also so that, following their example, we might die at our posts to which we are called and chosen, so to speak, by the very voice of the State. All were educated and zealous men, schoolmasters worthy of emulation. I won't speak of the others. As for Sevenus, your father-in-law, you can judge for yourself, since he left behind him many learned students, amongst whom you may also be counted a disciple as well as son-in-law. If he had wished to think more of his own interests than of the interest of other people, he would have left to you his son-in-law and to his own children a larger inheritance, and I would have had as tutor, fewer debts and worries. But he was a man born to think of others, not of himself: it is up to us to help his children with all our power and with all our means and to ask for help from the magistracy, if we wish to avoid a great scandal and not to set an example of lack of piety. I do not need to urge you, still less do I beg you to imitate him; it is for you do it spontaneously and you are capable of perfecting all that one asks of you. I ask only that you continue in this path and support your colleagues in their labor, Doctor of Theology Marbach and Visitor Conrad Dasypodius, of whom I doubt not their zeal, conscience, nor determination.

I am glad that you are teaching Aristotle's doctrine starting with Porphyry's *Elements*. I am also glad that your first concern is teaching your pupils the words used by that writer, his style and the gist of his teaching, followed by your elucidations of Aristotle's manner of explanation and proof, saving your own examples for the last. Of Philip Melanchthon, besides his innumerable qualifications, what especially pleased me about him in my youth and what was always most helpful to me, was that in everything he taught, he used appropriate examples that proved his erudition. If you wish to profit by this method, don't be ashamed of using examples that permit you to explain Aristotle, especially in the logical part that deals with probable arguments. In the other part called "Apodictic," Philoponus is the foremost commentator, excellent and succinct, but Doctor Jakob Schegk has treated these demonstrations at length very learnedly. These books can be useful for you and can lighten your load. Our friend, the mathematician Dasypodius, will also help you, as will our doctors—Andernach, Sebald, Lubert Estheius, Obrecht, Sigismond Rot, Chelius, Gallus—all of whom will provide you with many examples of proofs drawn from Galen and from Hippocrates. You will see for yourself what conclusions of an apodictical sort can be obtained without a guide from amongst the other sciences, different from the conclusions drawn from logic, that is to say, probable up to the point that the former cannot compare to the latter in terms of dignity. Our friend Toxites thinks that Paracelsus also gives some true demonstrations. You have him at your disposition and he is desirous of winning approval from our contemporaries for these new theories of Theophrastus (i.e., Paracelsus).

Martin Bucer I always admired during his lifetime for his activity, learning, experience and judgment in all theological disputes. Amongst other qualities, he had this one that was praiseworthy and worthwhile imitating: he divided all the topics he proposed for discussion into two parts, separating necessary propositions from those which were only probable. In this manner he taught young people to distinguish what was necessary from what was probable, so that they might know what was necessary to maintain and to defend earnestly in church and state, and on what one could make some concessions if circumstances so dictated. But once he had designated some point as necessary and the other party had shown him that it was merely probable, he gave in in such a manner that one never knew if he had made this concession out of natural goodness, or if he had only made his point in order to test his adversary. In the same way that he conducted himself in every dispute, so it seems to me that you too must conduct yourself in your teaching and in the principal propositions of arguments and in the forms of argumentation, so that the students may know what points and what lines of reasoning apply to things that are plausible and probable, and which are suitable to that which is necessary and perpetual.

You will borrow examples of proofs from the mathematical sciences or where they are lacking from doctors such as we have mentioned above. The writings of philosophers and of orators, of Plato, Aristotle, Demosthenes and Cicero are full of logical reasoning that will be helpful to you for your work. In fact, these writers are so gallant that they will be very happy to perform whatever you ask them to do, and are so learned that they will be able to answer your questions.

But since the disputations are part of your task, be careful, I beg of you, that we get quite a few of them, and that they are substantial. It is not necessary that you go over them and correct them all. Those you do correct and do re-work, should be held in a public place open to everyone. The others may be read behind closed doors among the disputants, several masters being called in as arbiters, sometimes before the class so that the spirit of emulation does not grow cold, but that there prevails a fervent zeal which often is the stimulus to virtue. It is not needful to recite these speeches from memory. The students will have done their duty if they write carefully, so that the purity of style is apparent and so that there are brilliant flourishes. Let it be considered praiseworthy if one or the other recites from memory, but it is not obligatory.

Be supportive of your two colleagues when it is necessary to admonish and to encourage the classroom teachers to adhere to our program and not to let a day pass without their realizing it, without fulfilling their duty. For we must all regulate our life, live and work in such a way that we think in terms of rendering an account of everything, not only of our life, but also of our professional responsibilities.

Farewell
Strasbourg, in this month of March.

* * * * *

19. 1565, March. Strasbourg.
Johann Sturm to Valentine Erythraeus, Professor of Ethics.

Although, o Erythraeus, you are entrusted with Aristotle's and Plato's works on ethics so that you can explain them in our school, nonetheless I am glad you are not giving up teaching rhetoric that shaped you from your early years, not the speeches of Demosthenes and Cicero. I am satisfied with your analysis of rhetoric, but I hope that shortly, when the staff have committed themselves to the path I am tracing in these several letters, it will not be necessary to cut those speeches of Cicero and Demosthenes into bite sizes. We will be able to speed up and advance to higher levels, since our students will be arriving from the lower grades to our public courses which form their crown better provided with a host of words and terms, composition and diction rules, and numerous and diverse examples of all that dialecticians and rhetoricians are in the habit of assigning and teaching. You will be able to move at times from the philosophers' library to the orators' perfumery. Now that will be even easier since Michael Beuther will be teaching, I hope, history in our gymnasium. He will not refuse to add to his task as historian the political books of Plato and Aristotle. Whenever you deem it best to turn to the orators' podium, it will be up to him to leave by the wayside his historian's sanctuary for the shaded Academy and the brilliant Lyceum. In that way, our young people will benefit doubly. Beuther will add to the philosophical precepts many important examples drawn from the historians concerning the governance of states, and you will teach them from the philosophical sources of Cicero and Demosthenes how orators have drawn the water wherewith they have irrigated the seedbeds of their imagination.

You will not need to translate word for word; you will be able to parcel out amongst your students a whole speech cut into equal portions if they are equally skilled in elocution and in the practice of language; if not, by unequal portions, so that having come to class they bring you the translations that they did at home from the Greek into the Latin in Greek raiment, or perhaps translate these two tongues into their native one, reproducing from memory, or reading out loud. In such a manner they will make the greatest progress, and you will be relieved of the grammatical labor of word for word translation, while the young people will better understand what they have prepared and repeated at home, and will also retain better. You may add any of the other observations which with your vast and extended experience you have made in the philosophical and oratorical works.

I am putting these translations of speeches in as substitute for the speechmaking activity, in order to establish their emulation as much as to show us their zeal for applying themselves to polishing their style. In fact, this practice of reading and writing was also that of the poets, as one can see in Martial and in Persius. Historians tell us that Homer had that constant habit, and the rhapsodies in the *Iliad* of that same poet prove it; they have been brought together from the different places where he recited his poems and then reassembled and redistributed into twenty-four books called rhapsodies by the Aristarchs and by the Greek grammarians, people gifted with a great erudition and a penetrating critical ability. You will thus help our Hertel, so that there is never a week, an afternoon, an ides or a calends when one isn't reciting from memory or reading from some text in hand something that has put one's fingernails in jeopardy, according to the words of a celebrated writer.

Farewell, my dear Erythraeus.
Strasbourg, in this month of March.

* * * * *

20. 1565, Strasbourg.
     Sturm to Wilvesheim, Teacher of Greek

The letter I have sent to Erythraeus, dear Wilvesheim, may do as well by you as by him. For although he is teaching the public lectures and we have given you two sections that meet together at noontime, yet since his students are in part those who were recently graduated from the first class, it seems to me that it is not necessary to make distinctions between your students and his and that the same method will do very well for them. These lunch hours very often produce sleepiness because of the heat and the meal, (and) it is important to rid oneself of it by a question and answer period. This kind of interchange is more useful at times like those than that other method of constant presentation such as teachers are given to and prefer—why, I don't really know—more than any other. You will refer then to the letter to Erythraeus and will follow it I don't doubt at all, for I know your nature and your devotion to me.

I will not enumerate the authors that you will lecture on. You know indeed that you will have to deal either with historians such as Herodotus and Thucydides (Xenophon, it is true, is easier to understand, better suited to that division of labor of which I spoke in the letter to Erythraeus, especially in the first months), or poets amongst whom you will take into consideration their difficulty in the first six months. Later on I give you permission to proceed to the more difficult writers, whether they be historians or poets. It is after all on these two kinds of expression that we need to exercise our youngsters yet beardless.

> "For it will be most important to know in what manner and with what habits you will raise them. The stork feeds her young on snakes, on lizards found in distant fields. And these young when their feathers have grown in look to dine on the same animals." (Juvenal, *Satire* IV)

In fact, such as we wish our young people to be the rest of their lives, such must be the instruction we give them as well as the food we give their bodies.

Farewell, my dear Wilvesheim,
Strasbourg, in this month of March.

* * * * *

21. 1565, March. Strasbourg.
Johann Sturm to his friend Elie Kyber, Teacher of Hebrew

It is by design that we have not begun the teaching of Hebrew in the grades, first because in my opinion, he has made great progress who before the age of sixteen has a fair command of two languages while at the same time having learned rhetoric and dialectic; who has studied in class in addition to the church catechism the *Evangiles* and the apostles' epistles; who has practiced singing psalms and who can recollect the other sacred literature about which one has spoken during daily assignments for the whole of his student experience. In the second place it is because I mean to have taught on the side a course in Hebrew grammar during one of those hours where there is no classroom instruction and where it is permitted everyone to learn what he wishes outside the program, provided that the subject is fit for an honest man, doesn't shock good manners, and doesn't interfere with the regular course of study. Finally, while yet regretting that I delayed the study of this language until my fifty-ninth year, I would not wish to force others to do what I never did myself. Nevertheless, I encourage everyone to add this language to the two other classical tongues following my own example, for last summer, all by myself, I laid the foundations for the study of this language, to the extent that I hope to be able in a little while to finish the rest of the course without the help nor advice of a teacher.

As for you, my dear Kyber, I beg that you follow Horace's advice: "Let everything you teach be brief so that tractable spirits may quickly grasp your words and faithfully retain them" (Horace, *Letters*). Before Nicholas Clenard had begun to teach Hebrew at Louvain, the number of students of this language was quite small, and yet John Campensis taught it at the College of Busleiden, a capable and learned man, but not such a good teacher as was Clenard. But as soon as Clenard had published his Tables and had begun to explain them, it was astonishing to see so many men so quickly rush up to devote themselves to this study and attain in so short a time the desired end. And yet this Clenard whom I knew at Louvain and had as a friend at Paris never brought anything in the way of rules aside from his Tables that would permit one to acquire the knowledge of this language and the understanding of the sacred books. I am writing this to you Kyber in order to impress upon you the lesson of Horace on brevity, that is the paucity and the clarity of rules, two qualities that shine in Clenard's teaching.

Our friend Reuchlin who succeeded Michael Delius also made some Tables that are not without utility; take the ones you wish. Flegel, whom the plague carried off last year and whom you are following, was more prolix than it was necessary to be, better suited to those who already know the language than for those who wish to learn it. Of Jerome Massari who succumbed to the same epidemic, a learned man and a cultured physician, I own some substantial courses well done that he drafted ten years ago without having published. I will give them to Josiah Rihel so that he can publish them. But they are more suited for reading at home than they are for teaching. I confess I used them very much and think that without them I would have had more difficulty in learning the language. I thus used him as a teacher and at the same time I had available to me the translators and summarized commentaries of

Santo Pagnini published in Geneva, and also the dictionary of John Foster.

But if you listen to me, you will follow the route I lay down for our classes. Students ought not to arrange words according to the twenty-four letters of the alphabet, but to class them by type, and in each type by species and categories, a method that I also use in teaching and which in a few days will reveal what a richness of sentences and expressions there is in this language which seems to possess few words and to be quite impoverished. But why speak of that to a man of such a refined erudition, myself such a beginner and such a recruit in this language. But you know what a recruit needs, one nearly sixty years old, and that is good teachers, those who follow their young soldiers' nature and sustain them.

> Farewell.
> Strasbourg, in this month of March.

* * * * *

22. March, 1565. Strasbourg
Johann Sturm to Mathew Stiffelreuter, Music Teacher

"If you have a voice, sing," says Ovid, "if you have supple arms, dance." (Ovid, *Ars amandi*, I) At my age I can no longer either sing or dance. It is enough that I can judge who dances and sings according to the rules of the art. Music has been entrusted to you and I do not doubt that you will serve as a good experienced musician, capable of pleasing the church and our school. And here is what I would like to see your work preserve always for our Republic: first, that the choir sings without shrieking, and then that their mouths are not twisted by the low pitch of the sound and that they are not stretched up to their ears by the vowels and by barbarous diphthongs, so that one sees nothing ugly neither in their mouths nor in their throats. To sing glibly so that one is not jolted by measures too quickly attacked and so one does not hear intervals between them, that is what experts consider a charm and a result of art.

In order to spare musicians the need to shout, the Romans placed acoustical jars in their theaters intended to carry softness of sound to the spectators' ears, and to spare singers from the fatigue of shrieking and making efforts that disfigured them, and to permit each listener easily to understand the sense of what was being sung. The Belgians and the Celts had excellent musicians, they still have some laudatory ones. The people of Liège, too, I heard them twenty-nine years ago, modulate their songs harmoniously. At Tübingen the jurist Melchior Wolmar knew how to sing so well himself and taught his students how to sing so well that they did not seem to have been born where they were, so remarkably sweet was their singing.

But like the other arts, music too has its theory and its practice. It is up to you to work and sing. Still the students and pupils of the first and second classes, those closest to the public courses, will be able to grasp quickly, if they are singers at all, what the deepest tone called the "proslambanomenos" is; what the sharpest sound, or "netehyperboleon" is; and similarly what harmony, chromatic modulation, and the diatonic scale are, and he will be able to understand the variations of all these tones.

Boetius brought to this subject many things that deserve to be learned by young people, that are honorable for them to know. Let them not sing the Psalms by random chance but especially in church and in class by the rules of art. It is your duty to teach them thus. But I trust you teaching these things that are so honorable and leave up to you and Conrad Dasypodius the task of deciding at what moment it will be necessary to explain some of these to the adolescent young people and which things deserve to be explained.

But why am I discussing this sort of thing with you? "If you have a voice, sing, if you have supple arms, dance!" Dance if you are equipped to do so and sing if you can do it, but with art and with modesty, for the good of our instruction, not for injuring it, and not to damage religion in any way. As for me, I do not hope for either the throat or the voice of Aristoxenes.

Farewell.
Strasbourg

* * * * *

23. March 29, 1565.
Johann Sturm to Simon Ostermann Eller, Jurisconsult,
Rector of the Lauingen Gymnasium

That which you asked of me, adding to your regulations whatever I felt must be added, I could not send you before the Frankfurt fair, for I wrote it the fourth day before the calends of April at daybreak. Not having been able to finish our regulations, I took up the old ones as you will see. While writing that I am reminded of a verse that Conrad Goclenius put into an epigram about a learned man who was lecturing on the treatise on duty by Cicero, and who erred only on one point, not through lack of wit, but through physical deficiency. Here is the last verse of the epigram:

"He who teaches about duty does not do his duty."

I am afraid that happens to me, too, for I told others what their duty was and I did not undertake any myself. And just yesterday, and three days ago, I was asked to undertake some hendecasyllables and remind myself of the obligation; but I did not do it, and I cannot; for my printer is waiting for the last part of my treatise.

With this letter I pledge myself to those fine men and to our magistrate to consider as my duty, not only teaching and thinking, but also practicing and doing what I teach. Also, I will not let another day pass without thinking of the school, without teaching, without writing, without going to inspect the classes, without myself showing in the lessons that what might seem impossible to some is realizable, and that even in the smallest classes, and greater still in the larger ones. Our learned friend, Doctor Marbach, whose earnestness in work you know, and Conrad Dasypodius are in agreement with me, and I'm sure the same goes for Leonard Hertel. They are the Visitors for what I dare call our Academy and for our Lyceum. It is to them that I shall turn, every time there is need, it is by their advice and help that I shall profit. For it is their task as it is mine, to watch that all do their duty, to inspect the classes every day to prevent the teachers from coming late to school and to class; and from leaving before time is up, and for seeing that they are not disturbed during the lesson, and to entrust the youngsters who come from afar to preceptors. These last must watch out for them; conduct them to their lodgings; get the promise of the lodgings' supervisor that they will make personal acquaintance with them and not permit any young man who is his lodger any action unworthy of the education given in our school and will not permit him to leave or to change lodgings without the permission of the Visitors.

Such is the task of the Visitors, and mine as well, to be sure. For it is up to all of us, rector, Visitors and teachers to see to it that discipline suffers no damage and that nothing is done that we cannot account for to the magistrate and to good men, and always to remind ourselves of these verses:

> "Telephe or Peleu, if you speak badly what one has given you to say either I will fall asleep, or else I will laugh; sad words are fitting for a somber visage, (while) threatening ones bespeak an angry one." (Horace, *Letters*, I.3.2)

That is why I will read, teach, or write every day something that can serve as an example. Here is what I have decided to add to our regulations: we make known for the moment as engraved in marble these ancient laws—born with our gymnasium, but useful—and we render them worthy of being engraved in letters of gold, if you continue in your resolve. The help of the Visitors is necessary and I advise you to join with the theologian Frederick Celestinus, the mathematician Cyprian Leovitius and Doctor Martin Roland not only so that you may have collaborators, but even more witnesses of your conscientiousness and zeal, in order that you have a way of communicating every occasion to that best of Princes your actions and thoughts.

> Farewell.
> Strasbourg, March 29.

* * * * *

24. Johann Sturm to Simon Ostermann, Jurisconsult.

In the month of March I had no time to send you the written regulations as I would have wanted. For Josiah Rihel, our book publisher, was insistent and was hurrying me, and you know how demanding and impatient these editors are about their work. But since all the copies were sold and the work is once again in the press, I remembered your request and I have added to our statutes some points concerning your teaching, and ours which seemed to me lacking in our regulations. I am not suggesting my rules or ours, but your Lauingen gymnasium, which is as close to my heart as ours, and which I do not cherish less than a father his young and beautiful daughter, who shows the sparkling signs of her beauty and virtue. Besides your concern is so dear to me because I hope that in the progress of that school you gain the esteem of the whole world and will be praised by fine men.

Farewell, my dear Ostermann.
Strasbourg, in the month of June, 1565.

11
Academic Letters
(1569)

Introduction

Johann Sturm's second published collection of letters was originally entitled *Academicae epistolae urbanae* (Strasbourg), exc. Iosias Rihelius, s.d. [1569]. Though much of their contents is analogous to the *Classical Letters*, the focus is somewhat different, for it centers on academic administration and counsel to some of his most outstanding professors. The letters are addressed to the Strasbourg senate, to the scholarchs, to Karl Mieg, councilor and scholarch, followed by letters to faculty, a doctor of jurisprudence, two mathematicians, the board of examiners, a logician, a rhetorician, a physicist, a jurisconsult and doctor of ethics, a grammarian, and to a special assembly. This collection of letters clearly reveals the administrative relation of the rector to the authorities above him and to the faculty in his charge.

The most readily available edition of the academic letters remains Reinhold Vormbaum, *Die evangelischen Schulordnungen des Sechzehnten Jahrhunderts* (Gütersloh: Druck und Verlag von C. Bertelsmann, 1860), pp. 709–723. The various reprints or editions are listed in Jean Rott's "Bibliographie des oeuvres imprimées de Jean Sturm (1507–1589)," *Investigationes Historicae*, II (Strasbourg: Librairie Oberlin, 1986), p. 366. Special attention should be directed to the splendid new history of Strasbourg, Georges Livet and Francis Rapp, eds., *Histoire de Strasbourg des Origines à Nos Jours* (Édition des Dernières Nouvelles de Strasbourg, n.d.), Livre IV, "Préréforme et humanisme Strasbourg et l'Empire (1482–1520)," pp. 177–254, by Francis Rapp; Livre VI, "La Réforme à Strasbourg" by Marc Lienhard, pp. 365–540. One could easily add to Sturm's own selection of "academic letters," for example, see "Une lettre de Jean Sturm, Premier Recteur du Gymnase et de L'Académie Addressée aux Scolarques (fin mars 1565)," presented and analyzed in Francis Rapp and Georges Livet, eds., *Grandes Figures de l'Humanisme Alsacien Courant Milieux Destins* (Strasbourg: Librarie Istra, 1978), pp. 175–182).

Academic Letters
of the Urban Rector
Johann Sturm
Book I
(1569)

Letter I
To the Senate:

There was once the Republic of the Athenians. It was remarkably praiseworthy, for it was established by Solon with good laws the authority of
which prevailed at home and in the field. It had a high reputation in
military valor and, in the realm of all Greece, with few exceptions, it
once was supreme; in literary studies it enjoyed the highest reputation
and was considered to be the inventor and creator of every art.

Though it shared its reputation for military valor with the Lacedae-
monians, in the case of Phillip and Alexander, its fortune was rather
poor and in the end it lost what reputation it had. At Rome the laws of
Solon were partially changed by the praetors themselves. Laws were
also framed more wisely by the Romans who held in their esteem the
greater part of the laws longer than those very people from whom the
laws had been transferred to Rome for the Septemvirs.

Now that so many centuries have passed from the time when Athens was overthrown, truly the glory of their letters is on the lips of all
men of letters and the greater the esteem among us for their letters, the
less capable we are than those famous men in teaching them. But, what
is more important, while the laws of the state are nearly all antiquated,
nevertheless surpassing monuments of literature have been left us from
poets, historians, mathematicians, and philosophers.

Surely, if one may compare the ordinary with the greatest, I shall
now be allowed to speak about our city-state. You especially, Senators,
who are of the highest rank, are able to judge whether my words are
true with a view to acquiring praise or false, composed with the aim of
flattery.

Moreover, the ordinary may be compared with the best because virtue lies in the mean and does not fear mortality on account of being

ordinary. Indeed, the moderate wealth of cities has stood longer than the great and vast power of the people.

Our elders waged wars in such a way that they seemed only to protect their own goods and not to seek the goods of others. When they received their laws and powers from their ancestors, they preserved for posterity up to our times, emended laws, and increased powers. They made increased powers in a way that the powers were established through self-restraint and prudence rather than by force of arms. They made the corrected laws so that they did it driven by the rule of religion rather than by the will. God wishes this method and truth wishes this moderation (*mediocritas*) to be permanent—indeed even immortal, if nature permits anything to be immortal.

Letters remained alive in our city. Our ancestors, content with an elementary school, preferred to get them from neighboring academies just as the Romans did from the city of Athens. You also sent your children outside instead of establishing something complete at home as the circumstances at that time suggested.

Now those who were thoroughly educated for life, morals, dangers and custom have resolved that the benefits of this kind of education and teaching be shared with others rather than be taken from those neighboring academies—which once was the fortune of the Athenians. For there was in Athens a shrine of Hercules that was named Cynosarges in which bastard boys were fed free of charge. But not only were these boys educated there but also the children of citizens were instructed in the discipline of letters. There were in this place schools of letters before the Academy of Plato or the Portico of the Stoics, or before the Lyceum of Aristotle. Moreover, since they were satisfied with this place, they seemed to need nothing more perfect.

So you also, being satisfied now for thirty-two years with classes, have decided that enough has been made available to your children and shared with those from outside the city.

But, two years ago, after the benefit was bestowed by the Emperor and the new academy was founded by me, you seemed to prescribe, as it were, what we should add to the classical exercises.

Therefore the writing of these academic letters has been assigned to me so that at my discretion I might explain in letters to my friends what I think about the foundations of the academy.

In this matter I have done your good will and agreement about what has been outstandingly done and I value that above even a military triumph. For a battle, as soon as it has been fought, ceases to be. But the establishment of a lyceum or a stoa or academy, once it has been formally organized, begins to be and promises long duration and hopes for immortality; and from these seeds of labor, brings forth daily fruits of glory forever as long as earth remains. What, therefore, has been entrusted to me and undertaken by me, I shall never leave until I shall have brought it to you completely finished.

Although nothing that I write is different from what I related in the Book, *The Correct Opening of Elementary Schools of Letters*, nevertheless I shall here ascend a little higher and shall move forward a bit farther so that it will be evident from these statements what I hoped for at that time and what I provided.

I shall indeed give an account of that most splendid city Athens which once had the most brilliant military leaders and the greatest interpreters of their deeds, as well as the most excellent poets and perfect orators, and, in three places, the greatest families of philosophers—in the Academy, the Stoa, and the Lyceum. Those were great men in their industry, diligence and teachings—judging by the books they wrote. Since they were enumerated by Diogenes Laertius and Suidas, they can be understood from the authority of their extant writings.

In composing this writing, whatever it is to be, I think that you call and summon me to show to men that you are the patrons of the liberal arts and that what we establish and what we do, we undertake with you as the founders.

Farewell. At Strasbourg.

* * * * *

Letter II
To the Scholarchs Heinrich Mühlheim, Karl Mieg, and Frederick Gotesheim:

It is a great honor to be called "Master of Liberal Arts and of Philosophy"—even more glorious than the title "Philosopher." For the knowledge of all things and wisdom itself are properly the possession and faculty of God and the study of these things has always been considered an honest undertaking. The man who tries to aspire to the limits of all things does not exceed the boundaries of modesty. Therefore all men may inquire into the nature of the universe and may learn everything that the natural scientists have handed down about the world and all its parts and all of its embellishments, and about the first principles of matter from which everything has arisen. Also, men may know what was produced by great authors about the first philosophy. They may elevate the mind higher and reduce into teaching both forms of matter (as if to abstract them from their bodies) and whatever involves many units. The multiple forms of whatever is figured may be partitioned. Men may consider as well the modes of speech in themselves and arrange them in various ways. They may observe the motions of the heavens and separate them. Finally, it is the duty of an industrious youth and even of a noble elder not to be ignorant of whatever the natural scientists, the first wise men, and the mathematicians have handed down.

Not only is it praiseworthy to wish to know these things, but also glorious to teach concerning life and morals, so that the part of philosophy that is called contemplative (θεωρική) may not remain alone but may walk with its companion which is named practical (πρακτική). He will teach this and also how to cultivate fields, plant vineyards, feed flocks and keep bees—all of which agriculture claims for itself—and not unlike this is what is called domestic economy (οἰκονομική). Even Pallas Athena will found citadels for herself and will build sacred temples and establish theatres and will make other buildings and instruct architects. She will even teach emperors to raise an army, to train raw recruits, to draw up a battle line, to besiege cities, to fight battles—which belong to the art of war. For not only did Minerva, herself from the brain of Zeus, bring with her her own brain, but she also sprang into life armed and provided with a spear. The heavenly muse Urania, Jove's daughter, encompasses the locations of the stars, their risings, their settings and returns—a teaching that is called Astronomy. But she will also teach physicians and instruct even sailors and will make them able to predict (προορητικός), as it were, the occurrences and signs of the universe. Apollo himself will know all the causes and cures of disease and will first teach Aesculapius to free mortals from sickness and torments. These things are all a part of nature and it befits a free-born and liberal man to know the works of those who are called natural scientists (*physici*). To practice these arts is in general fruitful—even necessary for mankind.

But since all human things were created by grace, not only the body is to be cared for (the concern of physicians) but much more must the spirit be cultivated by virtue and the mind must be adorned with good morals. The famous man Socrates, when he learned from his teacher Archelaos certain principles, and, as it were, seeds for the doctrine of morals, handed on these teachings neglected by the natural scientists to Plato and to his other disciples, so that Plato himself and his student Aristotle with his other disciples released this teaching in literary monuments and left us treatises on duties and explained the laws and set forth all kinds of civic matters and were conspicuous as teachers, as it were, of kings, lawmakers, magistrates and judges. This art that is called ethics crowns all these works. Its most powerful part is politics which cannot exist apart from economics. For I distinguish ethics itself in its pure form and then ethics in politics and then in economics, as Plato and Aristotle called it.

Truly, no kind of republic is more holy than that of the Christians and no one can instruct better about the kingdom of God than theologians. Therefore, there is this fourth kind of teaching which is appropriate to theology and it has learned teachers, not only God Himself but also prophets, apostles, evangelists and those who are called the fathers. In this kind of teaching we surpass all philosophers of former ages, every academy, and the Athenians themselves. The true ethics is the teaching of the morals of these Christians. It was unknown to the seven wise men of all Greece and not known by Thales and the Ionians, not understood by Pythagoras and the Italians, known neither by Socrates, nor perceived by the men who followed Socrates, i.e., the Academicians, the Stoics, the Peripatetics. These things are of such a kind and so great that they appear to be not at all human or transitory, but all appear to be divine and immortal and they are such as they seem to be.

What I have related up to this point is relevant to our academy which you have founded. For we have divided the third part which has to do with speech and language and the art of composition and the ability to speak, as we have logically divided them in the *Classical Epistles*; and we have cultivated them with the result that they are and are considered almost characteristic of our schools.

How indeed those two kinds of superior studies—one of which belongs to the realm of nature and the second to the realm of morals—can be taught in a way that can yet be understood and learned by everyone although everything cannot be read and explained in schools, since you have entrusted this duty to me, I have undertaken to set forth in my *Academic Letters*, not so as to propose laws to anyone but so that I may reveal my opinions and leave the final judgment to each individual.

The account of this plan I shall follow, if it pleases the Senate—a thing that I would wish at this time. If not, nevertheless, since it is your mandate, I shall not act contrary to my duty to observe the rules, the firm defense of which is sufficient against censure for shamelessness.

Farewell.

* * * * *

Letter III
To Karl Mieg, Councilor and Scholarch

Since it is the program of our academy that we try to teach everything that the human spirit can grasp, we teachers ought to have learned everything—something that we have not yet achieved. I do no see that any one of us could promise this for himself and, as I perceive it, no one has promised it. Or if he promised it, he did this more from zeal or eagerness than from an understanding of the difficult and arduous task.

If someone should read all the books of Plato, Aristotle, and Plutarch, would not all but a few think that they had not heard, examined, and understood everything? How many important subjects did they miss? I believe, and truly believe, if all the philosophers, whether they are Epicureans, Academicians, of the old or new Academy, or Stoics—I say of them all and of the other wise men of all Greece—if anyone collects their teachings and puts them in a sequence, he will see, nevertheless, that they made more categories than they explained—whatever their philosophy claims!

Most of all, surely, they were able to say nothing about God, nothing about the creation of the world, nothing about the nature of man, nothing about the return of men to life. The poets ventured to name the sons and daughters of Jupiter. But how much they and the philosophers erred in the search for the true Son—to say nothing about their understanding of Him! Now many things have been discovered in the natural sciences and mathematics by later generations that were unknown to the earliest wise men. Even though this is so, nevertheless, since one philosopher professes, as it were, all subjects and all have struggled to achieve this so that they may know all subjects and hand them on, why should not the same be granted to us as them? Or why should not we, no less than they, be able with industriousness to succeed? Do we lack books? or leisure? or stipends or abilities or, finally, intellect? For if we yield to the ancients in this, the corruption of learning would occur more from our own faint-heartedness than from our natural capability, the excellence of which is no less a gift and benefit from God than are fruits and the annual supply of food. Obviously ages have advanced, some in one way and others in another, and men are more numerous and keener witted and more learned just as some years are surpassed by one year and other years by another in regard to fruitfulness. The Arabs may have more men of genius than Germany may have, yet the benevolence of God must not be denied, for He is the Illuminator of the human mind. For every light of genius comes from God.

So Athens was a learned city and poets, mathematicians, and philosophers prospered there. Nevertheless they did not always prosper in
the same way. Since that was granted to them before us, it does not
mean that it is forbidden to us. They left us monuments of literature that
teach us how many important subjects they encompassed in their teachings. Learned men know these subjects and how much has been added
to the earliest posterity and how much can be contributed to posterity
by us. There are those who consider and reflect by what road may one
come to this ability. "Two walking together,"[1] as that famous man says,
there is need of (συζητήσει) (joint inquiry). And as that famous man
says,[2] "In an evil situation, let us talk as if in a good situation," the efforts
must be made by us mutually so that if we individually cannot achieve
everything thoroughly, nevertheless individually we can achieve individual things in an ordinary way. Let each one carefully cultivate set
individual tasks according to his own talent. Let him engage in as much
as he can and learn from his other colleagues so that all together
(*universi*)[3] may possess what they do not have as individuals. Therefore, if you would wish to be advisors to me and my colleagues, you
would be able to bring it about that we divide up among ourselves the
arts and books that we read so that in a few years, everything would be
apportioned among us not in books and libraries but in our minds and
memories and we would possess as understood and learned what
indeed has been preserved in the books of the ancients. Therefore let
the theological writers whom they read at home be divided up among
them whether they be Greek as are the church historians like
Chrysostom, Basil or Gregory of Nazianen and others, or Latin, like Tertullian, Lactantius, Cyprian, Jerome, Augustine.

Let the mathematicians and natural scientists do the same with their
writers. I shall this year willingly use in comparison to the precepts of
speaking and in comparison to Cicero and Demosthenes, the books of
Plato and Aristotle on the republic and on the laws, and what they have
handed down on morals. Likewise others should work hard on historians and poets so that having been instructed by them, they make
known, in meetings and daily conversations, in disputations and in
schools in rhetorical declamations, as many important subjects as the
human mind can grasp, if it tries. If the mind of man enters upon the
right method and plan, what great advances it is able to make by sharing
studies, by dividing up the work, by distinct divisions of hours, in sum,
by a reasonable method and a good plan!

*   *   *   *   *

Letter IV
To Lawrence Tuppius, Doctor of Jurisprudence:

I believe that it must be burdensome for you to repeat the *Institutes* of
the Emperor Justinian so often and, for those who hear you, unpleasant
to learn nothing from you except the *Institutes*. It even impedes the
praises of our Academy that we have so few interpreters of the law in
our gymnasium. I know that it was set up this way by our forefathers
and that the same policy was continued, namely to have only one interpreter of laws—and I know that they believed that students of law were
more morally lax than the rest of the students who devoted their energies to literature and theology.

Even if in other academies some who cultivate this study lead their
lives in a more unruly fashion—although why do I say "cultivate"? Students do not cultivate study who live shamefully. Rather they defile it
with vices and neglect one of the first precepts of this discipline. But
what precept is that? To live honestly! Therefore, though there are some
who live in a more unruly fashion, we can nevertheless control them by
our regulations.

We find out by experience that because of the small number of class
hours not only the young men but even the teachers themselves are misled by their free time and become apathetic so that they leave us before
it is useful for either of them. I am silent about the fact that the small
number of class hours, which is like a lack of wealth, harms even the
children of our citizenry.

So, if my counsel had any weight, I would urge that you, together
with Beuther and Hugo Blotius and Wilvesheim should divide up the
Pandects so that we may be comparable to the rest of the academies
also in this part of philosophy.

You have the sources of your law in the books of the philosophers
on the republic and on morals, which will hereafter be diligently
explained in our schools. You will do extremely well if you follow back
your streams to their origin, and they divert water from their fountains
to your streams. In this way and by this method, the study of law would
flow forth more pleasant, the work would be easier, and the teaching
of law would become richer. For just as the sight of fountains is more
splendid and their taste more pleasant than the sight and taste of
streams, and just as the fish in those rivulets that flow down from the
fountains are more healthful and delicious than the salted fish or eels of
our native country, so those imbued with the precepts of philosophy

learn their own as well as this art with greater pleasure and they bring sounder judgment to settling controversies. They do this with less work and with easier disagreement because of the arguments of the dialecticians that the philosophers convey and which they follow in the discipline of morals and of the law.

Is what I ask a good case? What of the fact that main sections of your law have been, up to now, mutilated? If not the fact that there were more practitioners (πραγματικοί) than knowledgeable men (ἐπιστημονικοί) and since the former were preoccupied with specifics, they could not see the subject as a whole and divide the whole into parts. Since they did not know the parts, they did not taste from the fountain of the philosophers and were content with their own stagnant waters abounding in their own kinds of fish. They wished to acquire wealth and resources rather than cultivate wisdom and perfect teachings. Cicero, or Crassus in Cicero's *De Oratore* (*On the Orator*) in the first conversation promises wisdom after a few months of law. This assurance could not have been made had he not been trained in the arts of philosophers and dialecticians. I have held these opinions that I would write to you at this time in view of our need. As for you, if you should have something better, "Share your thoughts frankly," as Horace says; if not, "Practice these along with me."[4]

* * * * *

Letter V
To Doctor Michael Beuther

I shall explain my opinions to Dasypodius about the three volumes of our Academy which contain the universal teaching of the mathematicians so that anyone by means of these precepts may be able both to learn in private and to teach in public the mathematics which remains available. Furthermore, I have decided that it would be useful for our program for the first two volumes to be explained in the two upper classes and the third be taught publicly to everyone. Since this plan was approved yesterday by you, outside the regular agenda, in your council, I once more certainly voice approval and wish that this be a felicitous and holy plan for our citizens and for foreign nations.

I am of the opinion, moreover, that the four principles of the arts be included in the first volume: geometry, logic, astronomy, and geography. I call these principles or (στοιχεῖα) basic which are taught before the problems and theorems, as are the definitions, divisions, axioms and postulates.[5] By these principles, obviously, the things that follow are proved and propositions are demonstrated, or they are directed toward something that must be accomplished or understood.

In the second volume, moreover, the very important teaching of arithmetical computation will be handed on and the rules of computation will be included—not only of day to day computation, but also that which you call astronomy. The body of knowledge of astronomy is very full, dealing with the prime mover of the sphere and the motion of the sky; the location of the land, the celestial orbits, the rising and setting of stars, the difference of days and nights. There are descriptions of the zones and climates, also some explanation of the eclipses of the sun, but not so that they are proven the way mathematicians prove them, but so that they may be identified for what they are and what type they are. For we know that distinction of yours of what is and why it is (τοῦ ὅτι, καὶ τοῦ διότι).

Now the third volume ought to include the apodictic explanation (ἀποδεικτικὴν *explicationem*) of all the above and the analyses (ἀναλύσεις) of the six books of Euclid and the proofs of the arithmetical precepts and the *Canon* (Κανόνα) of Geber; also the astronomical conclusions of the prime mover and the theoretical descriptions of the planets. Although there are three volumes, nevertheless it is not necessary to devote three hours to each book, but one hour to each, for there are three distinct qualities for three distinct different levels: the first and second classes and the public lecture hall. For you will concede to me, Beuther, that in our program I may use the discourse of Quintilian and of Pliny. Therefore, space has been allotted for these very classics for the remaining subjects that the plan for speech and composition requires. Since the lectures called public have been arranged for this one hour, they will be able to add three—even more—of the remaining hours to the other studies for which a careful schedule must be maintained. What is learned every day must be kept distinct from those subjects for which there may be a digression of a few hours. Ethics, physics, and the dialectics of Aristotle ought to be taught daily, if it can be done. But it is enough for you to give two hours apiece to your two spheres: the one that belongs to astronomers and the other to the geographers.

But I desire that the classes that we summon be as erudite as possible. For on them rest the foundations of our architecture and the bases of our agriculture. From them there ascend to the public tribunal the men who prescribe for us who are called the public lecturers, how many subjects we ought to know and how we ought to teach them. For whoever is delighted by a large assembly of students who listen, and who-

ever wish to help and teach them, these men ought to do something
that is more excellent than what they learned in classes.

In regard to what concerns the teaching of mathematics, we have
been adequately instructed by Dasypodius, especially with your assistance. Both of you can teach mathematics outstandingly and both of you
are interested in languages and desirous of elegance of expression,
unfriendly to impurities of language and enemies of barbarisms; and
both of you wish for our academy that its cause, its growth, and its
praise last forever. For we wish to benefit not only the living, but also
to hand down to our posterity what is permanent and eternal.

Farewell, my Beuther.

* * * * *

Letter VI
To Conrad Dasypodius, Mathematician

I remember that in a certain letter to Capito, once a theologian of our
city, Martin Luther wrote that of all of his writings he approved of nothing except his *Catechism* and something else [*On the Bondage of the
Will*] which I do not wish to name because of the hostile and destructive
disagreements of the churches in our time. With me the memory of
Luther is most sacred and so I freely use his authority, as it were. I assert
that there is nothing in this program of our academy that pleases me
more than the very beginnings that appeared in a book that I published
thirty-two years ago *The Correct Opening of Elementary Schools of Letters*
and which I renewed in my *Classical Letters*.

Certainly, were I asked whether I would prefer to eliminate the classical program or to withdraw from the program of the Academy, if I had
to do without one or the other, I would prefer to keep what has existed
now for thirty years, approved and praised by all. Even though, in preference to all else, classes have been established in those arts that are
called "logic" (λογικαί), yet this power of pure, true, and skillful speech
is being handed on in these classes in a way that the basic principles of
the rest of the sciences are taught along with them and their precepts
understood; especially since the selections from among the poets, orators, and historians that the students interpret, are chosen from the rivulets of the philosophers.

But for all that, a splendid addition has been made to the program through a new benefaction from the august Emperor Maximilian. If it could have been obtained at the time of the magistracy of Jacob Sturm and of the other magistrates, counselors, and theologians whose authority was great throughout all Europe, we should already have the perfect program that we are now seeking for our academy. But this program must be set up so that the integrity of the classes may not be neglected and so that nothing be taken away from the classes themselves of all the material that has been taught from the very beginning up to now.

First, therefore, I earnestly beg you that the principles of the mathematicians be taught in the last two classes with those two volumes about which we have spoken. We have the second volume from you which will be for the second class. We also await another volume by you to be completed for the first class, so that those who will advance from the first class may be able to dispose of and finish in two years what remains in these studies.

To these basic principles I add the first book of Euclid as it is recommended in my book about the schools of letters. For since the art of proof (ἀποδεικτική) is explained in the first class, why is this first book of Euclid not included? It is the only book of all those which are taught in this part of logic that contains examples. Nothing obscures teachings more than the lack of examples. Indeed from Euclid's *Elements* it is impossible not to understand the art that is called apodictic (ἀποδεικτική).

Therefore, this is the one thing I would not wish to be removed from the classes. Rather I would wish material to be added so that something may be explained more fully and that everything that must be learned in this part of our gymnasium may be understood very clearly. My second point is that the purity of Latin speech should not be corrupted because of the addition of mathematics. All sciences have their own names of things that are either incorrectly understood in Greek or are barbarously altered. Just as spoiled yeast corrupts until it is unhealthful and loathsome all the flour which should be leavened so as to be healthful and delicious, so they could contaminate language and spoil pure speech.

But I ask, what of the praise our school has now had for years which is for our teaching in morals and for elegance in speaking and writing? Therefore, it is agreeable to me for you to do what you have decided to do: to explain *The Sphere* of Proclus and the material that is useful in Sacro Bosco's ...*Sphere*[6] as well as material not annotated by Proclus that you have derived from Greek writers. But since you have retained Greeks or even translated them separately in the back of the book more purely than they are given in Sacro Bosco's work, it is agreeable to me for you to explain authors whom you know to be of that type: Ptolemy, Achilles Tatios,[7] Proclus himself, Cleomedes, Hipparchus the Bithynian, the *Phaenomena* of Euclid and the *Spherics* of Theodosius. Theon also will supply not a few needs.

I know that you deal with these writers. But deal with all this material with a good method and in a way that will not tire the minds of students with its very magnitude or lack of order. Brevity needs to be applied amid many and diverse topics. Amid this diversity that famous work of Horace must be remembered.[8]

> "Whatever you will teach, be brief so that minds may attentively grasp and faithfully retain what is said quickly. Everything superfluous flows from the full mind."

Just as whatever is poured into a full jug of water flows away, so whatever is superfluous in teaching escapes from the memory which refreshes and delights itself with brevity.

But, so that you may achieve and accomplish this, a description of the hours will be required. We will discuss this between us. I recommend that you use six hours each week: two in the second class on the first volume, just as many on the first and second volume. You should also lecture publicly two hours on the third work. For the art of foreknowledge (Προγνωστικὴν) which Laertius calls "prediction" (Προορητικὴν), it seems useful for you to teach it privately out of class so that you may summon sharper minds to the love of these disciplines. That is what I think Philipp Melanchthon wished to have done.

But I would wish to have you pardon me for the burden I impose on you which is greater than the pay you will receive. For all of us must do this: namely, undertake more work than custom formerly required. I truly have always praised your industry and diligence that you have demonstrated by many proofs to me as long as you were Prorector.

Farewell. Strasbourg, 1569

* * * * *

Letter VII
To Conrad Dasypodius

You ask me Dasypodius, who I think is the master teacher of philosophy and what person is worthy of such a great title. For the title is certainly great and far more glorious than the title of philosopher itself, since whoever claims the study of wisdom for himself, is afraid to claim to possess wisdom. For I believe that a master teacher of philosophy, if you think of the word (*magister*) is a man who yearns to know everything a philosopher knows whether divine or human. He knows all these subjects, I say, and has learned them; he knows and can teach them. You know this word of evangelical wisdom, "Art thou a master of Israel and knowest not these things?" (σὺ εἶ διδάσκαλος τοῦ Ἰσραὴλ καὶ ταῦτα οὐ γνώσκεις;).[9] Jesus Christ was the eternal wisdom and image of the Father, because he wished to call himself a teacher. Nicodemus sought from the teacher himself knowledge of a thing that was unseen and unheard of by most men: the "rebirth" (Παλιγγενεσίαν) of men, a noun which the philosopher Pythagoras invented, though he was ignorant of the thing itself and the cause. On the contrary, he did not even think of it! He inquires after all things who insistently seeks the highest.

But I believe that this perfection and consummation of wisdom must rather be hoped for than prescribed for our people. Satisfied with the mean in teaching, not with perfection in teaching, I measure this talent by eagerness and intellectual strength. I consider a man a master teacher of the arts and disciplines if he has comprehended them, can teach what philosophers have discovered and shared with us in their monuments of letters. Even if less so, he is still able to understand for himself and to teach others. For the Greeks call him a master (διδάσκαλος), that is, teacher (*doctor*). What kind of man he is cannot be understood by a student although learning (μάθησις) and teaching (διδασκαλία) belong to the same man and the same ability. Those who have almost perfect knowledge are called mathematicians. Nevertheless, none of them has been able to square a circle. Archimedes did not know what he sought before he exclaimed "Eureka!" (εὕρηκα). Was he then for that reason not a mathematician? By no means! For he was the greatest and nearly perfect. For it was enough to have been able to make a discovery. All philosophers before Socrates were ignorant of teaching about morals which embraces many great subjects. For interwoven with it are not only the teachings about morals and the virtues of men, but also of states. This they call the science of politics (πολιτική) in which is also contained the art of law (ἡ νομική), the teaching of jurists, and economics (οἰκονομική), the management of individuals' private property.

Although these all were not explained before Socrates, all men did not refuse to be called philosophers. But were they therefore not philosophers? Not at all! For there is always something to be learned. More than forty years now I have been teaching the arts of speaking and this is the sixty-third year of my life. Every day I observe something in these arts and make a note of what had previously escaped my notice. Therefore let us grant to the stupidity of men that the term "master teacher" is like the word "honor" so that they may decide that the philosopher teaches more important material than the master teacher of philosophy. We describe the duties of a master teacher by his zeal, vigorous diligence, ability, and ordinary learning. We propose that he is a man who brings from the schools of grammarians pure, very clear speech; from the debates of dialecticians, Aristotle's precepts of composition as explained in his logical treatises; who brings from the workshop of the rhetorician, ornate and apt speech and an aptitude for writing and speaking.

Let him keep to what is included by you in our gymnasium. I assert, I have decided, that a man has been trained enough by the equipment of philosophy so that he can learn by reading and thinking the essential material handed down by mathematicians and philosophers and can explain them by speaking. I also think that the same man must be admitted to this title and to this position of honor. But material that is extraordinary must not be omitted. I am speaking of the appropriate material from the Socratics about ethics, politics, and economics about which I just spoke; also the *Physics* of Aristotle, definitions, partitions, and other things of this sort that pertain to nature. For this task our colleague Bruno is the director (see Epistle 10). I trust him to explain Aristotle so that youths retain the essential information in their memories and understand the controversies; but also so that they may turn their minds with pleasure to the arguments by which this author refuted false things. The knowledge of this, the distinction and separation of our Aristotle from the fallacies of the sophists must be taken up. To judge from my observation of this dim art, nothing could be more unproductive than Aristotelian debates, nothing more loathsome. I say that to have learned this material or to be learning it day by day oneself, is, I deem, the special talent and duty of a master teacher.

But this future teacher (*doctor*) will be more useful to human society if he teaches what he has learned. For it is truly the nature of knowledge and doctrine to have learned, while it is the nature of virtue and

duty to explain. For the students of our academy require not only theory
(θεωρετικόν) but also earnestly seek the practical (πρακτικόν). This
work is supported by the student by learning, but is explained by a preceptor by teaching.

* * * * *

Letter VIIB
To the Board of Examiners

I hear that yesterday the question was referred to your board about
approval of those who are to be given the baccalaureate degree. About
them nothing certain can be decided unless one knows what subjects
the master teacher of philosophy professes to teach. Yesterday I wrote
to Conrad Dasypodius concerning the duty of a master teacher. In that
letter I expressed my opinion that the man can teach these subjects who,
through understanding, either possesses all those traditions that we
have from philosophy or as much as is adequate from a teacher for
learning the rest on one's own. For no one has ever lived who knows
everything. We grow old learning and the more someone achieves
through conscientiousness, the more he is considered more learned and
more perfect than others. Certainly, you who are called examiners, as it
were, inquisitors and approvers of talent, seem to me to carry not the
least burden on your shoulders.

Your function does not begin only at the time when graduation
exercises must be held (and these are about to happen because of
autumn), but must be extended from the start of the year along with the
loyalty of the master teachers who teach and the conscientiousness of
the young men who hear them. For you must know what subjects the
master teachers teach and by what methods they explain them, whether
then pass them on by continuous lecturing (*perpetua oratio*) or explore
the subject by questioning (*interrogatio*).

Then also you must weigh the talents and abilities of the students
by their own weight so that, before an honor may be given to each class
and before you begin to question and interrogate, a test has been made
on the scale, as it were, of conscientiousness and skill as to what judgment you must make. Even as bees drive off their own swarms, the parents drive out the offspring, for example, to a new colony, but they
themselves remain in their own hives. But you must do the opposite:
push the older ones out and put the younger in their place as if they

were new offspring. However, there is this similarity in your function: bees lead their offspring to other places where they can seek hives and are able to produce honey. As soon as they enter into the new beehive, they are able to construct honeycombs, make beeswax, and separate out among themselves the foundations of their individual domiciles, so that even their wax (κόμμωσις) is distinct from that of the propolis (πισσοκήρω)—indeed, it is separated by the propolis. So as to form a republic, they bring a king with them and set up leaders and councils. They carry with them the teaching from their parents and from their native land, as it were, into a new region of the world into which they bring with them food and sustenance, so that as soon as they have entered into their new hive, they may set up their quarters into which they fly an hour later and which can be seen to be divided up into little nests.

Just so, those whom you will test and on whom you will bestow the baccalaureate crown, must carry with them to a higher grade that by which they may be aided in the building of the temples of wisdom in which all things both divine and human can be contemplated.

Therefore you will require of them first of all pure and clear Latin that they have learned from the grammarians. Next, it must be adorned according to the teaching of the rhetoricians, which the first class teaches; then the rule of truth—not the popular scale (*trutina*) but the steelyard (*statera*) of the dialecticians which they receive in the two highest classes. To these will be added two volumes of mathematics which can be explained in one year by the same interpreter. A third volume has been prepared for those who wish to be called "masters of arts" which can be expounded in two years by the same instructor who teaches the two volumes in the second and first classes.

These volumes are so different that all three may be taught in six hours each week and yet each student may devote only two hours each week with no work, not even any trouble or any impediment from other studies. Indeed, more than anyone else, I abhor abridgments, especially those which depart from the words and order of the authors. I disapprove even of those who teach authors in bits and pieces (ἐπιτομικῶς) and, as it were, disconnectedly. For authorities and precepts ought to be taught in the very words of their authors and should contain the whole meaning and all the reasons that are in the author, not only in the teachings of the mathematicians, but also in the discipline of morals and in the exposition of nature. But these three volumes of which I am speaking nowhere depart from the authors. The same teachings are retained, the same definitions and distinctions are repeated, the same theorems and problems with the same words and terms of the best authors and also of the Greek authors, even at times with complete books. I return to your examination and those who have carried away the laurels of these two volumes from the highest class to the public schools. They can from these seeds, if they should sow them, cultivate laurels with lasting fruits so that nothing will be difficult for them in the third volume. Once this is understood, there is nothing so obscure or recondite in these studies that they could not learn and teach, as they say, by their own Mars,[10] which we consider to be the duty of the master teacher. If these things should be omitted, what distinction, I ask, will our academy have? Or how shall we be able to aspire to or ascend to that height that we have set for ourselves?

* * * * *

Letter VIII
To Johann Reinhard, Dialectician

I greatly rejoice that my advice to you about the three volumes pleases the mathematicians. For I see what the future will be: that the second year after our students will have graduated from classes, they may be able to be called "master teachers." For if we shall achieve this in mathematics, why should we not be able to arrange the same thing in those arts that we call dialectics (λογικὰς)?

For in the first and second classes, the useful, and almost all the basic precepts of dialectics are explained—indeed briefly but nevertheless clearly. In these classes, moreover, I have not failed to touch broadly upon Aristotelian teaching by following Aristotle himself and his commentators, whose rules I have enumerated rather than expounded in many places so that those who now hear you expounding the *Analytics* will recognize nothing new, nothing unheard, nothing not in some way known beforehand. But as in mathematical, so also in rhetorical and in dialectical precepts, there ought to be two men who teach these arts. In rhetoric, our school has Erythraeus and me; but you lack an associate and colleague. As for Hertel, otherwise a learned and most useful colleague while he was well, chronic gout keeps the man at home away from our gymnasium, so that we must seek for another, if the scholarchs should not return Speccer to us. I see that that cannot be obtained because of his daily services in the church. I would urge this advice, if it has any place: that they should add Theophilus Golius and another should be sought to whom the first class should be entrusted. The rest should go on to the upper three classes—a thing which can be done with less cost as well as with the joy and delight of all those who advance.

If Golius were explaining the *Prior Analytics*, you would expound the *Posterior Analytics*. From you we would receive every year those who could be said to be and who are held to be master teachers and teachers of dialectics. If this could not be attained, which I do not think is the case, the time must be doubled and the curriculum of studies lengthened. This would cause a delay for some, trouble for the dialecticians, and greater expenses and costs for all, and would do no little damage to the treasury of the academy.

There is no need for me to advise you about the method of teaching and the elegance of exposition. You know the best way of teaching is founded on the explanation of Aristotelian words, on examples, then on the proofs of the mathematicians, then on the dialectical conclusions of ethics, for which our Plato will provide a great supply. Philipp Melanchthon, whom I name with honor, not only has written many other things clearly but also was acute and penetrating in the explanation of examples. You will recommend his books to the students to read them at home, for his books need only a rather careful reader and do not require someone to explain at great effort.

What shall I write you about eloquence? For as much as I, you love clarity, strive for purity, seek embellishment, and ask for what is fitting and proper in speaking. For there are two things for which our schools have been praised now for many years: the seriousness of the teaching and the study of eloquence. Unless we preserve them both, all is wasted and the praise that we found in past years we would lose with this new program.

But if we retain them and if we add these academic philosophies, and if we gladly return to the old gymnasium of the Athenians, if there were no envy, I would gladly say that we would be able with the approval of all good men to achieve something outstanding and unique, an ornament to our city.

* * * * *

Letter IX
To Valentine Eurythraeus, Rhetorician

I have often observed that the task of those who teach publicly in our schools (*scholae*) and explain the poets, historians, and orators, is arduous and difficult. I have often wondered why the attendance is larger in classes (*classes*) than in the public schools (*publicae scholae*) of rhetoricians and poets—indeed often the professors in these schools are without an audience. Moreover, I have observed one cause to be that in the assemblies (*curiae*) which we convene, even the unwilling are kept by the need for teaching (*disciplinae necessitudo*) and by the schedule of hours and classes (*temporis et tribuum descripto*). A second reason is that in these lower classes (*loci inferiores*) writers of every kind are taught.

For they have the Greek poets Homer, Pindar, Sophocles and Euripides, besides the Latin poets, Vergil and Horace. The historians in both languages are expounded there as well as the most important writings of Demosthenes and Cicero. So, having progressed to our open schools (*liberae scholae*), they bring with them subjects and every kind of language and if they should not learn anything from us that is new and not previously heard, they will slip away or slip away to others who teach new subjects. When they are lawyers, of whom we have had so few, they surrender themselves to leisure because of their small number and waste their time in leisure. The rest of the teachers are indeed able to keep a large attendance, as do the lawyers themselves—of whom I hope we shall have more—and the expounders of ethics, physicists, and the rest of the mathematicians through whom students get no visible commodities. We indeed offer the same subjects and unless we enhance them differently than is done in the classical assemblies (*classicae curiae*) those very disadvantages emerge which we saw emerge for others.

Certainly those who came to us from other places have worked very hard in this area, yet few have kept large attendance. Up to now we continue to exist, perhaps because we offer something more dialectical (διαλεκτικώτερον) and more rhetorical (ῥητορικώτερον).

I have always observed that our students are delighted with brief partitions in the individual sections of an oration and in each kind of arrangement of arguments and that they derive satisfaction from the comparisons of examples. They get the most enjoyment if the kinds of thoughts are traced to their origins and those kinds that they teach are separated from the others which they either take over or adapt, and if the democratic thoughts are differentiated from the royal aristocratic ones. Above all, the elegance of these thoughts pleases, especially if we first point out in what kinds of subjects a similar arrangement and ornamentation ought to be and can be used. In this Hermogenes indeed helps us, but, with fine precision. It is Cicero who truly helps eloquently and with ornamentation. From him we take examples of the very things that he teaches. What could be more ornate, what fuller, than the three books of *On the Orator* (*De Oratore*), than the *Ideal Orator* (*Orator Perfectus*), or *Concerning Famous Orators* (*De Claris Oratoribus*)?[11] I willingly confess that I am steeped and trained in these. But while we ought to do something more excellently than they do in the assemblies (*curiae*), we ought in the meantime not to promise too much with respect to the abilities and teaching of our students.

For recently in teaching the Milonian oration of Cicero, I felt that even several of the more erudite were pleased by that analysis (ἀνάλυσις). When I divided the first part of the exordium into four types of persons—friends of Cicero, of Pompey, and, as Plautus says, of the patrons and of Clodius—so that I assigned the latter part to the presentation (καταστάσει) which includes the extraordinary circumstances, I was clearly taking a middle position artistically (τεχνικῶς) with this distinction. But what followed I felt was more to be approved: I pointed out the approach to the refutation itself. But before I come to this speech, I was pointing out the Clodian argument (κεφάλαιον): "They deny that it is right for him to see the light of day...."[12] Then I added Cicero's rebuttal (ἀντιπροβολή): "In what city, pray...."[13] Afterwards I pointed out this very type of refutation. Its argumentation I divided into two forms of headings, one of which is the analogical (παραδειγματική) and like the induction (ἐπαγωγή) of the philosophers. I enumerated the six authorities and examples[14] and I pointed out the coherence (συνέχεια) of these examples which is characteristic of the organization. After briefly demonstrating this kind, I proceeded to the second kind which is the argumentative (θετικόν) and syllogistic (συλλογιστικόν) and I passed over the first premise which dialecticians call the major premise (ὁ μείζων). "And if there is any occasion..."[15] and I pointed this out by the fitting example of the young soldier and since this example is different from the previous examples, I did not omit it.[16] From there I proceeded to the minor premise (ἐλ'ττω) and its proof: "For the man waiting in ambush and the highway robber...."[17] Then I came to that elegant discussion (ἐξεργασία) of each premise: "For this law, O judges, is not written, but was constituted spontaneously."[18] Then I inserted that brief digression (ἀπόστασις) regarding the opinion of the law-giver.[19] For the final conclusion, I stated briefly that passage, "Therefore let this remain in the case for the defense, O judges."[20] When they see how the reasoning of a deceitful adversary has been refuted by an opposite reasoning and by the well considered organization of each point, and after I took note of the kinds of words and observed the ornamentation of these at the same time, and after I noted briefly their remarkable and similar excellence and after I showed how far the practice extends or to how many subjects this form can be applied, it seems to me that the students saw how greatly Cicero differs from other writers and how great is the distinction between the forensic type of speaking and that of philosophers and historians.

You will pardon me that I write to you, a veteran soldier and a vigorous old (almost!) man, looking toward the curse of Hercules, a steed fierce with the reins, champing at the bit and not yet panting with broken wind.[21] Moreover, I write because those exercises (προγυμνάσματα) of my first age still please me and because I think that they will bring benefits by their own example. So that, if I as an old man do not neglect them, the men who come after me in age may think that nothing is unbecoming to any age that can benefit youth in any way and which has to do with the duties of life and of public office.

* * * * *

Letter X
To Johann Bruno, Physicist

I do not doubt that, if you wish, you can achieve remarkable work in physics. Moreover, I know that you wish not only that you may be useful to the fatherland, fulfill the expectations of the Prefect, and respond to my wishes (for you know that our schools are dear to me) but also, first of all, that you may both confirm the good opinion we and all men have of you and also may increase it for eternal memory. We have no doubt about your ability, for you are capable by nature and you are very interested and very learned in these arts and you studied with the Wittenberg professors after you left us for those regions. At Wittenberg, I say, and in Italy, you had the most cultured and learned men, especially that man Cardanus, most skilled now in all philosophy, but then especially skilled in your field, whose friendship, as I have often felt, was wont to delight you even in those places very far from here. Nevertheless, through your will, industry, and ability you uphold an arduous and difficult duty, as long as you teach and explain Aristotle's teachings. For although the author teaches with the best method and reasoning and is, as we now believe, methodical above other writers of all times, nevertheless his eloquence has been compressed into brevity, so that from a clear writer he has become obscure and since all his teaching is not set forth eloquently, but is detailed concisely, it has been rendered more subtle. This subtlety has produced shadows by which understanding is impeded and memory wearied unless it obtains an artist who dispels all difficulty with some new pleasure which, I think, lies in four subjects, and I judge that you also take note of them.

Of these four subjects the first is an account in such a way that the meaning of his words is understood and retained in every explication. I am accustomed to be so concerned about this that I do not usually depart from Aristotle or proceed beyond the paraphrase of Themistius.

The second is an account based on the introductions themselves of the disputations which the rhetoricians in their cases call καταστάσεις (the presentations)—I mean the problems of the whole coming debate. If these can be so described that the arrangement is noted, the complete form understood, and the subjects themselves are seen, and everything is recalled to memory in the final part of the debates, the difficulty will be removed, the shadows will be dispersed, the burden that seemed to be very heavy before it was understood, will become very light.

The third is the account in the refutation of contrary opinions which he shows to be true or to be false or that their suppositions can not be proven or made or cannot be true—obviously τὸ ἀδύνατον (the impossible), as the logicians and the physicists call them.[22] It is pleasing to understand from the preceptor the causes of error from sophistical refutations and the truth of those reasons which Aristotle brought against them into the open. But at this point prolixity must be avoided, for nothing brings greater light than brevity which lies not only in the explanation of the teacher but also in his questions. For in this kind of philosophy, a continuous oration is not always useful. Often the mind must be excited and taught by questioning.

The fourth is in the proof of Aristotle's teachings. The previous arguments are ἀνασκευαστικά (subject to destruction by refutation). These, however, require κατασκευήν (constructive reasoning) and need the corroboration of argumentation and an indication of logical sequence (*ordo*) in which definitions and logical divisions and the problems and theorems that are inferred from them are linked together. In the discussion of these, since it involves two kinds of argumentation one of which is συλλογισμός (syllogism) and the other ἐπαγωγή (induction), they must be illustrated with some eloquence so that the parts, order, and number of each individual argument may be retained.

But why do I bring these birds to your library and your Athens, like owls to Athens? I do not write these things to teach you, but so that you may see that I too at times philosophize and so that all may understand what plan of teaching has been proposed in this new academy of ours.

* * * * *

Letter XI
To Hugo Blotius, Jurisconsult and Doctor of Ethics

Yesterday you told me, Blotius, that your students are annoyed first that you took up the beginning of Aristotle's fifth book of the work *Concerning Ethics*, and second that you lecture on this teaching in the fourth hour of the afternoon. I believe both to be true and I marvel that with this double inconvenience you nevertheless retain a large number of students.

I am happy, nevertheless, because you teach in such a way that neither the shadows of night nor the cold of winter reduces either your diligence or the attendance of your students. However, in our conversation of yesterday you seemed to request another distribution of hours and a division of subjects other than what has been established. Indeed, the manner in which these things ought to be prescribed and divided in the public schools, I have set forth in the book *Concerning Schools of Letters* and in my *Classical Epistles*.

These *Academic Letters* of ours also shed some light on the subject. Nevertheless, I shall briefly explain to you my opinions. If any teacher demands his own hour and, moreover, wishes to teach in the same subject which others are already teaching who have been appointed prefects in the public schools, many could not teach and many subjects could not be expounded in a year. That would increase his own authority rather than seek the advantage of each individual. If all should wish the same large attendance to be given to themselves and the same students, they are demanding something unfair and they confuse types of talent and in the same manner as the previous ones, they are seeking their own advantage.

If one thinks that in two years he can explicate the *Organum* of Aristotle properly or can teach the doctrine of nature fittingly, or can dispose of the discipline of morals and of public affairs as the magnitude of the subject requires, he does not seem to me to view the magnitude of the subject correctly, but rather places upon his own shoulders more than his strength can sustain and bear.

Why could not the same plan be retained or established in other arts and teaching that exists in the schools of grammar and in classes? For in six assemblies, all teach at the same hours so that no one leaps over his own territory and seizes or obstructs another's possession. In the fourth and third class, authors are explained so that neither of the two preceptors obstructs or impedes the other. In the second and the first class, dialectical precepts are taught without any impediment, although the age of the boys and the frailties of that age require more preceptors and a greater division of labors. Yet, even though the more advanced teachings of the public schools cannot be satisfied by one teacher, they can be taught by a few. And so I think that even if the authority were mine, I would also decide that dialectics, rhetoric, and mathematics would be expounded by two teachers daily in two years to the public students. By this plan certainly I think that many more hours daily would be enough for accomplishing this, if, as in the classes, both teachers teach at the same hours in classes separated into their own types—after a distinction has been made in the books and the abilities so that easier subjects are taught to the less able students and the more difficult subjects would be explained to the abler students.

For it cannot happen that one teacher may teach the whole ethics of Aristotle in two years properly or either the physics or even the dialectical *Organum*. Our duty lies ἐν τοῖς δυνατοῖς, in the possible, and it is foolishness to invest labor ἐν ἀδυνάτοις in the impossible. But since even a summer day cannot supply enough hours, if one wishes free time to be given for oneself, the same hours must be shared with two or three others. For why should not the jurisconsultants teach the two or three hours in which the theologians teach, the one teaching the *Institutes* and the other the *Pandects*? Why should not two mathematicians teach the first hour, why not two ethicists the second hour, and two physicists the third hour? If books are separated by their difficulty or easiness, so may not students also be sorted out according to their abilities and natures and by the skill and progress of their studies? For just as the same nourishment is not suitable for a sick and a healthy person nor the same food for a boy and a man, so also one plan of teaching cannot be used for both the learned and the unlearned. In the Campus Martius some are teachers of beginners, some of veterans, some of gladiators and pugilists, some of equestrian games, and the swimmers have their own coaches, more often all on one day rather than separate individuals on different days. Since this is done in less serious matters, could it not and should it not be retained in more difficult matters? This conjunction of duties and separation of hours should for the first time make it possible for someone to complete his course in two years.

Thereafter, the mixing of abilities should be avoided and the learned should be separated from the unlearned, the less erudite from the erudite. Then, too, the observation of defects that need to be corrected will be easier, and every day virtue will hear its own praises and there will be no less discipline among the public scholars than there is in the regular classes. These have now publicly become lax, confused by a certain capriciousness and license since lectures are not only interrupted, but often omitted resulting in much contempt for the teachers and the ruin of the students themselves. Finally, studies would be dealt with more aptly, if someone would teach his own field to his own students with his own good plan. Nevertheless, I do not deny that professors of the same subject can be separated even by hours and that minor physics can be combined with greater ethics and that minor ethics can be joined with higher physics for an hour each day, so that both who are more diligent may be able to hear both, but not in such a way that those less learned may be intermingled with the more learned, but so that strictness of order and discipline may be retained. I have maintained these things, my Blotius, which I set forth to you concerning the assignment of hours since we have spoken about the matter privately and you who are a jurisconsult can easily understand them.

For your emperor and legislator Justinian has set forth every doctrine and notion of jurisprudence for Justinians and specialists in the *Pandects*, whether praetors and Papianists, Lytists and Prolytists and the five kinds of students and of professors. I would wish also that the exegesis of the Bible be divided in this way: the evangelists separated from the apostles, the Pentateuch from the historical and prophetic books, and that everything of this kind be separated for the teachers as well as for the students. For just as they now read so for many previous years they taught. The Greeks, by far more industrious before Troy, finally in the tenth year took the city. I ask how many are the academies that in fifteen years have done or accomplished this? But you are more industrious, especially like the Toulousians who run through all the laws in the third year. The teachers at Bourges are swifter, for they reach their goal in two years, but I do not know whether they do so more laudably than the Toulousians. Parisians give testimonies of five years in their decrees that are not neglected each year by students. But up to now I have heard of no student who could say that everything specified in the decrees had been taught and set forth in the school within this time.

But I love the Aurelians who require four years and the Justinians add up five years in these same studies. These must not be evaluated in terms of the things to which time ought to be applied so that each subject and each duty in explaining the subjects may be completed in its own time. A poet is scorned by Aristotle who creates a play lasting longer than one day only. An actor is derided who cannot act a good tragedy in the course of a day. Since this is required in plays, why should it not be required in the true and most serious subjects? Farewell.

* * * * *

Letter XII
To Jonas Bitner

Even though I was pained that the classical sequences were curtailed, nevertheless I am forced to confess that it is useful for you to be kept in this assembly. For since the youths, your students, bring grammatical precepts of both languages to your classes, someone ought to be put in charge of this fourth class who has been educated from boyhood in our schools and has been in charge for some years of the education of boys—as both you and our Golius have been. Both of you have taught usefully for forty-eight years up to the present time. Truly this assembly that you lead needs to hear not only orators, but also poets and historians, and to be furnished with all the equipment of words, and to have a supply of words not only stored up, but also organized so that the vocabulary of orators and poets are kept distinct and students may see placed before them the words appropriate to historians and the distinctions between them and their various meanings. You and Junius ought to apply your energies to this study in the third assembly, so that students may be able to bring with them to the upper two assemblies pure and clear speech and be armed against barbarisms. Barbarisms in language are wont to insinuate themselves from barbarous commentaries and from the depraved usage of some who teach and who say it is wisdom to speak barbarously and to follow practical business men (πραγματικοὺς χρηματιστὰς) rather than the leading writers in the arts. Thomas Aquinas pleases them more than Aristotle; Scotus more than Lactantius and Jerome; Bartolus and Baldus rather than Scaevola or Justinian; the voices of Averroes and Avicenna rather than of Hippocrates and Galen. These voices resound from the jaws of teachers through the academies in the ears of the students up to the present time, so that even in Italy, eloquence begins to be neglected and is reduced to just a few men. The Latin language has been corrupted by the defects of its interpreters and impurity is cultivated in the place of ornamentation. The ethicists and jurisconsults substitute barbarism for prudence, the physicists substitute it for truth, the medical doctors for practice, theologians for piety. You must resist these evils in the assemblies, especially you and Junius, so that aided by you, we can keep the students on the paths of the old academicians and Peripatetics which used to create among them fountains, rivulets, and streams of Greek purity, ornamentation, eloquence, and an impressive style, far removed from putrid swamps and unhealthful marshy places. Elegant only in the clothes on our bodies, and with impure language and the barbarous sound of words, we truly are compelled by this depraved judgment and by the corruption of old usage, to sink into the mire.

Moreover, your comic and tragic plays will be appropriate for this academy of ours. For these exercises are for everyday usage of the Latin language, yes, more sure than was the everyday speech of Romans and Athenians. The theatre and scenes preserve the praises of eloquence longer than do the forum and lawsuits.

I also recommend to you three volumes of music that were summarized by David Napheletha as well as by Dasypodius. As in stage plays, so also you should be present at the practice of music so that we have no silent muses but seem to worship Camena[23] who sings and is delightful. For just as I hate barbarism in language, so also I hate melancholy in our schools. Nothing strengthens and adorns studies more than cheerfulness. I believe that the darkness of countenance of Pallas was prejudicial in the judgment of Paris and that Juno was spurned in the same judgment because of the sadness of her eyes which jealousy had summoned up.

* * * * *

Letter XIII
To the Special Assembly

I hear that you have given permission to Erythraeus to teach a certain plan of writing letters, although that plan is an obstacle to the one by which the two of us are ordered to teach alternately the art of speaking and the orators. Nevertheless, I do not alter what you have done, and, so that this matter may be fruitful for our academy, I hope and pray to

God that he may profitably accomplish what he has undertaken. Truly, debates and declamations are being postponed to a too distant time—a thing which ought not to have been done. The practice in debating would not be difficult to establish if, for confirmation, the discipline of the Romans and the Greeks were recalled. The practice of declaiming has indeed languished in all the schools and academies and has always had a cold reception in ours. I see that there are and have been two causes of this misfortune. The first of these is that it is naturally difficult for young men to write and for preceptors to correct what has been written by the students. Second this task has been entrusted to many teachers so that they select for themselves boys who do not all have the same capability.

Often orations have been presented before the public that are different from each other not in their quality (that would be wished for in our schools) but in defects and barbarisms not only because of the nature of the individual abilities, but also because of the usage of many which weakens the purity of words, neglects the nobility of sentences, despises orderly sequence, does not respect elegance which should be retained in every part of eloquence. The result from this plan is that neither I, nor Sevenus, nor Erythraeus, nor Hertelius, nor Reinhard shall have found a remedy for this evil.

There is also a third cause: namely that either the defects have not been corrected for the young men by those to whom they had been entrusted, or they have been carelessly revised, or whole orations have been composed by the preceptors. So the result has been that nothing was presented that is either perfected by the student or the student's own work.

A fourth cause indeed embraces everybody and includes all kinds of faults: For while we have lost the manner of speaking of the old rhetoricians both among the Romans and the Greeks because of the infelicity of our elders and we are not regaining it because of our neglect, it is necessary that we, in this particular, either lie prone in the mud, if we try nothing; or are stuck in mud, if we do not renew this training unimpaired. What then was that training? Everyday there presided over these exercises one man who chose the appropriate students for this skill and excluded the inept. He assigned certain arguments that could be handled extemporaneously, some which required a few hours of reflection, some also which demanded preparation for several days. I, moreover, mean by "arguments" ὑποθέσεις (hypotheses), that is the cases themselves whose commonplaces (*loci*) he pointed out along with the principal arguments of the commonplaces and their position throughout all the parts of the case. But students did not fly to this oratorical power;

rather they came to it by stages. If any one of these stages is cut short, serious incidents of inarticulateness usually result. The preceptor did not, however, premasticate everything, but he prescribed the principal tasks that would be in the students' assignment to do and to work out at home and then present in the classes of declamation. Once the skill of the speakers was evaluated and their strengths confirmed, the preceptor allowed them to approach the circle of those who would be the audience and he summoned the judges and censors to his tribunal. Just as an important case is dealt with, they make a judgment about the skill of the speaker. Among those who were speaking there was a great rivalry for honor.

Where will we find this preceptor, you may perhaps ask? Or from where will we summon him? He must be sought for by you for whatever pay you wish, especially for the first two years within which time, if this training is correctly established, there will not be a lack in our academy of men who can preserve and cultivate the tradition. For they have talents, just as plants have growth so that from one plant, if it has found a good farmer, by planting and grafting, a great abundance is produced. Thus a few talents, well trained by one man usually produce many like him, as e.g., from one Socrates, how many philosophers? From one Isocrates, how many orators? From one Hippocrates, how many kinds of physicians? Has not each one of these possessed something which is extraordinary? But Socrates and Hippocrates could not be alone in their kind. Isocrates, if he had lived, would surely have freely extended the laurel to Demosthenes, just as poets who followed Homer freely would always concede the palm to him, except perhaps the Zoiluses whom nothing is apt to please.

Moreover, once this manner of writing, preparation, and delivery has been restored to use for our academy, I hope that it will come about that the many who will follow after us will surpass the students and teachers who preceded them. This is my opinion and to do this I wish my epistle to be a testimony. May what the Senate, the Scholarchs, the Council, and you resolve be fruitful and fortunate! Farewell!

12
Bibliographical Essay: Johann Sturm Perceived

Although the name Johann Sturm (1507–1589)—educator, humanist, scholar, diplomat—is familiar to most European scholars of Renaissance humanism, he has not received much attention from their American counterparts. The few amongst them who have shown some interest in Sturm have done so because of their interest in the career of two of Sturm's contemporaries whose lives were intertwined with his own— namely Roger Ascham, the English humanist and longtime correspondent of Sturm's, tutor to Queen Elizabeth I,[1] and Peter Ramus, the French logician and rhetorician who was Sturm's former student in Paris and later his colleague at the Gymnasium of Strasbourg,[2] where Sturm was Rector for forty-three years.

Among the reasons why Sturm has too often been ignored by modern scholars is the fact that the bulk of his voluminous writings on pedagogical and humanist topics (let alone diplomatic) has not until now been translated from the Latin.[3] There has been, however, a steady if not abundant literature on him in French and German ever since Charles Schmidt's biography of him appeared in 1855.[4] Much of that output, however, has been in the form of articles that appeared in journals of a restricted or local circulation not widely available in most American university libraries, even the best provisioned.

Furthermore, the very nature of Sturm's major pedagogical interest—the revival of Latin as a spoken as well as a written language must be counted among the reasons why American scholars have shown little interest in him; an elitist, classical education seemed to call into question our democratic, liberal philosophy. Besides, when the first nineteenth-century works on Sturm were appearing in France and Germany, a new industrialism was emphasizing not merely democratic but also pragmatic values. Latin eloquence seemed irrelevant to an America still in its heroic stage.

European comment on Sturm's pedagogy did not entirely escape the influence of complex social and economic changes. A number of European educators and academics also weighed the merits of a classical curriculum and found it wanting. Their attitudes concerning Sturm's neglect of vernacular instruction reflected perhaps their own national loyalties as well as the educational imperatives of a changing social order. Of course eloquent Latin was hardly the personal crotchet of Johann Sturm. Latin was the common mode of expression of churchmen, humanist scholars and diplomats and hence a practical and indeed, a necessary tool for all learned men. But its heyday was passing in the mid-sixteenth century and there was ample evidence that the vernacular tongues were on their way to becoming literary. It was unforgivable according to some modern critics that Sturm once referred to the fact that children began to learn in the mother tongue rather than in Latin as "a public calamity."[5] Charles Schmidt was the first to remark on Sturm's neglect of vernacular instruction, stating that he had abandoned German to the chances of taste and individual need, leaving it to become a colorless instrument in the hands of its native speakers.[6] This "flaw" in Sturm's educational program was remarked on by others.[7]

As in the case of Latin, so with respect to such perennial topics as discipline and methodology, the passage of time and changes in values and practices have inevitably affected the commentary that relates to Sturm's pedagogy. We believe whipping students is inhumane. He felt it was a useful and a normal means of discipline providing the whipping was used as a last resort and only on the express recommendation of the Rector himself.[8] Memorization, repetition and imitation of passages of prose or poetry or of grammar rules[9] are techniques for learning which have increasingly been frowned upon as sterile and non-productive, certainly as boring and tending to discourage creativity on the part of students. Although Sturm has been congratulated on the use he made of memory in learning[10] many moderns view memorization as unacceptable and passive drudgery.

Yet such criticisms as nineteenth- and twentieth-century commentators have made of Sturm's approach are not of such magnitude that they hide the enormous respect and admiration for his accomplishments as a classroom teacher,[11] as a gifted and sensitive administrator, as an educational theorist, as a creative scholar and publisher-author of textbooks. Sturm was something of an efficiency expert. His textbooks and exercises were designed to help students learn more in a shorter time. He wanted them to be independent, productive participants in society. Far from being, as cast by some modern commentators, an illiberal, tedious, impractical pedant of an irrelevant educational movement devoid of interest for us, the bulk of comment singles Sturm out for praise. He is generally portrayed as an exceptionally gifted educator whose concern with humanist learning combined with Christian devotion (*pietas litterata*) was to become his greatest legacy to Europeans from many different countries.[12]

Recently, the authors of a study on Strasbourg during the Reformation affirmed that Sturm's influence as a European educator of his times cannot be underestimated.[13] Another observer has used Sturm, as well as Johannes Tauler,[14] Geiler von Kaisersberg,[15] and Albert Schweitzer to represent the kind of traditionalism—positive and fraternal, yet critically acute—which he feels characteristic of the cosmopolitan city of Strasbourg. His estimation of Sturm's contributions includes a statement to the effect that Sturm's positions and values retain their vigor and relevancy into the present age.[16] Such enthusiasm reminds us that Johann Sturm has received a very warm press traditionally from Strasbourg savants who periodically, on the occasions in which they celebrate the founding of their Gymnasium in 1538, find it appropriate to review the career of Johann Sturm and his significance for Strasbourg education and culture.[17]

American educators who are only a little less apt to question their own effectiveness than is the general public will find Sturm an inspirational figure. Not only was he convinced in the rightness of his methodology when conscientiously applied,[18] but he was also an indefatigable publicist for his program.[19]

That program was not in its major outlines invented by Sturm, for he was from the first quick to acknowledge the influence which his three years of schooling at the College of St. Jerome in Liège, a school run by the Brethren of the Common Life, had on him (see note 47 below). His school was a reflection of all the intellectual factors to which he and his contemporaries had been exposed in their own youth, forces that were in part humanist, but in part scholastic, too, and which had shaped not their world only, but that of their fathers, their grandfathers, and even some of their more remote ancestors' intellectual and spiritual development. Although it used to be thought by historians that the humanist movement was wholly opposed to all that was scholastic,[20] recent works on Reformation scholarship and pedagogy have been responsible for a basic re-assessment.[21] It is now thought that Protestants were able to draw on humanism and yet not reject scholasticism.[22] It would probably be helpful to view Johann Sturm as a scholar who was re-integrating traditional knowledge with new, a man not at war with his intellectual heritage but willing to innovate, to adapt, and submit all traditional knowledge to a re-examination wherever it seemed profitable to do so. The application and re-application of new and old ideas, new and old ideals, into a practical and concrete form of school program could never have been achieved so handily had not the intellectual climate of Europe been prepared beforehand. Sturm's success at Strasbourg was fortunate, not fortuitous.

The major preparation for educational reform was owing in large measure to the spread and development of humanism as a literary and philosophical movement that began to affect the way thoughtful men regarded themselves and their historical heritage. "Humanitas" in Cicero's day—and Cicero was the prime inspiration for educational reformers like Sturm—meant education, or what the Greeks had called "paideia." Never has any intellectual movement been more self-assured when confronting their own perception of truth than humanism. Humanists regarded the "humanities"—poetry, rhetoric, history, etc.—as means by which men could develop their rational capacities and learn the Truth, as men had once done in classical times. Only in knowing could man be truly liberated. If, in reading some of Sturm's works, the modern student sometimes feels that he exaggerated the significance of a given proposition, or labored it unduly, he must reflect on the degree of passionate conviction which humanist scholars like Sturm brought to their studies. They were not involved as mere aestheticians, but as disciples of truth, as participants in an exciting liberation movement designed to release their fellow men from ignorance, superstition, and barbarism. Humanism was an important factor in Johann Sturm's intellectual development.

Because humanist philologists had taught scholars of language that the centuries following the classical period had distorted the nature of historical truth, filtering it through the prism of scholasticism, humanists determined to exercise stricter controls over language and to ferret out such abuses as they believed had occurred. Sturm was of this mind as well. He insisted that his students learn to speak and write a pure classical Latin. He sought to free them from misapprehensions caused by scholastic modes of reasoning. In the latter connection he produced a work[23] that was a major contribution to the new logic, one that aimed at making eminently practical a study that had formerly served the esoteric purposes of medieval clerks. Sturm, like the fifteenth-century logician, Rudolph Agricola, whose work *De inventione dialecticae* he popularized when he was a lecturer at the Collège de France in Paris, believed logic could serve every man's purpose, helping him solve problems not only of logic, but of a moral and natural sort too. The desire of late fifteenth- and sixteenth-century rhetoricians to apply logic to rhetoric meant that increasingly, written exercises in the classroom began to replace oral disputation—so characteristic of the medieval university. Sturm's logic was intended for literary or rhetorical excellence, and Sturm has been associated in such endeavors with Philipp Melanchthon, teachers who believed that knowledge of the real world—"of things"—had to be joined with that of logic or style—"Facultas dicendi."[24] Lately, the contributions which Sturm made to logic have clarified the position he may be said to have held with regard to that of his predecessor Agricola. Two historians have studied Sturm's contributions to logic and have found that he was more creative and innovative in his approach than had once been thought.[25]

Part of the problem of assessing Sturm's humanism lies in the fact that humanism was a bifurcated movement. While Italian humanism influenced northern Europeans in the direction of linguistic purity and remained a primarily aesthetic and literary preoccupation, northern Europeans moved steadily in the direction of practical ethics and spiritual inquiry. They applied new methods of logical analysis to subjects not primarily literary or classical, but to ideals of virtue and of justice and to those spiritual truths they believed classical authors held in common with Christianity. Sturm's modern critics may appear harsh in assessing his humanist credentials or more frequently, in assessing the humanist spirit of his gymnasium in Strasbourg, because they consider more authentic, or more valuable to the history of letters and culture Italian Renaissance modes of thought. Where to place Sturm's educational program—with those schools which offered a full exposure to classical humanism, or with those which offered a truncated humanist education bound about by the requirements of a particular religious point of view—has presented Sturm's commentators yet another opportunity to disagree.

Before we attempt to sketch in the major outlines of the controversy concerning the relative place of religion in the educational program as it developed in Strasbourg's gymnasium and how it affected the curriculum there it is useful to keep in mind two facts. One is the fact that as the sixteenth century progressed, the influences we call humanist diminished,[26] and the other is the fact that Johann Sturm began his intellectual career during the lifetime of men who were undoubtedly humanists (Erasmus, Melanchthon) but died long after that golden generation in 1589. He was poignantly aware of that fact. The difficulties which mere survival presented Sturm revolved upon the fact that he outlived the humanist era. Anton Schindling describes the Lutheran faculty in the Strasbourg Academy in the latter half of the century as of "une certaine étroitesse et immobilité provinciale,"[27] a provincialism, one must add, that offered the most direct challenge to a cosmopolitan and liberal career which Sturm had pursued on several different fronts (political, intellectual, pedagogical, religious) throughout a lifetime of service to Strasbourg, to the reformed cause, to European peace generally. Yet despite this kind of confessional rigidity, Sturm remained, says Schindling, a humanist educator.[28] Pierre Mesnard makes a similar judgment in an analysis of the way in which religion influenced Sturm's teaching.[29] He believes Sturm tried to keep a narrow confessionalism out of the instructional program in order to avoid a new Protestant scholasticism. In this view he aligns himself with the earlier works of Henri Strohl and Ernst Hoepffner. Strohl described the friendly cooperation between Sturm and Martin Bucer, Strasbourg's liberal religious reformer, on the eve of the re-organization of the Strasbourg school system circa 1537–38 and found that Sturm called upon the reformer in 1537 to help him write a system of instruction based on classical studies as a preparation for Christian life. Strohl felt both men believed a classical program was indicated because God had shown so much favor towards pagans of classical antiquity.[30] Hoepffner described Sturm as "un humaniste accompli" fighting to preserve the independence of his educational system from Lutheran domination.[31]

More recently, the nature of Martin Bucer's contribution to founding the Strasbourg school system has been given a prime rather than accessory interpretation. Ernst-Wilhelm Kohls[32] has determined that Bucer wrote a proposal for a Latin school that supplied courses in mathematics, languages, theology and music and also provided for the education of clergymen at public expense—an institution which in fact became the new Strasbourg Gymnasium in 1538. This work insists that Sturm's memoir to the scholarchs of 24 February 1538 was simply an accessory after the fact since Bucer's project, first submitted in 1533 to a church synod and given definitive form in 1534, was the base upon which the new school was erected. This view sets Strohl's (and virtually all earlier commentary) on its head, but does nothing to change the picture of Sturm's humanism.

Along with humanism, and inextricably linked to it as a basic impetus for educational reform, was the spiritual revival that began to manifest itself at the end of the medieval period. Continuing throughout the fifteenth and sixteenth centuries, this revival found its most dramatic expression, though not its only one, in the Protestant Reformation. The fact that Martin Luther was an educational as well as a religious reformer whose interests were supported and put into effect with the most brilliant results by his friend and colleague, Philipp Melanchthon, reminds us of one of the most important results of religious reform—reformed education. In its turn, reformed education sought to preserve the classical spirit which to such a large degree had engendered the religious revolution.

The best way to view the nature of John Sturm's pedagogical inspiration is to remember that for him, as for Erasmus, Melanchthon, Luther and indeed, all those who were anxious to improve education, learning was wasted on those who were not also imbued with sound Christian values. The exact relationship in Sturm's thought of these twin influences, humanism and reformed Christianity, has been a subject of controversy among Sturm's modern commentators. Some have concluded that piety outweighed humanism in the program of the gymnasium and have thus called into question or minimized the legitimacy of his humanism, though not of his Protestantism. This attempt to downplay the humanist aspect of Sturm's system was already noticeable in Charles Schmidt's biography, for Schmidt had emphasized the fact that Sturm put moral and religious education first, literary education second, and the knowledge of the real world—"un interêt très-accessoire"—last.[33] Schmidt's work was not free from ambivalence. He admired the degree to which Sturm had labored to restore the classics to the curriculum:— "un de ses grandes mérites"[34]—but he left an indelible stamp on some subsequent critics. R.R. Bolgar for example, though selecting Sturm as one of the "four leading exponents" of the *pietas litterata* movement that typified Protestant pedagogy, noted that the success and influence of the four leaders (Erasmus, Melanchthon, Sturm, and Mathew Cordier) "was in inverse proportion to their humanist zeal," and thus, finds Sturm "a less competent thinker" than the first two leaders, though a more competent one than Cordier.[35] A more flattering view for those who insist on Sturm's genuine humanist contributions is that of Andreas Stegmann, who feels that Sturm was not the less of a humanist because of his attraction to reformed ideas; his "irenisme" or broadmindedness explains the furor as well as admiration that his program inspired. The attractions of classical humanism were not determined according to narrow religious or philosophical lines, says Stegmann, but were instead "beyond philosophical and religious quarrels about which even modern criticism is not always detached."[36] The latter observation—that religious prejudice or at least rivalry—permeates the literature that pertains to the reform movement of sixteenth-century Europe is especially helpful to students of education who may wish to examine the pedagogy of this period, but who are unaware that the Reformation has not ceased to influence the way modern scholars perceive their sixteenth-century subjects.

An important factor—probably the most important factor—in shaping Sturm's educational program was his own experience as a student at the College of St. Jerome in Liège (1521–1524), one of many schools run by the Brethren of the Common Life. These men, continuing a tradition set by Gerard Groot of Deventer and his friend, Florentius Radewyn, in the late fourteenth century, lived in communities without monastic vows, devoting themselves to study and particularly to the education of youth, in a setting of poverty and without shunning hard physical labor. Their schools were notable for their attention to the classics and for a host of methods and practices that were later faithfully incorporated by Sturm into the Strasbourg Gymnasium.[37]

Because Johann Sturm owed so much to the Brethren by way of precept and inspiration—most writers agree on this point—it has not followed that there are no controversial topics dividing them when they attempt to clarify Sturm's indebtedness to them. Much of the difficulty is owing to the fact that historians are not in agreement about the nature of the Brethren. Were they primarily ascetic and anti-intellectual, deriving their strength from the mystical resources of their *devotio moderna* or were they intellectual humanists genuinely classical in their approach to education or were they both classical and pietistic? The classic study of the Brethren is that of Bonet-Maury,[38] who found the Brethren to be essentially humanist in their educational program. This view did not convince R.R. Bolgar who refuses to regard them as humanist just because they happened to use a grammar (by Despauterius) which many humanists had praised or "because Sturm praised the curriculum of a school with which they were connected."[39] Erasmus after all was convinced that Deventer, the Brethren's school attended by him, was backward with respect to its pedagogy.[40] Lucien Richard in a book concerning Calvin treats the Brethren as a basically anti-intellectual, ascetic movement.[41] These views are rejected by Kenneth Strand[42] who noted that "the Northern humanist generally (including Erasmus) and the *Devotio* looked back to ancient sources for religious thought as well as for practice." Strand emphasized Johann Sturm's indebtedness to the Brethren but primarily in the sense of methodological borrowings, which does not take into account the religious element at all. Jean Rott observed that the *devotio moderna*, together with the blending of the classical ideal of "vir bonus et doctus"—the Ciceronian concept of the orator, so revered by Johann Sturm—were most significant to Sturm's development;[43] unfortunately, he did not explain in detail how Sturm's program derived from the *devotio*. Léon E. Halkin, a scholar who has devoted much time to the study of the College of Liège denies altogether that there was anything more than an apparent connection between Johann Sturm's program and the *devotio moderna*. He has written: "Jean Sturm et Jean Sleidan… furent élèves des frères; je ne vois pas ce qu'ils retinrent de la *Devotio Moderna*."[44] Halkin believes that Protestant reformism swept a very Catholic *devotio* out of sight, and that only after the fact did Protestants view the Brethren's piety as a pre-Protestant phenomenon. On the other hand, Halkin suggests that such elements as a balanced view, a concern for methodology, especially those methods that had proved effective as well as carefully regulated exercises of religious worship were (besides the *devotio*) characteristic of the Brethren.[45] Such things as these as Halkin states in another place[46] did find their way into Sturm's program. But such things as those have rarely been contested.

Aside from the religious influence of the Brethren, controversy has centered on the exact nature of the College of Saint Jerome twice referred to by Sturm, once in a memoir to the scholarchs of 24 February 1538 [the *Advice*] and once in the *Classicae Epistolae*—in the letter to the Prince Bishop Gerard de Groesbeek—in which Sturm mentioned some teachers he had had at Liège.[47] Halkin rejects an old charge made by Heinrich Veil in 1888 in which Veil said Sturm's portrayal of the success of the College of Liège was a fabrication or at least, a gross exaggeration made in order to persuade the Strasbourg school authorities to create the kind of school which Sturm had in mind.[48] Halkin regretted that Veil's contention had been copied by several other German writers, namely by Friedrich Paulsen[49] and by Theobald Ziegler[50] and Ernst Hoepffner.[51] Halkin finds the accusation "Injuste à la fois pour la mémoire de Jean Sturm et pour le valeur pédagogique de ses maîtres liégeois."[52] He defends the school at Liège as having had a fairly sophisticated curriculum and clears Sturm of any such "Machiavellian" disingenuousness as Veil's thesis might have implied.

No consideration of Sturm's own program could afford to omit at least a cursory review of his religious beliefs, since, as must be apparent, religion assumed a preponderant role in the development of every aspect of intellectual expression in this period. The nature of Sturm's faith is less a matter of dispute than the possible effects it had on his commitment to humanist education, his selection of texts for instructional purposes, and his commentary on them. The relationship of his faith to his pedagogy shades off also into a consideration of his non-discriminatory admissions policy. Sturm was in favor of accepting students and teachers of different religious views at the Strasbourg school.

Sturm's great critic, the Rev. Johann Marbach,[53] believed Sturm represented a Calvinist element within the church, perhaps because Sturm was a good friend of John Calvin's, and had been a member of the French parish church in Strasbourg—and its treasurer as well—during the period when Calvin was the pastor of French refugees in Strasbourg, 1538–1541.[54] The belief that anyone who professed Christ ought to be treated as a brother was typical of Bucer and shared by Sturm. This is the opinion of Richard Zoepffel's analysis of Sturm's religion.[55] This author emphasized the reluctance of Sturm to engage in unproductive quarrels—"unnutze Gezank" that contributed nothing to the scholar's peace of mind. Sturm is viewed not as a champion of free thought, but rather as one whose practical "Bibelchristenthum" was both evangelical and Augustinian,[56] and that Sturm's adherence to the Tetrapolitana was because Sturm viewed it as the most likely statement of belief to produce brotherhood between Lutherans and other reformed believers.[57] A useful discussion of the practical uses to which Sturm put his faith can be found in Robert Faerber's analysis of Sturm's religious thought.[58] This writer finds Sturm to have been a theologically minded polemicist of academic stamp whose theological writings (15 original works and 14 prefaces to the works of others) are noteworthy for their tolerant spirit rather than for any original contributions of a theological sort. The results of Sturm's ecumenism, says Faerber, was to produce engaged Christian citizens. Hence, Sturm put logic and rhetoric at the service of faith.

Even those who, like Zoepffel and Faerber, admire Sturm's tolerance are aware that this was not absolute. Roger Zuber noted that while Sturm was more tolerant certainly than men like Marbach and François Hotman,[59] his was not toleration for its own sake—"Par principe"—for toleration in that sense was not yet known. Sturm's friends believed that his tolerance was a practical virtue, but it was yet a virtue limited by the strongest sanctions that could be levied against those beliefs that appeared too threatening. It has not been widely commented upon in the literature that has reviewed his remarkable career, but Sturm's toleration did not extend to Michael Servetus.[60] A few months after Servetus had been burned in Geneva Sturm wrote a letter to Calvin in which he aligned himself with the opinion of his old friend,[61] the historian Johann Sleidan,[62] and with Melanchthon too, approving of the way the Swiss reformer had dealt with the blasphemous heretic.[63]

Prospective educators and students of education generally may wonder why we have taken Sturm's religious beliefs and his view of religious toleration into consideration. The answer is that we wish to present a balanced view. It is obvious that humanists and religious performers made great strides in developing educational theory and practice accustoming large segments of the population to regard schooling as an essential requirement for the good life. It must be remembered, however, that these educators and the institutions they created had not put their faith wholly into free inquiry for its own sake. They were still defenders of received opinion to a larger or lesser degree. The literature on Sturm does not, however, address itself directly to such considerations, although several writers have remarked on the diminished secular spirit towards the close of the century. Even if Sturm's tolerance was less than absolute, he was palpably more liberal minded than many of his contemporaries. Indeed, one of the leading authorities on Sturm in our generation has declared that Sturm's absence of hostility to scholars of other faiths was astonishing. He chooses to explain this fact by associating Sturm's political idealism—"politique irenique"—with his dedication to an equally ecumenical pedagogy.[64] Obviously, Sturm's world was not a parochial world, nor was Strasbourg's school parochial as long as he was able to direct its policies.

Though we are not able to describe Sturm's long service in diplomacy on behalf of Protestant and Catholic co-existence in this bibliographical essay, it should be noted that his objective in diplomatic relations, not unlike his efforts in education, was to create a kind of European environment where peace and piety might prevail, a place where reason and justice might be reflected on earth as he thought they prevailed in heaven.[65]

When Johann Sturm at the behest of the school authorities of Strasbourg presented them (February 24, 1538) with his famous memoir concerning the re-organization of the city's school system, he not only rehearsed some of the characteristics he had admired in Liège, but revealed as well a Renaissance confidence in the value of education to civilized society:

> Such an institution will be useful to citizens, liberal towards neighboring cities and states, necessary for our posterity. All the hope of states lies in the good education of their youth, and in their early education is the only way to bring poverty to an end....[66]

The curriculum of the Strasbourg *Hochschule* or high school (the term gymnasium was applied only to those classes in which attendance was compulsory)[67] is easily described. The first four years of a boy's education were devoted almost wholly to the mastery of Latin grammar, style, vocabulary, and their rhetorical and dialectical uses. Sturm was determined to keep students away from specialized (technical or practical) subjects until they had become thoroughly imbued with the Latin language. Greek was introduced in the sixth year when the boys were about eleven years old and Hebrew was studied in the last two years. Theology and some legal theory were studied then as well. Of course, to some degree the students were introduced to the study of history and of the natural order through their reading of the classics. Modern critics of this literary education have questioned the degree to which such knowledge could have had any practical value, however. Not only does such a charge reflect a predilection on the part of many modern scholars for technological or scientific education, but also a feeling that the quality of life of pre-technical and pre-scientific cultures such as Sturm's was necessarily less valid than it might have been had contemporaries turned to pursuits and concerns that were not yet developed! In other words, anachronism on the part of some observers who appear most critical of sixteenth century educational content.

Sturm's first biographer was the first of the modern writers who objected to this literary and classical aspect of Renaissance education, and especially to its impractical nature.[68] During the later nineteenth century few writers took any other position. One of those exceptions was Mathieu Gaufrès, who observed that the classics were not regarded as merely literary sources by Renaissance men, but that gradually the earlier, and sensible point of view became perverted.[69] Gaufrès associated Sturm with that early practicality, and Sturm's Jesuit imitators as the perverters and corrupters of it. Twentieth-century commentary on the practicality of Sturm's curriculum continues to reflect this division of opinion. "Pas réele" is the summary dismissal of Sturm's approach given by J. Gessler.[70] William Melczer, on the other hand, finds it displayed a wise equilibrium between "connaisance empirique" (empirical knowledge) and theoretical knowledge. He uses the term "juste proportion" to describe Sturm's program.[71] Despite the fact that Sturm once abandoned the study of medicine (in Paris) before obtaining a doctorate in the subject, Ernest Wickersheimer makes it clear that those studies had considerable impact on Sturm's pedagogy.[72] Students in the Gymnasium received sporadic instruction in medicine; those in the public lecture program were encouraged to attend medical lectures of general interest; and medicine was taught sporadically at the Academy too, though on a rather elementary level. Such information enables us to perceive the degree to which a practical science found expression in a curriculum largely devoted to the humanities.

A different kind of practicality, political rather than biological, is explored by Herman Gumbel. He explains Sturm's position as a kind of intensification of certain traits that earlier had characterized men such as Brant,[73] Murner,[74] and Wimpheling.[75] For none of these men was antique classicism the main objective. They were all more concerned with themes of piety and good conduct. To Wimpheling's concern for good Latin—*Wissenschaft*—and good behavior—*Tugend*—Sturm added a developed political sense to produce what Gumbel calls "eines bewusst politischen Humanismus"[76] in which the mastery of oratory was prime. Practical methodology combined with logic and rhetoric were intended to secure the education of the nobility (Gumbel says the nobility was a weakness—*(Schwäche)*—of Sturm's) and a more apparent stress on facts—*(für Tätertum)*. Gumbel sees political education as the key to understanding Sturm's program. For him Sturm was an innovator of humanist education precisely because his political interests resulted in the creation of a practical school.[77]

We have already noticed how some commentators have deemed Sturm's approach insufficiently humanist, the result of its having been excessively Christian. The same approach has been accused of being excessively humanist. This idea, which seems to be a variant of the criticism of insufficient practicality, is in the main that held by Preserved Smith, an early twentieth-century historian of Reformation Europe. Smith, commenting on the type of educational offering typical of Strasbourg (though not specifically on Sturm's own) said that while the pedagogy of sixteenth-century writers seemed thorough, "then, what does it all amount to, in the end, but Latin and Greek?" He was willing to acknowledge that a little arithmetic, geometry and astronomy were admitted into such programs, but believed that "the knowledge of things was valued chiefly for the sake of literary comprehension and allusion."[78] A more recent but equally dim view of the humanist curriculum is that held by Georges Snyders. His assessment of the Renaissance period is that it witnessed a revival of classicism, but was coupled with a restraint: "une volonté de ne plus proposer certain des problèmes les plus difficiles, de ne plus se laisser tenter par l'ambition d'encyclopédisme."[79] This is perhaps the first hint in this literature that the classical Renaissance was less challenging to the intellect than the scholastic period. Snyders believes that the preponderant activity of sixteenth-century schooling was a waste of time, in part because students were not capable of doing the tasks they were given.[80] Neither Snyders nor any other commentator who has condemned the humanist curriculum as ineffective because of its excessively literary and verbal nature has founded their opinion on research into the productivity and success of students who were graduated from schools such as the one at Strasbourg.

When we turn away from the curriculum of the period to consider methodology, we enter into an area of pedagogy which, more so than that of subject matter, seems to have been one pre-eminently Sturm's own. This is not to say that he was the only Renaissance educator to concern himself with methods of teaching, but rather, that he was the first to develop a consideration of method in an explicit manual of logic or dialectics, the first to treat methodology as a separate subject.[81] The dialectical aspect of Sturm's methodology was a logical extension of his belief that understanding is from word to thing, that is, without a proper understanding of the word, the knowledge of the material world is useless or damaging. Friedrich Hahn has pointed out that while Erasmus had as early as 1512 written that knowledge required both word and thing, and though Melanchthon had followed suit, Sturm gave the method a pedagogical application by tying together words and things via memorization.[82] Hahn believes the object of real knowledge was not inappropriately associated with a method as verbal or "formal" as Sturm's. This rift in modern opinion concerning the aptness of Sturm's method and its ability to produce practical knowledge fit for politically active men has continued from the 19th century. Friedrich Paulsen, writing in 1885,[83] reproved one K. von Raumer[84] for having been too critical of Sturm's verbal emphasis (that the word must precede the thing). Paulsen said that Raumer was wrong to blame Sturm for excessive verbalism because that was the common posture of all the humanists. Still another critic, Ernst Laas,[85] has tended to see Sturm's preoccupation with form (*verba*) as more exaggerated than that of Melanchthon, Agricola, and Erasmus. Paulsen on the other hand finds such exaggeration was more apparent than real and was owing to the fact that Sturm's exposition was intended for a less scholarly audience, while the other humanists mentioned wrote for a more learned group. As with the discussion over curriculum, this controversy on method raises again a question of practicality, and rightly so since the curricular and methodological aspects of Sturm's program were intimately related. F. Collard, describing Sturm's methodology, doubted its ability to do anything more than produce vocabulary. He did not believe it could lead to an understanding of ideas or facts.[86] Certainly Sturm himself believed that it could.

As Jean Rott points out, Sturm's goal was to produce active citizens whose knowledge of the real world would be adequate for purposes of leadership. Performance rather than passivity and "servile imitation" was a conscious requirement.[87] Sturm's classroom routine included imitating written models,[88] memorization, recitation, learning homilies,[89] keeping diaries (*copia verborum*),[90] directed conversations (*confabulations*) between students, and after 1565, the rehearsing of classical comedies.[91] Luther himself had recommended to a Silesian schoolmaster the dramatization of the plays of Terence. These techniques are frequently alluded to by commentators, but rarely analyzed from a pedagogical point of view. Sometimes they are cited as evidence that Sturm was an innovative teacher. Charles Schmidt took a dim view of these procedures and the majority of comment followed suit. Only a handful of writers who have noted these activities have written enthusiastically of them. Schmidt noted the general lack of enthusiasm of the students and teachers for oratorical exercises that he claimed were ineffective. Two nineteenth century commentators in particular expressed real enthusiasm for the educational methods chosen by Sturm and they are widely spaced. The earliest was also that first of the century's commentators, Adam Strobel, who remarked admiringly that Sturm's method was successful to a large degree because of the numerous practical exercises which he devised and which, according to this author, made students use continually and in a practical way what they had been taught by way of theory.[92] Strobel's admiration was not unlikely owing to the fact that he was himself a gymnasium teacher and had the practical experience as a classroom teacher which many subsequent critics lacked. The second was Charles Engel who believed that all students "même doué médiocrement" were able to achieve the rhetorical precision expected of them in a few year's time. He felt that only the most incapable students were ever obliged to repeat a grade and was enthusiastic over the twice yearly promotions that provided swift advancement for the gifted.[93] More recently, William Melczer has intimated that the methods used in the teaching of classical languages—daily speaking practice and the prohibition after an initial period of instruction in the maternal language—were creative approaches. He is particularly appreciative of Sturm's contributions such as the concept of balance "juste mesure"—a principle he thinks resulted in meeting each student's individual needs, and in what he describes as a dynamic view of the nature of memory.[94] If relatively few observers have applauded the classroom techniques Sturm used, a much broader group has approved of his tact, his sensitivity to the need of students for variety in their routine, and to the needs of young people for daily physical recreation, with from time to time, class excursions or forays into the countryside. Such activities could scarcely have failed to win the approval of students, even if classroom exercises did not. In fact, Sturm's techniques were not altogether popular with every member of his faculty and their charges. He was obliged to recognize the problem and sought to solve it, not by abandoning the methods previously utilized, but by urging stricter observance of them on the part of his staff. There seems to be much truth in the dictum given by Melczer that Sturm's attachment to his teaching methods was rather "cabalistic,"[95] for he clung all the more doggedly to them when later they came under attack.

Before we take up the exact nature of the problems Sturm encountered with regard to his methodology and the efforts made by him to deal with them, it must be pointed out that his attention was not limited to secondary education, even though most of the comment on Sturm's career has been preoccupied with the nature of his gymnasium. He was also concerned with post-secondary or superior schooling. The sixteenth century has been described as a period in which the differentiation between secondary and superior education was not yet agreed upon. Contemporaries did not make such distinctions everywhere on the same basis. Paul Porteau has written that in southern France, for example, some students undertook a five-year course of general studies between their *collège* or secondary schooling and their matriculation in the Faculties or university departments that provided professional training. This system, where it prevailed, was known as "publicae auditiones," or public lectures. Porteau notes that Sturm is generally considered to have invented the system of public lectures.[96] Ernst Hoepffner has pointed out that the public lectures were not originally Sturm's own invention, but had been devised by Strasbourg's preachers sometime before his arrival there as courses in theology and philosophy intended for prospective pastors. Hoepffner credits Sturm with expanding the courses to include letters, medicine, law and scientific subjects as well as theology and philosophy, all forming a five-year cycle.[97] The development of the public lectures is interesting because it seems to have pointed the way towards what we frequently refer to in American society as adult education, one of the most democratic features of our own society. Sturm's students of course differed dramatically from the kind of students who most typically availed themselves of night school and adult education courses in the early years of the present century. Such courses were intended for disadvantaged adults, many of them immigrants, for whom a regular high school diploma was out of the question. Strasbourg's public lectures were designed to complement the education of students who had been privileged to attend the gymnasium. Yet there remains the philosophy of general as opposed to technical education characteristic of both the public lectures and the concept of the comprehensive high school—a strong conviction that to general education should be added a knowledge of practical things. Is it too far-fetched to think that our approach to high school education, which we try to make both comprehensive and general, has been influenced by the philosophy that underlay the public lectures of Strasbourg during the sixteenth century? Haven't American junior colleges in many respects been created as were the public lectures to continue education along similar lines, providing a transition between secondary school and the university?

The lectures were not so successful as Sturm had hoped they would be. Part of the problem was due to a duplication of subject matter and the repetition of methods used in the gymnasium. Some of the students must have found the lectures less satisfying because of that. Another problem derived from the inability of the authorities to grant degrees to those who attended the lectures. It was because of a general dissatisfaction then that Sturm requested the magistrates to press for imperial permission to transform the high school into a university with all faculties, an action they did not support.[98] The much more limited Academy was instituted at Strasbourg in 1566 and could give only bachelor and masters of arts degrees. Theological, law, and medical degrees had to be taken at the universities. Yet Sturm had the satisfaction of seeing the new Academy become a distinguished humanist institution where all instruction was imparted according to the methodology (humanist and rhetorical) originally laid down for the gymnasium.[99] As for the public lectures, they continued to exist alongside the new Academy, for in 1569 Sturm undertook at the magistrates' request, to write a work analogous to the *Classicae Epistolae* of 1565. The *Epistolae Academicae* (1569) were intended to inspire his colleagues at the Academy with a renewed sense of their educational mission.[100] Since the Academy was transformed in 1621 into the University of Strasbourg, Sturm may be said to have been that university's founding father.

When we attempt to analyze the nature of Sturm's success as an educator we are immediately struck by the fact that the bulk of his contemporaries revered and lionized this man whose life seemed proof that humanist studies and Christian principles were no handicap to achievement in both scholarship and citizenship. Sturm's personal prestige was great enough to protect his credibility as an educator, even when he became somewhat isolated during the 1560s—the last survivor of the original group of reform-minded preachers and humanist scholars and magistrates who had together molded the Strasbourg school system. Sturm was recognized outside of Strasbourg as well as within. He was the consultant for re-organizing or creating a number of schools in Germany, including Schulp-forta (1545); Lauingen (1565); Hornbach/Pfalz and Trarbach/Mosel (1573). Many others were influenced by his works, including those at Basel, Dortmund, Flensburg, Geneva, Nîmes, Cracow, Werwatow, and Zemosc. His students were sought after as rectors or organizers of schools as well, and they found positions in many schools, including schools in Württemberg, Kurpfalz, Kursachsen, Braunschweig and at Pforzheim, Altorf, Augsburg, Memmingen, Hamburg and Thorn.[101] His works were collected and published in the last town in 1586, just three years before his death, when he was in retirement not of his own choosing, feeble, and blind. He must have taken great satisfaction in the publication undertaken by the faculty of Thorn's gymnasium. A second edition of his works appeared in 1730 in Jena.

Sturm's pedagogy was particularly appreciated in Bohemia and in Poland. In Bohemia Sturm's influence was derived in part from the activity of one of his former students, Cocinus, a man who became as well a collaborator and an editor of Sturm's work.[102] In Poland his influence coincided with a decline in power of the Jagellon family, with the result that other genteel and noble families found it expedient to send their sons to Strasbourg for the kind of education that would equip them to fill the political roles left vacant[103] Another essay on Sturm's Polish popularity is André Mazon's,[104] while Sturm's connection with Hungary has been studied by Alfred Temesi,[105] and with Romania by Henri Tronchon.[106] A partial list of Sturm's disciples reads like a roll-call of distinguished Renaissance teachers: Claude Baduel (founder of the Academy of Nîmes); Thomas de Platter of Basel; Michael Toxites of Württemberg; Johann Fabricius of Meissen; the Pole Jan Zamoyski, and Roger Ascham. All were Protestants, but there were Catholic educators as well: Jerome Gebysler (Hagenau); Matthias Schürer (Schlettstadt); and Heinrich Schor (Saverne). An interesting account by Jean Rott and Robert Faerber alludes to the somewhat off-hand manner in which John Hales, using Sturm's precepts, founded a school in England.[107] Even those commentators who are not the most attracted to the program of classical study are able to appreciate Sturm's enormous influence as a shaper of European mentality whose finest ambitions were to see the ideals of justice and humanity firmly founded in Europe.

One area of influence which Sturm wielded on the reform of education involves the many Jesuit schools and academies that proliferated after the 1560s and indeed, seemed to some contemporaries to threaten the prosperity of Protestant foundations. In 1565 Sturm wrote to the Scholarchs concerning (among other things) Jesuit education:

> I rejoice over this work for two reasons: first because the
> Jesuits support us and cultivate good letters, object of all of
> our pains and our great passion. In fact, I have seen the
> authors they explain, the exercises they use and their
> instructional method which is so close to ours, that it seems
> to be derived from our sources.[108]

Although the preceding leaves no doubt that Sturm himself felt the
Jesuit schools were modeled after his own, that very question has
proved another subject for debate. Gaufrès, writing towards the latter
period of the nineteenth century made an unfavorable comparison
between the products of Jesuit education and Sturm's program. He took
a very pro-reformed (Protestant) position and insisted that while Protestant education sought to release man's imagination, Jesuit imitators
sought to bind it to their own (nefarious) purposes.[109] Even Sturm gave
voice to certain apprehensions as it became apparent to him that papal
authoritarianism posed a real threat to intellectual freedom. The work
of J.B. Herman, S.J. was the first to make a concerted effort to disprove
the assumption made by most commentators before him that the Jesuits
had copied Sturm.[110] Herman reproved such authors as A. Siccard[111]
and Otto Kaemmel[112] for making easy connections between the two
types of programs. Herman believed the differences between Sturm and
the Jesuits were profound despite superficial resemblances, and affected
"non l'extérieur du programme, mais son âme, son principe même."[113]
He felt that such confusions had arisen because both Sturm and the
Jesuits had drunk from a common source, namely, the Brethren of the
Common Life and the humanism of the Low Countries.

Herman's theme was refined by another Jesuit historian, Gabriel
Codina Mir.[114] While not denying the influence of the Brethren over
both Sturm and the Jesuit educators, Codina Mir points out that the latter
were more indebted to their experience of Parisian teaching methods
than they were to the Brethren while the reverse was true of Sturm.
Though he finds that certain Jesuit colleges in the area of Strasbourg
were directly influenced by Sturm's Gymnasium, that influence was
local and belated. Yet his concession is not inconsequential. Most commentators continue to connect Jesuit techniques with those used by
Sturm and to compare the *Ratio Studiorum* (Jesuit plan of study) with
Sturm's *De Literarum Ludis Recte Aperiendis* (On the Correct Opening
of Schools of Letters) (1538). This is not to say that the connection made
is always complimentary. Recently, R.R. Bolgar has weighed both programs and found them wanting. He thinks Jesuits and Protestants alike

watered down the humanistic heritage;[115] while Roger Chartier, M.M. Compère and D. Julia found no practical differences to have existed between Sturm's school and those run by his methods, and the Jesuits ones.[116] Instead, similar methods, sources, and goals (piety and eloquence) based on classical models were common to both kinds of institutions, according to these authors.

After one has reviewed from all sides the pedagogical career of Johann Sturm, and most particularly, the impact that his writings and practices had on his contemporaries, it seems almost pickwickian to raise the question of his ultimate success as an educator. Was not his influence on educational institutions and on educators, indeed, on all those who were educated, great enough? Still the question has been raised by most commentators because of two related events of the 1560s, namely, the re-organization of the Lauingen school program in 1564 and the publication of the *Classicae Epistolae* which followed in 1565.

As for the first event, Sturm responded to the plea of Duke Wolfgang of Zweibrücken to recognize the school of Lauingen, which was small and could be provided with only five teachers instead of the dozen or so who normally taught in Strasbourg's gymnasium. The plan which Sturm prepared[117] caused him to direct his attention towards maximizing efficiency. He consulted other teachers at length and the result was a paring away of texts not deemed absolutely essential for achieving the goals of Latin eloquence and a reading knowledge of Greek.[118] In the course of this effort, Sturm was obliged to re-evaluate the effectiveness of his methods and curriculum generally. The facts seem to indicate that the goal of eloquence in Latin speech had not been reached at Strasbourg or at least not by all pupils, and that the methods by which it was supposed to be attained had frequently been ignored by the masters there. The *Classicae Epistolae* was the result of this re-examination initiated in Lauingen.

This work was composed of twenty-four letters to Sturm's faculty as a kind of review of the educational goals each teacher was to achieve and the ways (methods) by which this should be done. The letters are, as Jean Rott observed in his French edition, full of good sense and enthusiasm.[119] They are also models of charm, tact, and good will that testify not only to Sturm's sense of mission, but also to his kindly and humane bearing vis à vis his staff and his students. When one reflects on the fact that these letters were written in recognition of certain weaknesses or failures one is all the more impressed. Melczer notes that these letters were intended as required reading by all the faculty; that the prevailing message was that of urgency plus a conviction that the educational reform had been thoroughly prepared and the actualization of the program should proceed at once.[120] Jean Rott's introduction to his edition makes plain that Sturm's frequent absences from Strasbourg in the period after 1553 due to diplomatic business proved inconvenient to the school, encouraging a breakdown of discipline, inferior teaching and a diminished learning environment. Rott observes also that the period was further troubled by increasing polemics between theologians and professors, the result of the introduction of a new, more orthodox catechism.[121]

We would probably be correct to view the period of the 1560s as one of "rolling readjustment," a period in which, after an initial enthusiasm and unity of purpose, a certain disenchantment and laxness had set in. Anton Schindling remarks that the faculty in its early years prided itself on the methodology that its exponents regarded as "une méthode scientifique unique."[122] It is easy enough to imagine that the founding of a new school and a new educational philosophy would be sustained in the first and more exciting years by the expectations of its idealistic staff and the plaudits of an intrigued group of informed spectators, but that at length, enthusiasm waning, the routine—grown too familiar—might seem less attractive. Teaching and learning too are even in the best of circumstances enterprises which involve much heroics in the form of unremitting drudgery not always deemed worthwhile. What is certain is that Sturm was fortunate to have the loyal support (until 1581) of the magistrates, who made adherence to his methods statute law in Strasbourg from 1568 to 1604, after which time the methods were gradually abandoned.

To assess the degree to which Sturm's program was or was not successful we must balance the facts against a variety of conflicting modern opinion. We might, it seems, reject the hasty negativism of such observers as "Lehrer" Schmitz, who found it quite tragic that Sturm's admitted teaching skill had been so nearly wasted—"beinahe verschwendet wurde" because of the inappropriateness of the goal—Ciceronian eloquence.[123] Had Sturm's contemporaries felt that way, they would not have expended so much energy and wealth in the creation of schools—Catholic as well as Protestant—with similar objectives. Nor is there any reason to believe that mere circumstances peculiar to Strasbourg's size or geographical location or political influence and irrespective of the dedication, administrative talent and gifts of Sturm himself, account for the reputation of his school program.[124]

It is not necessary to turn a blind eye to the weaknesses of Sturm's system. It is true that not every teacher or every student was always willing to sacrifice his own ease or his own creativity to the requirements set down by the Rector for his class. These may have had more insight into the needs of the hour, and may have been more effective left to their own devices than the Rector was able to recognize. What administrator has not underestimated his staff's creative powers? What teacher has not underestimated his students? Still, a close reading of the twenty-four letters makes it clear that Sturm did not intend to take all creative liberty from the teachers. He was unwilling, however, to give up the method he had spent nearly three decades perfecting.

In reviewing the literature on Sturm it is obvious that he did not escape criticism altogether. He was, in fact, dismissed from his position as "lifetime" Rector of the Gymnasium. The reason seems to have had nothing to do with his teaching or pedagogical principles, but rather to have reflected the political situation in the Empire and the vulnerability of the Strasbourg magistrates to pressure from the Elector Palatine, which was the culminating factor for his enforced resignation.[125] Such criticism as he was subjected to then was largely restricted to the school in Strasbourg itself and did not damage his reputation elsewhere.

To that reputation we return when we try to understand Sturm's importance to sixteenth-century education. He was, in the words of Alphonse Roersch, indeed, "un éducateur de race," a born educator.[126] He had in such bountiful measure so many of the requirements that are necessary for every good teacher: enthusiasm, respect for the needs of youth; an unflagging attention to the practical aspects of teaching and learning, not the least of which were clear lesson plans and achievable classroom objectives. His sense of responsibility to students, families, faculty and the community at large was deeply civic and also deeply religious. He was willing to review and to correct his own opinions even if he was not willing to abandon them altogether. He had an unstinting willingness for the hard work involved in writing and publishing textbooks and illustrative exercises, and an investigative curiosity into the very nature of the learning process which in many respects appears to have been rather advanced. Sturm was not it seems to us merely a pedagogue, nor merely an administrator, but a theoretician and (rare combination) a practical classroom teacher. What was more—and this may have been the most important attribute any great teacher has—he was himself a lifelong student, undertaking at an advanced age to teach himself Hebrew.

Jean Rott, who has as much as any scholar in the twentieth century increased our knowledge of Sturm's multi-faceted career and scholarship, noted that the criticisms of his methods and techniques are those commonly leveled at humanist educators of his era, but points out that Sturm was so full of good sense and so convinced of his mission that his stature remains one of real human significance.[127] Such attributes are not common in any age, and must be counted heavily in any estimation of his success and influence, which in retrospect, seem to us deservedly great.[128]

Notes

Introduction
(pages 11–18)

1. Woodward, *Vittorino da Feltre and Other Humanist Educators* (Cambridge, 1918), pp. 102, 106.
2. Paul F. Grendler, *Schooling in Renaissance Italy: Literacy and Learning 1300–1600* (Baltimore and London: The Johns Hopkins University Press, 1989). See the review by Margaret King, *Renaissance Quarterly*, LXIV, 1 (Spring, 1991), pp. 107–10. Paul F. Grendler, "The Organization of Primary and Secondary Education in the Italian Renaissance," *The Catholic Historical Review*, LXXI, 2 (April, 1985), pp. 185–205. See also Anthony Grafton and Lisa Jardine, *From Humanism to the Humanities: Education and the Liberal Arts in Fifteenth- and Sixteenth-Century Europe* (Cambridge: Harvard University Press, 1986); reviewed by Ronald Witt, *Renaissance Quarterly*, XLI, 3 (Autumn, 1988), pp. 479–82.
3. Woodward, *Vittorino da Feltre*, pp. 102–106.
4. The most thorough overview is that of Willy Moog, *Geschichte der Pädagogik der Neuzeit von der Renaissance bis zum Ende des 17. Jahrhunderts*, 8th edition (Ratingen bei Düsseldorf: A Henn Verlag, 1967). The basic older documents publication is that of D. Johann Michael Reu, *Quellen zur Geschichte des kirchlichen Unterrichts in der evangelischen Kirche Deutschlands zwischen 1530 und 1600* (Gütersloh: Druck und Verlag von C. Bertelsmann, 1911). See also Paul Oskar Kristeller, "Latin Schools in the Protestant Tradition," *Helios*, XIV, 2 (1987), pp. 161–64.
5. Lawrence V. Ryan, *Roger Ascham* (Stanford: Stanford University Press, 1963), pp. 116–117, 144–46, *et passim.*
6. The brilliant, though Fascist, Ezra Pound once pronounced that every cultural flowering has been preceded by an age of translation. See Ezra Pound, *Literary Essays* (New York, n.d.), p. 232. On Ezra Pound, Paul De Man, and modern "intellectuals" see Gene Edward Veith, Jr., *Modern Fascism: Liquidating the Judaeo-Christian Worldview* (St. Louis: Concordia Publishing House, 1993). On translations from the classics one should consult R.R. Bolgar, *The Classical Heritage and Its Beneficiaries* (Cambridge, 1954), pp. 506–41.
7. WA Br. 2, pp. 393–96, cited in James Kittelson, *Luther the Reformer: The Story of the Man and His Career* (Minneapolis: Augsburg Publishing House, 1986), p. 175. As Luther discovered: "I have found translating to be such a laborious task! No one would have moved me by money or favors to trans-

late a book, if I had not done it for the sake of my Lord Christ." WA Tr 2, no. 2623, August, 1532. He worked on improving his Bible translation until his death in 1546. WA 10", 60, St. Louis, Walch Ed., 15, 1672.

8. Pierre Mesnard, "La Pietas litterata de Jean Sturm et le développement à Strasbourg d'une pédagogie oecuménique (1538–1581), in *Bulletin de la Société de l'Histoire du Protestantisme Français*, CXI Année (October-November-December), pp. 281–302. This is to be found in an abbreviated version as "La Pédagogie de Jean Sturm et son inspiration évangélique (1507–1589)," in the *Rapports du XII Congrès Internationales des Sciences Historiques* (Vienna, 1965), III, pp. 75–86. This excellent article is translated by Evelyn M. Hartmann as "The Pedagogy of Johann Sturm (1507–1589) and its Evangelical Inspiration," *Studies in the Renaissance*, XIII (1966), Publications of the Renaissance Society of America, pp. 200–19.

9. Kückelhahn, *Johannes Sturm: Strassburgs erster Schulrector* (Leipzig, 1872).

10. Michael Reu, ed., *Quellen*, 3 (I. Teil, II. Band, 2. Abteilung, 1911), p. 752.

11. On the Reformation in Strasbourg and its impact on education see the splendid chapters by Marc Lienhard, "La Réforme à Strasbourg. Les événements et les hommes," Livre VI, 362–540, in Georges Livet and Francis Rapp, eds., *Histoire de Strasbourg des Origines à Nos Jours*, II (Strasbourg: Éditions des Dernières Nouvelles d'Alsace, 1980). See especially pp. 406–12, "Le Rayonnement de Strasbourg dans l'Europe protestante. Le Gymnase et les problèmes de l'éducation de la jeunesse."

Johann Sturm (1507–1589)
(pages 19–44)

1. His first formal schooling was begun in the public school of Schleiden, not at the castle. His first teacher was Johann of Neuburg. *Classicae epistolae sive scholae Argentinenses restitutae* (Strasbourg 1565), edited and translated (into French) by Jean Rott, (Paris-Strasbourg, 1938), Letter to Abraham Feis.

2. Johann Philipson (1506–1556) studied at Liège, at the College of St. Jerome, a year or so before Sturm arrived. He studied languages and literature at Cologne, and law at Paris and Orleans. Like Sturm, he was a protégé of Cardinal du Bellay and a negotiator for an alliance between German Protestants and Francis I. His history of the reign of Charles V (*Commentariorum de statu religionis et reipublicae, Carolo V. Caesare*, 1555) was written from voluminous documentary sources. In the Karlsruhe Archives is a letter from the Count Palatine Otto Heinrich to Sturm (March 14, 1557) in which the Count proposed that Sturm continue Sleidan's *Commentary* for a salary of 100 gulden per annum. Sturm never found time despite the Count's urging.

3. "…the picture I have kept of Johann of Neuburg, my first teacher, of Jacob of Blumenthal, of Antoine Dalber, of Gerard Episcopius, whose student I

was in my home town and whom I so love, is such that it would be the greatest joy for me to be able to express my thanks to their children and grandchildren. As for Arnold of Eynatten, whose courses I followed at Liège, and at the College of St. Jerome, I love him so much that I am tied to him from the depths of my being" (Letter to Abraham Feis, 1565, in *Classicae epistolae*). Neuburg was a teacher in the school of Schleiden. Dalber was director of the Manderscheid family's school.

4. One of these was Nicholas Nickman; another, Henry of Bremen. He called them "dominus" and they were probably secular priests and not Brethren of the Common Life (Letter to Gerard Groesbeek, Bishop of Liège, May 18, 1563). On the Brethren, see R.R. Post, *The Modern Devotion* (Leiden: E.J.H. Brill, 1968), pp. 563–64. Post heavily quotes the authority on the Brethren's school of St. Jerome, Léon Halkin. See Halkin's "Une lettre inédite de Jean Sturm au Prince-évêque Gérard de Groesbeek" (pamphlet), (Liège, 1941); and "Les frères de la vie commune, etc." in *Bulletin de l'Institute archéologique liégois* (1945); and in the same journal (1949–50), "Jean Sturm et le Collège Saint-Jérome de Liège (1495–1594)." Post's detailed research finally resulted in his not being able to see the forest for the trees, so that he did not fully appreciate the impact of the Brethren's schools and their total role in the Northern Renaissance.

5. Erasmus attended a school at Deventer not run by the Brethren, but one that had benefited from their efforts. See Albert Hyma, *The Youth of Erasmus* (New York: Russell & Russell, 1968; 2nd edition), pp. 29–30.

6. Luther did not attend a school owned by the Brethren at Magdeburg, but some other school, possibly the Cathedral School in which the Brethren taught. See Eric W. Gritsch, *Martin—God's Court Jester* (Philadelphia: Fortress Press, 1983), p. 224, n. 9. There (p. 4) the author states that "nothing is known" about Luther's education at Magdeburg.

7. Post, *The Modern Devotion*, p. 558.

8. The memoir was dated February 24, 1538.

9. On the relationship between Sturm's secondary schools and Jesuit schools see *Classicae epistolae* letters to Albert, Duke of Prussia, and to the Scholarchs (nos. 1 and 2). Here it may be noted that there were elements of continuity as to method and curriculum throughout the sixteenth century and between Protestant and Catholic schools, a continuity to which post Tridentine Catholicism, humanism, personal piety and the reformed religion all contributed. The Brethren found themselves, for many reasons, unable to attract new students toward the end of the sixteenth century; see R.R. Post, *The Modern Devotion*, pp. 566–67.

10. In the *Classicae epistolae* (no. 11, to Johann Reinhard) Sturm recalled with obvious pleasure that he had taken the part of Geta in the play *Phormio* by Terence.

11. The College was conceived and endowed by Jerome Busleiden's testament (1518) and was part of the university at Louvain. Instruction was given in Hebrew, Greek and Latin. Erasmus defended the study of Hebrew in a written exchange with a member of the theological faculty (James Latomus)

who had questioned its utility. See Johan Huizinga, *Erasmus and the Age of Reformation* (New York: Harper & Row, 1957), p. 135.

12. Wackers (1489/90–1539) was born in Mengeringhausen in Westphalia, educated in Cologne and at Louvain, and taught at the College of Three Languages from 1519 until his death.

13. Martin Bucer (1491–1551) was a native of Schlettstadt in Alsace. A Dominican monk until 1521, he converted to the reformed religion and was a preacher in the Palatinate until settling (1523) in Strasbourg. There, with Mathew Zell and Wolfgang Capito, he worked to establish the new religion. Bucer held Zwinglian conceptions of the Eucharist, but was eager to effect a union of Lutheran, south German and Swiss reformed churches. He was author of the *Confessio tetrapolitana* or religious confession of Strasbourg, a supporter and colleague of Sturm's educational and diplomatic activities. Bucer was obliged to leave for England when the Interim religious settlement (conservative, Catholic) was established throughout the Empire (1548). In that country he obtained a professorship in divinity at Cambridge University and helped to revise the Anglican *Book of Common Prayer*. See J.V. Pollet, *Martin Bucer: Études Sur la Correspondance* (Paris: Presses Universitaires de France, 1958) and Robert Stupperich, *Bibliographia Buceriana* (Gütersloh: *Schriften des Vereins für Reformationsgeschichte*, nr. 169, H.2, 1952).

14. The works of Galen (circa 130–200 A.D.) of Pergamum, court physician to the Stoic Roman Emperor, Marcus Aurelius, remained the principal texts of medical education during the sixteenth century.

15. Vesalius (1514–1564) was a Belgian physician and anatomist whose expertise in human dissection proved to his own satisfaction that Galen's work was based on animal, not on human anatomy. See E. Wickersheimer, "Jean Sturm, Ami Strasbourgeois d'André Vésalé" in *Aktuelle Probleme aus der Geschichte der Medizin*," *Proceedings of the xixth International Congress for the History of Medicine* (Basel: 7–11 Sept. 1964); *Current Problems in the History of Medicine* (New York: S. Karger, 1966), pp. 25–32.

16. Budé (1467–1540) was one of the greatest Renaissance scholars. Secretary to Francis I, it was at his urging that the king founded the Collège de France. Budé was a Greek scholar and his work helped establish the study of philology. Other of his interests were Roman law and Greek and Roman numismatics.

17. Marguerite (1492–1549) was Queen of Navarre through her (second) marriage to Henri d'Albret, titular king of Navarre. She was a supporter of church reform and a few reformers in whom she took an interest (Calvin, Farel) became Protestants. She did not. A talented writer, her works included a collection of seventy-two stories (*Heptameron*), plays, poetry, and one work condemned by the Sorbonne faculty of theology entitled *Mirror of a Sinful Soul*. Although she died a Catholic, her influence over her brother spared many reformers from persecution.

18. Guillaume (1491–1543) was a diplomat in Francis I's service and was involved in negotiations with Henry VIII of England and with Protestant

princes of Germany. He was governor of Piedmont from 1537 to 1543. Jean (1492–1560) was not only a Cardinal, but also a humanist diplomat. He was sent on many missions to England, Rome, Germany. A religious moderate, he was frequently criticized for supporting Henry VIII's divorce.

19. Servetus had established contact with a number of leading reformers—as a young man Servetus was already opposed to the trinitarian conception of the Godhead—including Oecolampadius, Capito, Bucer, Calvin and possibly even Luther. After Servetus's trial and death at Geneva (1553) Sturm sent Calvin a letter condoning the deed.

20. Charles Schmidt, *La Vie et Les Travaux de Jean Sturm* (Nieuwkoop: B. de Graaf, 1970; first edition, 1855), p. 10.

21. Huysman or Agricola (1443–1485), "father" of German humanism, helped train a whole new generation of German anti-Aristotelian (anti-scholastic) scholars, among whom were the Hebraist Johannes Reuchlin, great uncle of Philipp Melanchthon, and Conrad Celtis, first poet-laureate of Germany; see Lewis W. Spitz, *The Religious Renaissance of the German Humanists* (Cambridge: Harvard University Press, 1963), chap. 2, "Agricola, Father of Humanism."

22. Peter Ramus (1517–1572) was holder of a chair in rhetoric and philosophy in the Collège de France after 1551, despite criticism from the Church for his anti-Aristotelianism. He was forced to flee France in 1568 during the religious wars, and declined a job offered him by Sturm at the Strasbourg Academy. He returned to France in 1570, but was murdered during the St. Bartholomew's Day Massacre in 1572.

23. Bartholomaeus Latomus (1490–1570) was born in Arlon, Luxemburg and was a friend of Erasmus who travelled with him through Alsace in 1521. He taught philosophy in Trier and Cologne before coming to Paris. In 1534 he was called to Trier by the Elector Ludwig Von Hagen to be his Counselor; there he became engaged in anti-Reformation polemics. Latomus wrote a long (fifteen pages) letter to Sturm in 1540 after Sturm had been Rector at Strasbourg for two years in which he urged the need to prevent religious dissension in Germany in order to fight the Turks. Sturm's answer—that the Germans were already peace-loving—and Latomus's letter were published by Sturm under the title *Epistolae Duorum Amicorum Bartholomaei Latomi et Joannis Sturmii de dissidio Periculoque Germaniae et per quos stat quominas concordiae ratio inter partes ineatur* (Strasbourg, 1540 and 1564). In his last published work, Sturm set about to make a plea for the kind of ecumenical cooperation against the Turk which Latomus had urged forty-four years earlier.

24. So few learned women were honored by a Latin pen name!

25. According to Schmidt, *La Vie*, p. 12, Lewis Carinus came from Lucerne, and had met Bucer in Strasbourg along with other reformed intellectuals. Carinus may have interested Sturm in reading Bucer's works, but in any case, Sturm had already been exposed to Bucer's public lectures in Strasbourg, thus making it open to question whether it was Carinus who was instrumental in Sturm's conversion.

26. "...Cum rege diu de te locutus est, multa de tua integritate, eruditione, modestia... Exposuit omnem vestrae vitae et religionis rationem" [*Corpus Reformatorum*, Philippi Melanthonis *Opera Supersunt Omnia*, ed. by Cardius Gottlieb Bretschneider (Halis Saxonum (Halle): C.A. Schwetschke et Filium, 1838), II, pp. 855–60].

27. "Rex ingenio est per se acuto et prudenti, et natura facilis, et libenter admittit rationes..." [*Corpus Reformatorum*, V, p. 1031, Letter of July 9, 1535].

28. "...in vestra multa metuit priusquam omnem cognovit, propter eos tumultus, quos Germania iam crebros in multis locis est passa. Itaque, ne quid simile Galliae eveniat, mature consulit, et quoniam apud vos tranquilliorem esse respublicam audit, et te earum rerum magna ex parte authorem, cupit coram tecum colloqui. Hoc ego credo, Regis esse consilium, et eum monitum esse a prudentibus, et iam aliquid intelligere" [*Corpus Reformatorum*, V, p. 1032].

29. Jean Rott, *Classicae epistolae, sive scholae argentinenses restitutae*, translated with an Introduction and notes (Paris: Librairie E. Droz, and Strasbourg: Éditions Fides, 1938), Introduction, p. x.

30. Anton Schindling, *Humanistische Hochschule und Freie Reichsstadt. Gymnasium und Akademie in Strassburg 1538–1621* (Wiesbaden: Franz Steiner Verlag GMBH, 1977), p. 22.

31. Sebastian Brant (1457–1521) was a humanist who taught law at the University of Basel. *Das Narrenschiff* served as a vehicle by which Brant castigated all the human vices and foibles. See Eckhard Bernstein, *German Humanism* (Boston: Twayne Publishers, 1983), pp. 47–48, and Edwin H. Zeydel, editor of Brant's *Ship of Fools* (New York: Columbia University Press, 1944), pp. 29–34.

32. Johann Geiler (1445–1510) was dean of faculties of Philosophy and of Arts at the University of Basel, and a lecturer in theology before serving as Rector at the University of Freiburg in Breisgau, or as preacher at the Strasbourg Cathedral (1478). In the last post he took pains to speak to common people in simple terms, stressing the unity of the Catholic tradition and the power of believers to prepare themselves for grace and salvation. Although regarded as a fore-runner of the Reformation, he was really an orthodox, reform-minded Catholic. See Jane Dempsey Douglass, *Justification in Late Medieval Preaching: A Study of John Geiler of Kaisersberg* (Leiden: E.J. Brill, 1966) and Richard Newald, *Elsässische Charakterköpfe aus dem Zeitalter des Humanismus* (Colmar: Alsatia Verlag, undated).

33. Wimpheling (1450–1528) was the Alsatian preacher at Speyer cathedral. His interests were primarily in the reform of clerical morality and public virtue and in the protection of German culture against French expansion. He was not keen on pagan classical learning. See Newald, *Elsässische Charakterköpfe*, pp. 55–84.

34. Schmidt, *La Vie*, p. 26 points out that the city government had asked Melanchthon for his opinion on their plans to reorganize public instruction in Strasbourg as early as 1526. Melanchthon had just then opened up the

gymnasium at Nuremberg, and was widely hailed as Praeceptor Germaniae. His reply, if any, is unknown.

35. Beatus Rhenanus (1485–1547) edited (without permission) Erasmus's works, and wrote a biography of their author. Rhenanus' *Rerum Germanicarum libri tres* (1531) was based on documentary evidence and was highly regarded.

36. *Vita Beati Rhenani*, in *Beatus Rhenanus, Rerum germanicarum libri* III (Basel 1541).

37. Alexander Hegius (1433–1498) was a learned master of the school at Deventer, a friend of Agricola's and a teacher of Erasmus.

38. Wolfgang Capito (Köpfel) (1478–1541) was a humanist of irenic temperament who worked with Bucer to unify the churches of Germany, France and Switzerland. He was a victim of the plague; see James M. Kittelson, *Wolfgang Capito from Humanist to Reformer* (Leiden: E.J. Brill, 1975).

39. Caspar Hedio was another Strasbourg reformer.

40. Schindling, *Humanistische Hochschule*, p. 29.

41. This is the same memoir referred to above (n. 8).

42. Calvin (1509–1564) spent three years in Strasbourg, from 1538 to 1541. He had known Sturm from Paris when Sturm taught at the Collège de France. Bucer invited Calvin to Strasbourg where Calvin spent part of his time preaching to the French reformed, a church to which Sturm also belonged and served as its treasurer. This does not mean that Sturm became a Calvinist, however, for Calvin himself still subscribed to the Tetrapolitan Confession (*Confessio tetrapolitana*), a formula of faith designed to accommodate Strasbourg's less rigoristic Lutherans. Calvin also served on the staff of Sturm's Gymnasium during the plague years, accompanying the school on its plague retreat to the Black Forest area and to Wissenburg where it was temporarily lodged.

43. Vermigli (1500–1562), an Italian, joined the Augustinian canons and became prior of an abbey in Lucca, but as he adopted a symbolic interpretation of the Eucharist, he was obliged to flee north. He taught at the Strasbourg Gymnasium twice, once in the early 1540s and again between 1553 and 1556, having returned from a six-year stint as professor at the University of Oxford. He spent the years 1556 until his death as a professor of theology in Zurich.

44. Beyond the physical disruption of academic life was the loss of four teachers to the plague. Besides Capito, Bittelborn, Bedrot, and the French Hellenist, Claude Féréus, all died of the disease, and among reformers' children, the enrolled sons of Zwingli, Hedio and Oecolampadius (Schmidt, *La Vie*, p. 76).

45. *Ibid.*, p. 77.

46. On their friendship, see Karl Hartfelder, *Philipp Melanchthon als Praeceptor Germaniae* (Nieuwkoop: B. De Graaf, 1964), pp. 148–50. Hartfelder says that while Melanchthon was acknowledged by Sturm as the greater Latinist, he was free of any envy and had in 1556 offered Melanchthon a position in the Strasbourg school teaching theology, an

offer refused because of Melanchthon's attachment to his beloved Wittenberg. Sometime in November, 1542 Melanchthon wrote Sturm urging him to stay in teaching because nothing was more glorious or profitable than teaching God's truth in God's creation: "...tamen te adhortor, ut hoc praesertim tristissimo tempore, sapientiam esse statuas et domicilium illud, quod contigit, boni consulas, et magno animo docendi laborem profuturum posteritati perferas... Minus est splendida scolastica vita; sed revera melius de genera humano meretur. Quid est enim utilius, addo etiam quid gloriosius est, quam teneras mentes salutari doctrina de Deo, de Natura rerum de bonis moribus imbuere. Id lumen est unicum vitae..." Melanchthon added that Sturm's school, unlike his own school in Wittenberg, was famous for its good discipline: "Quodque in his nostris conventibus, quod saepe deploro, disciplinae vincula nimium laxata sunt, vos vestrum gregem facilius et regitis et corectis, et hac in re legibus et authoritate gubernatorum adiuvamini" [*Corpus Reformatorum*, IV, pp. 904–905].

47. The gymnasium had 624 students enrolled in 1546 (Schmidt, *La Vie*, p. 79).
48. This was a provisional religious settlement of a very Catholic sort. The reaction to it in largely Protestant Strasbourg was quite unfavorable.
49. Erasmus of Limbourg was a Baron who became a prominent Catholic clergyman, and was canon and treasurer of the Grand Chapter, and in 1541, Bishop of Strasbourg. It was partly due to Limbourg that Sturm had been appointed Rector of the Strasbourg gymnasium, and hence understandable that despite some differences of opinion, Sturm remained the Bishop's loyal defender.
50. Schmidt, *La Vie*, pp. 82–83.
51. On this first meeting see the Preface to *Dialogi in partit. orat. Ciceronis*, Sturm to Wolfgang, Count Palatine, March 10, 1539, and in Sturm's *Prolegomena, hoc est praefationes in optimos quosquo utriusque linguae tum bonarum artium tum philosophiae scriptores* (Zurich, 1556).
52. Jakob Sturm (1489–1553), no relative to Johann, was also a Scholarch or School Committee member, and one of the founders of the Strasbourg Gymnasium. He had been Wimpheling's pupil and was a friend of educational reform. Johann Sturm commemorated him in his *Consolatio ad Senatum Argentinensem* (1553).
53. Joachim Camerarius (1500–1574) was born in Bamberg and educated at Leipzig, Erfurt, and Wittenberg. He drank deeply of humanism under the learned Mutianus Rufus and of Lutheran reform from his association with Melanchthon. He persisted in working for reconciliation with Rome until the 1560s. See Eckhard Bernstein, *German Humanism*, p. 138. See also Friedrich Stähelin, *Humanismus und Reformation im bürgerlichen Raum: Eine Untersuchung der biographischen Schriften des Joachim Camerarius* (Leipzig, 1936).
54. Pierre Mesnard, "La Pietas Litterata de Jean Sturm et le Développement à Strasbourg d'une Pédagogie Oecumenique (1538–1581)," in *Bulletin de la Société de l'Histoire du Protestantisme Français*, Jan.-Mar., 1965, and in

English, "The Pedagogy of Johann Sturm (1507–1589) and its Evangelical Inspiration," Evelyn M. Hartman, trans., *Studies in the Renaissance*, Vol. 13, (1963), pp. 200–19.

55. Contarini (1483–1542) was a Venetian nobleman and member of the Great Council of Venice; Venetian ambassador to the court of Charles V in 1530; after 1535 a Cardinal, and in 1536 appointed by Paul III to a reform commission. Of Erasmian temperament, he worked with Melanchthon on a verbal formulation of the doctrine of justification by faith, but was frustrated by Luther's firm stand and by papal suspicion. When he died he was under investigation for heresy.

56. They were invited to do so by the Elector and Archbishop of Cologne, Hermann von Wied (1477–1552). Hermann began his career as both Elector and Archbishop in 1515 by instituting certain diocesan reforms. In 1541, with support from the estates of his electorate, he needed help, and the two Strasbourg reformers were called in. In 1543 he invited Melanchthon to assist him. He was summoned before the emperor and the pope, deposed and excommunicated by Paul III in 1546. He resigned his office in 1547 and retired to Wied.

57. This resulted from adherence (after 1532) of the Vaudois churches to the reform. The region was anciently associated with heresy and had preserved a tendency to emphasize scripture since the twelfth century. In 1487 Pope Innocent VIII raised a veritable crusade against the inhabitants, opposed by Louis XII of France. After 1532 (Synod of Angrogna) the Vaudois were considered Lutherans, and were ordered (1545) by the Parlement of Aix to abjure or vacate territory under its jurisdiction. Those who refused were massacred by mercenaries hired for the purpose. The towns of Cabrières and Mérindol were brutally treated. Over three thousand Vaudois were massacred, many burned alive in their own churches or barns; 650 were summarily executed. The butchery aroused general indignation in France, and Henry II put the chief instigators on trial before the Parlement of Paris. On the repression of heresy in France see G.R. Elton, ed., *The New Cambridge Modern History*, II, *The Reformation 1520–1559* (Cambridge, 1990), pp. 251–61.

58. The account of Sturm's diplomatic activities is drawn largely from Schmidt, *La Vie*, chap. VI.

59. In 1550, Frederick II, Elector of the Palatinate, bestowed his personal protection on him. In 1555 Charles V granted him a patent of nobility for his service and talents. In 1555, too, the successor of Frederick II, Otto Henry, offered him a pension in order for Sturm to complete Sleidan's history, but he refused (see n. 2 above).

60. In 1557 he was appointed to a second Colloquy of Worms, dissolved before it convened.

61. Schmidt, *La Vie*, p. 92, notes that the Venetian ambassador offered him a rich gift, and that on November 10, 1555, he was elected provost of the Chapter of St. Thomas.

62. Fagius (Büchlein) (1504–1550) was born in Rheinzabern and educated at Heidelberg between the ages of eleven and eighteen. From there he went to Strasbourg where he took a job teaching, met Wolfgang Capito, and learned Hebrew by studying with a Jewish teacher named Eliae Levitae. In 1544 Fagius was a preacher and a professor of theology. He was given a teaching post at Cambridge, where he published translations from the Hebrew Old Testament into Latin. See Marie-Joseph Bopp, *Die Evangelischen Geistlichen Theologen im Elsass und Lothringen*, 3 vols. (Neustadt a.d. Aisch.: 1959), p. 148.

63. Jules Bonnet, *Letters of John Calvin*, compiled from the original manuscripts and edited with historical notes (Edinburgh: Thomas Constable and Co., 1857), Vol. II, p. 187.

64. Ascham (1515–1568) was a humanist scholar of Latin and Greek and a master of prose style. His service as Elizabeth's tutor (1548–1550) completed, he spent several years on the continent as a diplomat. He was Queen Mary's Latin secretary, and was a devoted disciple of Sturm's educational and humanist writings.

65. Ascham would not live to see this work published. Sturm's *Aristotelis Rhetoricorum libri III* appeared only in 1570, two years after the Englishman's death.

66. "Non enim tibi concedam, ut tu me plus ames quam ego te diligam" [Sturm to Ascham, July 22, 1553, in *Ascham Epistolarum Libri Quatuor* (Oxford: Typis Lichfieldianis apud Henricum Clements, 1703), pp. 389–90].

67. "Nisi quod tu me sis in scribendo crebrior, in judicando prudentior, et experientior usu, tractandoque res nostri seculi" [*Ibid.*].

68. "Quo nihil vidi in hoc genere acutius, atque utinam stylus meus, ut tuum ingenium. Nam est aliquando hebetior. Itaque ubi confecero, mittam tibi, ut acuas et emendes" [*Ibid.*].

69. Ascham's letter concerning imitation revealed his great deference to Sturm in professional matters; see Ryan, *Roger Ascham*, pp. 244–45.

70. *Nobilitas literata ad Werteros fratres* (1549 and 1556; a third edition under an amended title was printed in Jena in 1680).

71. *De laudibus Graecarum literarum oratio* (Strasbourg, 1551). Heresbach (b.?–1576) also published a history of Anabaptism, a Life of Strabo, another on Christian jurisprudence, a commentary on rural life (*re rustica*) and a Latin translation of the Psalms. He taught for a time in Sturm's school.

72. Elizabeth's note read in part: "De tuo religios, studio, ex libris tuis intelligimis. De tuo ite multiplici rerum usa atq.; prudentia, ex sermone multorum accepimus: accepimus etiam id quod libenter quidem accepimus, magna te, & observantia nos & benevolentia nostros, iam diu esse prosequutum" [in *Rogeri Achami Angli, Regiae Olim Maistate a Latinis Epistolis Familiarium Epistolarum. Libri III* (Coloniae Allobrogum: Petrum Roverianum. 1611), pp. 26–27].

73. According to the count made by Jean Rott, "Bibliographie des Oeuvres Imprimées du Recteur Strasbourgeois Jean Sturm (1507–1589)," *Bulletin Philologique & Historique Comité Traveaux. Actes 95è Congrès Nationale*

Société des Savantes (Reims: 1970, 1975), Vol. I. (Paris: Imprimerie Nationale), pp. 319–404, Sturm's output was 155 works (in 503 editions).

74. Farel (1485–1565) was one of the reformers of Meaux, France, fleeing to Switzerland in 1533, where he set the Geneva reform movement in place. Farel begged Calvin for help. Both men left in 1538, Farel for Basel and Neuchatel, Calvin to Strasbourg. Farel rejoined Calvin in Geneva in 1541.

75. Bèze (or Beza) (1519–1605) was a French aristocrat who succeeded Calvin as the chief theologian of the Calvinist faith after the founder's death in 1564. Bèze took part in the Colloquy of Poissy in 1561; he also wrote theological tracts, a poor and idealized biography of Calvin, and helped edit the Greek and Latin editions of the New Testament.

76. Hotman (1524–1590) was a French jurist and Calvinist convert whose writings—the most famous was *Francogallia* (1573) because it attributed sovereignty to the French people rather than to the monarchy, which he deemed elective—covered a variety of subjects: criminal punishment; usury; the primitive church's priesthood; Roman law and administration; the Eucharist; etc. It was Calvin who brought him to Sturm's attention, arranging for him to teach (1555) at the gymnasium, and encouraging him to dedicate his latest book (a commentary on Cicero) to Sturm. See Donald R. Kelley, *François Hotman: A Revolutionary's Ordeal* (Princeton, NJ: Princeton University Press, 1973).

77. Schmidt, *La Vie*, says both Calvin and Sturm were ignorant of this plot of Amboise (p. 103) and that Sturm only learned of it through friends in France (p. 104). Hotman accused Sturm of having had prior knowledge of the conspiracy and of betraying the plotters to the Cardinal of Lorraine (p. 130). Sturm retorted that Hotman's anti-Guise tract known as the *Tigre* had aroused Guise suspicion (pp. 130–31). Sturm must have persuaded Hotman of his innocence for they were later reconciled, which would have been unlikely if Hotman continued to regard Sturm as a traitor to the reformed cause.

78. Gaspard de Coligny (1519–1572) won military honors in the Italian wars of the 1540s. In 1552 he was made Admiral of France. He converted to Protestantism in 1559, and together with Louis, Prince of Condé, commanded the Huguenot forces after the massacre of Vassy. He negotiated the treaty which ended the war (1568–70), between the Huguenots and the Court (Treaty of St. Germain, 1570) and was the favorite advisor of Charles IX until, to check that influence over the king, he was assassinated by order of Catherine d'Medici and François de Guise, the first victim of the infamous St. Bartholomew's Day Massacre (1572). See *Actes du Colloque l'Amiral Coligny et son Temps* (Société de l'Histoire du Protestantisme Française, 1972). On the St. Bartholomew's Massacre, see Alfred Soman, ed., *The Massacre of St. Bartholomews: Reappraisals and Documents* (The Hague: Martinus Nijhoff, 1974).

79. François d'Andelot (1531–1569) was one of the Protestant leaders in the French religious wars.

80. Bèze wrote: "Ego hanc occasionem arripui tanto magis urgendi, ut cum videat se periculoso morbo premi, tempestive conscientiam suam liberet. Itaque spero omino fore ut brevi ab his molestiis libereris. Utinam aliquid possem amplius" [Letter of August 24, 1565, in *Correspondance de Théodore de Bèze*, collected by Hippolyte Aubert, Alain Dufour *et al.*, editors and publishers, vol. VI (1565) (Geneva: Librarie Droz, 1990), p. 149.

81. Anthony Cook was Edward VI's tutor obliged to seek refuge in Strasbourg at the advent of Mary Tudor to the throne.

82. "Mihi magnopere dolet: usque adeo me spoliatum esse fortunis meis a Domino Royana: ut hunc virum mea pecunia non potuerim apud me retinere... Mitto tibi exemplum epistolae meae ad Reginam, ut videas quo modo queas.... Coactus sum intercessionem nostroreum Principum implorare, qui scripserunt omnes, etiam praefecti miliares: implor etiam Reginae Regisque auctoritatem jus meum jure persequar vel civili, vel detrimentum enim egestatem mihi attulit, et periculum fidae meae quam ego pro crudelissima muliere obligave creditoribus. Si Regina Angliae graviter pro me scriberet, plurimam mihi prodesset: et gratissimum faceret. Principibus nostris" [Letter from Sturm to the "Nobillisimo et Clarissimo Viro D. Antonia Cooko" (October, 1565), no. xxv in Pr 2201 E2 1703 (Stanford Rare Book Room, Division of Special Collections, Name of book missing)].

83. Thirty years after Sturm's death, the Condé family paid eighty thousand livres to Sturm's heirs as settlement. The letter of Bèze to Sturm (August 24, 1565) testified further to the urgent need of Sturm for repayment; see note 80 above. The editor of this volume states that the sum Sturm had advanced to Madame de Roye was twenty thousand florins, p. 149, note 1.

84. Johannes Marbach (1521–1581) studied in Strasbourg and in Wittenberg and was one of Luther's own students. Invited to Strasbourg by Bucer, he became a pastor in 1545 at St. Nicholas and a professor of theology in the gymnasium. He was present at the Council of Trent in 1551. In 1552 he succeeded Caspar Hedio as President of Convocation. In 1556 he was made a School Visitor and Superintendent of Schools as well. His group of young Lutherans opposed the Heidelberg reform movement and with the support of the conservative Scholarch, Karl Mieg (after 1570 *Ammeister*) reduced the control over discipline especially formerly exercised by the teachers of the gymnasium and the Academy. See Schindling, *German Humanism*, pp. 34–35 and 122–33.

85. This Concord was a formula of faith signed on May 26, 1536 by twenty-one theologians, including Bucer, Luther and Melanchthon, who intended to create unity thereby. It could not mask basic differences of opinion regarding rites and doctrine, and held little appeal for those with symbolic interpretations of the Eucharist. The Concord asserted the true body and blood of Christ were present in the bread and wine the communion service. The Wittenberg Concord, drafted primarily by the Wittenberg University theologians, not as was once thought by the conciliatory Strasbourg group led by Bucer, played a role in the pre-history of the Formula and the Book of Concord. See F. Bente, *Historical Introductions to the Book of Concord*

(St. Louis: Concordia Publishing House, 1921; reprint, 1965), pp. 8, 26, 49, 55, 60.

86. Zanchi (1516–1590) had been a Regular Canon in Bergamo (1531–41) when he met Peter Vermigli in Lucca and began reading works by Melanchthon, Bucer and Calvin. Leaving Italy (1555) he went first to the Grisons, and then to Strasbourg, where he was hired by the Scholarchs to teach theology, to the dismay of conservative Lutherans. He claimed he was neither Lutheran nor Zwinglian nor Calvinist: "Christianus igitur sum non sectarius." Nevertheless, he was unquestionably sympathetic to both Zwinglian and Calvinist theological positions. In Strasbourg Zanchi treated with the papal nuncio Delfino concerning Protestant participation at the Council of Trent, with no success. In 1563 he took upon himself the governance of a Protestant community at Chiavenna, leaving in 1568 for Heidelberg, where he taught for ten years. His works were published posthumously in 1617 and 1619 at Geneva. See D. Cantimori, *Eretici Italiani Del Cinquecento* (Florence, 1939).

87. The work was by Tilemann Hesshusius and entitled *Responsio ad praejudicium Melanchthonis de controversia Coenae Domini* (1560), which Schmidt, *La Vie*, (pp. 120–21) described as a "pamphlet." It was a polemic against French and Swiss reformed and against Frederick III, Elector Palatine, who protected them. Sturm wrote to Frederick criticizing the work and expatiating against the most materialistic interpretations of the Eucharist which he felt divided the European reformed community.

88. Specker (d. 1569) was a professor of theology from Isny in Swabia and a preacher at St. Thomas in Strasbourg. He was a severe critic of Sturm.

89. Schmidt, *La Vie*, p. 118, claims the book was never actually published. Schmidt stressed Sturm's role vis à vis the intransigent "pueri" as that of a man determined to preserve the cordial interaction between Calvinists and Lutherans which had existed in the days of Bucer, Capito and Hedio, who refused to let doctrines like predestination or the real presence weaken the ranks of Protestantism. In this sense, Sturm emerged as a conservative, one who was preserving a valid tradition of reformed religion in its Strasbourg context. It is also apparent that the religious behavior of the parties involved was heavy with political significance for the fate of Protestantism in Europe.

90. "Miserum seculum nostrum; miserum, inquis, sed quibus de causis? Nostra culpa, nostra, inquam, cupiditate, ambitione, stultitia, impudentia, crudelitate nostrum praecipuorum? Sed utinam eximii illi essent eis artibus quae Ecclesiis sunt pernecessariae!" [Sturm's letter to Bèze, February 20, 1558, in *Correspondance de Théodore de Bèze*, collected by Hippolyte Aubert (Geneva: Librairie Droz, 1980), Vol. II, p. 175].

91. The work was entitled *Nova vetera quatuor eucharistica scripta Buceri. J. Sturmii vetus renovatus dolor de hoc dissidio Eucharistico, ad. D. Antonium Cookum* (Strasbourg: Theobald Berger, 1561).

92. Schmidt, *La Vie*, pp. 124–25. Be it said that most of the writing on the question of Bucer, Sturm, Zwingli, Marbach, Pappus and the rest has been done

by authors of an anti-orthodox or French Calvinist persuasion, corrected in part by such Reformation scholars as James Kittelson, who has studied and published on the Zanchi, Pappus, Marbach, and Sturm controversies.

93. Robert Faerber, "La Pensée Religieuse et Théologique de Jean Sturm", in *Strasbourg Au Coeur Religieux du XVIe Siècle, Hommage à L. Febvre.* Actes du Colloque Internationale (Strasbourg: 1975). Faerber says Sturm wrote fifteen original theological works and translated or prefaced fourteen more and calls him a polemicist of academic stamp (pp. 111–41).

94. *Ibid.* Faerber sees three main characteristics of Sturm's faith: 1. Christian unity 2. A Bucerian view (symbolic) of the Eucharist 3. belief in the "Chrétien dans la cité" or the engaged Christian who is active in his community. Points one and two are related to civic issues; only the second point has any theological significance.

95. This was Schmidt's conclusion, *La Vie*, p. 125; Schmidt is not to be accepted uncritically.

96. Frederick II, Elector of the Palatinate.

97. Christoph, Duke of Württemberg.

98. Catherine (1519–89), widow of Henry II, was regent for her son Charles IX in 1562. She entertained a conciliatory policy towards the Huguenots after taking Michel l'Hôpital as her chancellor in 1560.

99. See Donald R. Kelley, *François Hotman: A Revolutionary's Ordeal* (Princeton, NJ: Princeton University Press, 1973), pp. 134–35 for a brief discussion of the French irenicists in the years before Poissy.

100. Brenz (1499–1570) was the provost of the collegiate church of Stuttgart, appointed by his patron, Ulrich Duke of Württemberg. A strong Lutheran, he was opposed to the death penalty for Anabaptists and other heretics.

101. Jacob Andreae (1528–1590) enjoyed the patronage of the Dukes of Württemberg. A champion of the ideal of Lutheran unity, his work was a polemical struggle against very conservative Lutherans, Melanchthon admirers and Calvinists. He denounced Sturm as an impious Calvinist during the Zanchi disputes, and prayed for Strasbourg's deliverance from this evil influence. Sturm compared him to a new Egyptian plague. See Robert Kolb, "Jakob Andreae, 1528–1590," in *Shapers of Religious Traditions in Germany, Switzerland, and Poland*, Jill Raitt, ed. (New Haven: Yale University Press, 1980), pp. 53–68; Robert Kolb, *Andreae and the Formula of Concord. Six Sermons on the Way to Lutheran Unity* (St. Louis: Concordia Publishing House, 1977).

102. "Brentius praeter alia dixit Sturmio, primum: Non debuisses, inquit, facere partialem in hac causa; deinde: Miror te in ista senecta velle fieri theologum. Ad primum, sic Sturmius: Vere me feci partialem, quia partitus sum aures meas, et unam dedi Marbachio, et alteram Zanchio. Defendere autem Zanchhium, ne inauditus damnetur, tenebar diplicis collegii vinculo, etc." [*Correspondance of Beza*, Vol. IV, p. 62, Zanchi to Bullinger, February, 1562].

103. Vassy, in Champagne, was the site of a Calvinist church. On his way to Paris from the meeting at Saverne, Duke Francis of Guise's troops attacked

worshippers at prayer and over three hundred were killed. The incident riveted European attention on the internal policies of France toward her religious dissidents and triggered the beginning of the religious wars.

104. Among those attending were Jacob Andreae, Cunman Flinsbach, Superintendent in Zweibrücken; Simon Sulzer, Rector of the University of Basel, and Ulrich Köchlin, a pastor of Basel; see Schindling, *German Humanism*, p. 361, n. 90.

105. See F. Bente, ed., *Triglot Concordia: The Symbolical Books of the Ev. Lutheran Church* (St. Louis: Concordia, 1921), p. 201, introduction. Predestination was a critical issue dealt with in Article XI, *Triglot*, pp. 1063–1095. Calvin remarked that the *Formula* did not deny, but rather veiled the doctrine of election. Jacob Andreae played a key role for Lutheranism for both the Strasbourg Consensus and the Formula of Concord. See Robert Kolb, *Andreae and the Formula of Concord: Six Sermons on the Way to Lutheran Unity* (St. Louis: Concordia, 1977).

106. On restructuring the Hornbach school see Anton Schindling, "Humanistische Reform und Fürstliche Schulpolitik in Hornbach und Lauingen," in *Neuberger Kollektaneenblatt Jahrbuch* 133; 1980; (Würzburg: Heimat-verein-Historischer Verein, 1981) Vol. 43. Würzburger Diozesan Geschichtsblätter, pp. 141–86; and also, *Humanistische Hochschule und Freie Reichsstadt Gymnasium und Akademie in Strassburg 1538–1621* (Wiesbaden: Franz Steiner Verlag GMBH, 1977), pp. 39–42.

107. According to Schmidt, *La Vie*, p. 147, Sturm remarked that the magistrates had chosen the route of respectable mediocrity ("honnête médiocrité" in voting only to support a limited faculty of philosophy rather than a full-scale university.

108. Châtillon (Odet de Coligny) (1517–1571), Cardinal of Châtillon, was the eldest of three Coligny brothers, all of whom embraced the reform. Gaspard became an Admiral and was murdered during the St. Bartholomew Day Massacre in Paris, 1572. François, the youngest, was Lord Andelot (Seigneur d'Andelot). Odet was obliged to seek refuge in England during the religious wars in France, and looked to Sturm for financial support. See Nancy Lyman Roelker, "Family, Faith, and Fortuna: The Chatillon Brothers in the French Reformation," chapter 9 in Richard L. DeMolen, ed. *Leaders of the Reformation* (London: Susquehanna University Press, 1984).

109. Wolfgang of Palatine-Zweibrücken, though a minor prince, contributed what he could to the Protestant defense fund. See Erich Hassinger, *Das Werden des neuzeitlichen Europa 1300–1600* (Braunschweig: Georg Westermann Verlag, 1959), p. 311.

110. Elizabeth contributed a subsidy of 20,000 pounds sterling in spring of 1569 (Schmidt, *La Vie*, p. 157). She was well aware that if the Guises managed to ally with Phillip II of Spain and crush the reform in France and the Lowlands, English prosperity and liberty could only suffer.

111. Jeanne (1528–1572) was the Protestant daughter of Marguerite de Navarre, the mother of Henry of Navarre, later Henry IV of France. Unlike her husband, Antoine of Bourbon, she remained a loyal supporter of the Huguenot

party and enemy of the House of Guise. See Nancy Lyman Roelker, *Queen of Navarre Jeanne d'Albret 1528–1572* (Cambridge: Harvard University Press, 1968).

112. Anjou (1551–1589) was the leader of the Catholic party during his brother, Charles IX's reign. He was the victor of several important battles against the Huguenot forces (Jarnac; Moncontour). He refused to marry Elizabeth I on religious grounds, and in 1573 was elected King of Poland, but returned the next year at his brother's death to ascend the French throne.

113. Schmidt, *La Vie*, p. 170.

114. Sturm certainly remembered his correspondence with Latomus about repelling the Turks (see n. 23 above). Obviously, Sturm talked freely about political problems to colleagues whose religious beliefs made them suspicious of his proposed solutions.

115. The last charge grew out of Sturm's habit of stating that there were many virtuous men in the Catholic fold, and that one of the reasons they were not attracted to the reform was the disunity which characterized the reform. He had cordial relationships with many prominent Catholic churchmen, and he had given his blessing to the school in Saverne founded by the local bishop. He never abandoned his plea that both groups ought to participate in universal church councils in an effort to reconcile their differences. This ecumenical attitude was held against him in some circles (Schmidt, *La Vie*, pp. 181–84). See also Walter Sohm's *Die Schule Johann Sturms und die Kirche Strassburgs in ihrem gegenseitigen Verhältnis 1530–1581. Ein Beitrag zur Geschichte deutscher Renaissance* (München und Berlin: R. Oldenbourg, 1912); Sohm says the quarrels between the two men were based on a profound difference in their educational and religious views, namely, that Sturm continued to revere the humanistic ideal of learned piety, and to associate religion with eloquence, whereas for Marbach, this was to threaten a substitution of ethics for faith (pp. 112–13).

116. Sturm approved of Calvin's behavior in the death of Servetus and wrote to tell him so.

117. Marbach was President of the *Kirchenkonvent* or pastoral corps.

118. These *Academicae epistolae urbanae liber I* (1569) reiterated Sturm's adherence to the basic principles of humanist education expressed by him as early as 1538 in the memoir on the new Gymnasium program.

119. Anton Schindling, *Humanistische Hochschule*, p. 52, suggests that Marbach was in fact an able school politician: "In einer für das konfessionelle Zeitalter charakteristischen Verbindung war der Kirchenkonvents präsident Marbach zugleich auch ein ruhiger Schulpolitiker" (p. 54).

120. *Ibid.*, p. 54 and n. 44. Schindling, referring to Robert Holtzmann, *Kaiser Maximilian II bis zu seiner Thronbesteigung* (Berlin: 1903), pointed out that there was a seeming willingness on the part of the emperor to create new kinds of institutions of higher learning, and that in fact, is what happened in Würzburg in 1575.

121. *Academicae Epistolae*, Letter 1, To the Senate.

122. *Academicae Epistolae*, no. 2, To the Scholarchs, etc. In this letter Sturm began by saying that, while it was a great honor to be called Master of Liberal Arts and of Philosophy, it would be even more glorious to be able to earn the doctoral degree.

123. Matthias Flacius Illyricus (1520–1575) was the director of a group of Lutheran scholars who compiled a history of the world up to the thirteenth century known as the *Magdeburg Centuries*, which began to appear in 1559. Although the work was supposedly the product of research into original sources, it was nonetheless propagandistic and aimed at discrediting the claims of the papacy to have received its authority from Christ.

124. Schmidt, *La Vie*, pp. 180–82. Among the more famous English Protestants with whom he was in correspondence: William Page, John Hales, William Cecil (Lord Burghley), Francis Walsingham; among the Catholics were the Cardinal du Bellay, Bishops Jean de Fresse and Sebastian de Laubespine, Bishop Johann Manderscheid, and Henri Schol, provost of Surbourg (a childhood acquaintance.)

125. Johannes Pappus (1549–1610) was a Lutheran theologian who succeeded Marbach as President of the pastoral corps. He was Sturm's opponent and disapproved of the *Confessio tetrapolitana*. He worked hard to get the Formula of Concord accepted in Strasbourg. See Sohm, *Die Schule Johann Sturms*, chap. 7, "Der Sieg der Orthodoxie und Sturms christlicher Humanismus."

126. Lucas Osiander the Elder (1534–1604) was a holder of various church offices until he became Court Preacher at Stuttgart in 1567. He wrote polemics against Jesuits, Calvin, Zwingli, Flacius Illyricus and Melanchthon. He was one of the contributors to the *Magdeburg Centuries*, and was also a noted Lutheran hymnist.

127. Schmidt, *La Vie*, p. 190.

128. See Jean Rott's bibliography on the various editions of *Antipappi*. The edition used here is *Antipappi tres, contra D.J. Pappi charitatem et condemnationem christianam*, S.1 (probably, Geneva, 1579, in 4°).

129. Sturm was Melanchthonian but not a Calvinist.

130. Pierre Bayle (1647–1706), *Dictionnaire Historique et Critique (1695–1697)*, "Sturmius" (Paris: Desoer ed., 1820), 16 vols., vol. 13, Rem E., maintains, that Sturm's dismissal was the culmination of a train of events which had begun in 1561 when Bayle sided with Zanchi concerning the nature of the Eucharist. He points out that immediately after the dismissal, the "Calvinist" ministers (i.e., those who were Sturm's sympathizers, or who were themselves heterodox or liberal) were deprived of their jobs in Strasbourg. Bayle thought that the real reasons for Sturm's dismissal were too embarrassing for the pastors to handle, and they saved themselves discomfort by alluding to his age.

131. Schindling, *Humanistische Hochschule*, p. 143.

132. Bayle, *Dictionnaire Historique et Critique (1695–1697)*, Rem. C.

133. The details of this suit are found in the *Correspondance de Théodore de Bèze*, Vol. X, p. 28, n. 2.

134. Sturm's second wife was Marguerite Wigand, Sapidus's step-daughter. His third was a member of the patrician Hohenburg family. Five children were born to him, but none lived to be even one year old. Schmidt, *La Vie*, pp. 214–15 and n. 3, p. 214.

135. Sydney (1554–1586) served in several diplomatic missions on the Continent, and was fatally wounded in the Battle of Zutphen. Only after his death were his poetic works published.

136. "Quaere, si placet, exterarum nationum studiosos juvenes, cuius gratia, molestiam, de qua alius ne cogitassent quidem, longitineris susceperint? dicent Sturmii Interroga Ungaros, Gallos, Danos, Polonos, Boemos, qui alios quos voles, cuius huc se contulerint gratia? Sturmii, Sturmii inquam respondebunt omnes…" from Oratio Joh. comitis ab Ostrorog, etc., recitata cum discessurus Argentina publice academiae… valedicerret. (Strasbourg: 1581, in 4°).

137. The student was one Bartholomew Chericus of Saxony. His poem was entitled "D.Jo. Sturmii communis praeceptoris" (Strasbourg, 1581, in 4°.)

138. Schmidt, *La Vie*, p. 220, noted that a young Thuringian scholar asked for permission to do this but Sturm did not think his letters to him were worthy of publication.

139. Stroband was a Scholarch at Thorn and a Senator of that town as well. At his insistence, Sturm's work was published by the professors of the Thorn gymnasium (1586), under the title *Institutiones literatae, sive de discendi atque docendi ratione*, in 3 volumes, of which Sturm's works form the first.

140. The selection was made by Phil. Glaser, Professor of Greek in the academy. They were titled: *Manes Sturmiani, sive epicedia scripta in obitum summi viri D. Joh. Sturmii, una cum parentaliis eidem memoriae et gratitudinis ergo factis a diversis amicis atque discipulis* (Strasbourg: 1590, in 8°).

141. Schmidt, *La Vie*, p. 220, n. 3, says that even two generations after his death, his talent and virtue were still being praised, but that his dogmatic quarrels were passed over in silence in the interests of good taste.

142. In the Introduction (unpaged) to *De Amissa Dicendi Ratione, ad Franciscum Frassium Jurisconsultum. Libri duo.* Argentinae apud Wendelioeum Rihelium. 1538. Sic optime constitutae Resp. non solu millitiae & liberorum etiam rationem summam habuerunt, neque utilitatibus modò, veram etiam honoribus literarum dicendi magistros provocarunt…. et per annos multos perpetuata vitae meae ratio delectatione et voluptate retineret, nisi respicerem quo me Deus in hominem genere vivere velit, & ad quas res me miserit, iamdudum fortasse commutarem hoc docedi munus cum quaestuosa et hisce moribus avara alicuius artis professione. Sed vivendum mihi in literis est, et acquiescendum ei institutioni cui me mea natura atque Deus addixit.

143. Bayle, *Dictionnaire Historique et Critique (1695–1697)*, Rem. F, states that Sturm praised both the second edition of Calvin's *Institutes* in 1539 and the third edition of 1543.

Johann Sturm's Method for Humanistic Pedagogy
(pages 45–58)

1. Jacob Burckhardt, *The Civilization of the Renaissance in Italy* (New York: Random House, 1954), pp. 199–208. This chapter is used by permission of *The Sixteenth Century Journal* editors, specifically Robert V. Schnucker, the managing editor. See vol. XX, no. 1, Spring, 1989, pp. 23–39.

2. Pierre Grappin, "L'Humanisme en Allemagne Après la Réforme Luthérienne," in *L'Humanisme Allemand, (1480–1540)*, (Paris: Vrin, 1970), pp. 593–605: "Selon la thèse communément admise, le succès de la Réforme a marqué la fin de l'humanisme. Luther a contribué à cette fin rapide, son succès a étouffé la renaissance dans le pays allemand" (593). More recently, Benjamin G. Kohl, "Humanism and Education," in Albert Rabil, Jr., ed., *Renaissance Humanism* (Philadelphia: University of Pennsylvania Press, 1988), vol. 3, pp. 5–22, claims that the "repudiation" of humanism came with the Lutheran Reformation, which deflected classical interests because of its need for educated officials and Lutheran clergymen to preach reformed theology (p. 19). This statement narrowly reflects the source from which Kohl draws this conclusion, Gerald Strauss's *Luther's House of Learning: Indoctrination of the Young in the German Reformation* (Baltimore: Johns Hopkins University Press, 1978). Strauss does not, however, treat Sturm's pedagogy at all, surely an omission which seriously affects the usefulness of that work as a guide for determining the influence which Lutheran educators had on humanism and on secondary education in Protestant Germany. See Marilyn J. Harran, ed., *Luther and Learning: The Wittenberg University Luther Symposium* (Selinsgrove, PA: Susquehanna University Press, 1985) with its excellent chapters by Harran, Leif Grane, James Kittelson, Daniel Olivier, and others. On the relation of humanism and the Reformation, see the work edited by Manfred Fleischer of the University of California, Davis, *The Harvest of Humanism in Central Europe* (St. Louis: Concordia Publishing House, 1992). Among the many positive reviews, see that of Alister McGrath, *The Journal of Theological Studies* (April 1993), pp. 414–16, and David W. Lotz, *The Sixteenth Century Journal*, XXV, no. 2 (Summer, 1994), pp. 427–30.

3. *The Classics and Renaissance Thought* (Cambridge: Harvard University Press, 1955), pp. 9–11.

4. Sturm's biography was written by Charles Schmidt, *La Vie et les Travaux de Jean Sturm* (Nieukoop: B. de Graaf, 1970), reimpr. of the 1st (1855) ed.

5. The authority on Sturm and the College of Saint Jerome is Léon Halkin, "Jean Sturm et le Collège Saint-Jerome de Liège, (1495–1594)," in *Bulletin de l'Institut Archéologique Liégeois* 67 (1949–50).

6. Sturm, in Marcel Fournier & Charles Engel, *Les Statuts et Privilèges des Universités Françaises Depuis Leur Fondation Jusqu'en 1789* (Bologna: Scientia Verlag Aalen, 1970), reimpr. of the Paris (1894) ed. 4, number 1977, p. 19.

7. Budé (1467–1540) was a great Renaissance scholar and secretary to Francis I, who founded what came to be called the *Collège de France* at Budé's urging.

8. Marguerite (1492–1549) had the ear of her brother, Francis I. A prime patroness of reformed scholars and reforming clergymen, she had offered Sturm a teaching position in her new University of Béarn. He refused.

9. Du Bellay (1492–1560) was a moderate Catholic, a humanist, and a diplomat working to cement a Valois alliance against the emperor.

10. Schmidt, *La Vie*, says Sturm was persuaded to reform by the Swiss physician, Louis Carinus, a friend of Melanchthon, Bucer, and Erasmus (pp. 11–12). Carinus later (1546) became a canon of Saint Thomas in Strasbourg, where Sturm was Provost. See Peter G. Bietenholz, "Ludovicus Carinus," *Contemporaries of Erasmus IA-E* (Toronto: University of Toronto Press, 1985), pp. 266–68.

11. A good summary of the affair is Donald R. Kelley, *The Beginning of Ideology* (New York: Cambridge University Press, 1981), pp. 13–19.

12. Sturm, *Commonitio oder Erinnerungsschrift* (1581), p. 16. He visited Strasbourg and met Bucer there in 1528.

13. For cultural development before Sturm's arrival in Strasbourg see Miriam Chrisman, *Lay Culture, Learned Culture; Books and Social Change in Strasbourg 1480–1599* (New Haven: Yale University Press, 1982), chs. 1–3.

14. Grappin, "L'Humanisme Allemand," p. 596, views Strasbourg as in cultural decline due to the advent of the Reformation.

15. Sturm's dismissal was preceded by increasing differences between the humanists and orthodox Lutheran pastors. Since the 1560s Sturm's religious latitude had been at issue. In the 1570s this took on political coloration. The young pastor Johann Pappus, alarmed by what he viewed as Sturm's Calvinist theology, persuaded the city magistrates to silence him in the interests of Strasbourg's domestic tranquillity and of its alliance with the Lutheran Palatine ruler, Ludwig VI. For the earlier (1560s) conflicts between Sturm and orthodox Lutherans see James Kittelson, "Marbach vs. Zanchi: The Resolution of Controversy in Late Reformation Strasbourg," *The Sixteenth Century Journal* 8 no. 3 (1977), pp. 31–44. Kittelson notes the institutional as well as the confessional implications of this conflict. For the Sturm-Pappus controversy see Anton Schindling, *Humanistische Hochschule und Freie Reichsstadt; Gymnasium und Akademie in Strassburg 1538–1621,* (Wiesbaden: Franz Steiner Verlag, 1977), pp. 132–40, who stresses the primarily political, only secondarily confessional character of Sturm's ouster. A lucid account of the religious issues which underlay it is in Walter Sohm, *Die Schule Johann Sturms und die Kirche Strassburgs* (Munich: Oldenbourg, 1912), chap. 7. None of these sources dwell on pedagogical issues, for Sturm's removal as rector was not pedagogically motivated.

16. Fournier & Engel, *Les Statuts et Privilèges*, 4, no. 2144, 291–337, (sec. 27, parag. 9), p. 315.

17. *De literarum ludis recte aperiendis*, 1538. (The edition used in this chapter is the Lyons, 1542, ed. Bibliographical information on all the treatises is taken from Jean Rott, "Bibliographie des Oeuvres de Jean Sturm," in *Investigationes Historicae: Églises et Société au XVIe Siècle* (Strasbourg: Oberlin, 1986), vol. 2, pp. 471–556. This work lists 155 different publications of Sturm, and 503 separate editions. The *De literarum ludis* was reprinted six times in its own century; once in each of the two subsequent ones. The structure introduced in this treatise was reaffirmed by Sturm in 1567, after the Academy was established. See Fournier & Engel, *Les Statuts et Privilèges*, 2, no. 2040, pp. 109–14; and again in 1604 (see n. 16 above).

18. Sturm, *De literarum ludis*, p. 150: "Propositum a nobis est, Sapientum atq; eloquentem pietatem, fine esse studiorum."

19. Sturm, *De literarum ludis*, p. 185.

20. *Ibid.*, p. 174.

21. *Ibid.*, p. 175.

22. *Ibid.*, p. 179.

23. *Ibid.*, p. 181.

24. *Ibid.*, pp. 180–81.

25. *Ibid.*, p. 184.

26. *Ibid.*, p. 187.

27. *Ibid.*, pp. 194–95.

28. *Ibid.*, p. 133.

29. *Ibid.*, p. 148.

30. Sturm, *De amissa dicendi ratione* (Lyon: 1542), 1st ed., 1538. Six printings in the sixteenth century.

31. Sturm, *De literarum ludis*, p. 132.

32. *Ibid.*, p. 133.

33. Jean Rott, "Jean Sturm, Le Premier Recteur du Gymnase et de L'Académie de Strasbourg (1507–1589)," in *Strasbourg au Coeur Religieux du XVIe Siècle. Hommage à L. Fèbvre. Actes du Colloque Internationale* (Strasbourg: 1975), pp. 185–88, reminds us that Sturm's motto was a variation of Cicero's oratorical ideal, "vir bonus dicendi peritus."

34. James Kittelson, "Les Valeurs Non-Dogmatique et la Réforme Strasbourgeois: le cas de Wolfgang Capiton," in *Strasbourg au Coeur Religieux*, pp. 99–108, notes that Capito regarded humanist knowledge as one of the useful instruments a theologian might use but without any intrinsic merit.

35. Jean-Claude Margolin, "Otto Brunfels dans le Milieu Evangélique Rhénan" in *Strasbourg au Coeur Religieux*, pp. 111–41, associates Brunfels' pedagogy with that of Erasmus, Agricola, and Melanchthon, and all to the thought of Cicero and Quintilian, Seneca and Saint Jerome. His description of this liberal humanist pedagogue is a useful gauge by which we can better assess the work of Sturm and of the other pedagogic figures of the Renaissance.

36. Henri Strohl, "Théologie et Humanisme à Strasbourg au Moment de la Création de la Haute-École" in *Revue d'Histoire et de Philosophie Religieuse*, 17 (1937), pp. 435–56. Strohl associates Bucer and Sturm in the belief that

the ancients were divinely inspired and therefore the pagans were helpful in explaining religious truths.

37. Sturm, *De literarum ludis*, p. 177.

38. Fournier & Engel, *Les Statuts et Privilèges*, 2, no. 1980, *The Rules for the Gymnasium*, p. 25: "Das End volkummenes studirens ist die Religion Gottis und gottlicher Ding erkantnüss. Die Religion wird mit ler und wol red gezieret."

39. Pierre Mesnard, "La pietas litterata de Jean Sturm et le développement à Strasbourg d'une pédagogie oecumenique (1538–81)," in *Bulletin de la Société de l'Histoire du Protestantisme Français* (Jan.-Mar., 1965), pp. 281–302, says that Sturm's conception of what the study of classical literature could do for religion—"pietas litterata"—was the essential principle of the pedagogical Renaissance of the mid-sixteenth century (p. 298). That this was achieved by keeping religious education out of the curriculum was, he believes, a matter of policy for Sturm. While this is the perception of the present chapter, it throws no more light on the problem of how piety was in fact handled in the context of literary discussion and explication. The most obvious answer is that individual teachers handled these questions on an individual basis as they arose in the classroom. Such treatment is necessarily hard to substantiate.

40. Sturm, *De literarum ludis*, p. 150.

41. The Brethren generally contributed to the northern Renaissance classical revival and they tended to emphasize religion of the heart and minimize the importance of sacerdotal ritual. In this sense, Sturm and many other Renaissance figures were in agreement. Perhaps Sturm's irenicism owed something to their emphasis on brotherly love.

42. Sturm used many elements of Agricola's logic while teaching at Paris (1529–36). In 1539 he published his study on logic, *Partitionum dialecticarum libri duo.* This was printed twenty-four times during the sixteenth century, including five times in tabular form. These figures are not included in note 81 (below), which tallies only the pedagogical treatises. The book was of great influence in teaching logic, for which it was a standard textbook.

43. Sturm, *De literarum ludis*, p. 140.

44. For a discussion of the trends in rhetoric and in dialectic (logic) in this period see John Monfasani, "Humanism and Rhetoric," in *Renaissance Humanism*, ed. T. Rabil, vol. 3, pp. 171–235. He notes that Melanchthon, along with Agricola, Erasmus, and Sturm's former pupil Peter Ramus, were waging a "counter-revolution" in humanist rhetoric which involved giving over to logic some of the tasks which classical authors reserved for rhetoric. Hence, he points out that Melanchthon soon transferred the loci to dialectics (p. 201). He names Sturm as "the most important classicizing authority on rhetoric in northern Europe in the sixteenth century" (p. 203), and points out that Sturm "covered all five of the classical parts of rhetoric in his *Partitiones oratoriae* and "reasserted the full classical range of rhetoric" (p. 204). Monfasani says the Jesuits were more successful in their classical

rhetorical approach than Sturm was because Sturm was obliged to compete with a number of more "pragmatic" rhetoricians, among whom Melanchthon and Ramus are numbered (p. 205).

45. William Melczer, "La Pensée Éducative de Jean Sturm dans les *Classicae Epistolae*," in *La Réforme et l'Éducation*, ed. Jean Boisset, (Toulouse: Édouard Privat, 1974), pp. 125–41. He credits Sturm with developing an innovative theory of memorization; notes his concern that memory not be wasted on unprofitable material (pp. 135–37).

46. Walter Ong, S.J., *Ramus Method and the Decay of Dialogue* (Cambridge: Harvard University Press, 1958), pp. 232–34.

47. Melczer, "La Pensée Éducative," p. 130.

48. Some, but not all, of the schools, were in Germany, e.g., Lauingen, Hornbach, Hagenau, Schlettstadt, Meissen, Saverne, and the Jesuit academies at Molsheim and Messina (but for Jesuit schools see n. 49 below); in France, the Academy of Nîmes; in Switzerland, Calvin's school at Geneva; in Poland, the Catholic academy of Zamosc; the anti-Trinitarian academy at Chmielnik; plus a number of Calvinist schools and schools established by the Moravian Brethren.

49. Herman, S.J., *La Pédagogie des Jésuites au XVIe Siècle* (Paris: Picard, 1914), said, however, that many elements of Sturm's method were used at Paris where Loyola noted them with approval. Gabriel Codina Mir, *Aux Sources de la Pédagogie des Jésuites* (Rome: Institutum Historicum, S.I., 1968), pp. 218–33 *et passim* says the order was mainly influenced by the Brethren of the Common Life, especially their techniques used at Zwolle; that while Jesuit schools near Strasbourg were "tardily" and "minimally" influenced by Sturm, the differences between them were great.

50. Sturm, *Epistolae classicae*, Letter to the Scholarchs, (no. 2), in Jean Rott's annotated ed.: Jean Sturm, *Classicae epistolae sive Scholae Argentinenses Restitutae* (Paris: Droz, 1938) (1st ed. 1565). Twenty-four letters; French trans. to right of Latin original (p. 12). The *Epistolae* were printed four times in the sixteenth century; once in each of the two following.

51. Sturm, *De amissa dicendi ratione* (see n. 30 above).

52. Two early twentieth-century critics were F. Collard, "La Pédagogie de Sturm" in *Mélanges d'histoire offerts à Charles Moeller* (Louvain: Bureaux du Recueil, 1914) who termed Sturm's emphasis on Latin eloquence a "rêve chimérique" (p. 159); and Preserved Smith, *The Age of Reformation* (New York: Holt, 1920), who thought Sturm's program amounted to nothing but Latin and Greek, with a bit of arithmetic and astronomy (p. 667). Such negative views were already apparent in Schmidt's *La Vie et les Travaux de Jean Sturm*, chap. 3, p. 239. Schmidt felt modern subjects had been sacrificed to the art of "bien parler."

53. *Ad Werteros fratres, Nobilitas literata*; printed five times in Sturm's century; four in the next; once in the eighteenth.

54. *Ibid.*, p. 40. The edition used is that printed by Wendel Rihel at Strasbourg, 1549.

55. Sturm's *De educatione principis* (1551) appeared in the first edition (used here) with Conrad Heresbach's *De laudibus graecarum literarum oratio* and with Sturm's correspondence with Roger Ascham, *De nobilitate anglicana* (1551). It was printed five times in the sixteenth century; twice in the seventeenth, and once in the eighteenth century.

56. Heresbach (1496–1576) was responsible for editing Herodotus and Thucydides. Tutor to Prince William, Sturm praised him highly in the *De educatione principis* (p. 385).

57. Sturm, *De educatione principis*, pp. 383–84.

58. *Ibid.*, p. 382.

59. *Ibid.*, p. 383.

60. *Ibid.*, pp. 376–78.

61. *Ibid.*, p. 376.

62. *De nobilitate anglicana* included the first letter of Ascham to Sturm (April 4, 1550) and Sturm's reply (Sept. 9, 1550). See Lawrence V. Ryan, *Roger Ascham* (Stanford: Stanford University Press, 1963), pp. 116–18, for a description of Ascham's letter. This exchange appeared with the *De educatione principis* (see n. 55 above) and with Ascham's *Familiarium epistolarum libri tres* five more times in the sixteenth century—ten in all; three in the seventeenth and twice in the eighteenth.

63. *De nobilitate anglicana*, (above ed. of 1551; see n. 55 above), p. 47.

64. *Ibid.*, p. 42.

65. *Ibid.*, p. 48.

66. Sturm, *Scholae Lavinganae* (1565). Printed three times in the sixteenth century and once in extracts (in 1585); once in the eighteenth century.

67. H. de Chelminska, "Sturm et la Pologne," in *L'Humanisme en Alsace* (Paris: Soc. d'Édition Les Belles Lettres, 1939), pp. 52–63. The Strasbourg school drew many Poles. Sturm, patron of Calvinists, was influential in Polish circles. Jan Zamoyski (1542–1605), the statesman and humanist, founded an academy on Sturmian principles in his native land. The Hornbach school in Germany adopted the Lauingen plan in 1573, replacing an earlier (also Sturmian) model prescribed for it by Dr. Marbach (Schindling, pp. 40–41).

68. Sturm, *Classicae epistolae, sive Scholae Argentinenses restitutae*, 1565. (See n. 50 above).

69. Sturm, *Classicae epistolae*, Letter to the Scholarchs, (no. 2), p. 20.

70. *Ibid.*

71. *Ibid.*, pp. 28 and 30, Letter to Heinrich Schirner, second year teacher, (no. 4).

72. *Ibid.*, Letter to Dr. Johann Marbach, (no. 13), pp. 78–79.

73. *Ibid.*, Letter to Abraham Feis, first year teacher, (no. 3), p. 22.

74. *Ibid.*

75. *Ibid.*, Letter to Theobald Lingelsheim, (no. 6), pp. 40, 42, 44. With regard to David Chytraeus's catechism, see Rott, *Jean Sturm, Classicae epistolae*, p. 44, n. 5. He says that by 1564 Marbach had used this as a replacement for Bucer's less orthodox catechism (in the six upper grades). But see also Theodore R. Jungkuntz, *Formulators of the Formula of Concord* (St. Louis:

Concordia, 1977), p. 84, whose treatment of Chytraeus suggests that he was far from being a rigid Lutheran himself, and was, like Sturm, accused of flirting with Calvinists. It is not certain from this letter that Sturm objected to Chytraeus's orthodoxy. It appears rather that he did not want the boys to waste time on catechetical learning.

76. *Ibid.*, Letter to Conrad Dasypodius, Mathematician, (no. 17), p. 94.

77. *Ibid.*, Letter to Elie Kyber, Teacher of Hebrew, (no. 21), p. 116.

78. Fournier & Engel, *Les Statuts et Privilèges*, 4, no. 2032, pp. 89–97. The document terms the method "leichten und wolverstendigen" and its classical grammar instruction "das fundament der andern obern freyen Kunsten."

79. *Ibid.*, no. 2033, pp. 97–98. "also das unser ludus vor vilen andern (doch ohn ruhm zuschreiben) wol instituiert oder angeordnet ist."

80. *Ibid.*, 2035, pp. 98–100. "quod superioribus annis ex schola ipsorum multi praeclari et celebres virl in omni genere doctrinae tamquam ex equo Troiano prodierunt, qui nunc in aulis magnorum principum et in insignibus rebus publicis clarent et quasi ad gubernacula sedent...."

81. *Academicae epistolae urbanae* (1569), thirteen letters. Printed twice in the sixteenth, and once in each of the next two centuries. The total number of printings of all of the eight pedagogical treatises discussed in this chapter are as follows: 42 separate appearances in the sixteenth century; 14 in the seventeenth century. The eighteenth century had only 1 printing of all these works, with the exception of the treatise *De amissa dicendi*, which was left out of an edition entitled *De institutione scholastica opuscula omnia* (Jena: Hallbauer, 1730).

82. *Academicae epistolae urbane*, Letter to the Scholarchs, (no. 2), p. 710, (Gütersloh: Vormbaum, 1860).

83. *Ibid.*

84. *Ibid.*, Letter to Lawrence Tupplus, (no. 4), p. 712.

85. *Ibid.*, Letter to Michael Beuther, (no. 5), p. 713.

86. *Ibid.*, Letter to Conrad Dasypodius, (no. 6), p. 714.

87. *Ibid.*, Letter (the second) to Conrad Dasypodius, (no. 7), p. 715.

88. *Ibid.*, Letter to Valentine Eurythraeus, Rhetorician, (no. 9), p. 719.

89. The late seventeenth-century era of German university life and studies was described as "that melancholy period" when Latin was learned, but used mostly in a theological context with commentaries from a post-classical age, and when Greek was studied scarcely at all, or at most, with regard only to the New Testament. This period was followed by a genuine classical revival. See Frederick A. Lange, *The History of Materialism* (London: Routledge & Kegan Paul, 1950) (1st ed., 1865), pp. 143–45, in chapter "The German Re-Action."

90. Sturm, *Classicae epistolae*, Letter to the Scholarchs, (no. 2), March 1565, observed on the matter of the school's founding: that the school was the Strasbourg senate's foundation, but that he had been its first organizer and form giver: "non constituti (nam sua sponte eo Senatus properabat), sed hac ratione instituti, (ut) quod bene a me institutum esset, perficerem si quid mihi deesse videretur."

91. Lange, *History of Materialism*, pp. 143–44, n. 106, pointed out that the classical revival was put into motion in the early eighteenth century by men
trained in the "traditions of Sturm, e.g., the zeal in the imitation of Cicero
at this period must not be regarded as mere traditional veneration of Latin,
but as a newly awakening sense of elegance and beauty in language."

The Correct Opening of
Elementary Schools of Letters
(pages 69–118)

1. We have translated *ars differendi* as the art of divisions here and on pages
   172 and 185 of the Latin (where the phrases are *ratio differendi*) since it
   appears to be the equivalent of Cicero's *Partitio and divisio* in the
   Herrenian treatise Sturm uses so much. Both ancient rhetoricians and
   philosophers used the term to indicate a method of making distinctions or
   a method of classification.
2. Plato uses the phrase χωλὸς φιλοπονίᾳ in the Rep. 534 d.1 "lame in attentiveness."
3. Sturm uses the word *gymnasium*.
4. *Protagoras* 230.d.4.
5. *Cyropaedia* I.2.3.
6. It is Homer in Book 13, line 237 of the *Iliad* who uses the phrase for which
   Sturm gives at first only the Greek, but then translates into Latin as
   "coniunctae vires" which I in turn have translated as "united effort."
   Poseidon uses the phrase in a speech in which he says that even poor
   soldiers in a united group have prowess.
7. *Phaedrus* 230.d.4.
8. *Gymnasia* in the Latin of Sturm.
9. Again Sturm uses *gymnasium* as well as in the next sentence.
10. Sturm uses the Latin phrase *sapientiae et linguae studia*.
11. *The Republic* 537a.
12. Sturm uses the Latin word *curriculum*.
13. Sturm uses the Latin phrase *grammatices partitio*.
14. Sturm uses the adjective *liberalis*.
15. Sturm uses the Latin phrase *ratio resolvendi* and in the chapter on *The
    Analysis of Orators* discusses the *loci* or topics (*topoi*) which serve as
    "headings" for memory storage.
16. Cf. *spero hercle ego quoque* (*Heau. 553*); *ego dicam tibi* (*Ad. 646*).
17. *De Or.* 2.154.
18. Sturm uses the phrase *inventionis ratio; inventio* is the substance of
    speech, the first of the five parts of Rhetoric: invention, arrangement, style,
    memory, and delivery.
19. *Partitiones Oratoriae*.
20. Of the *Rhetorica ad Herennium*.

21. Sturm uses the Latin phrase *De Resolutiones Oratorium*; see note 18 of this treatise.
22. *loci verborum... rerum... artis*, which he proceeds to explain in detail.
23. "Someone cultivates something" and "someone cultivates friendship" are the natural ways to understand what in Latin are ambiguous constructions, because *aliquid* and *amicitiam* by virtue of their class would not naturally be the subjects of the verb *colere*.
24. The number of categories enumerated by Aristotle varies in several passages, but include substance, quality, place, activity/passivity, relation, quantity, time, position, and state.
25. Sturm uses the Latin word *particulae* which seems to be the equivalent of Greek μέρη.
26. Earth, Air, Fire, Water.
27. Sturm uses the phrase *De Ratione commentandi*. *Commentatio* seems to be a technical term for the exercise in speech-making described below.
28. *Commentatio.*
29. *differendi ratio*, see note 18.
30. *status* = στάσις = basic issue (in Hermogenes' Περὶ Στασέων edited by H. Rabe, 1913, Leipzig).
31. Cicero in *De Oratore* I.153 uses the expression as though it means "to stop rowing," but later in his letter to Atticus 13.21.3 (= Shackleton-Bailey p. 351) acknowledges that he has just learned its true meaning.
32. Cicero in his letter *Ad Fam* 16.17 (= Shackleton-Bailey p. 186) objects to the inappropriateness of using the Latin *fideliter* as the adverb modifying the phrase *inservire valetudini* which his secretary Tiro has apparently used when something like *diligenter* (conscientiously) would be the apt adverb.
33. This is the speech *On the Crown* (*De Corona*) already referred to, where Demosthenes defends his career against Aeschines by speaking on behalf of Ctesiphon's bill to award Demosthenes the honor of a golden crown.
34. Sturm here uses the term *ars* which covers a variety of subjects as well as what the modern mind considers arts.
35. Though he uses the title "De Naturalium Rerum Auscultatione," Sturm probably is referring to the treatise "De Mirabilis Auscultationibus" (Περὶ Θαυμασίων Ἀκουσμάτων) on phenomena chiefly connected with natural history. It is generally not considered part of the Aristotelian corpus now.
36. *ratio differendi*, see note 18.
37. *ratio differendi* is also used here, see note 18.
38. Probably his treatise Περὶ ἰδεῶν.
39. Sturm's phrase in Latin is *differendi dicendique scientiae*, see note 18.

Liberally Educated Nobility,
for the Werter Brothers
(pages 133–73)

1. *differendi et dicendi ratio.*
2. *Odyssey* Book I lines 1&3: Ἄνδρα μοι ἔννεττε, Μοῦσα, πολύτροπον, ὅς μάλα πολλὰ πολλῶν ἀνθρώπων ἴδεν ἄστεα καὶ νόον ἔγνω,
3. *civilis scientia quam Graeci* politicen *nominant.*
4. *doctrina civilis.*
5. Cicero's speech for Milo is often considered Cicero's masterwork as an oration. We do not have it as delivered in court (Cicero's usual eloquence failed in the face of Pompey's soldiers who filled the courtroom) but as published after Milo's condemnation.
6. Probably Sturm means Dionysus of Halicarnassus (1st century B.C.) best known for his *Antiquitates Romanae.*
7. Sturm uses the terms *audiendi, legendi, commentandi.*
8. Shackleton-Bailey *Ad Att* #12.4 (=I.12): *Nam puer festivus, angagnostes noster Sositheus. decessart...* (Greek *anagnostes* ἀναγνώστης = Latin *lector.*
9. Herodian of Syria wrote a history in eight books of the emperors from Marcus Aurelius to Gordian III (A.D. 180–238).
10. After the digression on the choice of a teacher, Sturm resumes his discussion of what system is to be followed below.
11. Sturm uses the words *viros bonos* which in Cicero refers to the *nobiles.*
12. Sturm changes from "we" to the 2nd. person singular "you" as though talking to the two brothers as one.
13. Now usually called the *Memorabilia,* a less accurate translation of the Greek title than *Commentaria* which Sturm uses.
14. Sturm's Latin for the last phrase reads: ...*semper exploratrices dialecticae regulae sunt applicandae.*
15. The three discourses are the three books of Cicero's *De Oratore.* Triarius is an auditor in Cicero's *De Finibus Bonorum et Malorum* (*On the Limits of Good and Evil*).
16. Sturm writes "*inquit ille*" but seems to recall a common proverbial saying. Cf. Terence *Phormio* line 454: *Quot homines tot sententiae* (As many opinions as men); also Horace, Sat.2.1.27/28. *quot capitum vivunt totidem studiosum milia* (As many thousands of interests as living souls).
17. Cicero, *Pro Roscia.* (In defense of Roscia).
18. Sturm uses the Latin word *locus,* "place" or "passage" representing the Greek τόπος, "place" or "topic."
19. *animadversio.*
20. *comparatio.*

21. Sturm uses the Latin *membrum* which is the usual translation of the Greek κῶλον, in rhetoric, the part or phrase of a period.

22. Cicero *De Oratore* 2.63.

23. These lines (84–86) from Lucilius are quoted in Cicero's *De Oratore* 3.171.

24. Apparently one of the syllables does not count—perhaps the "i" of *gratia* with the "tia" being pronounced as one syllable, or perhaps the "a" of *gratia* was elided before *et*.

25. Vergil *Eclogue I*, lines 1–5.

26. Sturm uses the Latin transliteration of the Greek word *antistrophe*.

27. In the first four and one half lines of the *Georgics*, Vergil summarizes the contents of the poem by explaining the topics he will take up.

28. Vergil's first seven lines of the *Aeneid* form a period ending with the emphatic word "Rome."

29. line 13 of *Eclogue I*.

30. *a/g anc / eti*: elision of the final vowel "o" of *ago* before initial vowel "a" ("h" does not count as a consonant) of *hanc*.

31. The Greek and Latin meter which depends on syllable length and not stress was ill-understood at this early time.

32. Antonius, frequently mentioned by Sturm is Marcus Antonius, praetor in 102 B.C. who figures in Cicero's *Brutus* and *De Oratore* as a fine orator. He is the grandfather of the triumvir, Mark Antony.

33. Cicero's six books *De Republica* were known to Augustine, Lactantius, and others but were later lost (except for the *Dream of Scipio*, part of the 6th book) until large fragments were recovered in 1819 in a palimpsest.

34. Cicero, *De Oratore*, 2.64...*fusum etque tactum et cum levitate quadam aequabiliter profluens sine hac iudiciali asperitate et sine sententiarum forensibus aculeis*...(diffuse and drawn out and with a kind of lightness, evenly flowing forth without the harshness of courts and the forensic barbs of sentences...) We hope Sturm's *imitatio* was not missed by his students.

35. *Inst.* I.5.56 and VIII.1.3.

36. The text has "*immutationis*" but is here translated as if a misprint for "*imitationis*."

37. Horace, *Epistle* II (*Ars poetica*) lines 38–40. The standard text of Horace reads *Sumite...vestris...scribitis* (O you who write, take a subject equal to your strengths...).

38. Sturm wrote *modi*, a translation of Greek τρόποι = tropes.

39. More usually in Greek rhetorical writings it is μιμητικόν.

40. Horace *Carmina* 4.2.1–4; in line 2 the standard text reads *Iulle*, name of the mythical ancestor of the Julian *gens*.

41. Horace *Carmina* 4.2.5–8.

42. Horace *Carmina* 4.2.27–32; the standard text in line 32 reads *Carmina fingo* (I fashion poems).

43. The Julius Antonius to whom the 2nd ode of book 4 is addressed is the son of the triumvir, Mark Antony. He was a writer of both prose and poetry.

44. Cicero *Brutus* I.1: ...*cum de...morte esset allatum opinione omnium maiorem animo cepi dolorem.* (...when the report was brought about the death... I conceived a sorrow of mind deeper than anyone supposed.)
45. This translation reads *satietatem* in place of what the text has: *varietatem*.
46. Sturm writes: *est verborum & rerum vicaria operatio* (substitute action...).
47. *Eclogue* I, lines 1–5.
48. *Eclogue* I, lines 6–8.
49. *Idyll* I.4–6.
50. *Eclogue* I, line 11.
51. *Idyll* I.62; the standard text reads κοὔτι τυ κερτομέω (I do not mock you). Some mss. do have the reading Sturm gives.
52. αἰπόλις, transliterated *aepolis* in Latin means "goatherd." In the idyll of Theocritus the goatherd is not named.
53. In line 1–3 of Theocritus' first *Idyll* the text is Ἁδύ τι τὸ ψιθύρισμα καὶ ἁ πίτυς, αἰπόλε, τήνα / ἁ ποτὶ ταῖς πι, μελίσδεται, ἁδὺ δὲ καὶ τὺ / σύριδες· (Sweet is the whispered music of that pinetree by the springs, O goatherd, and sweet too your pipings.)
54. Sturm's text reads *Troiae* while the standard text of Vergil reads *Romae*.
55. Quintilian *Inst* 4.2.45 & 10.1.32 ...*illa Sallustiana brevitas qua nihil...potest esse perfectius...* (that famous brevity of Sallust than which nothing can be more perfect...).
56. The text has *velle-*; we read *vel*.
57. *Rhet.*1408 a 10–11.
58. *Ody.* 16.273.
59. *Ody.* 6.230: μείζονα τ᾽ εἰσιδέειν καὶ πάσσονα, κὰδ δὲ κάρητος....
60. *Ody.*8.20: καὶ μιν μακρότερον καὶ πάσσονα θῆκεν ἰδέσθαι, (and she made him taller and mightier to see...). Sturm's quote combines 6.230 and 8.20.
61. *Ody.* 6.230 & 231. See note 59.
62. Cardinal Jean du Bellay (1492-1560) corresponded with Sturm in 1545; Cardinal de Guise was Charles de Lorraine, with whom Sturm had an extended correspondence over his French pension and other matters; Julius Pflug (1499-1564), Catholic bishop of Naumburg-Zeitz 1541, wanted peace with the Protestants and helped draft the Augsburg and Leipzig interims; Christoph von Carlowitz (1507-1578), Saxon Chancellor, an Erasmian.

On the Education of Princes
(pages 175–85)

1. Plato was not a commoner. He was a descendent of Codrus, 17th and last king of Athens and a member of an illustrious and noble family.
2. The great work on classical education is Werner Jaeger, *Paedeia: Die Formung des grieschischen Menschen*, 2nd ed. (Berlin: Walter de Gruyter,

1934); English trans. by Gilbert Highet, *Paideia*, 3 vols. (Oxford University Press, 1943–1945).

3. Minerva, Roman goddess of wisdom and the counterpart of Athena. In the *Odyssey* of Homer, inspiration for Sophocles' play, it was certainly Athena who advised Ulysses to disguise himself as a beggar upon entering his home in Ithaca. His diligence or cunning is contrasted to the laziness and stupidity of Penelope's suitors there, and since Athena represented wisdom, she would naturally appreciate diligence. The use by Sturm of the name Minerva rather than Athena is hard to explain, except that he was more steeped in Latin than in Greek literature.

4. Erucius of Cyzius (fl. 40 B.C.) was a Greek with a Roman name, author of epigrams. He was very likely a slave. Curtius Rufus Quintus was a Roman historian (fl. A.D. 41–54) whose ten-volume history of Alexander the Great was based on that of the late 4th century Clitarchus. Curtius' history held little insight and was instead a series of romantic adventures. Mamercus (d. 340 B.C.) was a tyrant of Catana who surrendered to Timoleon. His attempts to speak in public at Syracuse were received with hisses, upon which he dashed his head against a wall. Upon recovering, he was put to death as a robber.

5. Marcius was the eponymous author of a number of oracular sayings current in early Rome. Cicero thought them the work of several nobly born brothers but Livy disagreed, and said that only one *vates* (poet/prophet)—Marcius—was responsible for them. Zoilus (fl. B.C. 259) was a sophist and grammarian of Amphipolis. He was a ferocious critic of the works of Plato and poems of Homer, for which he was named Homeromastic, or, chastiser of Homer. He presented his criticisms to Ptolemy Philadelphus, who indignantly rejected them. Some say he was stoned to death or exposed on a cross by Ptolemy's orders; others that he was burnt alive at Smyrna.

6. Asellio, Gaius Sempronius, was a military tribune in Spain under P. Scipio Africanus in B.C. 133. He wrote a history of Rome from the Punic wars to his own era. He was probably not a Senator.

7. Thersites and Glaucius King of the Illyrian folk called Taulantians. He fought against Alexander the Great in 335 B.C. He opposed Cassander. In 316 he offered refuge to a tot named Pyrrhus, a descendant of Achilles, raised him tenderly and set him on the throne of Epirus when the child was about twelve.

8. Cornelius Scipio Aemilianus Africanus Minor,(185 B.C.), younger son of L. Aemelianus Paulus, the conqueror of Macedonia, was adopted by P. Scipio, son of Hannibal's conqueror. He devoted himself to the study of literature and may have assisted Terence in the composition of his comedies. His friendship with Laelius was immortalized in Cicero's treatise "Laelius sive de Amicitia." Laelius Gaius was Scipio's *legatus* in the decisive assault on Carthage in 146 B.C. He was *praetor* in Spain and in 132 B.C. helped the consuls in their persecution of the Gracchans. He was regarded as one of the ablest orators.

9. Numa Pompilius was a Sabine philosopher invited by the Romans to succeed Romulus, their founder. He was noted for his piety—he taught the Romans not to worship the Deity by images; established the college of the vestal virgins; and relied on a nymph named Egeria to sanction and inspire the laws he introduced. Ovid claimed Numa married her. Numa was admired for his humanity and moderation. He was supposed to have reigned 43 years, and died in 672 B.C.

10. Nestor was a grandson of Neptune and king of Pylos. He was a distinguished general and led his subjects to the Trojan War where he distinguished himself by eloquence, wisdom, and justice. Homer gives him the most perfect character of all his heroes. He was supposed to have lived three generous lifetimes—for a total of about 300 years. When the Greeks and Latins wished a long and happy life to their friends, they wished them to reach the age of Nestor.

11. Flora was an ancient goddess of flowers and gardens and was worshipped by Sabines and Phoeceans before Rome was founded in the eighth century B.C. Robigus was a goddess of Rome worshipped particularly by farmers, as she presided over corn, which she protected from blight. Lympha was a nymph of the woodland springs and of Greek origin. Bonus Eventus was a Roman god whose worship was first introduced by peasants. He was represented holding a cup in his right hand and corn in his left.

12. Marcus Terentius Varro of Reate, in Sabine country, was a pupil of the first Roman philologist and had studied at Athens with Antiochus of Ascalon. A praetor and partisan of Pompey's in Spain, he was later made keeper of the public library in 47 B.C. by Caesar. He was outlawed by Antony in 43 and suffered the loss of his libraries during the civil war then raging. By his 78th year he had edited 490 books. Only two of these have survived—his *Rerum rusticarum libri III* and his *De lingua latina*.

13. Ajax was son of Telamon, king of Salamis. In Homer's *Iliad* he is a great hero, who rescued the body of Achilles from the Trojans with the help of the goddess Athena, and then fought Odysseus for Achilles' armor, and lost. In the *Iliad* he fought a flock of sheep (not cows) while temporarily maddened by his loss to Odysseus. Finally, he slew himself from disappointment. Sturm clearly states *boves*—but sheep are not *boves* but *oves* in Latin.

14. The stepson of Aloeus. Ephialtes and his twin brother, Otho, were sons of Neptune.

15 Sturm ought to have referred to them by their Greek nomenclature (Poseidon and Athena), since he speaks here of Athens. He definitely preferred the Roman names for Greek gods.

16. The reference to couches in the Latin is *pulvinaria*, or couches with cushions set out in the street on which were placed images of the gods at the Lectisternium, or feast offered to the gods (Livy). Feasts of the dead were continued in the Christian era in memory of a deceased person, or at the consecration of a chapel dedicated to him.

17. It is hard to square this tolerant statement with the fact that Sturm sent a letter to Calvin after the execution of Servetus assuring him that he had done the right thing in supporting that execution.
18. Lictors were the public attendants and principal Roman magistrates who carried before them the *fasces*, an emblem of their criminal jurisdiction, and executed the sentence they pronounced.

Concerning the English Nobility
(pages 187–98)

1. *De oratorum conversionibus* appears to be a rhetorical treatise on the periodic sentences in oratory. The term *conversiones* (Gk. *periodoi*) is used by Cicero in his *De Oratore* 3.48.186 and 49.190.
2. Epistle 1.18.77: ...*ne mox/ incutiant aliena tibi peccata pudorem*... so that the faults of others may not soon strike shame into you....
3. *De Anima*.
4. Their orations *On the Crown*.
5. *sententiam*.
6. *verborum vim atque potestatem*.
7. *inventionem*.
8. Of Plato.
9. By *illos* Sturm appears to mean the authors he does teach, e.g. Cicero, Demosthenes.
10. The last part of the sentence ...*quibus sordida puris, utilibus spinosa fuerunt potiora* is difficult.
11. The image of Pallas Athena in Troy.
12. Sturm uses the noun *conspiratio* which means both "harmony" and "conspiracy."
13. *tempore ordineque*.
14. *temporis et linguae*.
15. *ut tecum ludum rhetoricos*.

For the Lauingen School
(pages 199–254)

1. Actaeon was a huntsman who saw Diana and her attendant bathing, for which he was changed into a stag and devoured by his own dogs.
2. Daedalus was an inventive genius, native of Athens, who escaped from prison with his son, Icarus, on wings made of wax and feathers. Icarus's wings melted when he flew too close to the sun. Sturm means to point out that incomplete knowledge is dangerous, as in the old saw, "A little knowledge is a dangerous thing."

3. Presumably, Sturm refers to variations in Latin pronunciation from one region to another. These were not infrequently considered perfectly standard by those from the region.
4. Proverb attributed to or perhaps just repeated by Cicero *Magnum vectigal est Parsimonia*, proverb used also by Cicero, Par. 6,3,49.
5. Cilicia—a region in Asia Minor.
6. *Verres* was a governor of Sicily who was accused of malfeasance. Cicero undertook the defense of the Sicilian people in a work entitled *Accusatio*. However, there is one other person it might be referring to, namely *Verrius Flacus*, a grammarian under Augustus and Tiberius. This man was tutor to Augustus's children.
7. Aristarchus. Famous grammarian of Samos, who spent most of his life at Alexandria, where he was tutor to the sons of Ptolemy Philometer. He wrote over 800 commentaries on different authors before his death in 157 B.C.
8. Cornelii—a Roman tribe whose most famous members included P. Cornelius Scipio Africanus (the older and younger as well), and Cornelia, wife of Tiberius Semproneus Graechus, mother of the Gracchi. Sempronian Law—a land distribution act passed in 133 B.C. under the sponsorship of Tiberius Gracchus, the Tribune, elder of the Gracchi. It was popular with the poor, but Sturm disapproves.
9. Prudentius Aurelius Clemens, a Latin poet of Spain who flourished during the latter part of the fourth century A.D. His poems were devoid of elegance and purity of style, but greatly valued for their theological content.
10. Aeschines—a rival of the more famous orator, Demosthenes. He was banished from Athens to Rhodes and died there (or at Samos) around 314 B.C. Isocrates—this orator was a pupil of Socrates and was a notable student of history. He committed suicide in 338 B.C. (so tradition has it) because he regretted Phillip II of Macedon's victory over Greece at Chaeronia.
11. *Publius Terentius Afer*, born c.185 or 195 B.C., died 159 B.C. Born in Carthage, he was a slave to the Roman senator Terentius Lucanus, who brought him to Rome and eventually freed him. Writer of comedies.
12. aediles—Officials in Rome who exercised authority over the streets, traffic, markets, public games, and last but not least, over theatres.
13. Juvenalis Decimus Junius (d. 128 A.D.), poet and satirist. In his 80th year he incurred the displeasure of Domitian, who sent him off to serve as governor of the Egyptian frontier. Having survived this exile, Juvenal returned to Rome, where he died in Trajan's reign.
14. Codrus was a poet in the reign of Domitian whose poverty became proverbial. Juvenal (3, v. 203) refers to the *Thesiad* of Cordus, whom Sturm mistook for Codrus.
15. Herennius Caius, perhaps, a man to whom Cicero dedicated his *De Rhetorica*; or, possibly a Phoenician called Herennius Philo, who wrote a book on the reign of Hadrian and composed a treatise concerning the choice of books. The *Rhetorica ad Herrenium* was not by Cicero, as Sturm

believed, though it was Ciceronian. Classicists from Joseph Scaliger (1540–1609) into modern times have been aware of this mistaken attribution.

16. Hubert Hettwer, *Herkunft und Zusammenhang der Schulordnungen* (Mainz: V. Hase & Koehler Verlag, 1965), compares the educational laws of various parts of Germany such as the Saxonies, Brunswick, Württemberg, Hesse, Weimar, Gotha, Waldeck, and other states. Pages 91–105 discuss Sturm and Strasbourg, the influence of Sturm on the Lauingen School, and on the Württemberg *Schulordnung* of 1559.

Academic Letters
(pages 309–39)

1. σαύτε δύ ᾧ ἐρχομένω is probably meant to be σύντε δύ ᾧ ἐρχομένω from the *Iliad* 10.224 of Homer where Diomedes, in response to Nestor, wants a companion for his mission.
2. Neither the man nor the quotation is identified.
3. Sturm is referring to the original significance of the term *universitas.*
4. Horace, in his poetic letter (I.6.67/68) on the Pythagorean precept "wonder at nothing" (*Nil admirari*) writes these two closing lines which Sturm recalls: May you live! Farewell! If you know anything more correct than these precepts, share your thoughts with me frankly. If nothing, practice these along with me." (*Vive. Vale. Si quid novisti rectius istis,/ candidus imperti; si nil, his utere mecum.*)
5. Sturm translates the Greek αἰτήματα into Latin *aetemata,* translated "postulates."
6. The Tractatus de Sphaera by Johannes de Sacro Bosco (John Hollywood) was first published in Ferrara in 1472. Proclus (d. A.D. 485) was a Greek Neoplatonic philosopher whose works include commentaries on mathematical writers.
7. The text incorrectly lists his last name as Statius.
8. *Ars Poetica* (*Epist.* 2.3.335–337).
9. NT John 3.10.
10. Mars' name is used in Latin for "Martial strength" or "prowess" as early as Ennius so that it is a Latin or Roman commonplace.
11. With these last two titles, Sturm is probably referring to Cicero's rhetorical treatises now known as *Orator* which was written in the latter part of 46 B.C. ostensibly to answer a request for a description of the perfect orator and the *Brutus,* written in the first part of 46 B.C., an historical survey of Roman orators, both major and minor.
12. From *Pro T. Annio Milo* 3.7. The whole sentence reads "They deny that it is right for a man to see the light of day who has confessed that a man has been killed by him."
13. From *Pro T. Annio Milo* 3.7 where the whole sentence is "In what city, pray, do the most stupid men make this argument?"

14. Cicero gives six examples, as precedent: M. Horatius, P. Africanus, Servilius Ahala, P. Nasica, L. Opimius, C. Marius (3.7–8).
15. *Pro T. Annio Milo* 4.9. The whole sentence reads "And if there is any occasion for killing a man justly—and there are many—certainly this is not only just, but also necessary: when aggressive force is defended by force."
16. Cicero, *Pro T. Annio Milo* 4.9–10, tells the story of the young soldier who killed a military tribune who had attempted to rape him. Though the tribune was a relative of the general Marius, Marius absolved the young soldier of his crime.
17. *Pro T. Annio Milo* 4.10. The whole sentence reads: "For the man lying in ambush and for the highway robber, what death can be brought that is unjust?"
18. *Pro T. Annio Milo* 4.10.
19. Cicero (*Pro T. Annio Milo* 4.10–11) gives a short excursus on homicide in self-defense.
20. *Pro T. Annio Milone* 4.11.
21. Sturm is alluding, probably, to Horace's first letter to his patron Maecenas, lines 9 and 10.
22. Sturm refers to the logical term ≤ εἰς τὸ ἀδύνατο ἀπαγωγή = *reductio per impossibile*.
23. The Roman muses.

Bibliographical Essay:
Johann Sturm Perceived
(pages 341–63)

1. In Ascham's famous treatise on education he referred to "Johannes Sturmius" as "the dearest friend I have out of England" and he acknowledged his intellectual indebtedness to him. See *The Schoolmaster (1570) by Roger Ascham*, Lawrence V. Ryan, ed. Charlottesville: University Press of Virginia, 1967, p. 118. See also Friedrich A. Arnstadt's *Roger Ascham ein Englischer Pädagog des XVI. Jahrhunderts and seine geistliche Verwandtschaft mit Johannes Sturm* (Oster: F.E. Neupert, 1881), which contains a useful methodological résumé. And Jean Rott and Robert Faerber, "Un Anglais à Strasbourg au Milieu du XVIe Siècle: John Hales, Roger Ascham et Jean Sturm," in *Études Anglaises*, n. 4 (1968), pp. 381–94, which relates the enthusiasm of the Cambridge circle of intellectuals for Sturm's scholarship on Aristotle and Cicero, revealing "la communion d'esprit et de coeur" between them. See the splendid volume edited by Georges Livet and Francis Rapp, *Histoire de Strasbourg des Origines à Nos Jours*, vol. 2, *Strasbourg des Grandes Invasions au XVIe Siècle* (Éditions des Dernières Nouvelles d'Alsace-Istra, 1981).

2. See Walter Ong, *Ramus Method and the Decay of Dialogue* (Cambridge: Harvard University Press, 1958). Discusses the intellectual indebtedness of Ramus to Sturm in some detail.

3. The many excellent studies of Strasbourg, Sturm and the academy by that great scholar and master of the Strasbourg archives, Jean Rott, have been published as *Investigationes: Églises et Société au XVIe Siècle. Gesammelte Aufsätze*, 2 vols. (Strasbourg: Librairie Oberlin, 1986). The splendid new edition of the works of Martin Bucer contains much information on Sturm and the whole Strasbourg context within which he labored. See J.V. Pollet, O.P., *Martin Bucer Études sur les Relations de Bucer avec les Pays-Bas, L'Élector de Cologne et L'Allemagne du Nord avec de nombreaux textes inédits*, I, *Études*, II, *Documents* (Leiden: E.J. Brill, 1985). See also Christian Krieger and Marc Lienhard, eds., *Martin Bucer and Sixteenth-Century Europe. Acts du Colloque de Strasbourg*, 28–31 Août 1991 (Leiden, New York, Cologne: E.J. Brill, 1993). It appears that only two of Sturm's 155 known works in 503 editions [figures from Jean Rott's *Bibliographie Des Oeuvres Imprimées du Recteur Strasbourgeois Jean Sturm 1507–1589*, in *Actes du 95eme Congrès Des Sociétés Savantes*, 1970 (*Philologie et Histoire*, vol. I), pp. 319–20] were translated into English. These were: *The Epistle that J. Sturmius... sent to the Cardynalles and Prelates*, R. Moysine, tr. T. Bertheleti, London, 1538; and *A Ritch Storehouse or Treasurie for Nobilitye and Gentlemen*, Tr. T. Browne, Henrie Denham, London, 1570. The former work was of no pedagogical interest. The second is the work *Joannis Sturmii Ad Werteros Fratres, Nobilitas literata*, 1549 (*To the Werter Brothers*), newly re-translated by the editors and included in this edition. Some letters of Roger Ascham to Sturm have been translated into English, *Letters of Roger Ascham*, translated by Maurice Hatch and Alvin Vos, edited by Alvin Vos (New York: Peter Lang, 1989), part five, Letters to Johann Sturm, pp. 156–223. See Pierre Fraenkel, "La Proposition chez Sturm et Lever," *Logique et Théologie au XVIe Siècle: aux sources de l'argumentation de Martin Bucer*, by I. Backus, P. Fraenkel, L. Giard, P. Lardet, W. Sparn (Geneva: Cahiers de la Revue de Théologie et de Philosophie, 5, 1980), pp. 41–52. Pierre Schang, director of the Chapter of St. Thomas, and Georges Livet, Scholarch of the Gymnasium, have published a beautiful volume, well illustrated and presenting the history, sources and documents of Sturm's Gymnasium, the Academy, and the University from the founding in 1538 to the year 1988, *Histoire du Gymnase Jean Sturm: Berceau de L'Université de Strasbourg 1538-1988* (Strasbourg: Éditions Oberlin, 1988).

4. Charles Schmidt, *La Vie et les Travaux de Jean Sturm* (Nieukoop: B. de Graaf, 1970) (reprint of the 1855 edition). Schmidt's work has been superseded by much recent scholarship. However, the first nineteenth-century work which included an extended reference to Sturm was Adam G. Strobel's *Histoire du Gymnase Protestant de Strasbourg*, (Strasbourg: Frederic Charles Heitz, 1838), the first of many subsequent commemorative writings on him (see note 17). Strobel's book emphasizes the similarities which prevailed amongst the reform-minded educators of Strasbourg

before Sturm and Sturm's own views. Such similarities included the conviction that sound morals must be combined with literary education, and that such education should have what we moderns call "transfer value," i.e. practical applications [see p. xxx]. Strobel's admiration for Sturm was unqualified. He believed the curriculum combined the necessary emphasis on classical tongues (the vulgar languages had made, he said, "si peu de progès en France et en Allemagne!" (pp. 14–15) and that the program offered an effective instruction which was as intellectual as it was moral. The sketch was more positive than the biography which followed Schmidt's in the subsequent generation. See also the late John D'Amico, *Roman and German Humanism 1450–1550* (Aldershot, Hants., England: Variorum, 1993), on Ulrich von Hutten, Beatus Rhenanus, and the development of textual criticism, to which Johann Sturm contributed a great deal. A recent book worth noting deals with Sturm on the education of princes, Bruno Singer, *Die Fürstenspiegel in Deutschland im Zeitalter des Humanismus und der Reformation* (Munich: Wilhelm Fink, 1980), pp. 271–86, on Johann Sturm's *De educatione principum*, 1551. The major work on pedagogy in early modern times remains that of Willy Moog, *Geschichte der Pädagogik*, vol. 2, *Die Pädagogik der Neuzeit von der Renaissance bis zum Ende des 17. Jahrhunderts*, 8th edition (Ratingen bei Düsseldorf: A. Henn Verlag, 1967). A book which sets this monograph into a much larger setting is that of Anthony Grafton and Lisa Jardine, *From Humanism to the Humanities. Education and the Liberal Arts in Fifteenth and Sixteenth-Century Europe* (Cambridge: Harvard University Press, 1986).

5. This was the expression Sturm used in 1565 in the *Classicae Epistolae* when attempting to explain why students had not made more satisfactory progress in Latin eloquence.

6. Schmidt, *La Vie*, p. 284. "au hasard des gouts ou des besoins individuels" was Schmidt's phrase.

7. Among them, F.V.N. Painter, *A History of Education* (New York: D. Appleton & Company, 1887); by F. Collard, "La Pédagogie de Sturm," in *Mélanges d'Histoire Offerts à Charles Moeller* (Paris: A. Picard et fils, 1914); and more recently, by Marc Lienhard and Jakob Willer, *Strassburg und Die Reformation* (Morstadt Verlag, 1981), the latter observing that the omission of German was a reflection of contemporary values: "Doch Sturms Programm entsprach den Erwartungen seiner Zeit. Vom Humanismus geprägt, hat er den klassischen Sprachen den Vorzug gegeben" (p. 64). Sturm himself did recommend the vernacular works of Petrarch, Boccaccio, Commines and was one of the first to recognize the linguistic significance of Luther's translation of the Bible, as Jean Rott has observed. See his Jean Sturm, *Classicae Epistolae Sive Scholae Argentinenses Restitutae*, Introd., (Paris: Librairie E. Droz, 1938), p. xvi. Rott notes also that on at least one occasion Sturm recommended the study of vulgar languages as well as of classical ones—in a preface to Albert d'Oelinger's grammar book. However, he did not include the vulgar authors in his curriculum. On the Reformation's impact on the lower classes, see Franziska Conrad, *Reformation in der bäuerlichen*

Gesellschaft: Zur Rezeption reformatorischer Theologie im Elsass (Stuttgart, 1984).

8. Critical, but providing insight into Sturm's concern for good discipline is Jean LeBeau's article "Jean Sturm, L'Alsace et l'Europe," in *Les Annales de l'Académie d'Alsace*, nouv. sér. n. 19, 1979. He terms the Strasbourg Gymnasium "un univers carcéral" whose austerity (like corporal punishment) was designed to combat "la barbarie multiforme" that Sturm felt characterized so much of his society (p. 8).

9. "Dryasdust" is the dictum of R.R. Bolgar on Sturm's emphasis on memorization and repetition: "endless spoken and written exercises." Although Bolgar concedes that Sturm himself was a popular teacher, he concludes his popularity was due to his dullness and that dull requirements made "an idiom suitable for everyday use which was within his pupils' power to learn." *The Classical Heritage and Its Beneficiaries* (Cambridge: The University Press, 1958), p. 351. More sympathetic is Pierre Mesnard, who while viewing memorization and imitation "un véritable conditionnement" says it was used for a good cause—to produce pious and good men; rather than the empty goal of mere Latin eloquence was the lofty one of obtaining men who could read Scripture correctly. "La Pédagogie de Jean Sturm et son Inspiration Évangélique (1507–1589)," in *XIIe Congrès International des Sciences Historiques. Rapport III* (Vienna: Verlag Ferd. Berger & Söhne, 1965), p. 96.

10. Sturm was not unaware of the dangerous aspects of unnecessary memorization. He warned Lingelsheim, a member of his faculty, that children should not be obliged to memorize what was not profitable to them. See William Melczer, "La Pensée Éducative de Jean Sturm dans *Les Classicae Epistolae*" in *La Réforme et l'Éducation,* Jean Boisset, Directeur (Toulouse: Edouard Privat, 1974), p. 128. Melczer believes Sturm held a dynamic view of the uses and function of memory.

11. Sturm was a great success in Paris (1529–1536) where he taught in the new Collège de France created by Francis I. His colleagues frequently deserted their own lectures so that they might attend his!

12. William Melczer finds Sturm's writings of great historical importance, offering a "véritable perspective Renaissance" (p. 139) and a "principe oecumenique" (p. 129) or desire to see his labor bear fruit in areas outside of Strasbourg. See "La Pensée Éducative de Jean Sturm dans Les Classicae Epistolae," in *La Réforme et l'Éducation*, Jean Boisset, Director (Toulouse: Edouard Privat, ed., 1974).

13. Mark Lienhard and Jakob Willer, *Strassburg und die Reformation* (Strasbourg: Mirstadt Verlag, 1981), note: "Sturms Einfluss auf das Europäische Bildungswesen seiner Zeit ist nicht zu unterschätzen" (p. 64). See also Lorne Jane Abray, *The People's Reformation* (Ithaca: Cornell University Press, 1985). On the Reformation in Strasbourg see René Bornert, *La réforme protestante du culte à Strasbourg au XVIe Siècle (1525–1598): approche sociologique et interprétation théologique* (Leiden: E.J. Brill, 1981). See also the monograph by William S. Stafford, *Domesticating the*

Clergy: The Inception of the Reformation in Strasbourg 1522–24 (Missoula, MT: Scholars Press, 1976).

14. Johannes Tauler (1300–1361), a Dominican monk in Strasbourg, was possibly a student of the mystic Meister Eckhart. Tauler believed that the love of God and the love of men are intimately associated. In this respect he does indeed seem a fitting precursor of the type of thought that was common to Sturm and to Schweitzer.

15. Johann Geiler von Kaisersberg (1445–1510). The "German Savonarola," Geiler was known for his forceful preaching style, and was given a special position preaching in the Cathedral of Strasbourg. He was reform-minded but not a dissident.

16. Robert Minder noted in attending the 425th anniversary of the founding of the Strasbourg Gymnasium (he had in 1913 attended the 375th!) that Sturm's teaching "a gardé sa vigeur et sa valeur jusque aux nos jours." "Un Foyer de Culture Humaniste le Gymnase Jean Sturm à Strasbourg," in *Saisons Alsace*, n. 10 (1964), p. 178.

17. Such occasions have produced a large proportion of the Sturm literature. The first commemorative item written on Sturm was Adam G. Strobel's *Histoire de Gymnase Protestant de Strasbourg*, published on the occasion of the 300th anniversary of the founding of the Gymnasium (F.C. Heitz, 1838). Strobel was a professor in the Gymnasium. The old classic work on education prior to Sturm's reforms is Joseph Knepper, *Das Schul- und Unterrichtswesen im Elsass von den Anfängen bis gegen das Jahr 1530* (Strassburg: J.H. Ed. Heitz, 1905). When the University of Strasbourg was re-organized by the German imperial government after the Franco-Prussian War had resulted in the transfer of Alsace to Germany, no fewer than three major works appeared on Sturm—ostensibly to re-associate his work in Strasbourg with German culture. These included L. Kückelhahn's *Johannes Sturm, Strassburgs erster Schulrector besonders in seiner Bedeutung für die Geschichte der Paedagogik* (Leipzig); Ernst Laas, *Die Paedagogik des Johannes Sturm* (Berlin); and F.-K. Kaiser, *Johannes Sturm, sein Bildungsgang und seine Verdienste um das Strassburger Schulwesen* (Cologne). All three were published in 1872. August Schricker's *Zur Geschichte der Universität Strassburg. Festschrift zur Eröffnung der Universität Strassburg 1. Mai 1872* (Strassburg: C.F. Schmidt, 1872). For the installation of Richard Zoepffel as Rector of the newly named Kaiser Wilhelms-Universität (later known again as the University of Strasbourg) in 1887 the new Rector chose as his speech topic, "Johannes Sturm, der erste Rector der Strassburger Akademie." The next year, 1888, marked the 350th anniversary of the founding of the Gymnasium and that year Heinrich Veil published *Zum Gedächtnis Johannes Sturms. Eine Studie über J. Sturms Unterrichtsziele und Schuleinrichtungen mit besonderer Berücksichtigung seiner Beziehungen zu dem niederländischen Humanismus. Festschrift Feier d. 350 jährigen Bestehens d. prot. Gymnasiums* (Strassburg, 1888). The 375th anniversary was graced (one year previously) by the publication of Walter Sohm's *Die Schule Johannes Sturm und die Kirche Strassburgs in*

ihrem gegenseitigen Verhältnis 1530–1581 (Monaco, 1912). The 400th anniversary in 1938 saw a large crop of important works published, among them: *L'Humanisme en Alsace,* Congrès de Strasbourg 20–22 April 1938. Published by the Association Guillaume Budé. Among the important articles are Jean Rott's "L'Humanisme et la Réforme Pédagogique en Alsace"; Léon Halkin's "Jean Sturm et le Collège Liégeois des Frères de la Vie Commune" and Ernest Hoepffner's "Jean Sturm et l'Enseignement Supérieur des Lettres à l'École de Strasbourg." (See also notes 102 and 103.) This year Jean Rott published his important translation of Sturm's *Classicae Epistolae* of 1565. Mathieu-Jules Gaufrès's 1876 article "Mémoire de Jean Sturm sur le Project d'Organisation du Gymnase de Strasbourg," originally published in the *Bulletin de la Société de l'Histoire du Protestantisme Français* (1876), pp. 499–505) was reprinted. Two works by Hermann Gumbel appeared as well: "Der elsässische Humanismus Johann Sturms," in *Germanisch-Romanische Monatschrift,* Jan.-Feb., 1938, pp. 135–41; and "Humanitas Alsatica. Strassburger Humanismus von Jakob Wimpheling zu Johann und Jakob Sturm," *Elsass-Lothringisches Jahrbuch,* vol. 17 (Frankfurt a.M.: Verlag Moriss Diesterweg). The 425th anniversary (1963) of the Gymnasium gave us Robert Minder's "Un Foyer de Culture Humaniste le Gymnase Jean Sturm à Strasbourg," *Saisons d'Alsace,* 1964, n. 10, pp. 175–80, while the inauguration of the 20th century foyer, Foyer Jean Sturm, at no. 2bis Rue Salzman in Strasbourg on April 29, 1967 was the occasion for publishing a collection of photographs of this remodeled home of Sturm, 1555–1589. The house was that in which Sturm welcomed John Calvin in 1556; it was later the home of Charles Schmidt, Sturm's biographer, Canon of St. Thomas, and historian 1860–1895. The commemorative volume reminds us that the house "continue sa longue tradition humaniste." See *Inauguration de Foyer Jean Sturm,* Salle des Alsatiques, University of Strasbourg library.

18. Sturm, writing in March 1565 to the mathematician Conrad Dasypodius, one of the members of the Gymnasium faculty, said that his current thinking on educational methods had not changed—"n'écartent pas non plus de la voie que j'ai tracée…" (in 1538 when he first devised the educational program at the bequest of the Strasbourg scholarchs). The letter is one of the twenty-four contained in *Classicae Epistolae.*

19. Jean Rott notes that the wide diffusion of Sturm's textbook editions, each containing a preface which explained the method and purpose of the subject covered, served also to publicize Sturm's pedagogy. These prefaces were addressed to influential persons in a position to persuade others to accept the views of their author. Jean Rott, *Jean Sturm Classicae Epistolae,* p. xx.

20. This older view was that taken by Charles Schmidt in his biography of Sturm. He believed the Brethren wholly rejected scholasticism and undermined the influence of the University of Paris. "Mémoire de Jean Sturm Sur le Projet d'Organisation du Gymnase de Strasbourg," in *Bulletin de la Société de l'Histoire du Protestantisme Français,* vol. 25 (1876), p. 499.

21. Wilhelm Maurer, *Der Junge Melanchthon Zwischen Humanismus und Reformation* (Göttingen: Vandenhoeck & Ruprecht, 1967–69) and Horst Dreitzel, *Protestantischer Aristotelismus und Absoluter Staat, Die Politica des Henning Arnisaeus* (Wiesbaden: F. Steiner, 1970).

22. This is the observation of Stephen Ozment, who reminds us that humanism and scholasticism were not "mortal enemies." *Continuity and Discontinuity in Church History, Essays Presented to George Huntston Williams,* F. Forrester Church and Timothy George, eds. (Leiden: E.J. Brill, 1979), p. 149. See also Leif Grane, "Luther and Scholasticism," in Marilyn J. Harran, ed., *Luther and Learning: The Wittenberg University Luther Symposium* (Selinsgrove, PA: Susquehanna University Press, 1985), pp. 52–68.

23. *Partitionum Dialecticarum Libri Duo (The Structure of Dialogue in Two Books),* Paris: 1539.

24. William Harrison Woodward, *Studies in Education During the Age of the Renaissance, 1400–1600* (Russell & Russell, 1965), pp. 237ff.

25. Cesare Vasoli says that Sturm was indeed indebted to Agricola, but claims Sturm was very inventive in developing his logic and that neither Cicero, nor Boetius nor Agricola himself had ever attempted on behalf of rhetorical clarity what Sturm attempted and accomplished. "Richerche sulle Dialettiché del Cinquecento: III. Sturm, Melantone e il Problema del Metodo," in *Rivista Critica di Storia della Filosofia,* vol. xxi, (1966), pp. 123–177. See also Walter Ong, *Ramus Method.* Ong finds Sturm's conception of method a first expression of a modern mentality. See also note 79 below. The issue is intelligently discussed in Maretta D. Nikolaou, *Sprache als Welterschliessung und Sprache als Norm: Überlegungen zu R. Agricola und J. Sturm* (Neuried: Hieronymus Verlag, 1984).

26. Stephen Ozment says that the "humanist influence attenuated in the later stages of the 16th century and Protestant confessions became intellectually narrower in the late 16th and 17th centuries, when men with little humanist training assumed positions of leadership…" (*Continuity and Discontinuity,* p. 149). New research, however, underlines the continuity of humanism and the reformers' endorsement and support. See, for example, Manfred Fleischer, ed., *The Harvest of Humanism in Central Europe: Essays in Honor of Lewis W. Spitz* (St. Louis: Concordia Publishing House, 1992).

27. "Gymnase et Académie dans la Ville Libre d'Empire de Strasbourg 1538–1621," in *Strasbourg au Coeur Religieux du XVIe Siècle, Hommage à L. Febvre* (Strasbourg: 1975), p. 552.

28. Anton Schindling, *Humanistische Hochschule und Freie Reichsstadt Gymnasium und Akademie in Strassburg 1538–1621* (Wiesbaden: Franz Steiner Verlag, 1977). This is a brilliant study of the educational scene and Sturm's role in it—a must for anyone wishing a complete description of the program and functions of educators in this city during the period. This work is ably and favorably reviewed by Thomas A. Brady, Jr. in *The Renaissance Quarterly,* XXXII (Spring, 1979), pp. 85–87. See also Anton Schindling, "Schulen und Universitäten im 16. und 17. Jahrhundert: Zehn Thesen zur Bildungs-Expansion, Laienbildung und Konfessionalisierung nach der Ref-

ormation," in Walter Brandmüller, Herbert Immenkötter, Erwin Iserloh, eds., *Ecclesia militans. Studien zur Konzilien und Reformations-Geschichte*, 2 vols. (Paderborn: Schöningh, 1988). See Lewis W. Spitz, "Luther and Humanism," and James M. Kittelson, "Luther the Educational Reformer," in Marilyn J. Harran, ed., *Luther and Learning: The Wittenberg University Luther Symposium* (Selinsgrove: Susquehanna University Press, 1985), pp. 69–114. See also Lewis W. Spitz, *Humanismus und Reformation als Kulturelle Kräfte in der deutschen Geschichte: Ein Tagungsbericht* (Berlin and New York: Walter de Gruyter, 1981).

29. "La Pietas Litterata de Jean Sturm et le Développement à Strasbourg d'Une Pédagogie Oecumenique 1538–1581," in *Bulletin de la Société de l'Histoire du Protestantisme Français*, (Jan.-Mar., 1965), pp. 281–302.

30. Henri Strohl, "Théologie et Humanisme à Strasbourg au Moment de la Création de la Haute-École," in *Revue d'Histoire et de Philosophie Religieuse*, vol. 17 (1737), pp. 435–56.

31. Ernst Hoepffner, "Jean Sturm," in *Quatrième Centenaire du Gymnase Protestante de Strasbourg, 1538–1938* (Strasbourg: Éditions "Fides," 1939), pp. 263–76.

32. Ernst-Wilhelm Kohls, *Die Schule bei Martin Bucer in ihrem Verhältnis zu Kirche und Obrigkeit* (Heidelberg: Quelle und Meyer, 1963). This book was positively reviewed by J.V. Pollet, editor of Bucer's correspondence, who concluded that Bucer should be awarded the "paternity" of the gymnasium, and called Sturm's mémoire "un projet complémentaire." A recent two-volume work describes the significant activities of Martin Bucer and the profound influence he exerted on his contemporaries such as Sturm: Christian Krieger and Marc Lienhard, eds., *Martin Bucer and Sixteenth-Century Europe. Actes du colloque de Strasbourg* (28–31 Août 1991) (Leiden: E.J. Brill, 1993).

33. Schmidt, *La Vie*, p. 238.

34. *Ibid.*, pp. 241–42.

35. Bolgar, *Classical Heritage*, p. 356.

36. André Stegmann, "Un Thème Majeur du Second Humanisme Français (1540–1570): l'Orateur et le Citoyen. De l'Humanisme à la Réalité Vécue," in *French Renaissance Studies, 1540–1570*, Peter Sharrat, ed. (University Press, Edinburgh, 1976), p. 220.

37. Other such methods were: the practice of marking by solemn ritual the passage of students from one grade to another; public interrogations of students, regularly scheduled and held before the presence of the city officials and of the boys' families; "enchainment" or coordination of secondary with superior education in the same establishment and the maintenance of a strict progressivity from the studies of one class to those of the next; the importance given to Christian values in the whole school program; the performance of classical plays; the division of classes into groups of ten students—"decuries"—each headed by a "decurion" chosen from among the best students and serving both as a monitor of discipline and a teacher's aide.

38. Gaston Bonet-Maury, *De Opera Scholastica Fratrum Vitae Communis in Nederlandia* (Paris: L. Cerf, 1889).
39. Bolgar, *Classical Heritage*, p. 341.
40. *Ibid.*
41. Lucien Richard, *The Spirituality of John Calvin* (Atlanta: John Knox Press, 1974).
42. Kenneth Strand, "Additional Note on Calvin and the Influence of the Brethren of the Common Life in France," in *Seminary Studies*, Andrews University Press, Spring 1977, n. 1, vol. XV, p. 54. See also his "John Calvin and the Brethren of the Common Life: the Role of Strassburg," pp. 43–48 in the same volume.
43. Jean Rott, "L'Humanisme et la Réforme Pédagogique en Alsace," in *L'Humanisme en Alsace*, p. 75.
44. Léon Halkin, "La 'Devotio Moderna' et les Origines de la Réforme aux Pays-Bas," in *Courants Religieux et Humanisme à la Fin du XVe et au Début du XVIe Siècle*, Colloque de Strasbourg 9–11 May 1957 (Paris: Presses Universitaires de France, 1959), pp. 45–51.
45. *Ibid.*, p. 49.
46. Léon-E. Halkin, "Jean Sturm et le Collège Saint-Jérôme de Liège," in *Bulletin de l'Institut Archéologique Liégeois*, vol. 67 (1949–50), pp. 103–10.
47. Léon-E. Halkin, "Un Humaniste Liégeois Oublié: Maître Nicolas Nickman (Namur: Maison d'Édition Ad. Wesmael, 1941), pp. 9–10.
48. Heinrich Veil, *Zum Gedächtnis Johannes Sturms*; a memorial address without place or date.
49. Friedrich Paulsen, *Geschichte des Gelehrten Unterrichts* (Leipzig: Verlag Von Veit & Comp., 1985). See also Lewis W. Spitz, "Humanism in Germany," in Anthony Goodman and Angus MacKay, eds., *The Impact of Humanism on Western Europe* (London and New York: Longman, 1990), pp. 202–19.
50. Theobald Ziegler, *Geschichte der Pädagogik*, 1913. Carl Engel, *Das Schulwesen in Strassburg von der Gründung des Protestantischen Gymnasiums* (Strassburg: Strassburg Program, 1886).
51. Ernst Hoepffner, "Jean Sturm et L'Enseignement Supérieur des Lettres à l'École de Strasbourg," in *L'Humanisme en Alsace*, Association Guillaume Budé, Congrès de Strasbourg (Paris, Société d'Édition Les Belles Lettres, 1939), pp. 84–94.
52. Léon-E. Halkin, "Jean Sturm et le Collège Saint-Jérôme de Liège," p. 106, in the above volume.
53. Johann Marbach represented anti-Bucerian Lutheran orthodoxy. He was Superintendent of the Strasbourg Church and a Visitor of the Strasbourg Gymnasium, as well as a professor of theology in the school. Tension between Sturm and Marbach (and his sympathizers) began in 1561 and lasted intermittently until Sturm was forced to resign in 1581.
54. See Jacques Pannier, "Calvin à Strasbourg," *Revue d'Histoire et de Philosophie Religieuse* (Strasbourg: Imprimerie Alsacienne, 1925), p. 21. Pannier points out that at the time, Calvin adhered to the *Confessio tetrapolitana*, a

moderate reformed position to which Sturm remained loyal long after Calvin's position had changed. See also Charles Borgeaud, *Histoire de l'Université de Genève: L'Académie de Calvin, 1559–1748* (Geneva, 1900), pp. 662ff.

55. Richard Zoepffel, "Johannes Sturm der erste Rector," p. 7. See note 17 above.

56. *Ibid.*

57. Sturm, says Zoepffel, viewed the Tetrapolitana as the "Palladium der religiösen Toleranz und die bewahrte Grundlage eines brüderlichen Einvernehmens zwischen Lutheranern und Reformirten" (p. 9).

58. Robert Faerber, "La Pensée Religieuse et Théologique de Jean Sturm," in *Strasbourg Au Coeur Religieux du XVIe Siècle*, pp. 189–95.

59. François Hotman (1524–1590), French jurist and humanist. Hotman took a doctorate in law (at Orleans) and taught there and in other Protestant schools in Europe, including in Sturm's school at Strasbourg. He was an opponent of absolutism. Roger Zuber, "Strasbourg, Refuge des Champevois," in *Strasbourg au Coeur Religieux du XVIe Siècle*, pp. 309–19.

60. Jean Rott, "Extrait de la Revue d'Histoire et de Philosophie Religieuses," (no. 4), in Jean Rott, ed., *Documents Strasbourgeois de France* (Presses Universitaires de France, Paris, 1964).

61. Sturm wrote (June 14, 1554) Calvin a letter aluding to approval of Calvin's treatment of Servetus. Sturm, in the interest of ecumenicity, supported his former colleague and friend as well.

62. Sleidan, born Johannes Philippson (1506–1556), was a lifelong friend of Sturm's from Schleiden. A Protestant, his *Annals* of the Reformation was a main source for the period until the archives were opened in the nineteenth century.

63. See Jean Rott's edition of Sturm's *Classicae Epistolae*, p. 332.

64. Pierre Mesnard, "La Pietas Litterata," observed that Sturm regarded Catholic humanists like Bembo, Sadoleto, Contarini and Pole as fellow-soldiers against idolatry. These men were the most liberal of the Catholic humanists. See also Pierre Mesnard, "La Pédagogie de Jean Sturm et son inspiration évangélique (1507–1589)," *XIIe Congrès International des Sciences Historiques. Rapports. III. Commissions* (Vienna, 1965), pp. 95–110. An example of the influence on the Melanchthon-Sturm approach to education is provided by Claude Baduel's reform of the academy of Nîmes. See Theodore Casteel, *The Academy and University at Nîmes: An Experiment in Humanistic Education in the Age of Reform* (Stanford University Diss., 1973). Baduel, like Calvin, had his Strasbourg educational experience with Sturm.

65. The most thorough account of Sturm's diplomatic career remains that given by Charles Schmidt (*La Vie*), who said that Sturm preferred diplomacy to education, having been equipped with the attributes which made for success in such service—eloquence and foreign contacts. Schmidt recognizes that Sturm's diplomacy was all in the interest of the Protestant reform movement, even if he collected pensions from Catholic monarchs (Francis

I, Charles V, Maximilian II) as well as Protestant ones (Elizabeth I and the King of Denmark). He died impoverished by his generosity to the Protestant cause. There is also some useful information in Jean-Daniel Pariset's *Les Relations Diplomatiques Franco-Allemandes au Milieu du XVIe Siècle* (Strasbourg: Librairie Istra, 1979). See also the Colloque du Strasbourg, 2–3 March 1973. "Charles Quint, le Rhin et la France. Droit Savant et Droit Pénal à l'Époque de Charles-Quint." *Actes des Journées d'Études de Strasbourg.* Istra, 1973. Jean Rott's introduction to *Classicae Epistolae* contains a topical outline of Sturm's diplomatic activities and Sturm's relations with the French Huguenots are treated in his article "Le Recteur Strasbourgeois Jean Sturm et les Protestants Français," in *Actes du Colloque l'Amiral Coligny et Son Temps*, Société de l'Histoire du Protestantisme Français, Paris: 24–28 Oct., 1972, pp. 407–25 and 435–37. The forthcoming work by Thomas A. Brady, Jr., *Protestant Politics: Jacob Sturm (1489–1553) and the German Reformation* (Atlantic Highlands, NJ: Humanities Press International, 1994) should prove to be of background interest to the story of Johann Sturm. Brady's earlier work provides useful social and political information, Thomas A. Brady, Jr., *Ruling Class, Regime and Reformation at Strasbourg 1520–1555* (Leiden: E.J. Brill, 1978). See especially pages 184–95, where he refers to Johann Sturm as a "learned flatterer" and "fiery rector of The Latin School."

66. Translated by the editors from Charles Schmidt's "Mémoire de Jean Sturm sur le Projet d'Organisation du Gymnase du Strasbourg," *Bulletin de la Société de l'Histoire du Protestantisme Français*, vol. 25, 2nd ser., 1876, p. 505.

67. That is, the first nine grades of the Gymnasium. A tenth was added around 1565. Depending upon when the boy began his education (between the ages of 5 and 7) he would graduate around the age of 16. At that point he was ready for higher education, either the Academy or some university.

68. Schmidt recognized that all Renaissance scholars put a premium on Latin but said Sturm exaggerated by demanding excellence in Latin oratory as well as an ordinary command of the language. He wondered why such a distinguished man could have so poorly assessed the educational needs of a new generation: "On s'est demandé comment il s'est fait qu'un homme aussi distingué ait pu entrevoir si peu les besoins des générations nouvelles." *La Vie*, p. 241.

69. Gaufrès noted: "Les classiques furent d'abord pour la Renaissance autre chose qu'une source de mots et de phrases; ils lui apparurent comme une réalité aussi positive et féconde que la découverte de Christophe Columb." "Histoire du Plan d'Études Protestant," in *Bulletin de la Société de l'Histoire du Protestantisme Français*, vol. 25, 1876, p. 498.

70. Gessler, *Histoire de la Pédagogie* (Louvain: S.A. De Vlaamse, 1948), p. 64.

71. Melczer, "La Pensée Éducative," p. 138.

72. Ernest Wickersheimer, "Jean Sturm, Ami Strasbourgeois d'André Vésale," in *Current Problems in History of Medicine*, Proceedings of the XIXth Interna-

tional Congress for the History of Medicine, Basel 7–11 Sept 1964 (New York: S. Karger, 1966), pp. 25–32.

73. Sebastian Brant (1458?–1521), German humanist and satirical poet. His *Das Narrenschiff* (*Ship of Fools*) (1494) pilloried corruption in clergy and laity alike. A professor of law in Basel 1489–1499, he was made an imperial councilor and given a title (Count Palatine) by Maximilian I. His work was a late embodiment of medieval piety and ideals. See Edwin H. Zeydel, *The Ship of Fools by Sebastian Brant* (New York: Columbia University Press, 1944).

74. Thomas Murner (1475?–1537), another German satirist and social critic. His style was popular, racy, broadly humorous. He was a Franciscan monk, teacher and administrator for his order. His anti-Lutheranism was apparent in his *Lutherische Narren* (1522), one of the ablest anti-Luther satires.

75. Jakob Wimpheling (1450–1528), German humanist. He studied law, theology, rhetoric and poetry and became a professor at Heidelberg in 1498. He was an earnest desirer of economic reforms in the Catholic church, and at first sympathized with Luther, though later rejected the reform's anti-ecclesiastical implications. In *Germania* (1501) he urged the magistrates of Strasbourg to found a school where besides Latin, geography, agriculture and military science would be taught. He was notable for his ardent patriotism (pro-Germanism). See Lewis W. Spitz, *The Religious Renaissance of the German Humanists* (Cambridge, MA: Harvard University Press, 1963), pp. 41–60.

76. Herman Gumbel, "Der elsässische Humanismus Johann Sturms," pp. 138–39.

77. *Ibid.* "Seine radikale Steigerung des Humanistischen lag nicht nur im Zug wimpfelingisch-elsässischer Anlage, sie war dieses Mannes Weise und Weg zu Tat und Wirkung."

78. Preserved Smith, *The Age of the Reformation* (New York: Henry Holt and Co., 1920), p. 667.

79. Georges Snyders, *La Pédagogie en France aux XVIe et XVIIe Siècles* (Paris: Presses Universitaires de France, 1965), p. 20. A much more positive assessment of the importance of the Renaissance for education is to be found in Paul F. Grendler, *Schooling in Renaissance Italy: Literacy and Learning, 1300–1600* (Baltimore and London: Johns Hopkins University Press, 1989).

80. *Ibid.*, p. 24.

81. Walter Ong, *Ramus Method*, pp. 232–34. He finds Sturm's fascination with methodology marks the starting point of the modern mentality. Ong is primarily concerned with dialectical aspects of method and not pedagogical ones. He describes Sturm's dialectics as a tripartite process proceeding from 1) resolution (analysis) 2) composition (synthesis) and 3) definition. As for the application of this process to Sturm's teaching procedure, Ong finds this relationship obscure.

82. Friedrich Hahn, *Die Evangelische Unterweisung in den Schulen des 16. Jahrhunderts* (Heidelberg: Quelle & Meyer, 1957), pp. 107–108. "Erst aus-

wendig lernen, das Verstehen folgt nachher. Denn so führt Sturm aus, die menschliche Natur lernt eher sprechen als denken und urteilen."

83. Friedrich Paulsen, *Geschichte des Gelehrten Unterrichts auf den deutschen Schulen und Universitäten* (Leipzig: Verlag Von Veit & Co., 1885). Paulsen said: "…er schrieb Anweisungen für den Schulunterricht. In solchen konnte er offenbar nicht umhin, diesen Gesichtspunkt in die vorderste Reihe zu stellen." *Geschichte des Gelehrten Unterrichts*, p. 255.

84. von Raumer, *Geschichte der Paedagogik*, vol. 1 (Gütersloh, 1877).

85. Ernst Laas, *Die Paedagogik des Johannes Sturm* (Berlin: Weidmann, 1872).

86. Collard, "La Pédagogie de Sturm," in *Mélanges d'Histoire Offerts à Charles Moeller*, vol. 2 (Louvain: Bureau de Receuil, 1914), pp. 149–67.

87. Jean Rott, "L'Humanisme et la Réforme Pédagogique en Alsace," p. 75.

88. Sturm wrote: "It has always and all times been granted to all mankind to endeavor to improve things. Imitation ought to be free, not servile." From *Liberally Educated Nobility* (for the Werter Brothers).

89. Sturm believed homilies were decorative and produced more graceful themes, if used.

90. The diaries or *copia verborum* were to be kept by students to remind them of their own progress as well as for review. So important did he consider new vocabulary (vocabulary building) that he wrote for students his *Onamasticon Puerile*—a collection of words under subject headings. He did not invent the device. A recent edition of Theophilius Golius's (Golius was a former student of Sturm) word book with a preface by Sturm has been edited by Gilbert de Smet. De Smet discusses the genre of word books in the early sixteenth century. See *Theophilius Golius, Onomasticon Latinogermanicum. Cum Proefatione Johannis Sturmii*, Gilbert de Smet, ed. (New York: Georg Olms, 1972).

91. Dramatic performances were allowed to lapse as early as 1539 at the Strasbourg school, but were revived with incredible success in 1565. Sturm thought the revival would be a useful re-inforcement of his goal of oratorical proficiency. The popularity of the comedies is accounted for by a growing interest in drama throughout Europe, only temporarily restrained by the onset of the religious reforms. The plays were at first performed by students in the last two classes of the Gymnasium. Eventually these were replaced by professional actors for the most part—the students were relegated to the chorus lines, while leading roles went to the professionals. See Charles Engel, "L'École de Strasbourg au XVIe Siècle," in *Revue Internationale de l'Enseignement*, 1896, pp. 451ff. Sturm encouraged dramatic productions by the students at the academy. See Johannes Crüger, "Zur Strassburger Schulkomödie," in the *Festschrift zur Feier des 350 jährigen Bestehens des protestantischen Gymnasiums* (Strassburg, 1888), pp. 307–54. See also James A. Parente, "Empowering Readers: Humanism, Politics, and Money in Early Modern German Drama," in Manfred P. Fleischer, ed., *The Harvest of Humanism in Central Europe* (St. Louis: Concordia Publishing House, 1992), pp. 263–80.

92. Adam G. Strobel, *Histoire du Gymnase Protestant de Strasbourg*, (Strasbourg: Frederic Charles Heitz, 1838), pp. 11–18. None of the methods named here were invented by Sturm, even if some authors assume he was their originator. Miriam Chrisman, for example, notes that these were "novel, pedagogical methods," in *Strasbourg and the Reform: A Study in the Process of Change* (New Haven: Yale University Press, 1967), pp. 271–72. The methods were not new. What was true of Sturm is that he urged the constant use of a variety of techniques never doubting that they were indispensable for student progress. Miriam Chrisman has contributed many fundamentally important studies of the intellectual and religious culture in Strasbourg in the sixteenth century. See by way of example her *Lay Culture, Learned Culture: Books and Social Change in Strasbourg 1480–1599* (New Haven: Yale University Press, 1982); Miriam Chrisman, *Bibliography of Strasbourg Imprints, 1480–1599* (New Haven: Yale University Press, 1982).

93. Charles R. Engel, *L'École Latine et l'Ancienne Académie de Strasbourg (1538–1621)* (Strasbourg: Schlesier & Schweikhardt, Éditeurs, 1900), pp. 80–81.

94. William Melczer, "La Pensée Éducative," pp. 137–39.

95. *Ibid.*, p. 131.

96. Paul Porteau, *Montaigne et la Vie Pédagogique de Son Temps* (Paris: Librairie E. Droz, 1935), p. 39.

97. Ernest Hoepffner, "Jean Sturm," pp. 263–72.

98. Charles Schmidt quoted Sturm's reaction to the reluctance of the Strasbourg magistrates to support a full university program: "Etiam in hoc genere ingenium nostrae civitatis sequimur, cujas vides in mediocritate positum…" (*La Vie*, p. 147). Sturm condemned their position as an example of mediocrity of spirit.

99. This is the opinion of Anton Schindling, "Gymnase et Académie dans la Ville Libre d'Empire de Strasbourg 1538–1621," in *Strasbourg Au Coeur Religieux*, pp. 551–56.

100. Schmidt says that Sturm tried to get his colleagues to feel "la grandeur de leur mission et de diriger leurs efforts communs vers le noble but d'élever des hommes utiles à la patrie et à l'Église." (*La Vie*, p. 154).

101. These are the schools cited by Rudolf Streubel, "Johannes Sturm der grosse Pädagoge des 16. Jahrhunderts," *Sonderdruck aus der Festschrift des Stadt Gymnasiums* (Schleiden, 1957), p. 7.

102. Stremooukhoff, "Les Humanistes Tcheques à l'Académie de Strasbourg," in *L'Humanisme en Alsace*, pp. 42–51.

103. de Chelminska, "Sturm et la Pologne," in *L'Humanisme en Alsace*, pp. 52–63.

104. André Mazon, "Mélanges André Mazon," in *Revue des Études Slavs*, vol. 27 (Tome jubilaire 1921–1951). Publiée avec le concours du Centre National de la Récherche Scientifique, 1951.

105. Alfred Temesi, "Humanisme Franco-Hongrois," in *Kulonlenyomat az Archivum Philologicum*. Egyetemes Philologiai Kozlony. evi 10–12 fuzetebol (Budapest, 1939).

106. Henri Tronchon, "La Reine Marie de Roumanie et l'Université de Strasbourg." Allocution Pronouncée par. H.T. Devant les Professeurs et Étudiants de l'Université Libre Latine à Brasov: le 19 juîllet, 1938.

107. Jean Rott and Robert Faerber, "Un Anglais à Strasbourg," *passim.*

108. Translated by the editors from Sturm's *Classicae Epistolae*, 2, letter of the end of March 1565, to the Scholarchs.

109. Mathieu-Jules Gaufrès, "Histoire du Plan d'Études Protestant," p. 496.

110. Herman, *La Pédagogie des Jésuites au XVIe Siècle Ses Sources, Ses Caracteristiques* (Paris: A. Picard et fils, Editeurs, 1914).

111. Siccard, *Les Études Classiques Avant la Révolution* (Paris, 1887).

112. Otto Kaemmel, *Geschichte des deutschen Schulwesens im Uebergange vom Mittelalter zur Neuzeit* (Leipzig, 1882).

113. Herman, *La Pédagogie des Jésuites*, p. 44. See also Aldo Scaglione, *The Liberal Arts and the Jesuit College System* (Amsterdam: John Benjamins B.V., 1986).

114. Gabriel Codina Mir, *Aux Sources de la Pédagogie des Jésuites* (Roma: Institutum Historicum, S.I., 1968), p. 317.

115. R.R. Bolgar, *The Classical Heritage and its Beneficiaries*, p. 364.

116. Roger Chartier, M.M. Compère and D. Julia, *L'Éducation en France du XVIe au XVIIIe Siècle*, p. 160.

117. *Scholae Lauinganae*, 1565.

118. Charles Engel remarked: "Ce séjour de Sturm à Lavingen fut de la plus grande importance pour le développment de son system pédagogique." (*L'École Latine*, p. 108.)

119. Jean Rott, *Jean Sturm Classicae Epistolae*, introduction, p. xxx.

120. Melczer, "La Pensée Éducative," p. 128.

121. Jean Rott, *Jean Sturm Classicae Epistolae*, introduction, pp. 21-22.

122. Anton Schindling, "Gymnase et Académie dans la Ville Libre d'Empire de Strasbourg 1538–1621," p. 553.

123. "Lehrer" Schmitz, "Ein berühmter Schulreformator des 16. Jahrhunderts aus der Eifel," in *Eifelvereinsblatt*, 21. Jahrgang no. 2, 1920 (mitte Feb.), Bullingen, pp. 17–18.

124. Such a geo-political interpretation was adopted by Friedrich Paulsen who observed that Melanchthon's *Plan für die Schule* (1528) would have had as great a success as Sturm's program, if Wittenberg had been as large as Strasbourg and not dependent on the small towns of Saxony. (*Geschichte des Gelehrten Unterrichts*, pp. 195–97).

125. Jean Rott, *Jean Sturm Classicae Epistolae*, introduction, p. xxix.

126. Alphonse Roersch, "Sturm," in *Dictionnaire Nationale de Belgique* (Bruxelles: G. Goemare, 1906), p. 210.

127. Jean Rott, *Jean Sturm Classicae Epistolae*, introduction, pp. xxix-xxx. See also Paul Oskar Kristeller, "Latin Schools in the Protestant Tradition," *Helios*, vol. 14, no. 2 (1987), pp. 161–64.

128. For a listing of the rich archival holdings of Johann Sturm manuscripts see the *Inventaire des Archives du Chapitre de St. Thomas de Strasbourg* (Strasbourg: Imprimerie Alsacienne, 1937), p. 98. See also the essays in honor of Jean Rott, *Horizons européens de la Réforme en Alsace. Das Elsass und die Reformation im Europa des XVI. Jahrhunderts.* Mélanges offerts à Jean Rott pour son 65e anniversaire publiés par Marijn de Kroon et Marc Lienhard (Strasbourg: Librarie Istra, 1980) by the *Société Savantes d'Alsace et des Régions de l'Est* Collection "Grandes Publications," Volume XVII.

Index of Names and Places

Academic Letters, second published collection of letters (1569), 309–39

Acontius, Melchior, humanist learning for women, 16

Actaeon, changed into an antlered stag, 217

Adrian, Cardinal, for care and diction in grammar, 225

Aeschines, orations, 191

Aesop, taught to seven-year-olds, 48

Agricola, Peter, preceptor in Neuberg, Bavaria, 201; great person and teacher, 205

Agricola, Rudolf (Roelof Huysman), influence on rhetorical dialectic, 22; a rhetorical rather than a deductive approach to logic, 51; Sturm's dependence on Agricola's rhetoric, 120; author of *De inventione dialecticae*, 344

Albrecht, Duke of Prussia (Albert), Sturm explains gymnasium teaching plan to, 255; Sturm's letter to Albert (1565), 257–60; Sturm recommends his plan for an academy in Koenigsberg, 258; son Albert Frederick, 258, son-in-law Prince Duke Johann Albert of Mecklenburg, 258

Alcibiades, failed to follow the counsel of Socrates, 149

Aquinas, Thomas, poor Latinist, 193; teacher and brother of Albertus Magnus, 200; pleases some more than Aristotle, 336

Aristarchus, dominant intellect, 228

Aristotle, *Organum*, in second class, 63; compared with Alexander the Conqueror, 178

Ascham, Roger, admires Sturm's writings on education: Ascham's *The Schoolmaster*, 30; Letter to Ascham published, 54; Ascham, 187–88; *Concerning the English Nobility* (1551), to Roger Ascham, 189–98; sends coin of Gaius Caesar, 198

Athenians, supported the teaching of all disciplines, 183; worshipped false gods, 184

Augustine, Ascham writing on Augustine, 192; less skilled in speaking than Chrysostom, 195; example in oratory, 244; Sturm held to be Augustinian, 350

Baduel, Claude, taught at Strasbourg and moved to Geneva and Nîmes, 12

Bedrottus, Jakob, with Hedio publishes report favoring a central school, 60

Bellay, Guillaume and Cardinal Jean du, Sturm's benefactors, 21; helps Sturm, 46; shining light in the College of Cardinals, 173

Bembo, Pietro, imitates Cicero's grief for Hortensius, 166; a light in the College of Cardinals, 173; places words over substance, 193; favors humanist education, 259

Beuther, Michael, letter to Beuther, doctor of law, jurisconsult, and history teacher, praises Melanchthon, 291–93; to help Lawrence Tuppius teach *The Pandects*, 317; on teaching mathematics, 318–20

Bèze, Theodore, concerned for Sturm's welfare, 43

Bither, Jonas, teacher of the fifth class, 276–78; instructed by Sturm on teaching, to be in charge of the fourth class, 336–37

* * * * *

It is true that a book without an index is like a person with one eye.
The references to certain classical and patristic writers are so numerous
that to list the page numbers would be quite redundant.

Index of Subjects